The Content Analysis *Guidebook*

Kimberly A. Neuendorf
Cleveland State University

Sage Publications
International Educational and Professional Publisher
Thousand Oaks ■ London ■ New Delhi

Throughout this book, the term SAS © is copyrighted by SAS Institute, Inc., SAS Campus Drive, Cary, NC 27513-2414; the term SPSS © is copyrighted by SPSS Inc., SPSS Inc Headquarters, 233 S. Wacker Drive, 11th Floor, Chicago, IL 60606.

For information:

Sage Publications, Inc.
2455 Teller Road
Thousand Oaks, California 91320
E-mail: order@sagepub.com

Sage Publications Ltd.
6 Bonhill Street
London EC2A 4PU
United Kingdom

Sage Publications India Pvt. Ltd.
M-32 Market
Greater Kailash I
New Delhi 110 048 India

Printed in the United States of America

Library of Congress Cataloging-in-Publication Data

Neuendorf, Kimberly A.
   The content analysis guidebook / by Kimberly A. Neuendorf.
      p. cm.
Includes bibliographical references and index.
   ISBN 0-7619-1977-5 (cloth: alk. paper)
   ISBN 0-7619-1978-3 (pbk: alk. paper)
   1. Sociology—Research—Methodology.   2. Content analysis
(Communication).   I. Title.
   HM529 .N47 2002
    301'.01—dc21   2001004115

03 04 05 06 07 10 9 8 7 6 5 4

Acquiring Editor:	Margaret H. Seawell
Editorial Assistant:	Alicia Carter
Production Editor:	Claudia A. Hoffman
Copy Editor:	Marilyn Power Scott
Typesetter/Designer:	Janelle LeMaster
Cover Designer:	Jane Quaney

Contents

List of Boxes

List of Tables and Figures

Foreword

Content analysis has a history of more than 50 years of use in communication, journalism, sociology, psychology, and business. Its methods stem primarily from work in the social and behavioral sciences, but its application has reached such distant areas as law and health care. I've been involved with studies using the various methods of content analysis for a quarter century. Over that time, many things have changed, and others have remained amazingly constant. We now use computers to organize and analyze messages and to conduct statistical analyses with great speed. Yet studies are still often conducted with little attention to theory or rigorous methods. With regard to content analysis, there seems to be a widespread but wrongheaded assumption that "anyone can do it" with no training, and there also seems to be another common misperception that any examination of messages may be termed a content analysis. There is a need for a clear and accessible text that defines the rules of the game and lays out the assumptions of this misunderstood quantitative research technique.

Forged through my own experiences as a coder, principal investigator, or advisor for at least 100 content analyses, I have developed a clear view of what content analysis can be when practiced with a "high bar." In my work, I have maintained a commitment to the centrality of content analysis to communication research and devoted my efforts to elevating the standards for content analysis. This book was written with two somewhat contradictory goals—to combine a strong scientific approach and high methodological standards with a practical approach that both academics and industry professionals will find useful. Five Resources provide the reader with guides to message archives and comparisons of text analysis computer programs. Other support materials can be found at the book's Web site, *The Content Analysis Guidebook Online*—for instance, sample codebooks, coding forms, dictionaries, bibliographies, and more information on archives and computer text programs (see Resource 5).

This book is designed for upper-level undergraduates and graduate students studying communication, sociology, psychology, and other social sciences. It should also be useful to academics and practitioners in such related areas as marketing, advertising, journalism, film, literature, public relations and other business-related fields, and all other areas that are concerned with the generation, flow, and impact of *messages*.

Acknowledgments

This book is the culmination of more than 20 years of research and teaching involving the method of content analysis. I owe a debt of gratitude to so many people whom I have encountered along the way.

First, special thanks go to Bradley Greenberg and M. Mark Miller for granting me the initial opportunities at Michigan State University that have led to my expertise in the methodology of content analysis.

I'd like to acknowledge the influence of my long-time Cleveland State University colleagues Sid Kraus, Sue Hill, David Atkin, and Leo Jeffres, whose encouragement and guidance in the circuitous process of drafting the book proposal and obtaining a publisher were vital.

The writing of this book sometimes required specialized knowledge beyond my experience. For generously providing support in their respective areas of expertise, sincere thanks go to Ellen Quinn, Lida Allen, Edward L. Fink, Tamara Rand, Rick Pitchford, George Ray, Vijaya Konangi, Eric Megla, and Steve Bretmersky.

Thanks go also to my manuscript reviewers and proofreaders—Deanna Caudill, Joe Sheppa, Jim Brentar, Jean Michelson, D. J. Hulsman, Jack Powers, Fariba Arab, Dorian Neuendorf, and the three fabulous anonymous Sage reviewers. Their critical and creative comments have resulted in a much-improved text. And I wish to acknowledge my content analysis students whose successes and frustrations have helped shape this book—Shawn Wickens, Ryan Weyls, Mike Franke, Debbie Newby, Dan Chuba, Mary Miskovic, Brenda Hsien-Lin Chen, Tracy Russell, Patinuch Wongthongsri, John Naccarato, Jeremy Kolt, Amy Capwell, Barb Brayack, James Allen Ealy, and Ann Marie Smith.

To those in the content analysis research community who have been notably generous with their time and in their willingness to share resources, I want to express heartfelt thanks—Joe Woelfel, Bill Evans, M. Mark Miller, Ken

Litkowski, Ann Marie Smith, Cynthia Whissell, Matthew Lombard, Cheryl Campanella Bracken, John Naccarato, Kathleen Carley, Harald Klein, Ian Budge and colleagues, and Mark West.

The professional staff at Sage Publications has been extremely helpful. Thanks go to Margaret Seawell for her solid advice in formulating the project, Alicia Carter and Claudia Hoffman for their guidance through the editorial process, and Marilyn Power Scott for her incisive editing skills (her stamp is most definitely on the final text) and her patience through the final edit.

And special thanks go to my colleague and co-author Paul D. Skalski, whose contributions to the development of this text are far too numerous to itemize. His abilities, enthusiasm, and support have been essential to the completion of this text.

CHAPTER 1

Defining Content Analysis

Content analysis is perhaps the fastest-growing technique in quantitative research. Computer advances have made the organized study of messages quicker and easier . . . but not always better. This book explores the current options in the analysis of the content of messages.

Content analysis may be briefly defined as the systematic, objective, quantitative analysis of message characteristics. It includes the careful examination of human interactions; the analysis of character portrayals in TV commercials, films, and novels; the computer-driven investigation of word usage in news releases and political speeches; and so much more. Content analysis is applicable to many areas of inquiry, with examples ranging from the analysis of naturally occurring language (Markel, 1998) to the study of newspaper coverage of the Greenhouse Effect (Miller, Boone, & Fowler, 1992) and from a description of how the two genders are shown on TV (Greenberg, 1980) to an investigation of the approach strategies used in personal ads (Kolt, 1996). Perhaps, one of the more surprising applications is Johnson's (1987) analysis of Porky Pig's vocalics from a clinical speech therapy standpoint. He examined 37 cartoons, finding that the per-cartoon stuttering ranged from 11.6% to 51.4% of words uttered, and certain behaviors were associated with the stuttering (e.g., eye blinks, grimaces). If you are unfamiliar with the range of content analysis applications, Chapter 9 presents an overview of the major areas of study—the main "contexts" of content analysis research.

The various techniques that make up the methodology of content analysis have been growing in usage and variety. In the field of mass communication research, content analysis has been the fastest-growing technique over the past 20 years or so (Riffe & Freitag, 1997; Yale & Gilly, 1988). Perhaps, the greatest explosion in analysis capability has been the rapid advancement in computer text content analysis software, with a corresponding proliferation of online archives and databases (Evans, 1996). There has never been such ready access to archived textual messages, and it has never been easier to perform at least basic analyses with computer-provided speed and precision. This book will explore the expansion and variety of the techniques of content analysis.

In this chapter, we will follow the development of a full definition of content analysis—how one attempts to ensure objectivity, how the scientific method provides a means of achieving systematic study, and how the various scientific criteria (e.g., reliability, validity) are met. Furthermore, standards are established, extending the expectations of students who may hold a prior notion of content analysis as necessarily "easy."

Is Content Analysis "Easy"?
Is It Something That Anyone Can Do?

There seem to be certain common misconceptions about the method of content analysis: Conducting a content analysis is substantially easier than conducting other types of research, content analysis is anything a scholar or student says it is, and anyone can do it without much training or forethought. It's also widely assumed that there is little reason to use content analysis for commercial or nonacademic research. Unfortunately, these stereotypes have been reinforced by academic journals that too often fail to hold content analyses to the same standards of methodological rigor as they do other social and behavioral science methods, such as surveys, experiments, and participant observation studies. Based on more than 20 years of involvement in over 100 content analyses, I would like to dispel common myths about this method before providing a full working definition.

> **Myth 1:**   **Content analysis is easy.**
>
> **Truth:**   **Content analysis is as easy—or as difficult—as the researcher determines it to be. It is not necessarily easier than conducting a survey, experiment, or other type of study.**

Although content analysis must conform to the rules of good science, each researcher makes decisions as to the scope and complexity of the content-analytic study. An example of a very limited—and quite easy—content analysis is shown in the summary graph in Figure 1.1, indicating how many prime-time network TV shows have dealt with medical issues over a period of 38 years. The unit of the analysis is the individual medically oriented TV program, with three simple variables measured: (a) length of show in minutes, (b) whether the show is a drama or a comedy, and (c) the year(s) the program was aired. The raw data analyzed were listings in a readily accessible source that catalogs all TV shows on the major networks since 1948 (Brooks & Marsh,

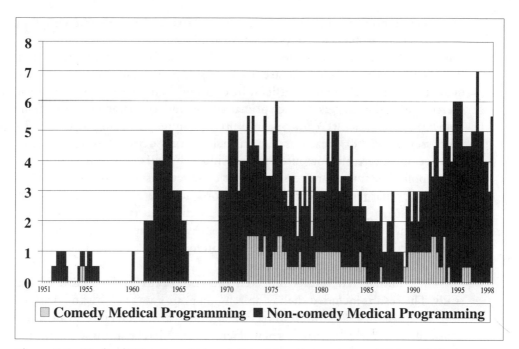

Figure 1.1. Medical Primetime Network Television Programming, 1951 to 1998 (number of hours per week)

1999). Figure 1.1 reports the findings by quarter year in a basic bar graph, indicating weekly total hours of prime-time network TV medical programming. By any assessment, this analysis would be considered easy. Correspondingly, its findings are limited in breadth and applicability. The interpretations we can make from the figure are basic: Over a 40-year period, medical shows have filled only a small portion of the prime-time period, averaging only about 4 hours per week. This has varied little over the period of study.

To make more of the findings, we must dig into the data further and examine the nature of the programs represented in the bar graph. Then, we may identify essentially two eras of TV health-related shows—the 1960s world of physician-as-God medical melodramas (e.g., *Ben Casey, Dr. Kildare*) and the 1970s-1990s era of the very human medical professional (e.g., *St. Elsewhere, ER*). Comedic medical shows have been rare, with the most successful and enduring among them being *M*A*S*H*. The 1990s included a potpourri of novel medical genres, ranging from documentary-form shows, such as *Rescue 911*, to historical dramas, such as *Dr. Quinn, Medicine Woman*, to science fiction (e.g., *Mercy Point*). Notice that these more interesting findings go beyond the content analysis itself and rely on qualitative analyses. The very simple content analysis has limited utility.

Near the tougher end of the easy-to-difficult continuum might be an ambitious master's thesis (Smith, 1999) that examined the gender role portrayals of women in popular films from the 1930s, 1940s, and 1990s. The sampling was extremely problematic, given that no valid lists (i.e., sampling frames) of top box office hits are available for years prior to 1939. For many years after that date, all that are available are lists of the top *five* films. The researcher made the analysis even more difficult by deciding to measure 18 variables for each film and 97 variables for each primary or secondary character in each film. Some of the variables were untried in content analysis. For example, psychologist Eysenck's (1990) measures of extraversion (e.g., sociable, assertive, sensation-seeking), typically measured on individuals by self-report questionnaire, were applied to film characters, with not completely successful results. One hypothesis, that female portrayals will become less stereotypic over time, resulted in the measurement and analysis of 27 different dependent variables. With four active coders, the study took 6 months to complete; it was one of the more difficult master's theses among its contemporaries and much more difficult than many surveys and experiments.

The multifaceted results reflected the complexity and breadth of the study. The results included such wide-ranging points as (a) across the decades (1930s, 1940s, 1990s), there were several significant trends indicating a decrease in stereotypical portrayals of women in films; (b) average body shape for women varied across the decades at a near-significant level, indicating a trend toward a thinner body shape; (c) screen women who exhibited more traditional sex-role stereotyping experienced more negative life events; (d) female characters who exhibited more male sex-role traits and experienced negative life events tended to appear in films that were more successful at the box office; and (e) screen women were portrayed somewhat more traditionally in films with greater female creative control (i.e., in direction, writing, producing, or editing) (Smith, 1999).

> **Myth 2:** **The term *content analysis* applies to *all* examinations of message content.**
>
> **Truth:** **The term does not apply to every analysis of message content, only those that meet a rigorous definition. Clearly, calling an investigation a content analysis does *not* make it so.**

There are many forms of analysis—from frivolous to seminal—that may be applied to the human production of messages. Content analysis is only one type, a technique presented by this book as systematic and quantitative. Even in the scholarly literature, some confusion exists as to what may be called a content analysis. On a number of occasions, the term has been applied erroneously (e.g., Council on Interracial Books for Children, 1977; DeJong & Atkin, 1995; Goble, 1997; Hicks, 1992; Thompson, 1996), and at times, studies that warrant the term do not use it (e.g., Bales, 1950; Fairhurst, Rogers, & Sarr, 1987; Thorson, 1989).

A complete review of all the types of message analysis that compete with or complement content analysis is beyond the scope of this volume. But the reader should become aware of some of the main options for more qualitative analyses of messages (Lindlof, 1995). One good starting point is Hijmans's (1996) typology of qualitative content analyses applied to media content (according to the definitions presented in this book, we would not include these qualitative procedures as content analysis). She presents accurate descriptions of some of the main qualitative analytic methods that may be applied to messages. Based on descriptions by Hijmans (pp. 103-104) and by Gunter (2000), they are as follows:

Rhetorical Analysis

For this historically revered technique, properties of the text (both words and images) are crucial. The analyst engages in a reconstruction of manifest characteristics of text or image or both, such as the message's construction, form, metaphors, argumentation structure, and choices. The emphasis is not so much on *what* the message says as on *how* the message is presented. There is detailed reading of fragments. There is an assumption that the researcher is a competent rhetorician. This technique has a *very* long history, with its principal origins in Greek philosophy (Aristotle, 1991), and is the legitimate forebear of many of today's academic disciplines. Rhetorical analysis has been widely applied to news content, political speech, advertising, and many other forms of communication (McCroskey, 1993).

Narrative Analysis

This technique involves a description of formal narrative structure: Attention focuses on characters—their difficulties, choices, conflicts, complications, and developments. The analyst is interested not in the text as such but in characters as carriers of the story. The analysis involves reconstruction of the composition of the narrative. The assumption is that the researcher is a competent reader of narratives. One of the most complex and interesting applications of this technique is Propp's exhaustive analysis of Russian fairy tales (Propp, 1968), which establishes common character roles (e.g., hero, helper, villain, dispatcher), an identifiable linear sequence of elements in the narrative (e.g., initial situation, absentation, interdiction), and particular functions in the narrative (e.g., disguise, pursuit, transfiguration, punishment).

Discourse Analysis

This process engages in characteristics of manifest language and word use, description of topics in media texts, through consistency and connection of words to theme analysis of content and the establishment of central terms. The technique aims at typifying media representations (e.g., communicator motives, ideology). The focus is on the researcher as competent language user. Gunter (2000) identifies van Dijk's *Racism and the Press,* published in 1991, as a clear example of a large-scale discourse analysis. According to Gunter, van Dijk analyzes the "semantic macrostructures," or the overall characteristics of meanings, with regard to ethnic minorities in the news media (p. 88), concluding that minority groups are depicted as problematic.

Discourse analysis has been a popular method for analyzing public communication, with analyses ranging from the macroscopic to the very microscopic. Duncan (1996) examined the 1992 New Zealand National Kindergarten Teachers' Collective Employment Contract Negotiations and identified two discourses—"Children First" and "For the Sake of the Children." Both discourses were evident in arguments used by each side in the labor negotiations, in arguments *for* teacher pay and benefits by the teachers' representatives, and in arguments *against* such expenditures by employers and government reps. Duncan's article presents numerous direct quotes from the negotiations to support her point of view. Typical of this method, she points out that her analysis "is *one* reading of the texts, and that there will be numerous other readings possible" (p. 161).

refute existing hypotheses

Structuralist or Semiotic Analysis

The focus here is on deeper meanings of messages. The technique aims at deep structures, latent meanings, and the signifying process through signs, codes, and binary oppositions. Interpretations are theoretically informed, and assertions are made on central themes in culture and society. Rhetorical or narrative analysis can be preliminary to this process. The assumption is that the researcher is a competent member of the culture. (See also Eco, 1976.)

Semiotics has been a valuable technique for examining cultural artifacts. Christian Metz's (1974) classic text, *A Semiotics of the Cinema,* applies the wide range of semiotic techniques to the specific medium of narrative film. He provides a "syntagmatic" analysis of the French film, *Adieu Philippine,* indicating the *structure* of the film in shots, scenes, sequences, and the like. He also offers a detailed semiotic analysis of the self-reflexive "mirror construction" of Federico Fellini's semiautobiographical film, *8-1/2.*

Interpretative Analysis

The focus of this technique is on the formation of theory from the observation of messages and the coding of those messages. With its roots in social scientific inquiry, it involves theoretical sampling; analytical categories; cumulative, comparative analysis; and the formulation of types or conceptual categories. The methodology is clearly spelled out, but it differs from scientific inquiry in its wholly qualitative nature and its cumulative process, whereby the analyst is in a constant state of discovery and revision. The researcher is assumed to be a competent observer.

Many of the systems of analysis developed by these methods are empirical and detailed and in fact are more precise and challenging than most content analyses (e.g., Propp, 1968). With only minor adjustment, many are appropriate for use in content analysis as well (e.g., Berger, 1982, 1991).

In addition to these qualitative message analysis types reviewed by Hijmans (1996), several others deserve mention.

Conversation Analysis

Conversation analysis is a technique for analyzing naturally occurring conversations, used by social scientists in the disciplines of psychology, communication, and sociology (Sudnow, 1972). The procedure has been described as a "rigorously empirical approach which avoids premature theory construction and employs inductive methods . . . to tease out and describe the way in which ordinary speakers use and rely on conversational skills and strategies" (Kottler & Swartz, 1993, pp. 103-104). Most typically, it relies on transcribed conversations. The technique generally falls within the rubric of ethnomethodology, scholarly study in which the precise and appropriate methods used emerge from within the process of study, with the clearly subjective involvement of the investigator. Examples of its applications have included an analysis of doctor-patient interaction (Manning & Ray, 2000) and an in-depth analysis of a notorious interview of Vice President George Bush by television reporter Dan Rather as they jockeyed for position in order to control the flow of a "turbulent" interview (Nofsinger, 1988/1989).

Critical Analysis

Critical analysis, often conducted in a tradition of cultural studies, has been a widely used method for the analysis of media messages (Newcomb, 1987). The area of film studies provides a good example of a fully developed, theoretically sound literature that primarily uses the tools of critical analysis (e.g., Lyman, 1997). For example, Strong's (1996) essay about how Native Americans are "imaged" in two mid-1990s media forms—Disney Studio's *Pocahontas* and Paramount's *The Indian in the Cupboard*—is influenced heavily by her own roles as mother, musician, American raised during a period when "playing Indian" was a childhood rite of passage, and anthropologist long interested in White America's representations of Native Americans. She acknowledges these various roles and perspectives, provides precise details to back her assertions (including many lines and song lyrics from the movies), and gives summative statements that bring the details into line with cultural frameworks. For example, she concludes that "Disney has created a New Age Pocahontas to embody our millennial dreams for wholeness and harmony, while banishing our nightmares of savagery without and emptiness within" (p. 416).

Normative Analysis

Some analyses are explicitly normative or proscriptive. For example, a guide to *Stereotypes, Distortions and Omissions in U.S. History Textbooks: A Content Analysis Instrument for Detecting Racism and Sexism* (Council on Interracial Books for Children, 1977), compiled by 32 educators and consultants, provides checklists for history textbook coverage of African Americans, Asian Americans, Chicanos, Native Americans, Puerto Ricans, and women. For each group, an instrument is presented with criteria for parents and teachers to use when examining children's history texts. For instance, in the Native American checklist, the following criteria are included: "The myth of 'discovery' is blatantly Eurocentric," "War and violence were not characteristic of Native nations," "The Citizenship Act of 1924 was not a benevolent action," and "The BIA [Bureau of Indian Affairs] is a corrupt and inefficient bureaucracy controlling the affairs of one million people" (pp. 84-85). The guide is certainly well intended and a powerful tool for social change. It does not, however, fit most definitions of content analysis.

Similarly, in their article, "Evaluation Criteria and Indicators of Quality for Internet Resources," Wilkinson, Bennet, and Oliver (1997) offer a list of 125 questions to ask about a Web site. Their goal is to pinpoint characteristics that indicate accuracy of information, ease of use, and aesthetic qualities of Internet material. The work is a normative prescription for a "good" Web site. Although they call their proposal a content analysis, it does not meet the definition given in this book.

In another case of normative recommendations for message content, Legg (1996) proposes that commercial films are an important venue for the exploration of religion in American culture, and she provides tips to religious educators for using movies in teaching. She contends that "in forms like contemporary films we can see the very pertinent questions with which our culture is really wrestling" (p. 401) and urges religious educators not to limit their use of film to explicitly religious films, such as *The Ten Commandments* or *Agnes of God*. Equally useful might be explorations of manifestations of good and evil in *Batman* or a discussion of dimensions of friendship, aging, Southern ethos, prejudice, and family in *Driving Miss Daisy* (p. 403). Such detailed analyses have obvious utility; however, this process does not attempt to achieve objectivity, as does a content analysis.

> **Myth 3:** **Anyone can do content analysis; it doesn't take any special preparation.**
>
> **Truth:** **Indeed, anyone can do it . . . but only with training and with substantial planning.**

While the person who designs a content analysis must have some special knowledge and preparation, a central notion in the methodology of content analysis is that *all* people are potentially valid "human coders" (i.e., individuals who make judgments about variables as applied to each message unit). The coding scheme must be so objective and so reliable that, once they are trained, individuals from varied backgrounds and orientations will generally agree in its application.

Clearly, however, each coder must be proficient in the language(s) of the message pool. This may require some special training for coders. To analyze natural speech, coders may actually need to learn another language or be trained in the nuances of a given dialect. Before coding television or film content, coders may have to learn about production techniques and other aspects of visual communication. To code print advertising, coders may need to learn a bit about graphic design. All this is in addition to training *with the coding scheme,* which is a necessary step for all coders.

For analyses that do not use human coders (i.e., those that use computer coding), the burden rests squarely on the researcher to establish complete and carefully researched dictionaries or other protocols. Because the step of making sure coders can understand and reliably apply a scheme is missing, the researcher needs to execute additional checks. Chapter 6 presents some notions on how this might be done.

Myth 4:   Content analysis is for academic use only.

Truth: Not.

The vast majority of content analyses have been conducted by academics for scholarly purposes. However, there has been growing interest among commercial researchers and communication practitioners in particular applications of content analysis. A law firm hired a respected senior professor to conduct content analyses of news coverage of their high-profile clients, to be used as evidence in conjunction with a change-of-venue motion (i.e., excessive and negative coverage may warrant moving a court case to another city in order to obtain a fair trial; McCarty, 2001). In response to criticisms, a Southern daily newspaper hired a journalism scholar to systematically document their coverage of the local African American community (Riffe, Lacy, & Fico, 1998). The marketing research unit of a large-city newspaper has begun the process of systematically comparing its own coverage of regional issues with that provided by local television news. Organizational communication consultants sometimes include a content analysis of recorded messages (e.g., e-mail, memos) in their audit of the communication flow in the organization. And the clinical diagnostic tools of criteria-based content analysis have been used in nonacademic settings by psychologists and legal professionals.

A Six-Part Definition of Content Analysis

This book assumes that content analysis is conducted within the scientific method but with certain additional characteristics that place it in a unique position as the primary message-centered methodology.

Box 1.1   Defining Content Analysis

Some of the main players in the development of quantitative message analysis present their points of view:

Berelson (1952, p. 18): Content analysis is a research technique for the objective, systematic, and quantitative description of the manifest content of communication.

Stone, Dunphy, Smith, & Ogilvie (1966, p. 5, with credit given to Dr. Ole Holsti): Content analysis is any research technique for making inferences by systematically and objectively identifying specified characteristics within text.

Carney (1971, p. 52): The general purpose technique for posing questions to a "communication" in order to get findings which can be substantiated. . . . [T]he "communication" can be anything: A novel, some paintings, a movie, or a musical score—the technique is applicable to all alike and *not* only to analysis of literary materials.

Krippendorff (1980, p. 21): Content analysis is a research technique for making replicable and valid inferences from data to their context.

Weber (1990, p. 9): Content analysis is a research method that uses a set of procedures to make valid inferences from text.

Berger (1991, p. 25): Content analysis . . . is a research technique that is based on measuring the amount of something (violence, negative portrayals of women, or whatever) in a representative sampling of some mass-mediated popular art form.

Riffe, Lacy, & Fico (1998, p. 20): Quantitative content analysis is the systematic and replicable examination of symbols of communication, which have been assigned numeric values according to valid measurement rules, and the analysis of relationships involving those values using statistical methods, in order to describe the communication, draw inferences about its meaning, or infer from the communication to its context, both of production and consumption.

This book: Content analysis is a summarizing, quantitative analysis of messages that relies on the scientific method (including attention to objectivity-intersubjectivity, a priori design, reliability, validity, generalizability, replicability, and hypothesis testing) and is not limited as to the types of variables that may be measured or the context in which the messages are created or presented.

Content analysis is a summarizing, quantitative analysis of messages that relies on the scientific method (including attention to objectivity-intersubjectivity, a priori design, reliability, validity, generalizability, replicability, and hypothesis testing) and is not limited as to the types of variables that may be measured or the context in which the messages are created or presented.

Box 1.1 presents some alternative definitions of content analysis for comparison's sake. More details on this book's definition are presented in the discussion that follows.

1. Content Analysis as Relying on the Scientific Method

Perhaps, the most distinctive characteristic that differentiates content analysis from other, more qualitative or interpretive message analyses is the attempt to meet the standards of the scientific method (Bird, 1998; Klee, 1997);

by most definitions, it fits the positivism paradigm of social research (Gunter, 2000)[1]. This includes attending to such criteria as the following:

Objectivity-Intersubjectivity

A major goal of any scientific investigation is to provide a description or explanation of a phenomenon in a way that avoids the biases of the investigator. Thus, objectivity is desirable. However, as the classic work, *The Social Construction of Reality* (Berger & Luckman, 1966), points out, there is no such thing as true objectivity—"knowledge" and "facts" are what are socially agreed on. According to this view, all human inquiry is inherently subjective, but still we must strive for consistency among inquiries. We do not ask, "is it true?" but rather, "do we agree it is true?" Scholars refer to this standard as *intersubjectivity* (Babbie, 1986, p. 27; Lindlof, 1995).

Another set of terms sometimes used is the comparison between *idiographic* and *nomothetic* investigations. An idiographic study seeks to fully describe a single artifact or case from a phenomenological perspective and to connect the unique aspects of the case with more general truths or principles. A nomothetic study hopes to identify generalizable findings, usually from multiple cases, and demands "specific and well-defined questions that in order to answer them it is desirable to adopt standardized criteria having known . . . characteristics" (Te'eni, 1998). Idiographic study implies conclusions that are unique, nongeneralizable, subjective, rich, and well grounded; nomothetic study implies conclusions that are broadly based, generalizable, objective, summarizing, and inflexible.

An A Priori Design

Although an a priori (i.e., "before the fact") design is actually a part of the task of meeting the requirement of objectivity-intersubjectivity, it is given its own listing here to provide emphasis. Too often, a so-called content analysis report describes a study in which variables were chosen and "measured" *after* the messages were observed. This wholly inductive approach violates the guidelines of scientific endeavor. All decisions on variables, their measurement, and coding rules must be made before the observations begin. In the case of human coding, the codebook and coding form must be constructed in advance. In the case of computer coding, the dictionary or other coding protocol must be established a priori.

However, the self-limiting nature of this "normal science" approach should be mentioned. As Kuhn's (1970) seminal work on paradigms has pointed out, deduction based on past research, theories, and bodies of evidence within the current popular paradigm does not foster innovation. Content analysis has a bit of this disadvantage, with the insistence that coding schemes be developed a priori. Still, creativity and innovation can thrive within the method. As described in Chapter 5, a lot of exploratory work can and should be done before a final coding scheme is "set in stone." The entire process may be viewed as a combination of induction and deduction.

Reliability

Reliability has been defined as the extent to which a measuring procedure yields the same results on repeated trials (Carmines & Zeller, 1979). When human coders are used in content analysis, this translates to *intercoder reliability*, or level of agreement among two or more coders. In content analysis, reliability is paramount. Without acceptable levels of reliability, content analysis measures are meaningless. Chapter 7 addresses this important issue in detail.

Validity

Validity refers to the extent to which an empirical measure adequately reflects what humans agree on as the real meaning of a concept (Babbie, 1995, p. 127). Generally, it is addressed with the question, "Are we really measuring what we want to measure?" Although in content analysis, the researcher is the boss, making final decisions on what concepts to measure and how to measure them, there are a number of good guidelines available for improving validity (Carmines & Zeller, 1979). Chapter 6 gives a more detailed discussion.

Generalizability

The generalizability of findings is the extent to which they may be applied to other cases, usually to a larger set that is the defined *population* from which a study's sample has been drawn. After completing a poll of 300 city residents, the researchers obviously hope to generalize their findings to all residents of the city. Likewise, in a study of 800 personal ads in newspapers, Kolt (1996) generalized his findings to all personal ads in U.S. newspapers in general. He was in a good position to do so because he (a) randomly selected U.S. daily newspapers, (b) randomly selected dates for specific issues to analyze, and then (c) systematically random sampled personal ads in each issue. In Chapter 4, the options for selecting representative samples from populations will be presented.

Replicability

The replication of a study is a safeguard against overgeneralizing the findings of one particular research endeavor. Replication involves *repeating* a study with different cases or in a different context, checking to see if similar results are obtained each time (Babbie, 1995, p. 21). Whenever possible, research reports should provide enough information about the methods and protocols so that others are free to conduct replications. Throughout this book, the assumption is made that *full* reportage of methods is optimal, for both academic and commercial research.

As Hogenraad and McKenzie (1999) caution, content analyses are sometimes at a unique disadvantage with regard to replication. Certain messages are historically situated, and repeated samplings are not possible, as with their study of political speeches leading up to the formation of the European Union. They propose an alternative—bootstrap replication—which compares and pools multiple random subsamples of the original data set.

Hypothesis Testing

The scientific method is generally considered to be hypothetico-deductive. That is, from theory, one or more hypotheses (conjectural statements or predictions about the relationship among variables) are derived. Each hypothesis is tested deductively: Measurements are made for each of the variables, and relationships among them are examined statistically to see if the predicted relationship holds true. If so, the hypothesis is supported and lends further support to the theory from which it was derived. If not, the hypothesis fails to receive support, and the theory is called into question to some extent. If existing theory is not strong enough to warrant a prediction, a sort of fallback position is to offer one or more research questions. A research question poses a query about possible relationships among variables. In the deductive scientific model, hypotheses and research questions are both posed *before* data are collected. Chapter 5 presents examples of hypotheses and research questions appropriate to content analysis.

2. The Message as the Unit of Analysis, the Unit of Data Collection, or Both

The unit in a research study is the individual "thing" that is the subject of study—what or whom is studied. Frequently, it is useful to distinguish between the *unit of data collection* (sometimes referred to as the *unit of observation;* Babbie, 1995) and the *unit of analysis,* although in particular studies, these two things are often the same. The unit of data collection is the element on which each variable is measured. The unit of analysis is the element on which data are analyzed and for which findings are reported. In most social and behavioral science investigations, the individual *person* is both the unit of data collection and the unit of analysis.

For example, when a survey of city residents is conducted to measure opinions toward the president and the mayor, let's say, the unit of data collection is the individual respondent—the person. That is, telephone interviews are conducted, and normally, each person responds alone. The variables (e.g., attitude toward the president, attitude toward the mayor, gender, age) are measured on each unit. The unit of analysis is also typically the individual person. That is, in the data set, each respondent's answers will constitute one line of data, and statistical analyses will be conducted on the data set, with n equalling the number of people responding. When "average rating of confidence in the president" is reported as 6.8 on a 0-to-10 scale, that's the mean based on n respondents.

Sometimes, the unit of data collection and the unit of analysis are not the same. For example, a study of marital discord may record interactions between married partners. The unit of data collection may be the "turn" in verbal interaction: Each time an individual speaks, the tone and substance of his or her turn may be coded. However, the ultimate goal of the study may be to compare the interactions of those couples who have received intervention counseling and those who have not. Thus, the unit of *analysis* may be the dyad, pooling information about all turns and interactions for each married pair.

In content analysis, the unit of data collection *or* the unit of analysis—or both—must be a *message unit*. Quite simply, there must be communication *content* as a primary subject of the investigation for the study to be deemed a content analysis. In the marital-discord example just described, the unit of data collection is a message unit (an interaction turn), and the unit of analysis is not. It may be called a content analysis. Chapter 4 provides more examples of unitizing.

3. Content Analysis as Quantitative

The goal of any quantitative analysis is to produce *counts* of key categories, and measurements of the *amounts* of other variables (Edward L. Fink, personal communication, March 26, 1999). In either case, this is a numerical process. Although some authors maintain that a nonquantitative (i.e., "qualitative") content analysis is feasible, that is not the view presented in this book. A content analysis has as its goal a numerically based summary of a chosen message set. It is neither a gestalt impression nor a fully detailed description of a message or message set.

There is often confusion between what is considered *quantitative* and what is considered *empirical*. Empirical observations are those based on real, apprehendable phenomena. Accordingly, both quantitative and qualitative investigations may be empirical. What, then, is *not* empirical? Efforts to describe theory and conditions without making observations of events, behaviors, and other "real" subjects, such as abstract theorizing, many aspects of the discipline of philosophy, and (perhaps surprisingly) certain types of scholarship in mathematics (ironically, quite quantitative in focus). Much of the social and behavioral science literature is based on empirical work, which may be quantitative or qualitative.

It should be made clear at the outset that this book takes the viewpoint that critical and other qualitative analyses that are empirical are typically extremely useful. They are capable of providing a highly valid source of detailed or "deep" information about a text. (Note that the term *text* is a preferred term in many critical analyses and denotes not just written text but also any other message type that is considered in its entirety. For example, the text of a film includes its dialog, its visuals, production techniques, music, characterizations, and anything else of meaning presented in the film.) The empiricism of a careful and detailed critical analysis is one of its prime strengths and may produce such a lucid interpretation of the text as to provide us with a completely new encounter with the text. Such an analysis may bring us into the world of the text (e.g., into what is called the *diegesis* of a film, "the sum of a film's denotation: the narration itself, but also the fictional space and time dimensions implied in and by the narrative, and consequently the characters, the landscapes, the events, and other narrative elements" [Metz, 1974, p. 98]). It may illuminate the intentions of the source of the text, or it may allow us to view the text through the eyes of others who may experience the text (e.g., as in providing an understanding of a child's view of the *Teletubbies,* something that may be essential to a full appreciation of such a child-centric television program).

When approaching a text—a message or message set—the researcher needs to evaluate his or her needs and the outcomes possible from both quantitative (i.e., content analysis) and nonquantitative analyses. For example, to identify and interpret pacifist markers in the film *Saving Private Ryan,* a critical analysis, perhaps with a Marxist approach, is in order. To establish the prevalence of violent acts in top-grossing films of the 1990s, a content analysis is more appropriate. The content analysis uses a broader brush and is typically more generalizable. As such, it is also typically less in-depth and less detailed.

The outlook of this book coincides nicely with the view presented by Gray and Densten (1998): "Quantitative and qualitative research may be viewed as different ways of examining the same research problem" (p. 420). This *triangulation* of methods "strengthens the researcher's claims for the validity of the conclusions drawn where mutual confirmation of results can be demonstrated" (p. 420). It is rare to find a single investigation that combines methods in this way, but such triangulated studies do exist. One study examined storytelling in Taiwanese and European American families, combining ethnographic fieldwork with content-analytic coding of audio and video recordings of naturally occurring talk in the home (Miller, Wiley, Fung, & Liang, 1997).

4. Content Analysis as Summarizing

As noted in the previous point, a content analysis summarizes rather than reports all details concerning a message set. This is consistent with the nomothetic approach to scientific investigations (i.e., seeking to generate generalizable conclusions), rather than the idiographic approach (i.e., focusing on a full and precise conclusion about a particular case).

The goal of some noncontent analysis message studies may be a type of microdocumenting, as in a syntagmatic approach to analyzing transcribed speech or written text (Propp, 1968). The computer program, NUD*IST

(Non-Numerical Unstructured Data Indexing Searching and Theorising computer software; see also *The Content Analysis Guidebook Online*), is primarily oriented to this type of detailed markup, retrieval, and description of textual content. It is based on the organization of coded text via a system of concept nodes, grouped hierarchically in a tree structure, which is displayed by the program. Buston (1997) gives a cogent description of the use of NUD*IST to organize and make sense of a set of 112 interviews with young people with chronic health problems (e.g., asthma). In addition, Buston provides reflections on the ways in which NUD*IST affects qualitative methodologies, concluding that using NUD*IST "is *not* exactly the same as working using manual methods only." On the positive side, it speeds up mundane, routine tasks. On the negative side, it may lead to " 'coding fetishism,' indexing anything and everything obsessively and unnecessarily" (p. 12).

Another program, HyperRESEARCH, a computer-assisted program for conducting qualitative assessments of multimedia, was demonstrated by Hesse-Biber, Dupuis, and Kinder (1997) to be useful for identifying and indexing (what they term *coding*) a broad mix of photographs, text samples, audio segments, and video segments. They also point out the program's utility in searching and reporting based on the codes. Again, though, the emphasis is on cataloging discrete exemplars of desired content in a manner that makes their retrieval and comparison easy. For example, after indexing is complete, the researchers might query the program to produce all examples that have been tagged "expression of self-esteem" (p. 7). These cases may be examined and cross-indexed according to other characteristics, but the responsibility for making sense of these interwoven networks of similarities rests with the researcher. This is somewhat different than the summarizing function of content analysis.

Historians have contributed a number of examples of very precise, fully explicated analyses that rely on original textual sources. Because these analyses are based on texts, we might be tempted to call them content analyses. But some of them display an obvious attempt to report all possible details across a wide variety of units of data collection rather than to summarize information for a chosen unit of data collection or analysis. One example is Kohn's (1973) book on Russia during World War I, in which he professes to attempt "an *exhaustive* inquiry into the vital statistics of Russia" (p. 3), ultimately to assess the economic and noneconomic consequences of the war on Russian society. The work is largely a reportage of numerical facts taken from a variety of textual sources. Another example, a book about the *Plantation Slaves of Trinidad,* brings the reader into the daily lives of these Caribbean slaves during the nation's slave period of 1783-1816 (John, 1988). Aggregate figures on slave mortality and childbearing are presented side by side with drawings of slave life on the Trinidad plantations.

In contrast, the content analysis summarizes characteristics of messages. In Kolt's (1996) study of personal ads in newspapers, he found 26% of them offered physical attractiveness, whereas only 8% requested physical attractiveness of the reader. Lin (1997) found that women in network TV commercials were nearly twice as likely to be shown as "cheesecake" (i.e., physical appearance "obviously alluring") as men were as "beefcake." These results summarize characteristics of the message pool rather than focusing on specific cases.

5. Content Analysis as Applicable to *All* Contexts

The term *content analysis* is not reserved for studies of mass media or for any other type of message content. So long as other pertinent characteristics apply (e.g., quantitative, summarizing), the study of any type of message pool may be deemed a content analysis. The messages may be mediated—that is, having some message reproduction or transmittal device interposed between source and receiver. Or they may be nonmediated—that is, experienced face to face. Although not attempting to create an exhaustive typology of communication purposes and context, the sections to follow give some examples of the range of applications of the techniques of content analysis.

Individual Messaging

Some analyses examine the creation of messages by a single individual, with the typical goal of making some inference to that source.

In psychology, there is a growing use of content analysis of naturally produced text and speech as a type of psychometric instrument (Gottschalk, 1995; Horowitz, 1998; Tully, 1998). This technique analyzes statements made by an individual to diagnose psychological disorders and tendencies, to measure psychological traits of the source, or to assess the credibility of the source (Doris, 1994). Nearly all these efforts stem from the work of Philip Stone (Stone, Dunphy, Smith, & Ogilvie, 1966) in the Harvard Department of Social Relations. His "General Inquirer" computer program was the first to apply content-analytic techniques to free-speech words (see Chapter 2). Rosenberg and others (e.g., Rosenberg & Tucker, 1976) applied the computer technique to the language of schizophrenics, with the goal of better diagnosis. In an example of a further refinement of such procedures, Broehl and McGee (1981) analyzed the writings of historical figures—three British lieutenants serving during the Indian Mutiny of 1957-1958—and on this basis developed psychological profiles for the officers. Even the Watergate tapes have been studied using content analysis to gain insights into the underlying psychological motives of the individuals involved (Weintraub & Plant, as cited in Broehl & McGee, 1981, p. 288).

Others in the field of psychology have continued to develop computer analyses that produce diagnoses from written or spoken text. For example, Gottschalk, Stein, and Shapiro (1997) compared results from standard psychometric tests, such as the MMPI (Minnesota Multiphasic Personality Inventory), with content analysis results from a computer analysis of transcripts of 5-minute speeches. Their study of 25 new psychiatric outpatients found strong construct validity—the speech analyses were highly correlated with corresponding questionnaire outcomes. They point out the potential value in being able to use ordinary spoken or written material for an initial, rapid diagnostic appraisal that can easily remain unobtrusive (i.e., the individual does not have to submit to a lengthy questionnaire administration; p. 427). The content analysis scheme used, the 16-part Gottschalk-Gleser Content Analysis Scales, is a software program developed and validated over a period of many years.

Another application of content analysis to the individual as message generator is the common method of coding responses to open-ended questionnaire items and in-depth interviews (Gray & Densten, 1998). Although the first steps in this process usually include a qualitative review of the message pool and the development of an emergent coding scheme based on what's represented in the pool, it must be remembered that the true content analysis portion is the subsequent careful application of the a priori coding scheme to the message pool.

In the fields of linguistics, history, and literature, some attempts have been made at analyzing individual authors or other sources. Most recently, computer text content analyses have been conducted either to describe a source's style, to verify a questionable source, or to identify an unknown source (Floud, 1977; Olsen, 1993). For example, Elliott and Valenza's (1996) "Shakespeare Clinic" has developed computer tests for Shakespeare authorship, and Martindale and McKenzie (1995) used computer text content analysis to confirm James Madison's authorship of *The Federalist*.

Interpersonal and Group Messaging

This book assumes a definition of interpersonal communication that acknowledges the *intent* of the messaging to reach and be understood by a *particular individual*. This may occur face to face, or it may be mediated, as in the cases of telephoning or e-mailing. It may occur in a dyad or a small group.

To study face-to-face group processes, Bales (1950) developed a content analysis scheme that calls for the coding of each communication act. A verbal act is "usually the simple subject-predicate combination," whereas a nonverbal act is "the smallest overt segment of behavior that has 'meaning' to others in the group" (Bales, Strodtbeck, Mills, & Roseborough, 1951, p. 462). Each act is coded into one of 12 categories: (a) shows solidarity, (b) shows tension release, (c) agrees, (d) gives suggestion, (e) gives opinion, (f) gives orientation, (g) shows antagonism, (h) shows tension, (i) disagrees, (j) asks for suggestion, (k) asks for opinion, or (l) asks for orientation. Bales's scheme has been widely used and elaborated on (Bales & Cohen, 1979) and has also been adapted for analyzing human interaction in mass media content (Greenberg, 1980; Neuendorf & Abelman, 1987).

Box 1.2   Analyzing Communication in Crisis

Perpetrator and Negotiator Interpersonal Exchanges

Most standoffs between police and perpetrators are resolved nonviolently. An analysis of 137 crisis incidents handled by the New York City Police Department revealed that in 91% of the cases, neither hostages nor hostage takers were killed (Rogan & Hammer, 1995, p. 554). Nonetheless, those crisis situations that end violently—such as the 1993 Branch Davidian conflagration in Waco, Texas—focus attention on the need to better understand the negotiation process. There is interest among scholars and police professionals alike in studying the communication content of negotiations in crisis situations so that outcomes may be predicted and negative outcomes prevented.

Rogan and Hammer (1995) had such a goal for their content analysis of audio recordings of three authentic crisis negotiations obtained from the FBI training academy. They looked at message affect, a combination of message valence and language intensity, across eight phases of each negotiation process. The unit of data collection was the uninterrupted talking turn. Each turn was coded by human coders for positive-negative valence and for Donohue's (1991) five correlates of language intensity: (a) obscure words, (b) general metaphors, (c) profanity and sex, (d) death statements, and (e) expanded qualifiers. The analysis was highly systematic and achieved good reliability (i.e., agreement between independent coders).

Total "message affect" scores were calculated for perpetrator and negotiator for each of the eight time periods in each negotiation. In all three situations, the negotiator's message profile remained positive throughout, whereas the perpetrator's score became more strongly negative during stages 2 and 3. Eventually, between stages 6 and 8, the perpetrator's message affect shifted to a positive valence, approaching that of the negotiator. In the one successful negotiation studied, the perpetrator's scores remained high and positive; in the two unsuccessful incidents (one culminating in the perpetrator's suicide), the perpetrator's scores began an unrelenting slide to intense negativity at stage 6 or 7.

The researchers point out certain limitations of the study—primarily, that the analysis was limited to message affect, with no consideration of other characteristics of the communicators, no examination of substantive or relational communication content, and so on. Nevertheless, just based on message affect, the results are striking. By looking at the charted message affect scores, you can *visualize* the process of negotiation success or failure. Although not useful at this point for real-time application to ongoing crisis situations, this content analysis technique shows promise for the development of such application in the future. And researching past negotiation successes and failures provides practitioners insight into the dynamics of the process. As Rogan and Hammer (1995) note, "ultimately, such insight could enable a negotiator to more effectively control a perpetrator's level of emotional arousal, such that a negotiator could take actions to reduce a perpetrator's highly negative and intense emotionality in an effort to negate potentially violent behavior" (p. 571), perhaps the ultimate useful application of the technique of content analysis.

Box 1.3   The Variety of Content Analysis

Religious TV—Tapping Message Characteristics,
Ranging From Communicator Style to Dollar Signs

In the 1980s, religious broadcasting reached a peak of popularity with the rapid growth of "televangelism" (Frankl, 1987). Concerned with a growing perception of religious broadcasting as invasive and inordinately focused on fund-raising, the organization of Roman Catholic broadcasters, UNDA-USA, commissioned a set of content analyses. During the mid-1980s, researchers at Cleveland State University conducted an extensive six-part project. All the components of the project were quantitative content analyses, and they drew on a wide array of theories and research perspectives.

A set of 81 episodes of religious programs provided the content to be analyzed. These episodes were three randomly sampled episodes for each of the top religious television or cable programs, as determined by an index of availability in a random sample of 40 U.S. towns and cities. These programs ranged from talk format shows, such as *The 700 Club,* to televangelist programs like *Jim Bakker* to narrative forms, such as the soap opera *Another Life* and the children's stop-motion animated "daily lesson" program, *Davey and Goliath.* Teams of coders were trained for five types of analysis:

1. The demography of religious television:
    With the unit of analysis the individual character (real or fictional), a dozen demographic variables were assessed (based on previous content analyses of TV characters, such as Greenberg [1980] and Gerbner, Gross, Morgan and Signorielli [1980]), including social age (child, adolescent, young adult, mature adult, elderly), occupation, and religious affiliation. An example of the results is the finding that 47% of the characters were mature adults, with 37% being young adults. Children constituted only 7% of the sample, with the elderly at only 5% (Abelman & Neuendorf, 1984a).

2. Themes and topics on religious television:
    Here, the unit of analysis was a period of *time*: the 5-minute interval. At the end of each 5-minute period, a checklist coding form was completed by the coder, with 60 measures indicating simple presence or absence of a given social, political, or religious topic within all verbalizations in the period (pulling from existing analyses of religious communication, e.g., Hadden & Swann, 1981). Also, both explicit and implied appeals for money were recorded at the end of

Organizational Messaging

Content analysis has been used less frequently for profiling messages within a defined organization than it has in other contexts. More often, messages within an organization have been scrutinized using more qualitative techniques (Stohl & Redding, 1987). An assortment of content analyses in the organizational context have used a variety of techniques.

each 5-minute period. Overall, $328.13 was explicitly requested of the viewer per hour across the sample of religious programs (Abelman & Neuendorf, 1985a, 1985b).

3. Interaction analysis of religious television content:
Using a scheme derived and adapted from Bales (1950), Borke (1969), and Greenberg (1980), interpersonal interactions among characters on religious television were examined. The unit of analysis was each verbal utterance (act), which was coded as falling into one of 20 modes (e.g., offering information, seeking support, attacking, evading). The results suggested age and gender differences in interaction patterns; most interactions were male dominated, and the elderly were often shown as conflict-producing individuals who were the frequent targets of guidance from those who were younger (Neuendorf & Abelman, 1987).

4. Communicator style of televangelists:
Drawing on the considerable interpersonal communication literature on communicator style, notably the work of Robert Norton (1983), this aspect of the project targeted the 14 televangelists in the program sample and used as the unit of analysis each verbal utterance within a monologue. Each utterance was coded for a variety of characteristics, including mode (similar to the interaction coding scheme), vocal intensity, pace, and facial nonverbal intensity. Based on an overall intensity index, the top three "most intense" televangelists were James Robison, Robert Schuller, and Ernest Angley (Neuendorf & Abelman, 1986).

5. Physical contact on religious television programming:
Drawing on work in nonverbal communication (e.g., Knapp, 1978), this portion of the content analyses examined physical touch. The unit of analysis was the instance of nonaccidental physical contact. Characteristics of the initiator and recipient of the touching were tapped, as were type of touch (religious in nature, nonreligious), anatomical location of the touch, and the recipient's reaction to the touch. A sample result was that there was a clear similarity with real-life touching along gender lines: Males were the primary initiators of physical contact, and it tended to be rather formal and ritualistic (i.e., a substantial portion of the contact was religious in nature, e.g., healing; Abelman & Neuendorf, 1984b).

Organizational applications of content analysis have included the analysis of open-ended responses to employee surveys (DiSanza & Bullis, 1999), the word network analysis of voice mail (Rice & Danowski, 1991), and the application of interpersonal interaction coding to manager-subordinate control patterns (Fairhurst et al., 1987). Developing a novel coding scheme, Larey and Paulus (1999) analyzed the transcripts of brainstorming discussion groups, of four individuals, looking for unique ideas. They found that interactive groups were less successful in generating unique ideas than were "nominal," noninteractive groups.

Mass Messaging

Mass messaging is the creation of messages that are *intended* for a relatively *large, undifferentiated audience*. These messages are most commonly mediated (e.g., via television, newspaper, radio), but they do not necessarily have to be, as in the case of a public speech.

Mass messages have been heavily studied by sociologists, social psychologists, communication scientists, marketing and advertising scholars, and others. Fully 34.8% of the mass communication articles published during 1995 in *Journalism and Mass Communication Quarterly,* one of the most prominent mass communication journals, were content analyses (Riffe & Freitag, 1997). The range of types of investigations is staggering, although some areas of study are much better represented in the content analysis literature than others; for instance, studies of journalistic coverage are common, whereas studies of films are rare.

Applied Contexts

In addition to the aforementioned means of dividing up message contexts, we might also consider such applied contexts as health communication, political communication, and the Internet, all of which transcend the distinctions of interpersonal, group, organizational, and mass communication. That is, content analyses within the health context might include analyses of doctor-patient interaction (interpersonal), the flow of e-mail among hospital employees (organizational), and images of medical professionals on TV (mass; Berlin Ray & Donohew, 1990). Yet all these studies would be better informed by a clear grasp of the norms, values, behaviors, legal constraints, and business practices within the healthcare environment. Thus, a special consideration of such applied contexts is useful. A number of these are considered in Chapter 9.

Some applications of content analysis may be highly practical. Rather than attempting to answer questions of theoretical importance, some analyses are aimed at building predictive power within a certain message arena. Box 1.2 highlights one such study. Rogan and Hammer (1995) applied a scheme to actual crisis negotiation incidents, such as hostage taking. Their findings offer insight into message patterns that may predict successful and unsuccessful resolutions to crisis incidents.

Another applied context is that of religious broadcasting. Box 1.3 describes a set of studies that took into consideration the special nature of religion on television. A variety of communication and religious perspectives informed the analyses, ranging from interpersonal communication theories to practical considerations of religious broadcasting.

6. All Message Characteristics Are Available to Content Analyze

This book takes a broad view of what types of messages and message characteristics may be analyzed. A few clarifications on terminology are in order:

Manifest Versus Latent Content

Much of the content analysis literature has concentrated on *manifest* content, the "elements that are physically present and countable" (Gray & Densten, 1998, p. 420). An alternative is to also consider the *latent* content, consisting of unobserved concept(s) that "cannot be measured directly but can be represented or measured by one or more . . . indicators" (Hair, Anderson, Tatham, & Black, 1998, p. 581). These two types of content are analogous to "surface" and "deep" structures of language and have their roots in Freud's interpretations of dreams.[2]

Although the early definition of content analysis by Berelson (1952) indicated that it is ordinarily limited to manifest content only, numerous others have boldly attempted to tap the deeper meanings of messages. For example, in the Smith (1999) study, the latent construct, "sexism," was measured by 27 manifest variables that tapped "stereotypic images of women," extracted from a variety of theoretic works (largely from feminist literature) and critical, qualitative analyses of film (e.g., Haskell, 1987).

In the case of Ghose and Dou's (1998) study of Internet Web sites, the latent variable, "interactivity" (conceptualized as related to "presence," or a sense of "being there"), was represented by 23 manifest variables that are easily measurable, such as presence or absence of a key word search, electronic couponing, online contests, and downloading of software. Although serving as the theoretic core of the study, interactivity is sufficiently abstract as to require that its more concrete elements be defined for actual measurement.

Gray and Densten (1998) promote the use of latent constructs as a way of integrating quantitative content analysis and qualitative message analysis. They used both methods to study the broad latent concept, locus of control (from Rotter's internal/external locus of control construct: An individual holding a more external locus of control feels that his or her life events are the product of circumstances beyond his or her personal control; p. 426). Their findings indicate a surprising correspondence between quantitative and qualitative methods in the discovery of new locus-of-control dimensions reflected in a variety of very specific manifest indicators.

A number of researchers have criticized any dependence on the manifest-latent dichotomy, noting the often fuzzy distinction between the two (Potter & Levine-Donnerstein, 1999; Shapiro & Markoff, 1997). It is perhaps more useful to think of a continuum from "highly manifest" to "highly latent" and to address issues of subtlety of measurement for those messages that are very latent (and therefore a challenge for objective and reliable measurement).

Another perspective one may take is that you can't measure latent content without using manifest variables. However, not all researchers would agree with this heuristic.

Content Versus Form Characteristics

Many scholars have differentiated between content and form elements of a mediated message (Berelson, 1952; Huston & Wright, 1983; Naccarato & Neuendorf, 1998). Content attributes—sometimes called *substance characteristics*—are those that may appear or exist in any medium. They are generally able to survive the translation from medium to medium. Form attributes— often called *formal features,* although there's usually nothing formal about them in the colloquial sense—are those that are relevant to the medium through which the message is sent. They are in a sense contributed by the particular medium or form of communication.

For example, the examination of self-disclosure by women to other women has been analyzed for movie characters (Capwell, 1997). The same measures of level and type of self-disclosure could be used to analyze naturally occurring discussions between women, interactions between characters on TV programs or commercials, or relationship building between characters in novels. The measures are *content* measures, applicable regardless of the medium. On the other hand, measurements of the type of camera shot (e.g., close-up vs. long shot) used when self-disclosure occurs in a film is a measure of *form,* how the content is treated in a particular medium.

Even though the distinction between content and form is an important one, the primary focus should not be on placing each variable in one category or the other. Some variables may be on the fine line between the two types, exhibiting characteristics of each. What's important is that both content and form characteristics of messages ought to be considered for *every* content analysis conducted. Form characteristics are often extremely important mediators of the content elements. Huston and Wright (1983) have summarized how formal features of TV influence the cognitive processing of TV content, notably for children. This speaks once again to the importance of the content analyst becoming well versed in the norms and syntax of the medium he or she chooses to study.

Text Analysis Versus Other Types of Content Analysis

You'll notice that some of the classic definitions of content analysis shown in Box 1.1 apply the term *only* to analyses of text (i.e., written or transcribed words). The view presented in this book is not so limiting. Content analysis may be conducted on written text, transcribed speech, verbal interactions, visual images, characterizations, nonverbal behaviors, sound events, or any other message type. In this book, the term *content analysis* encompasses all such studies; the terms *text analysis* or *text content analysis* refer to the specific type of content analysis that focuses on written or transcribed words.

Historically, content analyses did begin with examinations of written text. And text analysis remains a vibrant part of content analysis research (Roberts, 1997b). The next chapter will trace this history and show how, over time, the applications of content analysis expanded beyond the written word.

Notes

1. According to Gunter (2000), the "overriding objective" of the positivism paradigm is to "prove or disprove hypotheses and ultimately to establish universal laws of behaviour through the use of numerically defined and quantifiable measures analogous to those used by the natural sciences" (p. 4).

2. According to Gregory (1987), "Freud's approach to the interpretation of dreams was by way of the method of free association [from which Freud's psychoanalysis procedures would evolve]. . . . As in psychoanalysis proper, the subject is required to relax and allow his mind to wander freely from elements in the dream to related ideas, recollections, or emotional reactions which they may chance to suggest" (p. 274). The dream as reported was termed by Freud the *manifest content,* and the dream's underlying thoughts and wishes Freud called the *latent content.*

CHAPTER 2

Milestones in the History of Content Analysis

This chapter examines the motley history of content analysis and identifies prominent projects and trends that have contributed to enormous growth in the use of the method. Key players are identified in the development of content analysis as the prominent technique it is today.

The Growing Popularity of Content Analysis

Content analysis has a long history of use in communication, journalism, sociology, psychology, and business. Content analysis is being used with increasing frequency by a growing array of researchers. Riffe and Freitag (1997) note a nearly six-fold increase in the number of content analyses published in *Journalism & Mass Communication Quarterly* over a 24-year period—from 6.3% of all articles in 1971 to 34.8% in 1995, making this journal one of the primary outlets for content analyses of mass media. And the method of content analysis is more frequently taught at universities. By the mid-1980s, over 84% of master's-level research methods courses in journalism included coverage of content analysis (Fowler, 1986).

The growth in the use of content analysis over the past four decades may be seen in a simple analysis shown in Box 2.1, with highlights of important trends graphed in Figure 2.1. Box 2.1 contains tabled frequencies for library online index and abstract searches for the terms *content analysis* and *text analysis*. The indexes and abstracts were chosen for their ready availability and their potential relevance to content analysis in a social or behavioral science context.[1] The 20 indexes and abstracts used in the analysis cover a wide range of interests and publication types.[2]

Box 2.1 Content Analysis Timeline

Search for Keyword *Content Analysis* or *Text Analysis*

Index or Abstract	Begins	Total Number	1958	1959	1960	1961	1962	1963	1964	1965	1966	1967	1968	1969	1970	1971	1972	1973	1974	1975	1976	1977
ABI/Inform	1971	482														0	0	0	1	6	2	9
Anthropological Literature	1900	65	0	1	1	0	0	1	0	0	2	0	0	0	0	0	2	3	0	1	1	4
Arts & Humanities	1980	83																				
ComAbstracts	1966	265									1	1	0	0	0	1	0	0	0	0	1	1
Communication Abstracts	1998	292																				
Educational Abstracts	1983	1088																				
ERIC	1966	6022									12	27	58	111	103	121	160	176	198	192	236	207
HealthSTAR	1975	1305																		12	12	11
Historical Abstracts	1960	135	2	0	1	0	0	0	0	2	0	1	0	0	4	4	2	9	2	2	5	6
Humanities Abstracts	1984	213																				
Library Literature	1984	244																				
Medline	1966	1507								1	2	2	3	6	4	4	7	5	6	12	17	3
Music Index	1979	44																				
PAIS	1972	126															0	0	0	0	2	4
Periodical Abstracts	1986	404																				
ProQuest Digital Dissertations	1861	5832	4	5	6	8	3	5	6	9	12	12	10	17	25	23	18	25	29	26	23	19
PsychInfo	1887	4402	8	13	15	4	18	12	14	16	24	54	34	33	17	34	38	47	67	57	55	80
Social Sciences Cite Index	1980	1839																				
Sociological Abstracts	1963	3630						7	9	8	7	10	14	10	17	23	40	37	29	57	36	90
World Cat	1200	4225	11	25	22	34	21	32	18	37	48	64	61	62	98	85	101	90	92	98	98	126

Index or Abstract	1978	1979	1980	1981	1982	1983	1984	1985	1986	1987	1988	1989	1990	1991	1992	1993	1994	1995	1996	1997	1998	1999
ABI/Inform	2	9	11	9	13	15	22	14	19	23	22	21	27	17	36	42	38	33	28	29	13	24
Anthropological Literature	4	0	8	12	6	2	2	1	2	1	1	1	0	1	2	0	1	1	1	3	1	1
Arts & Humanities			1	5	2	1	5	1	2	7	3	4	9	12	19	17	15	15	14	9	10	3
ComAbstracts	1	2	0	1	0	2	1	0	3	1	4	5	27	29	11	17	22	19	29	24	26	31
Communication Abstracts																					145	147
Educational Abstracts						45	52	80	71	56	63	54	60	50	61	74	61	72	68	84	52	84
ERIC	211	229	238	235	233	230	230	276	251	225	202	204	185	159	189	199	202	205	239	226	183	129
HealthSTAR	11	10	10	10	20	20	11	29	24	16	35	55	78	82	76	88	106	98	139	126	129	173
Historical Abstracts		6	4	7	5	4	11	2	6	7	8	7	6	8	2	2	3	9	3	0	2	2
Humanities Abstracts							1	3	7	6	5	8	15	15	21	23	29	21	26	22	17	16
Library Literature						25	1	2	1	11	14	16	26	21	24	16	24	15	20	25	21	25
Medline	15	13	2	20	25	25	16	39	29	23	45	63	100	96	84	98	126	104	152	141	130	172
Music Index		3	3	2	6	4	4	5	4	8	7	8	11	6	7	5	12	8	8	9	3	13
PAIS	3	0	2	3	2	3	5	5	2	14	4	4	11	8	7	2	7	4	5	13	10	17
Periodical Abstracts									5	0	3	35	20	16	37	47	43	38	50	58	28	64
ProQuest Digital Dissertations	18	55	202	228	203	214	223	226	238	264	263	284	275	321	341	357	359	416	346	382	345	381
PsychInfo	67	53	93	84	145	108	94	147	165	138	155	157	189	207	211	249	244	257	289	327	279	310
Social Sciences Cite Index			20	15	27	29	21	23	21	28	34	31	30	55	149	153	163	183	201	266	217	275
Sociological Abstracts	88	65	56	58	75	63	90	135	202	178	160	160	179	184	192	201	256	272	287	211	125	122
World Cat	101	131	133	112	128	130	120	145	129	160	126	156	143	162	189	184	176	155	175	171	157	116

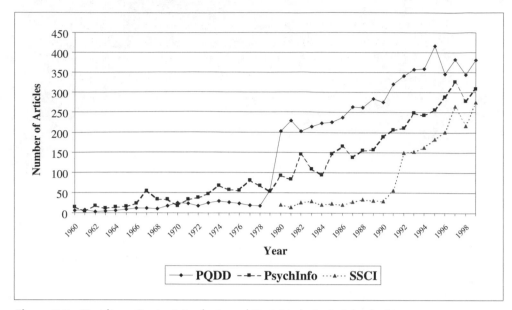

Figure 2.1. Timeline: Content Analysis and Text Analysis Articles by Year

The tabled numbers should be viewed cautiously and interpreted for what they are—the results of simple searches for terms, in publications available since 1958[3]—without full information about how the terms have been used by the researchers. That is, a number of so-called content analysis studies are actually qualitative studies, not what this book would define as content analysis at all. Second, the indexes overlap in their coverage. For example, a number of communication journals are indexed in both Communication Abstracts and PsychInfo. Third, some of the growth in content analysis applications shown is surely due to the expansion in the number of journals indexed (via new journals and cross-over additions). Taking these caveats into account, the evidence is still clear: Never has content analysis received more attention in the research literature than at the present time.

The expanding use of the technique is particularly notable in the searches of PsychInfo, the Social Science Citation Index, and ProQuest Digital Dissertations; results for searches of these three indexes are graphed in Figure 2.1. The growing use of content analysis as a technique for graduate theses and dissertations is particularly noteworthy. This expansion is shown in the rising numbers both for ProQuest Digital Dissertations and for World Cat (which includes many master's theses).

The history of the use of the various techniques called content analysis has been documented only piecemeal, with some histories emphasizing text analysis (e.g., Stone et al., 1966); some, computer text analysis (e.g., Diefenbach, in press); and others, specific applications (e.g., Rosengren, 1981), including communication (Berelson, 1952) and psychological diagnosis (Gottschalk, 1995). The field is in need of a comprehensive history that melds the various cross-influences, which are many. Unfortunately, this book, with its more practical bent, does not allow room for a comprehensive history. Instead, 10 milestones important to the history of content analysis have been selected, with an eye to those events, persons, institutions, and trends whose influence has transcended disciplinary and substantive boundaries. Following the model of Lowery and DeFleur (1995), both key historical details and important implications for the advancement of knowledge are given for each featured milestone.

Milestones of Content Analysis Research

Rhetorical Analysis

The first recorded message analyses were not content analyses. They were subjective, normative essays consisting of advice on effective speaking, and they were written about 4,000 years ago (McCroskey, 1993). In the beginning of message analysis, Aristotle applied his considerable energies to the study of rhetoric, the "art of discovering persuasive proofs" (Miller, 1987, p. 447). His tripartite analysis, focusing on the speaker, the audience, and the speech, put message content and form at the center of an argument—that we use communication to control our environment, including the actions of others (Aristotle, 1991). Over the subsequent millennia, rhetoricians have continued to conduct microscopic and theory-based analyses of persuasive communication. While rhetorical scholars prefer a logical, qualitative approach to message analysis, their techniques complement the quantitative approaches of social and behavioral scientists (McCroskey, 1993). And quite simply, we wouldn't be doing what we do if not for the influences of the early rhetoricians, who first took the art and practice of human communication seriously.

Biblical Concordances and the Quantification of History

Content analysis "learned its methods from cryptography, from the subject classification of library books, and from biblical concordances, as well as from standard guides to legal precedents" (Marvick, as quoted in Rogers, 1994, p. 214). Such systematic indexing of large message sets brought order and retrievability to the study of massive historical documents. Concordances, systems of cross-listings of terms and concepts so that themes might be readily accessed in a large text, were used centuries ago to organize scholarly studies of the Bible. Such concordances have been of use in organizing other historical documents, such as the Dead Sea Scrolls. (Obviously, the advent of the computer has made such tasks much easier.)

Another trend in the quantification of history is decryption, the identification of intended meanings for written symbols. The Rosetta Stone, discovered in 1799, contained three parallel script types—hieroglyphs, demotics, and Greek letters. Thomas Young was able to "translate" between the three scripts through a process of quantifying (counting) occurrences of signs on the stone and other ancient sources.

Other historians have applied statistical procedures to the task of organizing data from historical documents. The massive effort by Robert Fogel and Stanley Engerman (1974a, 1974b) to study American slave treatment, *Time on the Cross,* attracted both popular media and scholarly attention. The comprehensive analysis was based on historical documents containing pieces of evidence that included birth records; slave sale prices; the dimensions of slave cabins; and many measures of nutrition, health, and family life extracted from plantation records. Their analyses culminated in a report that concluded that American slaves enjoyed greater physical and psychological well-being than had previously been supposed (Sutch, 1975). Controversial in its conclusions from the date of publication (Sutch, 1975), *Time on the Cross* nevertheless succeeded in focusing attention on the meaning of "messages" sent, as it were, over time, and it stimulated interest in *cliometrics,* the quantitative measurement of historical events and trends.

While quantitative studies in history continue to be a viable part of the discipline (Dollar & Jensen, 1971; Jarausch & Hardy, 1991; Rowney & Graham, 1969), content analysis has not played as major a role in the field as have the more conventional techniques of historians (Carney, 1971; Floud, 1977). Still, content-analytic examples do exist in studies of history textbooks (e.g., Gordy & Pritchard, 1995; Holt, 1995), political documents (e.g., Anheier, Neidhart, & Vortkamp, 1998; Beriker & Druckman, 1996), news coverage of historical events (e.g., Switzer, 1990), and in other novel approaches capturing the tone of historical periods (e.g., Padilla's [1997] study of U.S. Army recruiting posters beginning in 1915 and Matcha's [1994-1995] study of early-20th-century obituaries in Ohio).

The Payne Fund Studies

In the days before television ruled the American scene, the most popular and compelling mass medium was narrative film. And before people were worried about the effects of violent television, they worried about the corruption of the nation's youth by movies. In the early years of sound films, the first major research efforts were made, backed with money from the Payne Fund. The studies looked at both movie content and effects, forging advancements in various methods of media study. Box 2.2 focuses on this milestone of an era "when movies were king."

The Language of Politics

The title of this subsection is appropriately taken from the name of Lasswell, Leites, and Associates' (1949) book, which explored the power of propaganda and the quantitative methods appropriate for examining the content of political messages. Harold Lasswell is very possibly the single most influential figure in the development of the systematic study of messages in the

Box 2.2   When Movies Were King

Studying the Power of the Moving Image

   In the late 1920s, virtually everybody in America went to the movies regularly . . . and that means *everybody*—whole families attended, unlike today's teen and date audiences. Children above 7 years of age attended movies an average of once a week (Charters, 1933). In this environment of common exposure to powerful, vivid, fictional representations, there was for the first time widespread public concern over the impact of negative images and behaviors on children. In 1928, William H. Short, Executive Director of the Motion Picture Research Council, coordinated the establishment of a major research project, funded by The Payne Fund. The researchers were psychologists, sociologists, and educators from the University of Chicago, the University of Iowa, Yale University, New York University, Pennsylvania State College, Columbia University, and Ohio State University. They launched what would be the most ambitious research project on the effects of entertainment media to date and for several decades to follow.

   The Payne Fund Studies have been identified as one of the landmarks of early mass communication research (Lowery & DeFleur, 1995). Through experimental and response studies, the movies' effects on children's learning and attitudes were studied. Surveys and interviews measured correlates of movie attendance among U.S. youth. Autobiographical case studies and experiments that employed galvanic skin response measures looked at the children's emotions as related to movie exposure. Even the effect of movies on children's sleep patterns was studied. The conclusions reached were that (a) movies were a potent source of education for children, and (b) although clearly an influence on children, movies were one among many influences that molded the experience of kids; the situation was complicated and in need of further study (Charters, 1933).

   Ohio State University was the home of the content analysis portion of the Studies. There, Edgar Dale (1935) conducted an analysis of the major themes from the written descriptions of 1,500 movies released in 1920, 1925, and 1930.[4] The films were classified into 10 types. Although the coding scheme for this variable was emergent, that is, devised from the film descriptions themselves rather than set in advance, good scientific procedures were followed when Dale used 300 films for a reliability check of the final 10-category measure, finding an average percent agreement of 87%. The results indicated a strong prevalence of both love and crime, with substantial representation by films emphasizing sex and comedy. The percentage figures for the 3 years were as follows:

	1920	*1925*	*1930*
Love	45	33	30
Crime	24	30	27
Sex	13	17	15
Comedy	12	13	16
Other	6	7	12
	100	100	100

(continued)

Box 2.2   Continued

Although this large-scale analysis gave the researchers important information about what movie content children were being exposed to, for Dale, this was just the beginning. He trained coders and sent them to theaters to watch 115 movies. They were armed with a coding guide that asked for information about nine major "social values" areas, with numerous variables under each one (e.g., nature of American life and characters; nature of foreign life and characters; motivation of characters; emotional appeals to audience; crime, delinquency, and violence; relations of sexes; military situations; depiction of underprivileged peoples; deportment). In the age before video, such real-time coding in the movie theater was limited to current releases and required that the coders sit "near a light . . . to make satisfactory notes" (Dale, 1935, p. 5). Given these challenges, it's understandable that a less-than-optimal coding protocol was established (i.e., the coders read reviews of the films before viewing to prime themselves for major themes, and the coding was what we might generously call "open-ended"— coders were to write as much as they could during the film and then continue their narratives shortly after viewing the film). On the other hand, Dale continued to attempt to apply rigorous standards. He trained the coders in contemporary standards for psychological observation and reporting and established independent reliability by accepting only those details reported by more than one coder. Moreover, he conducted an even more in-depth analysis of 40 of the films by obtaining dialogue scripts and sending stenographers to the movies to supplement the dialogue with descriptions of settings, characters, and actions. Again, he included reliability assessment. Throughout, when Dale was unable to achieve high standards, he was forthcoming about the study's limitations.

The numerous and diverse findings were summarized by Dale (1935) in a "balance sheet for motion picture content" (p. 229), which included the identification of the following emphases in 1930 movies: portrayals of life in the upper economic strata, rather than life among the middle and lower economic strata; problems of the unmarried and young, rather than problems of the married, middle aged, and old; problems of love, sex, and crime, rather than other problems of everyday life; motifs of escape and entertainment, rather than motifs of education and social enlightenment; individual and personal goals, rather than social goals; physical beauty, rather than beauty of character.

It's amazing how similar the findings are to those of contemporary analyses and criticisms of television and movies. Dale put his finger on the pulse of popular entertainment, and it still seems to be beating the same beat.

20th century. It was he who defined communication as "*who* says *what* to *whom* via what *channel* with what *effect*?"[5] He spent decades exploring the *whats* as well as the *effects* of the messages, with a focus on politically motivated communication.

Although trained as a political scientist, Harold Lasswell has been called the "da Vinci of the behavioral sciences" (Smith, 1969, p. 41) for his productivity and his renaissance-like interest and proficiency in a multitude of areas of study. He was "rambunctiously devoted to breaking down the man-made barriers between the social studies, and so acquainting each with the rest" (American Council of Learned Societies as quoted in Rogers, 1994, p. 203). He worked with linguists, anthropologists, law scholars, psychologists, and psychiatrists[6] on research that ranged from political behavior to psychoanalysis to culture (e.g., Lasswell, 1935; Rogow, 1969). He made an indelible impression on everyone who worked with him (Schramm, 1997).

Among all Lasswell's contributions, a standout is his influence on the development of content analysis as a quantitative technique. What's particularly impressive is his honest assessment of the weaknesses in his technique as his methods developed. In his progression, we can see the evolution of social and behavioral science methods in general and content analysis methods in particular. He called his 1927 dissertation a "content analysis" of World War I propaganda techniques, but it was actually very qualitative and critical (Rogers, 1994, p. 213). However, it *was* an empirical study and a first attempt at a classification of propaganda. (He studied leaflets dropped from balloons and airplanes and examined military recruitment posters.) Later, he was pointedly critical of his own anecdotal evidentiary style, noting that he didn't even report the "criteria for selection" of examples of the various propaganda styles he identified (Lasswell et al., 1949, pp. 41-42). Also, Lasswell proceeded to praise much-earlier endeavors for their "systematic definition and historical detail" of measurement (Lasswell et al., 1949, p. 44)—such studies as George Carslake Thompson's analysis of public opinion in the British population of the 1870s and several studies of newspaper coverage that used good representative sampling, topic coding, and column inch measures of coverage as early as 1900.

Lasswell made improvements to his own content analysis work and completed many quantitative studies of propaganda before and during World War II. During the war, he was chief of the Experimental Division for the Study of War-Time Communications in the U.S. Library of Congress, funded by the Rockefeller Foundation (Lasswell et al., 1949; Rogers, 1994). Later, he headed research efforts by Revolution and the Development of International Relations, a project at the Hoover Institute and Library on War, Revolution and Peace at Stanford University (Lasswell, Lerner, & Pool, 1952). Later in his career, motivated certainly by his wartime efforts to describe and predict Nazi communication activity, he seemed particularly enthusiastic about the possibility of discerning the Communist leanings of writers of pamphlets and other publications.[7]

Most of the lessons Lasswell learned in his lifetime about the utility of scientifically sound content analysis have been passed down to us. Lasswell declared that

> content analysis operates on the view that verbal behavior is a form of human behavior, that the flow of symbols is a part of the flow of events, and that the communication process is an aspect of the historical process. . . .

> Content analysis is a technique which aims at describing, with optimum objectivity, precision, and generality, what is said on a given subject in a given place at a given time. (Lasswell et al., 1952, p. 34)

He devised methods of pilot testing, coder training, and reliability assessment that have served as early models of current sound practice.

The study of political propaganda was advanced by other researchers as well and has continued to this day. Coming out of the Institute for Propaganda Analysis (founded in 1937 with social psychologist Hadley Cantril at the helm), *The Fine Art of Propaganda* (Lee & Lee, 1939) presented seven common devices of propaganda[8] still in use today. In recent decades, the Manifesto Research Group, established by David Robertson and Ian Budge in 1979 and now working in cooperation with the Research Unit in Institutions and Social Change of the Science Centre-Berlin (Budge & Hofferbert, 1996), has systematically content analyzed party platforms for elections in many countries, going as far back as 1922. An archive of their data from 20 nations covering the period from roughly 1945 to 1983 is housed at the University of Essex. In their analyses, the Manifesto group has pinpointed clearly contrasting emphases of competing parties; for example, in pooled analyses for national elections in Great Britain from 1945 through 1992, they found the Conservative Party to emphasize free enterprise and law and order much more so than the Labour Party, which emphasized economic planning and social justice. In analyses of the U.S. national elections from 1948 through 1992, they found the Republican Party focusing on a positive portrayal of the military, government effectiveness, and economic orthodoxy more than did the Democratic Party, which focused on peace and social justice (Budge & Hofferbert, 1996, p. 86).

The War at Home: Advances in Social and Behavioral Science Methods During World War II

As noted, Lasswell and others developed content-analytic techniques for uncovering enemy orientations that were useful during World War II (Rogers, 1994, p. 224). This was just one of a host of social and behavioral science advances spurred on by the war effort. The period was marked by unprecedented cooperation between private industry, government, and scholarly research bodies, joined for the noble cause of winning "the good war." The discoveries and advancements of this era jump-started research initiatives in all the sciences, including the social and behavioral sciences. Some have noted that advances during this time gave the social sciences a measure of acceptance they had long sought (Delia, 1987).

The U.S. War Department's Information and Education Division conducted a series of experiments on the effectiveness of some of the seven-part *Why We Fight* series of training and indoctrination films produced for the military by Hollywood director Frank Capra. Although the films tested had an impact on the acquisition of factual knowledge, they did not result in the hoped-for morale boost (the type of patriotism enhancement that is assumed to have resulted from the films of Nazi documentarist Leni Riefenstahl[9]). The film evaluation studies set new standards for communication effects research and established the importance of individual differences in audience members' responses to the persuasive messages (Lowery & DeFleur, 1995). Also, the captive population of military personnel afforded social scientists a great opportunity to apply theories of sampling and to refine measurement procedures with individuals as the unit of data collection (Babbie, 1995).

As Rogers (1994) notes, "The banks of the Potomac were an exciting place for social scientists during World War II" (p. 224). In the midst of this activity, content analysis experienced its share of advancements. Code breaking and other surveillance activities (what today we would call "intelligence activities") demanded the application of linguistic and psychological theories to practical predictions. During World War II, a group "connected with the BBC" (Lasswell et al., 1949, p. 49) systematically analyzed radio broadcasts from Axis powers and began forecasting Nazi policy and activities in real time. And Allied forces were able to estimate the concentration of German troops in various locations by comparing music played on German radio stations with music played elsewhere in occupied Europe (Wimmer & Dominick, 1994, p. 163).

As Delia (1987) notes, the wartime advances in research were solidified and guaranteed continuation by an "unparalleled expansion of American higher education in the postwar period. As educational opportunities were opened through government support, the universities became engines of social and economic transformation" (p. 56).

Speech as a Personality Trait

Taken from Edward Sapir's (1927) important essay, the title of this section denotes the contribution of a host of linguistic and psychological studies that took to heart Sapir's admonition that human personality traits might be discerned from communication content.

> If we make a level-to-level analysis of the speech of an individual and if we carefully see each of these levels in its social perspective, we obtain a valuable lever for psychiatric work. . . . If carried far enough, [it] may enable us to arrive at certain very pertinent conclusions regarding personality.[10] (p. 905)

As detailed in Chapter 9, a number of diverse yet overlapping areas of content-analytic study have grown up around this approach. In the following discussion, some of their common roots are considered.

The use of content analysis for both basic psychometrics (i.e., the measurement of psychological traits and states) and clinical diagnoses owes a great deal to the work of Gordon Allport (1942, 1965), who, although not engaging in content analysis per se, advanced the notion that the systematic inspection of personal documents (e.g., letters, diaries, open-ended responses on questionnaires) might be used for psychological measurement and in fact might shed light on theories of personality. In his editing and interpretation of the classic *Letters from Jenny* (Allport, 1965), he further posed the question of whether the study of a single case may fit the requirements of the scientific method. He argued that if the goals of science are to understand, predict, and control events, then to fulfill these goals for a single individual, we need to study the individual's own patterns of behavior and communication.

By the 1950s, true content analysis coding of verbalizations and individual texts was being used for a variety of psychotherapeutic purposes. Auld and Murray (1955), in their review of literature to that time, identified some of the more influential analysis schemes. Bales's (1950) interaction process analysis has been applied to exchanges between the counselor and the patient. Dollard and Mowrer's (1947) discomfort-relief quotient is a word-by-word content analysis system intended to measure the tension experienced by a patient involved in psychotherapy. Raimy's (1948) positive-negative-ambivalent quotient is another scheme intended to measure the patient's emotional reactions to the counseling process. These and other researchers established content analysis as a viable method for tapping individual traits and states.

Another innovative contributor to progress in content-analytic measurement of psychological constructs was David McClelland (1984), who developed a system of coding Thematic Apperception Test responses (from the work of Murray [1943]) to measure an individual's achievement motive (Winter, 1998). McClelland (1984) favored the development of standard, systematic content analysis coding schemes and was mystified by the field of psychology's initially slow progress in this regard: "perhaps it is the unusual sensitivity of the method to disturbances . . . [or] the time and trouble it takes to learn a coding system" (pp. 449-450). He compared psychology's reluctance to conditions in the natural sciences. "I knew that biologists were extremely careful in standardizing conditions for taking a measurement and would also spend hours making a single assay. Why couldn't psychologists take the same amount of trouble?" (p. 450).

By the 1950s, there was growing attention to methods of developing message-based personality measures from linguistic, historical, and emotional perspectives (Pool, 1959). Participants at the 1955 Allerton House conference at the University of Illinois came together to consider these and other issues. By the 1990s, psychologists' early reluctance had decreased to the point that dozens of standard content-analytic measures were in use (Smith, 1992).

Department of Social
Relations at Harvard

Harvard during the 1960s was a center of activity on the study of human communication behavior, with the establishment of the General Inquirer project. Philip Stone headed an interdisciplinary group that set out to use computer text analysis to content analyze written messages from linguistic, psychological, sociological, anthropological, and communication standpoints (Stone et al., 1966). With initial input from Harvard scholars Robert Bales and George Miller and supported by grants from the National Institute of Mental Health and the National Science Foundation, the project developed the first computer program designed to categorize language. The main dictionary was the Harvard Third Psychosociological Dictionary, which coded 3,564 different target words with 83 different tags (such as job role, clothing, and body part). As of 1965, Stone et al. noted 16 additional dictionary systems that had been developed for use with the General Inquirer, including the Stanford Political Dictionary, the Davis Alcohol Dictionary, two need affiliation dictionaries, and the Lasswell Value Dictionary (pp. 140-141). The program, with a high degree of flexibility to add and refine dictionary search and coding commands, is still actively used today, and the Essex Summer School features seminars in its use (see *The Content Analysis Guidebook Online* for links). And as Diefenbach (in press) notes, the system "still serves as the model for the method" of computer text content analysis (p. 14).

Television Images: Violence and Beyond

Just as film was the medium of choice in the 1920s and 1930s, television took over the hearts and minds of Americans in the 1950s. Perhaps for the first time since the Payne Fund studies, there was interest enough in the effects of entertainment media content to launch large-scale projects with big-time backing. The primary focus was violence on television, and numerous researchers would spend the next several decades documenting its presence and effects. Others would look at the portrayals of women, minorities, or the elderly. Some would even look at prosocial content on television (Greenberg, 1980; see also examples in Chapter 9).

Whereas many individual researchers looked at specific aspects of violence, the largest and most long-term effort was by George Gerbner and his Cultural Indicators Project team. Their studies on the frequency and types of violence on U.S. entertainment television began in 1967, with a grant from the National Commission on the Causes and Prevention of Violence, and has continued in some form ever since, funded by a host of governmental, nonprofit, and private institutions.[11] It has continually found levels of TV violence that far outstrip measures of violence in real life. And although the studies of Gerbner's team and others have supported the notion that TV violence does play a role in creating and perpetuating images of a violent and scary world, the upshot has been limited to simple debate and the institution of content warning systems. Contemporary studies of violence on TV continue to find that little has changed (National Television Violence Study, 1997). On the other hand, the high-profile Cultural Indicators Project has provided an invigorating model for generations of content analysts to come.

In the context of these projects, researchers honed their skills in analyzing the *moving image*. They had to move beyond simple text and develop new methods that considered nonverbal and other behaviors, artifacts (e.g., clothing), and even production techniques.

The Power of Computing

The General Inquirer, of course, demonstrated the use of computers to automatically analyze text messages, but its use was dependent on access to a powerful mainframe and some level of sophistication in computer use. And, the first demonstration of computer text analysis at a communication conference, by Rick Holmes and Joe Woelfel in 1982, was achieved via a 300-baud phone line connection of a "dumb" terminal at the conference with the UNIVAC mainframe at the University of Albany (Joseph Woelfel, personal communication, June 2000). Their demonstration of CATPAC heralded a changing research environment.

With the diffusion of the personal computer, both text analysis and data analysis have been brought to the desktop. PCs have revolutionized the means by which messages are created, stored and archived, disseminated, and organized. (Chapter 4 deals in greater detail with message management via computer, and Chapter 6 clarifies the important role that computer text analysis currently plays; see also Diefenbach, in press.) Huge databases of speech transcriptions or mass media messages can be analyzed at a keystroke. The availability of sophisticated data analysis techniques (for *all* purposes, not just for content analysis) is at an all-time high. Cluster analysis and multidimensional scaling are no longer the exclusive province of "techies"—CATPAC is now an extremely user-friendly, nicely designed PC application.

But we must remember that the notion of the completely "automatic" content analysis via computer is a chimera. As Diefenbach (in press) notes, "The maxim still holds, 'garbage in, garbage out' " (p. 5). The human contribution to content analysis is still paramount.

The Global Content Analysis Village

One of the many global villages[12] in evidence today is the community of scholars and practitioners of content analysis who communicate via the Internet. In past decades, there have been several efforts to reduce schisms and to cross-fertilize interdisciplinary approaches to content analysis. The 1955 Allerton House conference at the University of Illinois was an effort to invigorate the method of content analysis, perceived to be in decline at that time (Diefenbach, in press; Pool, 1959). A multidisciplinary gathering organized by George Gerbner at the University of Pennsylvania in 1966 (documented in Gerbner et al., 1969) was a truly amazing blend of individuals with diverse approaches and common goals. The publication of Ole Holsti's (1969) book, *Content Analysis for the Social Sciences and Humanities,* gave researchers a book carefully based in scientific method. And it reflects true interdisciplinary variety, as shown by his collection of research questions from the 1940s through the 1960s (p. 15); it encompasses music lyrics, literature, political communication, news coverage, advertising, authorship attribution, psychographics, and psychiatry.

After these advances, content analysts seemed to go their separate ways in the 1970s and 1980s. They tended to settle into disciplinary splits that were productive in the sense that they allowed specializations to be established and new areas of expertise to develop (e.g., methods particularly appropriate to communication; Budd, Thorp, & Donohew, 1967; Krippendorff, 1980; Smith, 1978). In the 1990s, the Internet and the World Wide Web changed that. With CONTENT, the e-mail listserv established in 1994 by Bill Evans at Georgia State University, contact was made.[13] Content analysts needed to learn to speak each others' languages again, and this process is apparent in the discussions that take place on the listserv. Today, CONTENT has more than 1,000 subscribers. Most are graduate students and faculty in university social science programs, but the mailing list also includes computer scientists, software developers, market researchers, political consultants, and public health professionals. Participants reside in the United States, Germany, Sweden, New Zealand, Canada, Great Britain, Japan—anywhere the Internet can reach. Bill Evans also went online with the first content analysis resources Web site in 1996; the reader may link to it from *The Content Analysis Guidebook Online* (see Resource 5).

What the 1955 Allerton House Conference participants discovered was a set of commonalities: Attendees across disciplines were concerned with issues related to using content analysis to make inferences about sources or receivers and with the trend toward going beyond "simply counting the frequency of words or other symbols" (Diefenbach, in press, p. 13). The next chapter revives these themes and attempts to incorporate them into a system of thinking, an "integrative" model of content analysis that demands that the researcher think outside of the box of describing content.

Notes

1. There is another "content analysis" in the discipline of chemistry, where the content is a compound for which chemical composition is analyzed.

2. The following are capsule summaries of the indexes and abstracts used in the creation of Box 2.1:

> *ABI/INFORM* (Global edition) provides abstracts from more than 1,300 business and management publications, including 350+ English-language titles from outside the United States. Complete articles for more than 600 sources are also provided. Topics covered in the abstracts and articles include business conditions, trends, corporate strategies and tactics, management techniques, and competitive and product information. Dates covered range from 1971 to the present.

Anthropological Literature index collects citations of articles and essays on anthropology, archaeology, art history, demography, economics, psychology, and religious studies. It includes English- and European-language articles, two or more pages long, published from the late 19th century to present.

Arts & Humanities Citation Index covers the journal literature of arts and humanities disciplines, including archaeology, architecture, art, Asian studies, classics, dance, folklore, history, language, linguistics, literary reviews, literature, music, philosophy, poetry, radio, television and film, religion, and theater. It currently indexes 1,144 discipline-specific journals plus relevant items from over 6,800 science and social science journals. Information from 1980 forward can be accessed through the index.

ComAbstracts (1979 to present) online database contains abstracts of articles published in the communication discipline. Approximately 50 journals are currently represented, with coverage spanning from 1979 to present (though coverage varies, depending on the journal). The full text of the abstracts may be searched by word, phrase, or author and synonyms for many search terms are automatically included in searches unless explicitly overridden (e.g., a search for "youth" will also return "teen" and "adolescent").

Communication Abstracts (1998 to present) includes references to literature in all areas of communication (mass, interpersonal, and more). It currently covers only the period from 1998 to the present.

Education Abstracts covers English-language periodicals, monographs, and yearbooks about the education discipline. Every article (of one column or more) in 423 periodicals and yearbooks is cited, along with books related to education (published in 1995 or later). Topics covered include contemporary education issues, such as government funding, instructional media, multicultural education, religious education, student counseling, competency based, and information technology. Dates covered are 1983 to present, though information from 1983 to 1993 is only indexed; abstracts begin in 1994.

ERIC, which stands for Educational Resources Information Center, is the world's largest source of education-related literature and information. Abstracts of journal articles and documents (e.g., reports, papers, books) on education research and practice are covered. In addition to the usual search features, ERIC includes a target audience code that identifies who a particular piece was intended for. It covers the period from 1966 to present.

HealthSTAR database focuses on Health Services, Technology, Administration, and Research literature. It contains bibliographic citations (plus abstracts, if available) to journal articles, technical and government reports, meeting papers and abstracts, books, and book chapters. The index covers topics with both a clinical focus (e.g., evaluation of patient outcomes and effectiveness of procedures, programs, etc.) and nonclinical focus (e.g., health policy, health services research). Information from 1975 forward can be accessed through the service.

Historical Abstracts includes references to more than 2,000 journals covering aspects of world history from 1450 to present (excluding the United States and Canada). Included are key historical journals, books, and dissertations, as well as social sciences and humanities journals of interest to history students and researchers. Historical Abstracts thus serves as a resource for researchers in fields such as history, sociology, multicultural studies, psychology, women's studies/gender studies, religion, interdisciplinary studies, anthropology and political science. Dates covered range from 1450 to the present.

Humanities Abstracts database cites articles since 1984 from approximately 468 English-language periodicals (journals and magazines) covering fields such as archaeology and classical studies, art and photography, folklore, history, journalism and communications, language and literature, literary and political criticism, music and performing arts, philosophy, and religion and theology. Some full-text articles are included.

Library Literature index includes references from 234 library and information science periodicals, plus books, book chapters, conference proceedings, state journals, theses, and pamphlets. Topics covered include the following: censorship, public relations, preservation, copyright legislation, automation, cataloging and classification, and electronic searching. The database covers the period from 1984 to the present.

MEDLINE database contains bibliographic citations and author abstracts from the fields of medicine, nursing, dentistry, veterinary medicine, health care, and preclinical sciences. More than 3,900 biomedical journals from the United States and abroad are represented; 88% of citations are in English, and 76% have English-language abstracts. The database comes from the National Library of Medicine (NLM), which indexes each article with NLM's controlled vocabulary, MeSH (Medical Subject Headings). The period covered is from 1966 to the present.

Music Index Online covers the journal literature of classical and popular music since 1979. Indexed topics include musicological or organological subjects and also book and record reviews, first performances, and obituaries. Articles from more than 640 international music periodicals are currently represented and organized within, according to an internal subject heading list.

PAIS International database indexes literature relevant to public affairs (e.g., current issues and actions affecting communities, governments, and people; topics that are or may become the subject of legislation). Subject areas covered include economics, political science, public administration, international trade, international law, international relations, demography, and social problems. PAIS International incorporates references to more than 425,000 journal articles, books, reports, Internet material, and more. Publications from more than 120 countries are indexed, in a variety of languages. Dates covered by the database are 1972 to the present.

Periodical Abstracts is a general index providing access to abstracts from general and academic periodicals covering a variety of disciplines. More than 1,800 periodicals are currently represented. Dates covered range from 1986 to the present.

ProQuest Digital Dissertations database contains citations of more than 1.6 million doctoral dissertations and master's theses published from 1861 (the date of the first accepted U.S. dissertation) to present. The full text of more than one million entries can be obtained in paper and microfilm formats, and the full text of 100,000-plus dissertations can be downloaded from the Web site. Although full-text privileges are restricted to institutional subscribers to the service, free 24-page previews of dissertations and theses (from 1997 forward) are freely available. In addition, citations for post-1979 dissertations include 350-word abstracts, and citations from post-1987 theses include 150-word abstracts. Around 47,000 new dissertations and 12,000 new theses are added to the index each year.

PsycINFO database collects citations from publications deemed psychologically relevant by the American Psychological Association, including journal articles, dissertations, reports, book chapters, and books (all English-language). In addition to psychology literature, the database includes literature relevant to communication, education, medicine, law, nursing, and social work. Dates covered range from 1967 to the present, with Historic PsychINFO going back as far as 1887 for some sources.

Social Sciences Citation Index covers the journal literature of a variety of social science disciplines, including anthropology, communication, history, industrial relations, information science and library science, law, linguistics, philosophy, psychology, psychiatry, political science, public health, social issues, social work, sociology, substance abuse, urban studies, and women's studies. Currently, more than 1,725 journals and 3.15 million articles are indexed, plus relevant items from approximately 3,300 scientific and technical journals. The database allows users to access information from 1980 onward, and author abstracts are available from approximately 60% of cited works. In addition, the index also cites references, allowing users to check the cited works in each article as well as the number of times the article has been cited in other works.

Sociological Abstracts collects research citations from sociology and related social and behavioral science disciplines. It includes information from 2,600 journals plus conference papers, books, and dissertations. The database covers research from 1963 to the present; however, only records after 1974 include in-depth, nonevaluative abstracts.

WorldCat, a general online database, includes references to any type of material cataloged by Online Computer Library Center member libraries (including master's theses). Areas covered include arts and humanities, business and economics, conferences and proceedings, consumer affairs and people, education, engineering and technology, general and reference, general science, life sciences, medical and health sciences, news and current events, public affairs and law, and social sciences. Around 40 million records are currently indexed, dating from the 12th century to present.

3. In Box 2.1, years are left blank for which no search is possible for an index. A zero indicates that the index is operable for that year, but no citations to content analysis or text analysis are found. For example, Humanities Abstracts begins with the year 1984; there is one content analysis/text analysis cite for that year.

4. The descriptions were provided by *Harrison's Reports,* a commercial reviewing service available to movie exhibitors. The Reports included a brief plot description for each film released. Dale did a validity check of the Harrison plot summaries.

5. Notice that there was no "why" component to the question. Lasswell's receiver (rather than source) orientation is well noted.

6. Lasswell trained in psychoanalytical methods with Elton Mayo at Harvard, and his subsequent psychoanalytical research was rejected by political scientists and Freudians alike. In the late 1930s, he made plans to establish an institute with Yale anthropologist and linguist Edward Sapir and psychoanalyst Henry Stack Sullivan, a plan cut short by Sapir's death.

7. In Lasswell's seminal work (Lasswell et al., 1949), one of his applications of content analysis was his "propaganda detection," a coding system to be used in support of the McCormack Act, a 1939 law that provided for the registration of foreign agents with the federal government (Spak, 1990). He notes, "In periods of crisis, it is peculiarly necessary to identify enemies of democracy, and to stimulate the members of the public to be on guard in evaluating what is said" (Lasswell et al., 1949, p. 175).

8. Lee and Lee's (1939) seven propaganda devices are (a) name calling, (b) glittering generality, (c) transfer, (d) testimonial, (e) plain folks, (f) card stacking, and (g) band wagon. This classification system is still used today (Severin & Tankard, 1997).

9. Riefenstahl's master works *Triumph of the Will* (1935) and *Olympia* (1937), artistically groundbreaking films documenting the 1934 Nuremberg Nazi Party Rally and the 1936 Berlin Olympics, respectively, are credited by popular and scholarly critics as having stimulated public support for Adolph Hitler (Kracauer, 1947).

10. Sapir (1927) identified five levels for "get[ting] at the personality of an individual" (p. 904) from speech characteristics: (a) voice, (b) voice dynamics (e.g., intonation, rhythm, continuity, speed), (c) pronunciation, (d) vocabulary, and (e) style.

11. Signorielli, Gerbner, and Morgan (1995) provide the following partial list: The Surgeon General's Scientific Advisory Committee on Television and Social Behavior, the National Institute of Mental Health, the White House Office of Telecommunications Policy, the American Medical Association, the Administration on Aging, the National Science Foundation, the W. Alton Jones Foundation, the Screen Actors' Guild, the American Federation of Television and Radio Artists, the National Cable Television Association, the U.S. Commission on Civil Rights, the Turner Broadcasting System, the Office of Substance Abuse Prevention and the Center for Substance Abuse Prevention of the U.S. Public Health Service (p. 279). The Cultural Indicators Project findings are reported in Gerbner (1972), Gerbner and Gross (1976), Gerbner, Gross, Signorielli, Morgan, and Jackson-Beeck (1979), Gerbner et al. (1980), Gerbner, Gross, Morgan, and Signorielli (1986), and Gerbner, Gross, Morgan, and Signorielli (1994).

12. Marshall McLuhan predicted a global village, linked by electronic technologies (McLuhan & Powers, 1989). Fred Williams (1982) refined this prediction to include *multiple* villages defined by communities of interest rather than geography, and this has indeed come to pass.

13. Bill Evans notes that he began CONTENT—the Internet mailing list for news and discussion of content analysis—"because I was lonely. I was at the faculty at Georgia Tech., where I was surrounded by colleagues with interests in research methods and computing. Unfortunately, none of my colleagues had more than a passing acquaintance with content analysis. . . . But I also knew many other researchers at other universities who felt similarly isolated." (William Evans, personal communication, June 2000)

CONTENT provides a forum for discussion among content analysts, and Bill Evans also sends informative content analysis "Publication Alerts" to the listserv subscribers.

CHAPTER 3

Beyond Description
An Integrative Model of Content Analysis

As noted in Chapter 1, this book takes the view that content analysis is (or should be) a research technique that conforms to the rules of science. Most closely related to the technique of survey research, it uses messages rather than human beings as its level of analysis. Issues that apply include those of validity (internal and external), reliability, sample representativeness, the principle of maximum information (Woelfel & Fink, 1980), and objectivity (or intersubjectivity). Before proceeding on a discussion of exactly how content analysis may be conducted to achieve these standards, a basic background on the ground rules and terminology of the scientific method is in order.

The Language of the Scientific Method

Whether explicitly stated or not, a primary goal of most scientific studies is to identify *causal relationships*. That is, we hope to discover at least one causal agent (X) that leads to at least one outcome (Y). Establishing a cause-and-effect relationship is rarely (many would say never) achieved in social and behavioral scientific study; it is almost impossible to meet all three criteria for causality: (a) a relationship, (b) time ordering (such that X precedes Y in time), and (c) the elimination of all alternative explanations. The second criterion—time ordering—requires either a study that has two or more measurement points over time (a *longitudinal* study) or an experiment. The third criterion—accounting for all alternative explanations—is generally impossible to fully achieve. However, the task is to do the most complete job possible, identifying and measuring as many *control* variables as possible.[1]

Given that the discovery of true causality is essentially an unattainable goal, we do not refer to "cause" and "effect." Rather, we refer to each "presumed cause" as an *independent variable* and each "presumed effect" as a *dependent variable*. A *variable* is a definable and measurable construct that varies, that is, it holds different values for different individual cases or units. For example, we may predict that gender is related to interrupting behavior, such that males will interrupt conversations more often than will females. Each unit (person, in this case) will hold a certain value on the independent variable (male or female) and a certain value on the dependent variable (e.g., 4 times in 5 minutes, 12 times in 5 minutes). These values must vary across units or there exists no variable for study; for instance, if all persons in the study are male, no comparison may be made with females, and therefore "gender" does not exist in the study as a variable; we could not assess the impact of gender on interrupting behavior. In this example, gender is the independent variable and interrupting behavior the dependent variable. In a *hypothesis,* we predict that one's gender affects one's interrupting behavior; the converse is clearly impossible in this case.

The main empirical, quantitative methods available to the social or behavioral scientist to investigate *hypotheses* or *research questions* about possible relationships between independent and dependent variables are the *experiment* and the *survey.* An experiment is an investigation in which at least one independent variable is manipulated or controlled. A survey is a study in which an attempt is made to measure all variables—independent and dependent—as they naturally occur. Note the simplicity of these definitions. Despite common expectations, an experiment does *not* have to take place in a laboratory setting (although many do). And a survey does *not* have to consist of a questionnaire (although most do). An experiment could be conducted in a "real" setting, such as a workplace. For example, a researcher might randomly assign employees in an organization to types of working conditions (e.g., face-to-face work teams vs. "virtual," online work teams), and then outcome variables could be measured.

Most surveys do involve the use of a *questionnaire,* that is, a set of questions that are presented to a respondent either as a self-administered paper-and-pencil booklet, as an online set of questions, or as an interview. However, many experiments also use a questionnaire, especially to measure dependent variables and control variables. And a survey that does *not* use a questionnaire is quite possible—it might involve direct observation of behavior: for instance, observing and tabulating a child's play behavior. Although the "self-report" nature of the study has been eliminated, it's important to note that the observation process also relies on subjective human reportage—in this case, a human observer-coder of others' behavior. As we shall see, this involvement of humans in the measurement process is of great concern in content analysis.

The relative advantages and disadvantages of the two research approaches —experiment and survey—are clear. An experiment generally enjoys a high degree of control and certainty about the validity of the independent variable(s) but is often artificial in its execution (i.e., higher on validity and lower on generalizability, which is sometimes called *external validity*). A survey is more true to life and tends to be more generalizable so long as a *random sample* is employed, but its measures are more suspect, especially when they rely on self-report questionnaire responses (i.e., higher on generalizability or external validity and lower on validity). Most scholars agree that the "best" approach is one of *triangulation*, that is, testing for a hypothesized relationship among variables with a variety of methods—experiments, surveys, and other, more qualitative methods. The various methods' strengths and weaknesses tend to balance out, and if all the various methods reveal similar findings, the support for the hypothesis is particularly strong.

Content analysis as a research method is consistent with the goals and standards of *survey* research. In a content analysis, an attempt is made to measure all variables as they naturally or normally occur. No manipulation of independent variables is attempted. Some type of random sampling of the units of data collection is typical, making the findings generalizable to a larger grouping or *population* of messages. Note that the units of data collection are simply different from those of the typical survey (i.e., messages rather than persons). And the questionable validity of the measures in a survey also applies to the content analysis. Just as the self-report nature of most surveys calls into question the objectivity and validity of their measures, so, too, the involvement of human decision makers in the content analysis process calls into question the validity of the coding or dictionary construction. In short, the content analysis enjoys the typical advantages of survey research and usually suffers its drawbacks as well.

How Content Analysis Is Done: A Flowchart for the Typical Process of Content-Analytic Research

As a form of scientific endeavor, content analysis ought to be conducted in line with procedures appropriate to good science. Box 3.1 contains a flowchart of the typical process of content analysis, with nine steps outlined. The model follows the common steps for research in the scientific method, applying appropriate terminology for content analysis whenever needed. Subsequent chapters will explore the steps: Steps 1 through 3 are treated in Chapter 5; Step 4, Coding, is included in Chapter 6; Step 5, Sampling, is the subject of Chapter 4; Steps 6 through 8 are addressed in Chapter 7; And Step 9, Tabulation and Reporting, is dealt with in Chapter 8. An important distinction apparent in the flowchart is the splitting off of human coding from computer coding at two junctures. At this point, it's important to understand the differences between the two.

Box 3.1   A Flowchart for the Typical Process of Content Analysis Research

1. *Theory and rationale: What* content will be examined, and *why?* Are there certain *theories* or perspectives that indicate that this particular message content is important to study? Library work is needed here to conduct a good literature review. Will you be using an integrative model, linking content analysis with other data to show relationships with source or receiver characteristics? Do you have *research questions? Hypotheses?*

2. *Conceptualizations:* What *variables* will be used in the study, and how do you define them *conceptually* (i.e., with dictionary-type definitions)? Remember, you are the boss! There are many ways to define a given construct, and there is no one right way. You may want to screen some examples of the content you're going to analyze, to make sure you've covered everything you want.

3. *Operationalizations (measures):* Your measures should match your conceptualizations (this is called *internal validity*). What *unit of data collection* will you use? You may have more than one unit (e.g., a by-utterance coding scheme and a by-speaker coding scheme). Are the variables measured well (i.e., at a high *level of measurement,* with categories that are *exhaustive and mutually exclusive*)? An *a priori* coding scheme describing all measures must be created. Both face validity and content validity may also be assessed at this point.

Human Coding   Computer Coding

4a. *Coding schemes:* You need to create the following materials:

    a. *Codebook* (with all variable measures *fully* explained)

    b. *Coding form*

4b. *Coding schemes:* With computer text content analysis, you still need a codebook of sorts—a full explanation of your *dictionaries* and method of applying them. You may use standard dictionaries (e.g., those in Hart's program, *Diction*) or originally created dictionaries. When creating custom dictionaries, be sure to first generate a frequencies list from your text sample and examine for key words and phrases.

Human Coding   Computer Coding

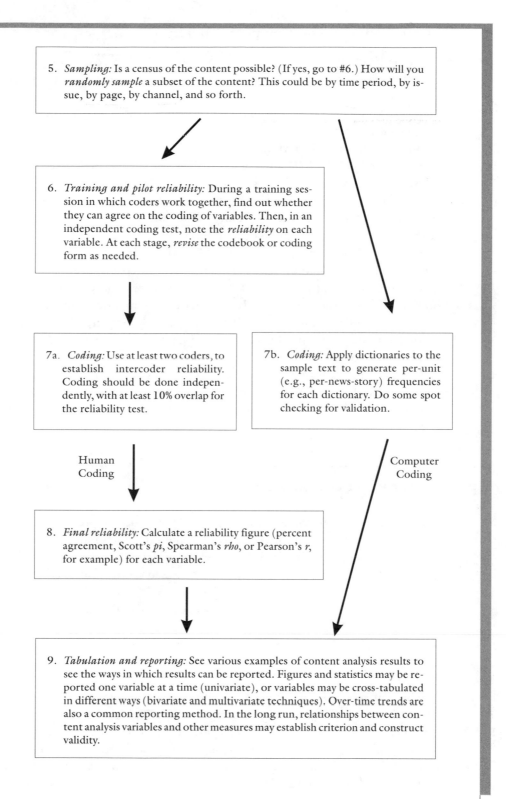

5. *Sampling:* Is a census of the content possible? (If yes, go to #6.) How will you *randomly sample* a subset of the content? This could be by time period, by issue, by page, by channel, and so forth.

6. *Training and pilot reliability:* During a training session in which coders work together, find out whether they can agree on the coding of variables. Then, in an independent coding test, note the *reliability* on each variable. At each stage, *revise* the codebook or coding form as needed.

7a. *Coding:* Use at least two coders, to establish intercoder reliability. Coding should be done independently, with at least 10% overlap for the reliability test.

7b. *Coding:* Apply dictionaries to the sample text to generate per-unit (e.g., per-news-story) frequencies for each dictionary. Do some spot checking for validation.

Human Coding

Computer Coding

8. *Final reliability:* Calculate a reliability figure (percent agreement, Scott's *pi*, Spearman's *rho*, or Pearson's *r*, for example) for each variable.

9. *Tabulation and reporting:* See various examples of content analysis results to see the ways in which results can be reported. Figures and statistics may be reported one variable at a time (univariate), or variables may be cross-tabulated in different ways (bivariate and multivariate techniques). Over-time trends are also a common reporting method. In the long run, relationships between content analysis variables and other measures may establish criterion and construct validity.

Human Coding Versus Computer Coding

Human coding involves the use of people as coders, with each using a standard codebook and coding form to read, view, or otherwise decode the target content and record his or her objective and careful observations on preestablished variables. Computer coding involves the automated tabulation of variables for target content that has been prepared for the computer. Typically, computer coding means having software analyze a set of text, counting key words, phrases, or other text-only markers. The term *CATA* has been adopted to designate the popular use of "computer-aided text analysis."

Until recently, some content analysts referred to automated coding as *machine coding*, leaving open the possibility of noncomputer automated coding. Are there currently any machines other than computers capable of conducting some type of automated content analysis? Not really. However, as will be described in Chapters 4 and 6, there are a number of video and audio technologies that may assist in the coding of visual and auditory content. In all likelihood, as their potentials for fully automated coding develop, all these technologies will be firmly linked with (controlled by, or merged with) computers. However, theoretically, machine coding could be conducted by a device other than a computer.

Chapter 6 presents some examples of codebooks and coding forms for human coding and dictionaries for computer coding via computer text content analysis. More examples are available at *The Content Analysis Guidebook Online*.

Approaches to Content Analysis

This book presents the view that content analysis is best approached as one tool for testing relationships within a basic communication model. The classic Shannon-Weaver (Shannon & Weaver, 1998) model provides the raw framework of *source, message, channel, and receiver.* Based on this, Berelson (1952) proposed five purposes for content analysis: (a) to describe substance characteristics of message content (essentially what are described in Chapter 1 as content characteristics), (b) to describe form characteristics of message content, (c) to make inferences to producers of content, (d) to make inferences to audiences of content, and (e) to determine the effects of content on the audience.

The view presented in this book does not accept the notion that it is appropriate to make conclusions about source or receiver on the basis of an analysis of message content alone. Carney (1971) expresses the view that there are three uses of content analysis: Descriptive, hypothesis testing, and *facilitating* inference. This book's presentation is more consistent with Carney's view, extending it somewhat to include the consideration of *extramessage* variables, that is, variables measured on source or receiver units.

This chapter will attempt to develop an integrative model of content analysis, which recognizes that whereas content analysis itself can only *describe* message characteristics or identify *relationships* among message characteristics, its methods are integral to a full understanding of human behavior and hence essential to social and behavioral science. When combined with results from other studies that use persons as units of inquiry (Shoemaker & Reese, 1990), content analysis can provide important missing links in multistep models of human communication behavior and of audience responses to mediated communication. Thus, whereas Berelson, for example, says that we may infer source characteristics or intent from examining message content, this book argues instead for the integration of content analytic studies with surveys of sources that give concrete evidence of source characteristics or intent. The goals of science are typically presented as *description, prediction, control,* and *explanation.* Only with an integrated approach to data collection can applications of content analysis aspire to the highest goal: explanation.

To date, the common approaches to content analysis may be categorized as descriptive, inferential, psychometric, and predictive.

Descriptive Content Analysis

Many content analyses describe a particular message pool in almost archival fashion. Researchers working in this vein are careful to limit their conclusions to the content being studied, although they may clearly be motivated by a desire to infer characteristics to the source(s) or to anticipate outcomes of the messages. These analyses are attractive in their clarity and parsimony. But they sometimes seem to be targets for those who question the scientific importance or sophistication of content analysis as a method.

An example of descriptive content analysis would be the ongoing research tracking sexual content in U.S. television programming (Kunkel, Cope-Farrar, Biely, Farinola, & Donnerstein, 2001). Whereas its origins are clearly in a concern over the effects of sexual content on viewers, the project never overstates its conclusions—they are purely content based. Key findings include an identified rise in sexual content over a 2-year comparison period, notably in shows featuring teenagers.

Also, a team at Temple University is currently involved in a long-range project to describe formal features of TV as they are presently employed (Lombard, Campanella, Linder, & Snyder, 1996). Motivated by the growing body of evidence concerning the physiological and psychological processing and impact of structural features of television (e.g., pace of editing, camera angles, sound effects, use of text and graphics), their work begins to document the state of the art of television production. Their descriptive goal is clear.

Another example of a purely descriptive content analysis is the Screen-Actors-Guild-sponsored analysis of prime-time television programming, the African American Television Report (Robb, 2000). A team led by Darnell Hunt at the University of Southern California examined a sample of 384 episodes of 87 prime-time series on the six broadcast networks, identifying a total of 6,199 characters. The study found that although African Americans composed 12.2% of the U.S. population at the time of the data collection, they accounted for about 16% of the characters. This "overrepresentation" was more marked in situation comedies, with more than half (50.5%) of all Black characters appearing in sitcoms.

It needs to be understood that *descriptive* does not always mean *univariate*, that is, describing results one variable at a time. There might be—and often should be—a predicted relationship among variables measured in the content analysis. A good example is Dixon and Linz's (2000) study of television news coverage of lawbreakers. They found a significant relationship between the race of the perpetrator and whether the crime reported was a felony. Thus, the bivariate (two-variable) relationship is

Race of perpetrator → Type of crime (felony or nonfelony)

Inferential Content Analysis

The view presented in this book does not endorse most explicit inferences made strictly from content analysis results, a view consistent with early admonitions by Janis (1949). Counter to this view, Berelson's (1952) 50-year-old encouragement continues to be invoked in cases where researchers wish to make conclusions about sources or receivers solely from content-analytic studies. Yet such unbacked inferences are inconsistent with the tenets of the philosophy of science—it is important to note that they are not empirically based.

It seems that interpersonal communication-type content analyses (especially those with known receiver[s]) tend to try to infer to the source, whereas mass communication-type studies (with undifferentiated receivers) tend to attempt to infer to receivers or receiver effects or both, although this observation has not been backed by data (e.g., a content analysis of content analyses). Clearly, however, there is great interest in going beyond description of messages. As we will see, there are alternatives to nonempirical inference.

Psychometric Content Analysis

The type of content analysis that seems to have experienced the greatest growth in recent years within the discipline of psychology is that of psychometric content analysis. This method seeks (a) to provide a clinical diagnosis for an individual through analysis of messages generated by that individual or (b) to measure a psychological trait or state through message analysis.

This particular application of content analysis might be seen as going beyond simple inference in that the measures are validated against external standards. Applying the notion of criterion validity as articulated by Carmines and Zeller (1979), the technique involves a careful process of validation, in which content analysis is linked with other time-honored diagnostic methods, such as observations of the subject's behavior (the "criterion"). Over a series of investigations, the content analysis dictionaries (sets of words, phrases, terms, and parts of speech that are counted up in a sample of the subject's speech or writing) are refined to improve their correspondence with the older diagnostic and psychographic techniques (Gottschalk, 1995; Smith, 1992). The ultimate goal is, however, to *infer* to a given source without having to apply these other diagnostic tools each and every time. But this is done only after substantial, careful validation with numerous sources.

Predictive Content Analysis

This type of content analysis has as its primary goal the prediction of some outcome or effect of the messages under examination. By measuring key characteristics of messages, the researcher aims to predict receiver or audience responses to the messages. This necessitates the merging of content-analytic methods with other methods that use people as units of data collection and analysis—typically, survey or experimental methods or both.

A good example of this type of study is Naccarato's (Naccarato & Neuendorf, 1998) combined content analysis and audience study that linked key print advertising features to audience recall, readership, and evaluations of ads. Box 3.2 tells the story of the research process, and Box 3.3 carries the process a bit further by applying the knowledge gained from the content analysis to a hypothetical creative process of new ad creation.

In a series of studies linking media presentations of violent acts and aggregate crime and mortality statistics from archival sources, Phillips (1974, 1982, 1983; Phillips & Hensley, 1984; Phillips & Paight, 1987) has established a long and distinctive record of research using simple predictive content analysis.[2] He has examined the incidence of homicides after network news coverage of championship boxing matches, the incidence of suicides after newspaper reports of suicides, and the occurrence of deaths due to car accidents following soap opera suicides. Although Phillips's attempts to draw causal conclusions have come under criticism (Gunter, 2000), his research approach has shown robust, replicable relationships between media reports and depictions of violence and real-life events.

Another type of predictive content analysis that has been gaining popularity is the prediction of public opinion from news coverage of issues (e.g., Salwen, 1986). Through a blending of content analysis and public opinion poll summarization, Hertog and Fan (1995) found that print news coverage of three potential HIV transmission routes (toilets, sneezing, and insects) *preceded* and was *significantly related* to public beliefs about those routes as expressed in polls. Key details of this innovative and sophisticated study are reported in Box 3.4.

Box 3.2   The Practical Prediction of Advertising Readership

After 20 years as an advertising professional, John Naccarato wanted his master's thesis (see Naccarato & Neuendorf, 1998) to merge theory and research with a practical application to his chosen field. In his capacity as a business-to-business ad specialist, he was accustomed to receiving reports from publishers and from other standard readership services regarding the level of readership for the ads he placed in business-to-business publications. Privately, he had always asked what he called the "why" question: *Why* did one ad perform better than another? What was it about a given ad that attracted the reader?

He settled on content analysis as a method of linking the already accessible readership data with ad characteristics. In this way, he would be able to find out if certain ad attributes bore a relationship to readership scores. If so, although causality would not be verifiable, he could at least make *predictions* from ad characteristics. Only a handful of studies had tried to do something along these lines; only a few of these analyzed print advertising, and none had examined the business-to-business context (Chamblee, Gilmore, Thomas, & Soldow, 1993; Donath, 1982; Gagnard & Morris, 1988; Holbrook & Lehmann, 1980; Holman & Hecker, 1983; Stewart & Furse, 1986; Wood, 1989).

Naccarato's needs were concrete—he wanted to find the best combination of ad variables that would predict reader response—but he did not ignore theory and past research in his collection. From persuasion theories, he derived measures of the ad's appeals (e.g., humor, logical argument, fear; Markiewicz, 1974). From earlier content analysis studies, he adapted indicators of form attributes, such as use of color, ad size, and other layout features. From practitioner recommendations found in advertising texts, he pulled variables such as use of case histories, use of spokespersons, and competitive comparisons. And from his own personal experience in advertising, John extracted such notions as the consideration of the role of charts and graphs in the ad layout. At the end of the process of collecting variables, he had a total of 190 variables.

Naccarato's codebook and corresponding coding form were lengthy (both may be found at *The Content Analysis Guidebook Online*). As a result of combining variables and

The Integrative Model of Content Analysis

Expanding on this notion of predictive content analysis, it is proposed that a comprehensive model for the utility of the method of content analysis be constructed.

To date, Shoemaker and Reese (1996) have been the most vocal proponents of integrating studies of media sources, messages, audiences, and media effects on audiences. They have developed a model of research *domains* for typologizing mass media studies. Their individual domains are as follows:

eliminating variables with low reliabilities or lack of variance, the final pool of variables was reduced to 54 form and 21 content variables for inclusion in analyses.

The population of messages was defined as all ads appearing in the trade publication, *Electric Light and Power* (*EL&P*) during a 2-year period. Sampling was done by issue; eight issues were randomly selected, with all ads in each issue included in the analysis (n = 247). All the ads in *EL&P* during this time period had been studied via the publisher's own readership survey, the PennWell Advertising Readership Research Report. This self-report mail survey of subscribers measured audience recall and readership and perceptions of the ad as attractive and informative. The survey sample sizes ranged from 200 to 700, and response rate ranged from 10% to 50%.

With the unit of analysis being the individual ad, data were merged to analyze the relationship between ad characteristics and each of the four audience-centered dependent variables. Stepwise regression analyses were conducted to discover which of the 75 independent variables best constructed a predictive model.

This approach proved to be fruitful. All four regression models were statistically significant. Variances accounted for were as follows: For ad recall, 59%; readership, 12%; informativeness, 18%; attractiveness, 40%. For example, ad recall seemed to be enhanced by use of a tabloid spread, greater use of color, use of copy in the bottom half of the ad, use of large subvisuals, and advertising a service (rather than a product). Recall was lower with ads that were of fractional page or junior page size, that used copy in the right half of the ad, and that used a chart or graph as their major visual (rather than a photo).

John Naccarato's practical interest in predicting audience attraction to business-to-business ads was rewarded with some powerful findings and resulted in a caution against taking practitioner recommendations too seriously. In only a small number of instances did such recommendations match up with the study's findings of what relates to positive reader reactions. For example, books by leading advertising professionals recommend such techniques as the use of a spokesperson, humor, calls to action, and shorter copy. Yet none of these was related to any of the four audience outcomes. On the other hand, copy placement and use of fear appeals were important predictors that practitioners usually ignore.

A. Source and system factors affecting media content

B. Media content characteristics as related to audience's use of and evaluation of content

C. Media content characteristics as predictive of media effects on the audience

D. Characteristics of the audience and its environment as related to the audience's use of and evaluation of media content

E. Audiences' use of and evaluation of media content as related to media's effects on the audience

Box 3.3   Creating the "Perfect" Advertisement

Using Content Analysis for Creative Message Construction

Box 3.2 shows how an integrative content analysis model can produce powerful findings with practical significance. By linking message features with receiver response, Naccarato and Neuendorf (1998) discovered specific form and content characteristics of business-to-business advertisements that led to recall, readership, and other indicators of message effectiveness. A logical next step would be to relate these findings back to the source level by constructing an ad that incorporates all of the successful predictors.

Just for fun, a sample ad has been created that does just that. The ad, shown below, is for the fictional product, *SharkArrest*. It incorporates all of the exclusively positive, significant predictors of business-to-business message effectiveness from the Naccarato and Neuendorf study into a single message.

Protect your resort with *SharkArrest*

Rows and rows of razor-sharp teeth. Five-thousand pounds of clamping pressure. These are just a few frightening attributes of sharks that can wreak havoc on a successful resort community. But now there's a solution to shark-related anxiety.

SharkArrest is a new service for the safety-conscious resort owner. The SharkArrest team of experts is specially trained to fend off sharks using advanced fish repellent techniques. The patented methods are scientifically proven and 100% environmentally & shark safe.

For more information and a free trial, call:
1-555-NOSHARKS

SharkArrest
www.sharkarrest.chomp

Form Variables

Headline placement, top: The headline, "Uninvited guests can kill your business . . .," is located at the top of the ad, making it the first distinguishable feature, from a top-down perspective. This placement relates positively to perceived *informativeness* of the ad.

Subject apparent in visuals: Sharks, the subject of the ad, is clearly communicated through the shark photograph in the top half of the layout. Making the subject apparent in visuals is a positive predictor of both *readership* and *informativeness*.

Color: The original SharkArrest ad (not reproduced in color here) includes two colorful photos, one of a shark and another of a beach, and also some color text. Color leads to both *recall* and perceived *attractiveness*.

Large size of subvisuals: The photo of the beach at the bottom is larger than a typical subvisual, which positively predicts *recall*.

Copy placement, bottom: Two paragraphs of copy appear in the bottom half of the SharkArrest ad. This layout predicts both *recall* and *attractiveness*.

Content Variables

Fear appeal: The ad uses a frightening photo of a great white shark and copy describing some threatening attributes of sharks, to strike fear in resort owners, because it makes sharks seem like a danger to both their businesses and their guests. Fear appeals positively predict both *readership* and *attractiveness* of ads.

Ad type—service: The ad is from a shark protection company that provides a service to business customers by keeping sharks away from their property. Ads for a service are significantly likely to be *recall*ed by business-to-business ad readers.

These features could all be included in a real-life business-to-business service advertisement, thus making it a perfect ad, in light of the Naccarato and Neuendorf study results. More important, this example shows one of the many creative possibilities opened up by an integrative content analysis approach.

These authors propose combining the five domains to produce a variety of broader domains of research, with domain A-B-C-D-E as the optimal "fully elaborated model of mass communication" (p. 257). Their model clearly distinguishes between message *effects* on audiences and audiences' more active *use* of media messages.

The Shoemaker and Reese (1996) model can productively inform our discussion of integrating content analysis with additional data. Domains A, B, and C clearly address the utility of content analysis data and hold similarities to the integrative model proposed here. But key differences do exist. The Shoemaker and Reese model is in some senses more restrictive (in its particular application to mass communication research) and in other senses more expansive (in its consideration of modes of inquiry other than content analysis). The integrative model developed in this chapter is designed with the simple goal of focusing interest on the role of *content analysis* in answering questions via social and behavioral science investigations.

This model uses the basic Shannon-Weaver communication model (Shannon & Weaver, 1998) as a guide. That model, developed by mathematicians at

Box 3.4   Approaching Causality—Does Press Coverage *Cause* Public Opinion?

The prevailing view of news coverage by those who report it is that the news *follows* public opinion, rather than *leads* it. That is, the public agenda is first established and then news reporters simply pick up on evident trends and document them. Many scholars have questioned this point of view, and numerous media effects studies have established the potential of media messages to change the opinions of individuals. Hertog and Fan (1995) took the novel approach of tracking aggregate public opinion in light of overall news coverage on a singular topic. Using techniques originally proposed in Fan's (1988) book on computer text analysis of news coverage, they collected public opinion poll findings and content analyzed news stories on the same topic over the same period of time.

All stories pertaining to supposed AIDS transmission via sneezes, toilets, and insects, from eight news sources (four major U.S. newspapers, three news magazines, and the UPI newswire) were collected for the years 1987 to 1991. The 166 stories were human-coded for coverage of the issue—"pro" (e.g., representing the view that you *can* get AIDS from toilets) or "con" (e.g., representing the view than you *cannot*). The results of 23 National Health Interview Survey polls were available for the same period, all of which included measures of public perception of the likelihood of AIDS transmission in each of the three manners. Data were merged by time period, with each poll representing one data point.

Using Fan's (1988) ideodynamic model, the relative impacts of both pro and con AIDS transmission stories were assessed. For example, for both sneezing and insects, pro stories seemed to carry more weight than con stories, resulting in a significant change in public perception toward the erroneous pro viewpoint.

Most important, Hertog and Fan (1995) used the Granger Causality Test to examine over-time relationships between news coverage of each AIDS transmission type and public opinion. For both sneezing and toilet transmission, they found news content to predict later public opinion. Public opinion did *not* predict subsequent news content. With a relationship *and* time ordering well established, these findings come as close to establishing causality as we have seen in content-analytic research.

Bell Laboratories in 1949, was designed to describe the flow of information in a mediated system and to mathematically model conditions for optimal system operation (e.g., reduce noise). The original model consisted of the identification of the following elements: source, message, transmitter, signal, channel, noise, receiver, and destination. The model was readily adopted by social and behavioral scientists as a descriptor of the human communication process, with source "encoding," receiver "decoding," and "feedback" from receiver to source as key additions.

Despite its explication in a wide variety of studies over a 50-year period, the Shannon-Weaver model (Shannon & Weaver, 1998) has experienced little adjustment for the changing information environment (e.g., Baran & Davis, 1995; Dominick, 1990; Schramm & Roberts, 1971; Straubhaar & LaRose, 1996). For example, current debate over what constitutes *message* and what constitutes *channel* in considering Internet Web sites (e.g., as when the site is so responsive to the user that the channel "interacts" with the receiver, creating a unique message pool and mode of presentation for each individual user) has not yet resulted in a popular revision of the model (Skalski, 2000). Generally, the Shannon-Weaver model (Shannon & Weaver, 1998) is a paradigmatic framework for most scholars studying communication activity.

The proposed integrative model of content analysis takes off where Berelson (1952) left off. Rather than engaging in overt inference making from content-analytic information alone, the integrative model calls for the collation of content analysis message-level data with other available empirical information regarding source, receiver, channel, or other contextual states. It requires that a content analysis study be examined within the framework of the basic communication model. Although this may seem rather mechanistic, it provides us with a clear picture of what components contribute to our understanding of the messages of interest, as well as the nature of the links between message variables and extramessage variables.

Evaluation With the Integrative Model of Content Analysis

The quality of the information from each component of the modeled study should be evaluated, as should the quality and strength of the *links* among components. We might think of these links between message variables and source or receiver variables in terms of how closely tied the data are. Although the strength of the ties between data sets decreases as we move from first-order to third-order linkage, all are improvements over simple description and unwarranted inference.

First-Order Linkage

The units of analysis are isomorphic (i.e., the same) for content analysis and source or receiver data. This one-to-one correspondence allows for strong relationships to be established. The one-to-one link may be a Type A, in which the precise messages analyzed in the content analysis are the ones created by the sources under study or are the ones accessed by the receivers under study. An example would be Naccarato and Neuendorf's (1998) study of print ads, in which the very ads that were content analyzed were the ads receivers responded to in a readership survey. Or the first-order link may be a Type B, in which the messages and sources or receivers are linked by a unit of analysis that is not a message under investigation—for example, if the messages and receiver characteristics are summarized and then linked by a time period, such as *year,* as in studies of news coverage and public opinion (e.g., Domke et al., 1997; Iyengar & Simon, 1993; Watts, Domke, Shah, & Fan, 1999).

Second-Order Linkage

In this case, a link is established without a one-to-one correspondence on some unit of analysis. Such links may be anecdotal or occasional—that is, every unit in the content analysis is not matched with a unit in a source or receiver study. An example shown later in this chapter is Andsager and Miller's (1992) study of news coverage of a public issue, which they link to intermittently occurring events in the sociopolitical environment.

Third-Order Linkage

Here, there are no one-to-one or occasional correspondences of units of analysis. Rather, there is an overall *logical* link between content analysis and other studies based on the variables selected for study. Studies identified earlier as descriptive might easily fit this description. A third-order link is simply a logical link, using evidence from source or receiver studies to provide a rationale for a content analysis or using a content analysis as motivation for source or receiver studies. For example, a set of studies on alcohol advertising found that two of the most common appeals in beer and wine ads (celebrity endorsements and sex appeals, as identified in a *content analysis*) were also significantly more attractive to teens than to older adults (as discovered in *experimental studies* of teens and adults, using newly created ads; Atkin, Neuendorf, & McDermott, 1983).

The integrative approach is a simple way of analyzing the role of content analysis in the investigation of the larger framework of the communication process. Examples that have linked content analysis data with extramessage source data and extramessage receiver data are considered in turn in the following discussion.

Linking Message and Receiver Data

Often, a goal in marketing and mass media research is to demonstrate an effect (e.g., greater audience attendance) of media message characteristics. For example, the Naccarato and Neuendorf (1998) study (see Box 3.2) could be modeled in the following way, with S representing source characteristics, M/Ch representing message (within a channel) characteristics, and R representing receiver characteristics. The double-headed arrow may be viewed as leading from message to receiver (indicating effects) or from receiver to message (indicating use or voluntary exposure).[3]

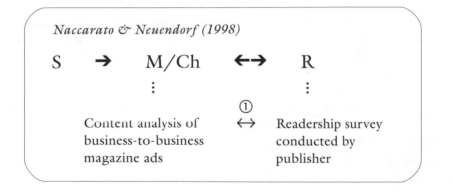

Data are linked one-to-one (first-order linkage, ①); the unit of analysis is the individual ad, for which both content-analytic and survey data are collected. Note that the units of data collection are different, however (unit = ad for the content analysis, unit = person for the readership study).

In evaluating this content analysis, we might criticize the low reliabilities of a number of measures and the inclusion of a relatively small number of content (vs. form) variables. The readership survey may be criticized for sampling problems and self-report issues typical of readership studies. On the other hand, the linkage is quite sound, given the one-to-one correspondence by individual ad. As noted in Box 3.2, the researchers were able to conduct multiple regression analyses to predict readership scores from ad characteristics.

In the case of Hertog and Fan's (1995) study (see Box 3.4), the original units of sampling or data collection are not the same, but the two data sets have some shared unit of analysis. The study could be summarized as

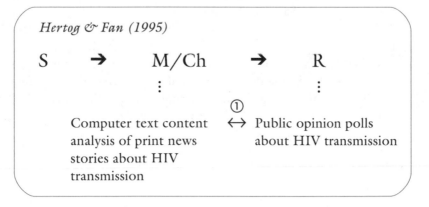

Data are linked by time period (first-order linkage); the units of analysis are time periods corresponding to 23 available National Health Interview Surveys between 1987 and 1991; the original units of data collection were the news stories for the content analysis and the individual respondents for the polls. Each study was well executed, and the tie between the two was fairly strong.

In an extraordinary study that ultimately linked pessimism in popular songs to the subsequent state of the U.S. economy (really), Zullow (1991)

also accessed publicly available data (public opinion poll findings and economic data) to link with his content analysis. This is also a wonderful example of the high level of sophistication to which content analyses may aspire. Both the coding scheme and the time-series analysis plan required a high degree of methodological and statistical expertise. Zullow found that as pessimistic rumination (i.e., negative descriptions or evaluations of an event) in popular songs increased, consumer optimism declined. Furthermore, he found that a decrease in gross national product (GNP) tended to follow. The flow from "bad vibes" songs to lowered GNP was found to occur over an average of 2 years. His study may be diagrammed as

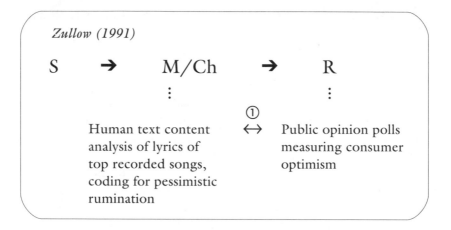

Data are linked by time period (year; first-order linkage). Each data collection was sound: The intercoder reliabilities for the coding of song lyrics were good, and the consumer polls were the highly regarded Index of Consumer Sentiment, conducted by the Survey Research Center at the University of Michigan.

Zullow (1991) has applied measures of pessimism and rumination in other contexts. In a human-coded content analysis of Democratic and Republican presidential candidate nomination acceptance speeches from 1948 to 1984, Zullow and Seligman (1990) found that the candidate who expressed more pessimistic rumination lost 9 of 10 times. Again, the study linked message characteristics and audience (receiver) responses in a clear and powerful manner.

Boiarsky, Long, and Thayer's (1999) study of children's science television provides a clear case of a *third-order linkage,* using content analysis to test the prevalence of key message characteristics that have previously been found to be important to the receiver's response. They chose three form characteristics that had been well studied in experimental work: content pacing, visual pacing, and use of sound effects. Past studies had found rapid visual or auditory change to increase children's attention to television programming (in some cases, resulting in enhanced learning) but on the other hand had found rapid topic switching to inhibit children's learning (p. 186). The Boiarsky team was interested in finding out whether contemporary children's programming that ostensibly had an educational goal—science programming—used devices that would maximize children's learning. Their mixed findings indicated a high number of attention-gaining features (e.g., sound effects, quick cuts) but also rapid pacing (e.g., cuts rather than dissolves, very frequent topic shifts) that would tend to inhibit children's learning. The study's linkage with previous work may be diagramed as

Boiarsky, Long, & Thayer (1999)

$$S \quad \rightarrow \quad M/Ch \quad \rightarrow \quad R$$

③

Human content analysis of formal features of children's science television   ↔   Experimental research identifying the impact of several key formal features of children's television

Again, the contents-analytic research and experimental studies, each well conducted in their own right, are linked only loosely, by a logical third-order connection (③).

Linking Message and Source Data

In content analyses in the field of psychology, a link between source characteristics and message characteristics is often desired. For a half century, Louis Gottschalk and colleagues have been involved in developing methods of measurement of psychological dimensions (with biological roots) in children and adults, through the analysis of the content and form of their verbal behavior (Gottschalk, 1995, p. 3). The early studies, especially, provided strong links between source and message; they were designed to validate content analysis measures against more traditional evaluative procedures—self-report scales, physiological measures, and psychiatric rating scales (assessed by an expert, trained observer).

In one study, the researchers measured brain activity, cerebral glucose levels, as well as levels of hopefulness and hopelessness in verbal reports of dreams following REM sleep, non-REM sleep, or silent, waking mentation (Gottschalk, Fronczek, & Buchsbaum, 1993). They concluded that there are "different cerebral representations for hopefulness and hopelessness during each [of the three] state[s] of consciousness" (Gottschalk, 1995, p. 14). Their study could be modeled as

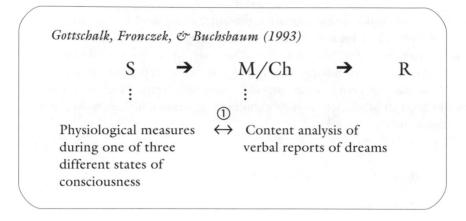

Data are linked on the individual subject (person), a first-order linkage.

In a study of interpersonal verbal behavior, Marche and Peterson (1993) refuted a substantial body of evidence indicating that males engage in the majority of interruptions when conversing with women. Their study looked at 20-minute structured conversations of 90 dyads, with same-sex or opposite-sex composition. With good intercoder reliability (87%-95%), conversation interruptions were identified by human coders. Interruption behavior did not vary significantly by age, by gender of the interrupter, or by the gender composition of the dyad: Males did not interrupt more often than did females. The study could be modeled

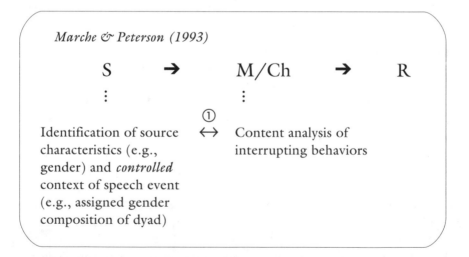

Data are linked by the individual subject (person).

In journalism, studies that link content analyses with source studies seem to be a bit rarer than those linking message and receiver data. Shoemaker and Reese's (1996) comprehensive volume on "mediating the message" is unique in its emphasis on the study of mass media sources and those source and structural factors affecting the production of media content. Notably, they rely on the Westley and MacLean (1957) model of the news-gathering process. This model is similar to the Shannon-Weaver (Shannon & Weaver, 1998) source-message-channel-receiver model but with a notable addition—a "universe of possible messages" from which sources select (Shoemaker & Reese, 1996, p. 34). But studies that investigate how sources make this selection are infrequent. Shoemaker and Reese have summarized scores of content-analytic studies that clearly intend to infer back to source intent without source data.

The few news studies that do include source data include Farley's (1978) study of magazine publisher gender and tone of coverage of the Equal Rights Amendment, in which female publishers produced more favorable coverage. Another source-integrative study is Shoemaker's (1984) investigation of special interest and other political groups, in which she combined content analyses of *The New York Times'* coverage of 11 political groups with survey data tapping U.S. journalists' attitudes toward those groups—the more "deviant" the journalists judged the groups, the less legitimately the publication portrayed the groups (Shoemaker & Reese, 1996, p. 90). Some studies of news coverage have measured source *organizational* variables rather than characteristics of individual authors or gatekeepers. For example, in a study of the impact of corporate ownership on news reportage, Pasadeos and Renfro (1988) compared the content of the *New York Post* before and after its purchase by media mogul Rupert Murdoch. They found that Murdoch ownership signaled a greater amount of page space devoted to visuals and a more sensational coverage style.

A content analysis that included a perfunctory survey of entertainment sources is Smith's (1999). Her study of character portrayals in female-focused films of the 1930s, 1940s, and 1990s (introduced in Chapter 1) included unobtrusive measures of the gender of key "sources" of the films—writers, directors, producers, and editors—as identified in film encyclopedic sources. Her findings included the identification of a somewhat surprising impact of female involvement behind the scenes, such that greater female creative control was related to a higher level of stereotypically feminine portrayals of women characters. Smith's combination of unobtrusive measurement of a key source variable (gender) and content analysis could be modeled in the following manner.

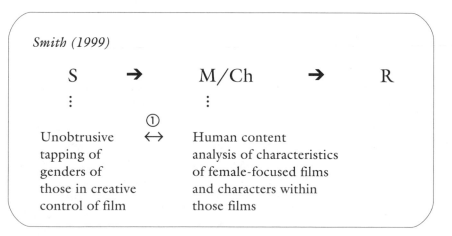

Data are linked by film (a strong first-order linkage). The survey of sources was as valid as the encyclopedic sources used, and the content analysis was generally quite competent but suffered from some low reliabilities.

In a mass media study exemplifying a somewhat more tenuous source-message link, Andsager and Miller (1992) explored a connection between newspaper coverage of RU-486, the so-called abortion pill, and events occurring in the environment that were likely to affect news coverage. Each of 998 news stories appearing in major newspapers between 1982 and 1994 was computer content analyzed. Several important framings of the abortion pill were discovered in a cluster analysis of 125 key terms—information, women's health, and policy. Producing a time line for each of these three clusters, the researchers identified peaks in the types of coverage. They provided proposed explanations for these peaks based on time-matched events. For example, a peak in women's-health-type coverage of RU-486 in 1989 coincided with the announcement of a University of Southern California clinical trial of the pill and a new campaign by the National Organization for Women to legalize RU-486 in the United States. Another peak, in 1993, co-occurred with the Food and Drug Administration's approval of testing RU-486 in breast cancer prevention trials. As Andsager and Miller point out, "the incorporation of time-sequencing plots adds to understanding of relationships among a variety of concepts involved in an issue over time. They also aid in interpreting what events and issues shape coverage" (p. 9). The study may be diagramed as

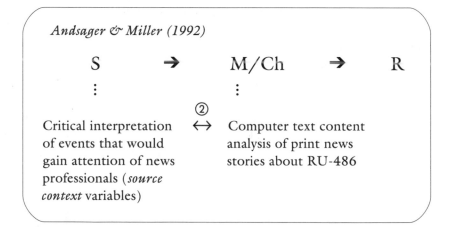

Data are linked by time sequencing (but with only a second-order linkage [②]: that is, without a one-to-one correspondence of units of analysis).

Developing New Linkages

To date, content analysis studies that engage in some sort of first-order or second-order linkage between message and source or message and receiver are the exception rather than the rule. And studies that link all three—source, message or channel, and receiver—are rare. Some collected research reports, such as the 1972 *Surgeon General's Report on Television and Social Behavior* (Comstock & Rubinstein, 1972) have at least *addressed* all three. In the five-volume report on media violence, the editors combined several television content analysis and effects studies with a chapter on source (e.g., interviews with producers, writers, and directors; Baldwin & Lewis, 1972).

Researchers should be encouraged to add source or receiver data collection to their content analysis studies whenever possible. And although not forgetting theory as the primary motivator for any study, researchers might be alert to the potential for adding a content analysis to already existing findings regarding sources or receivers. For example, Solomon and Greenberg (1993) studied choices made by professional television property masters in their selection of furniture, clothing, and other props for TV commercials. Their survey of 25 working professionals found evidence of high consensus in choices of props for characters of a particular social class and gender. A content analysis could confirm how widespread is this "collective selection among individuals responsible for constructing the 'worlds' present in television commercials" (p. 17).

Sometimes, findings regarding the *effects* of a certain type of message may just be sitting there, waiting for a content analysis to add to the knowledge base. For example, Chen and Rada (1996) conducted a meta-analysis of experimental studies on the utility of hypertext, synthesizing the quantitative findings of 23 studies. They found a significant positive relationship between nonlinearity of structure and effective user performance and a significant positive relationship between the presence of graphical maps and user performance. A logical next step would be for a researcher to see how prevalent these important hypertext characteristics are in the information pools of CD-ROMs and Web sites, for instance. The characteristics of nonlinearity and graphical representation have been found to be effective for users; now we may ask, are they being put to use in hypertext applications? Content analysis may bring closure to this issue and to others that could benefit from content-analytic data.

Notes

1. A *control* variable helps assess whether an alternative explanation to a true relationship between X and Y may exist. For example, we may wish to test whether an individual's television viewing (X) leads to the individual's aggressive behavior (Y), which we could diagram as X ---> Y. There may be reason to believe that the level of aggressive behavior in the home (Z) may be related to both X and Y, most likely in one of the following ways: (a) X ---> Z --->Y or (b) X <--- Z ---> Y. That is, perhaps (a) television exposure leads to aggression in the home, which in turn leads to an individual behaving aggressively, or (b) a climate of aggression in the home leads to both increased TV viewing and an individual in the home behaving more aggressively. In either case, X does

not directly affect Y, and any relationship found between X and Y is what we call *spurious*. Also, in either case, Z constitutes an *alternative explanation* for a relationship between X and Y. We might include a measure of Z in our study as a control variable. If, after including Z as a statistical control, a relationship between X and Y still holds, then Z may be eliminated as an alternative or competing explanation.

2. More recently, Phillips's work has examined mortality rates as related to other, nonmedia factors, such as living in or visiting New York City (Christenfeld, Glynn, Phillips, & Shrira, 1999), the symbolic meaning of an individual's initials (Christenfeld, Phillips, & Glynn, 1999), and whether a person's birthday has recently occurred (Phillips, Van Voorhees, & Ruth, 1992).

3. As a point of comparison, the typical nonintegrative (i.e., wholly descriptive) content analysis might appear like this.

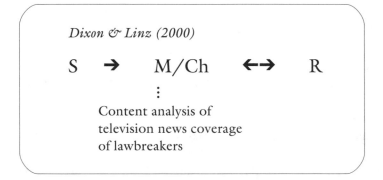

Dixon & Linz (2000)

S → M/Ch ←→ R

Content analysis of
television news coverage
of lawbreakers

In this model, no data have been linked from either the sources of the messages or the receivers of the messages.

CHAPTER 4

Message Units and Sampling

This chapter introduces the reader to the initial decisions necessary in content analytic research. Various types of units are considered, showing the range of choices in selecting the unit(s) for a given study. There is discussion of proper random sampling techniques, including the standard simple random sampling, systematic random sampling, cluster sampling, stratified sampling, and multistage sampling. Issues of access to sampling frames, message archive documentation (Resource 1), the use of the NEXIS database for text collection (Resource 2), and the management of the medium (e.g., the use of computer programs to unitize and mark-up video content) are explored.

Units

In content analysis, a *unit* is an identifiable message or message component, (a) which serves as the basis for identifying the population and drawing a sample, (b) on which variables are measured, or (c) which serves as the basis for reporting analyses. Units can be words, characters, themes, time periods, interactions, or any other result of "breaking up a 'communication' into bits" (Carney, 1971, p. 52).

As indicated in Chapter 1, these types of units are called units of sampling, units of data collection, and units of analysis. They are not always the same; for example, Lombard et al. (1996) have routinely used a random sampling of time periods, dates, and television channels to obtain a good representative sample of television programming. From this body of content, they analyze certain variables for each episode. For other, more microscopic variables, each randomly selected 10-second time interval within the episode ("timepoint") is used as the unit of data collection, and other units of data collection are also used (e.g., the segment, the shot, the transition, the single frame). Weyls (2001) collected news stories dealing with adult entertainment from the NEXIS online database and analyzed each story using the text analysis computer program, Diction (Hart, 1997). His ultimate goal, however, was to track changes in coverage by *year*, and his results are presented in that way. Here is a summary of the key points of the unitizing conducted by the Weyls and the Lombard et al. studies.

	Weyls (2001)	*Lombard et al. (1996)*
Unit(s) of sampling	News story	Time, date, channel
Unit(s) of data collection	News story	Episode, time interval, and so on
Unit(s) of analysis	Year	Episode, time interval, and so on

Two different perspectives exist regarding the unitization (i.e., the segmenting into units) of messages. They correspond to the classic distinction between *etic* and *emic* (as in "phonetic" and "phonemic"; Headland, Pike, & Harris, 1990). Much debate exists over the precise difference between these two epistemological perspectives. However, the general notion is one of etic referring to scientifically generated knowledge and emic denoting subjective knowledge or experience (thus, an etic approach seems more consistent with the techniques of content analysis). However, we may profit by considering both etic and emic approaches to unitizing. As Berry (1990) notes, "Etic units and classifications are available in advance, rather than determined during the analysis. Emic units must be discovered, not predicted" (p. 85). Just as critical content analytic variables may be discovered as well as prescribed by the researcher (see Chapter 5's discussion of emergent variables), so too may units emerge from the pool of messages. Through immersion in the message pool, the researcher may discover what units make sense within the world of those messages. Berry would refer to these as *derived etic* units (i.e., derived from an emic process). The only caveat is this: Actual content analysis coding should not commence until the final unit(s) of data collection have been defined, *after* the emic discovery process.

Although the researcher is ultimately the boss, so to speak, there might be pragmatic or methodological reasons for choosing one type of unit over another. For example, Gottschalk (1995) and colleagues have found the verbal *clause* to be the best unit of data collection—the one which is assessed for the presence or absence of many key markers in their psychologically based coding scheme. Their rejected alternatives include the word, the sentence, the paragraph, and the message as a whole. In their case, using the clause was found to be the smallest identifiable unit for which they could reliably code for their desired variables, thus providing maximal variance for these measures across the entire unit of sampling (a full 5-minute spoken message from one individual).[1]

The sampling unit should be large enough to well represent the phenomenon under investigation. For example, Gottschalk and Bechtel (1993) report that a verbal selection of 85 to 90 words is adequate for diagnostic purposes; with fewer than that, the results may be unreliable. Hill and Hughes (1997) used a rather unique and complicated ultimate unit of data collection—the thread of discussion, or the entire conversation, found in discussions by USENET newsgroups dedicated to American politics. They were interested in the dynamics of the interaction—sampling individual postings would not provide the full information they desired.

Unitizing a Continuous Stream of Information

There is good evidence that human actions are experienced by an observer (e.g., a coder) as coherent units, with clear beginnings and endings, and that there generally is consensus as to where those breakpoints are (Newtson, Engquist, & Bois, 1977, p. 849). That said, attempts to allow coders the authority to unitize (i.e., to separate a stream of actions into discrete units) are often met with failure. For example, Abelman and Neuendorf (1987) attempted to train coders to identify individual topic changes in discussions presented in religious TV programming. Coders were not able to do this reliably, due in large part to the fluidity of the conversations. A reasonable level of agreement for unitizing was not reached, and the researchers opted instead to use researcher-imposed *time-based* units—5-minute intervals. Thus, while viewing on videotape, the coders would pause every 5 minutes, according to the real-time counter, and indicate on a coding form the presence or absence of several dozen coded topics.

On the other hand, attempts to train coders to reliably unitize when more easily definable and *discrete* events must be extracted from a continuous stream on content are often more successful. Greenberg (1980) headed a large-scale content analysis project with more than 50 coders, most of who were charged with identifying unique instances of such TV content as antisocial behaviors, prosocial behaviors, sex-role behaviors, and verbal interactions. Wurtzel and Lometti (1984) reported success at reliable coder unitization of violent acts in television programming in their commercial research endeavors (social research at the ABC television network).

Others have also experienced success at unitizing, such as those using interaction analysis. As Folger, Hewes, and Poole (1984) note, "social interaction can be unitized into a variety of segments" ranging from 300 milliseconds to the entire theme of an interaction between two speakers (p. 118). Selecting the "act" as his unit of data collection, Bales (1950) had a good rationale: The act is "the smallest discriminable segment of verbal or nonverbal behavior" that a coder could code "under conditions of continuous serial scoring"

(p. 37). Hirokawa (1988) has identified four different unit-of-data-collection options for interaction analysis: thought units, themes, time intervals, and speech acts.

Defining the Population

The researcher gets to define the population for the study. The population is the set of units being studied, the set of units to which the researcher wishes to generalize. For content analysis, this is often a set of messages; it may, however, be a population of people, whose messages are then collected and analyzed (as is frequently the case in psychological and interpersonal communication applications of content analysis). Once the population is defined, it must serve as the basis for any sampling. Sparkman (1996) has identified a trend of serious violations of this precept in his study of 163 U.S.-based advertising content analyses published between 1977 and 1993. He found 97% of the articles to be based on samples that included regional and local advertising, yet almost all reported to be studies of "national" advertising. Sparkman reports on research showing significant differences in key variables among various regional and local ad populations, indicating that the location of the collection of the sample of ads will heavily influence the nature of the supposedly national sample. Again, if the population is defined as national print ads, then the sample needs to be taken from a roster of national print ads and should not include other types of ads.

The defined population may be quite large, such as all books ever published. It might be of a more limited size, such as parent-child interactions among participants at a co-op daycare facility. It may be narrowly defined, such as all female-directed films released in the United States in 1999. Lee and Hwang (1997) purposely limited their population—and therefore their sample—to movie ads in the *Los Angeles Times* for two specific years, 1963 and 1993. For their study of female images, they had clear rationales for the limitations they placed on their population definition (Los Angeles as home to the movie industry, 1963 and 1993 as key years in feminist history). Evans (1996) also had a narrow population definition—two groups of magazines that were most dissimilar in readers' household income but similar on readers' gender, race, and age.

In the case of a small population, there may be no need to draw a smaller, representative sample of the population. Rather, all units in the population may be included in the study, which would then be called a *census*. More commonly, the population is quite large (we like to generate knowledge about broad-ranging and important things, after all), and a sample is drawn from it. For future reference, the following table allows us to learn the terminology of populations and samples.

	Population	Sample
The study of its units:	Census	Survey, experiment, content analysis
The number of units in it:	N	n
A number that summarizes information about a variable and its distribution:	Parameter	Statistic
The mean of a variable:	μ	M or $\overline{X}$
The standard deviation of a variable:	σ	sd
The variance of a variable:	σ^2	sd^2

Sometimes, a population is defined by criteria set by the researcher, but he or she has no notion ahead of time as to how many messages might be in the population. For example, Breen (1997) searched the NEXIS database for all newspaper articles in major papers during certain time periods between 1991 and 1994 that included the key search terms, "catholic" and "priest" or "clergy" within two words of each other. The search resulted in a set of articles that served as the population from which he then drew a sample.

Jasperson, Shah, Watts, Faber, and Fan (1998) used a similar procedure to extract from NEXIS all relevant stories over a selected 7-month period in 19 selected U.S. newspapers. They used a detailed search string aimed at locating stories about the U.S. budget deficit. This resulted in an N of 42,695, from which they pulled a simple random sample of $n = 10,000$.[2]

Keenan's (1996a) study of network TV news coverage of public relations used the Television News Archive at Vanderbilt University as the initial sampling frame, executing a search for the terms "public relations" and "PR" for the period 1980 through 1995. A total of 79 stories were identified, and this entire population was studied in a *census* content analysis. Miller, Fullmer, and Walls (1996) analyzed all 995 journal articles obtained in a search for the keyword "mainstreaming" in the ERIC (Educational Resources Information Center) database in their census of messages.

In the case of content analyses of hard-to-find messages, such as historical documents, the population may be defined by the availability of materials. Shapiro, Markoff, and Weitman (1973) collected as many documents as they could to study communication at the beginning of the French Revolution (specifically, in the year 1789), resulting in a collection that included "virtually all the extant . . . documents produced by the Nobles and commoners at the final stage of the electoral process, and carried to Versailles" (p. 177).

Occasionally, messages that we think ought to be fully indexed are not, and we have to punt, so to speak. Rothbaum and Xu (1995) studied popular songs dealing with parents and their adult children and, unable to locate a useful index of such songs to serve as a sampling frame, surveyed students for nominations. This, then, became a study of "popular songs perceived by undergraduates to be about parents and their adult children." Note that another, much more laborious but appropriate technique would have been to select a very large random sample from a general list of popular songs (e.g., *Billboard's* rankings) and then screen for relevant songs.

Archives

An *archive* is a collection of messages, usually well indexed. This is to be distinguished from the index itself, which simply lists the titles and/or other identifying information about the messages. An archive contains the messages in their entireties.

An amazing variety of archives exists. Some annotated lists of archives have appeared in print, such as *Reruns on File: A Guide to Electronic Media Archives* (Godfrey, 1992), *Untapped Sources: America's Newspaper Archives and History* (Vanden Heuvel, 1991), and *Historical Information Systems* (Metz, Van Cauwenberghe, & van der Voort, 1990). Many archives are now accessible online. For example, the NEXIS database referred to earlier is an archive, part of LEXIS/NEXIS, a computer-assisted legal research service (LEXIS) and the world's largest database of full-text news and business publications (NEXIS; Emanuel, 1997). This is perhaps the largest message archive in existence, with more than 9.5 million documents added daily to over one billion documents already online (pp. 1-2). NEXIS is probably the largest message archive available online and certainly the most accessed for content analyses of news coverage (even though the developers of the service never intended for it to be used for this purpose). Resource 2 provides a short, practical guide to some of the dos and don'ts for using the NEXIS database for content analysis purposes.

The ERIC database is also very large, composed of over a million documents of relevance to the field of education. The ERIC database is a combination of older documents available on microfiche and newer additions available on CD-ROM.

In the fields of linguistics, languages, history, literature, and related fields, archives are often referred to as *corpora*. Each corpus (or "body") is typically a set of written materials representing a particular era and place (e.g., Louis Milic's [1995] *Century of Prose Corpus,* a compilation of samples of British English text written by 120 authors between 1680 and 1780). A corpus may be the collected works of one writer (e.g., Edmund Spenser) and may include a "concordance" or search faculty that generates linkages between texts based on common topics or terms (e.g., the "Concordance of Great Books"; see *The Content Analysis Guidebook Online*). Scholars working with corpora have established standards for the electronic storage and transfer of texts, called the TEI standards (Text Encoding Initiative; Ide & Sperberg-McQueen, 1995). Storing texts in electronic form allows complex applications that were not possible before the texts could be studied and summarized via computer. Lowe and Matthews (1995) used the complex Radial Basis Function neural network technique to compare texts written by William Shakespeare and his contemporary John Fletcher and were able to shed light on the probable authorship of disputed texts.

There are literally thousands of message archives out there. Think of any peculiar type of message content—from Three Stooges films to movie scripts to letters written home by Civil War soldiers—and there's an archive for it. The Internet has exploded our access to archives, both online databases and other, physical archives. Resource 1 provides a guide to some of the most enduring and active message archives. *The Content Analysis Guidebook Online* includes summaries for and links to additional archives and corpora. Some quick examples will show the range of options.

- WordNet and EuroWordNet (Alonge et al., 1998; Fellbaum, 1998; Vossen, 1998) are collections of words, organized in semantic networks, in which the meanings of nouns, verbs, adjectives, and adverbs are represented by links to other words and sets of words. Useful to those who study linguistics quantitatively (i.e., who work in the area of computational linguistics), these so-called lexical databases are available online.

- Archives of survey and interview data that include open-ended responses may be useful to linguists, psychologists, and others. The Henry A. Murray Research Center at Radcliffe College has hundreds of data sets available online for secondary analysis.

- The Television News Archive at Vanderbilt University in Tennessee is the world's most complete collection of television news, containing every evening news broadcast by the major U.S. networks since 1968. For a fee, custom compilation tapes may be ordered. And abstracts are available and can be analyzed using computer text analysis (e.g., Iyengar & Simon, 1993).

- Both the Steven Spielberg Jewish Film Archive and the National Center for Jewish Film contain collections of films relevant to the Jewish experience.

The Evaluation of Archives

Although the Internet has exponentially increased our ability to locate and access message archives, it is an unpoliced source of information, and many so-called archives are the selective collections of private individuals. For example, numerous joke archives exist that are simply collections of Web masters' favorite jokes. Even legitimate message archives may not be definitive or complete collections; for example, the Gish Collection at Bowling Green State

University is composed solely of the materials bequeathed to the university by sisters Dorothy and Lillian Gish, major stars of American silent films. This difference between *comprehensive* and *selective* message archives is important. When an archive is selective, that limitation may then narrow the definition of the population (e.g., as in "a study of the Gish Collection at Bowling Green State University").

Lee and Peterson (1997) consider the issue of content analyzing archived messages, cautioning that these messages are typically gathered for another purpose by other researchers. They recommend a careful initial screening of some units from the archive to determine whether the archived materials are suitable to the task at hand. They provide an excellent review of content analyses that have used archives in the field of clinical psychology. They identify several distinct advantages to using archived messages that seem appropriate to most content analysts.

- Longitudinal (over-time) studies may be conducted retrospectively. For example, Peterson, Seligman, and Vaillant (1988) analyzed attributional style (i.e., the pattern of attributing causes to outcomes) for historically archived essays completed by returning World War II soldiers. They were able to show a relationship between the men's attributional style and their state of health 35 years later.

- Content analysis may be conducted on messages from sources not readily available otherwise (e.g., U.S. Presidents, Hall of Fame athletes). Simonton (1981, 1994) has used this technique extensively, studying psychological attributes of famous composers, scientists, and writers from archived texts, in his studies of greatness.

- Various archived materials allow the study of messages at a variety of levels—the individual, the family, the organization, the nation. Access to cultural-level messages (e.g., mass media products, political statements) can aid in cross-cultural investigations, of which there have been many in recent years.

Medium Management

There has always been a need for the content analyst to understand the nature of the medium in which the target messages are found and the operation of equipment for delivery of the messages. This could be as simple as knowing how to find specific news articles in a newspaper's morgue, learning how to record and play back audiotape or videotape, or knowing how to use transcription equipment.[3] But with the explosion of options in electronic and digital media, new considerations have come into play.

The Brave New Digital World

The digital age has fundamentally changed the ways in which content analysis may be conducted. Digital technologies have changed—and continue to change in ways we can hardly anticipate—a number of tasks important to content analysis.

1. Archiving messages: Other sections of this chapter point out the advancements in electronic and digital archiving and the ease of locating message archives in the age of the Internet. Digitally archived messages are typically immediately available for computer text content analysis, as in Hogenraad and McKenzie's (1999) study of 110 European political speeches, which they downloaded en masse and analyzed with several CATA systems.

2. Searching for messages: Similarly, electronic archives and indexes give users unprecedented power to search databases and archives systematically.[4]

3. Preparation of messages for coding and message handling during coding: There are surprising new systems for such support functions as the transformation of messages to computer-readable form (e.g., voice recognition of news broadcasts), the mark-up of message sets in preparation for coding (e.g., the NUD*IST computer suite, typically used for qualitative work, can be used to notate texts in preparation for human coding), and the manipulation of messages during coding (e.g., Pettijohn and Tesser's [1999] use of the PhotoMagic software to help in the measurement of facial features of film actresses in a study of facial attractiveness). A number of other advances are outlined in the discussion to follow.

4. "Automatic" content analysis coding: The "ultimate" use of digital technologies in content analysis, automatic coding, has been achieved for only one type of content analysis research—computer text content analysis. Chapter 6 presents a review of current computer programs and procedures for computer text content analysis. The options are numerous and varied.

No true automatic computer coding of static or moving images has as yet been fully developed. There *are* a number of interesting new support functions available for analysis of visual content. These are applications relevant to the second and third points in the foregoing list, searching for messages and preparation of messages for coding and message handling during coding. Currently, many of these systems require special expertise and are designed for use by professionals working in video and television (e.g., using the Executive Producer software as a means of locating video clips for inclusion in a documentary). But as the ongoing convergence of video and computer continues,[5] the interfaces will become more user-friendly and accessibility will increase. The utility of these systems for content analysis is clear.

The following list of *new functions* available in the digital age includes these systems, as well as some of those dedicated to the preparation of text messages for content analysis. They are, in no particular order,

Automatic Transcription

This has been developed for transcribing broadcast news, using voice recognition software (Furui, Ohtsuki, & Zhang, 2000; Gauvain, Lamel, & Adda, 2000; Wactlar, Hauptmann, Christel, Houghton, & Olligschlaeger, 2000). Such programs as "Rough'n'Ready" (Kubala, Colbath, Liu, Srivastava, & Makhoul, 2000) are already showing promise at being more accurate than available closed-captioning.[6]

Grammatical Parsing

A number of systems have been developed for the identification of different parts of grammatical speech in computerized text and to segment the spoken or written word into clauses for further analysis (e.g., Gottschalk & Bechtel, 1993).

Voice Recognition

Voice recognition software for computers continues to improve rapidly, and two-way discussions between computers and humans are no longer the stuff of science fiction (Zue, 1999). The Galaxy architecture developed at the M.I.T. Laboratory for Computer Science purports to go even further—its five functions are (a) speech recognition, (b) language understanding, (c) information retrieval, (d) language generation, and (e) speech synthesis. This raises the possibility of future "auditory" text coding, with hands-off searching for desired texts. For example, we might be able to query our computer to "locate and read aloud all the open-ended responses that mention 'love.' "

The nonresearch applications of these technologies are awe inspiring (or chilling, depending on your viewpoint). For example, voice recognition systems are being used to analyze prisoner phone calls, replacing human monitors in searching for key words, such as "escape." Using this method, the California Department of Corrections has reportedly put a quick end to "all kinds of smuggling" (Weed, 2001, p. 24).

Object or Behavior Recognition[7]

A number of teams are working on perfecting systems, called OCRs (optical character recognition), that can identify individuals or characters appearing in a video or film presentation (Kubala et al., 2000). One of the most comprehensive of these is MAESTRO (Multimedia Annotation and Enhancement via a Synergy of Technologies and Reviewing Operators; SRI MAESTRO Team, 2000). MAESTRO is software intended to electronically archive and retrieve multimedia information using a wide variety of factors. For example, in a TV news archive, appearances by British Prime Minister Tony Blair could automatically be "identified in the news by his voice, his appearance, captions, and other cues" (p. 58).

One particular nonresearch application of this type of technology shows the potential power of the technique while it raises significant privacy issues. The surveillance system FaceTrac was used to scan the fans at the 2001 Super Bowl, comparing their facial characteristics to mug shots of known criminals (Grossman, 2001). FaceTrac positively identified 19 criminals, but no arrests were made.

Another suite of systems, the Virage Videologger, extracts text from video; uses voice recognition to transcribe speech; extracts closed-captioning, teletext, and other embedded texts; logs with user-provided annotation; and identifies characters' faces. In addition, Virage has begun to provide support for the retrieval of archived video, such as the British Parliamentary proceedings, now available online as on-demand streaming video.

Mehtre, Kankanhalli, and Lee (1997) report progress with a computer shape recognition system for the automatic retrieval of information containing targeted trademarks. Coming at the issue from a different direction, scientists at the Salk Institute in California have developed a computer system that recognizes human facial expressions (Golden, 1999). And EthoVision is a system for the automatic recording of activity, movement, and interactions of animals, to be used in behavioral science research.

Mark-Up [8]

Many systems are designed to simply assist the viewer in mark-up or annotation (i.e., adding notes) of message sets as they review them. The notion is that such annotation will assist in locating desired material later on. For text, the popular package, NUD*IST, most often used in qualitative studies, may also be used for complex, multilevel mark-ups of text. This annotation process is called *logging* in the video and television industries. The oldest of the video mark-up systems is Executive Producer, which allows annotation based on video time code.[9] Others include Excalibur Video Analysis Engine, Scene Stealer, and MacSHAPA (a sophisticated application developed by Penelope Sanderson at the University of Illinois, with aviation applications in mind, to assist in the observation of human physical behaviors). In addition, the MoCA Project (automatic movie content analysis) promotes the development of automatic video abstracts, "short clips containing the essence of a longer video." The abstracts could be useful in the organizing of multimedia archives and databases (such as the Internet Movie Database).

Event Segmentation

By programming a computer to recognize segmental markers, such programming segments as separate news stories (Boykin & Merlino, 2000; Kubala et al., 2000) or commercials (e.g., the MoCA Project) may be identified. This could be used to assist in unitizing a stream of video.

Metadata Applications

Metadata means "data about data" and could be anything that summarizes information about a set of data. The term has recently emerged as a hot topic in the debates over standards for digital television and video in the United States. Older video systems (such as the American standard NTSC) have allowed a small amount of metadata to be carried, such as closed-captioning and DVS (Descriptive Video Service, an oral description of action provided for the visually impaired) carried in one line of the vertical blanking interval, the area between video frames. The more recent digital systems have greatly expanded the opportunities for metadata, which in a digital system may be stored anywhere in the signal throughout the entire duration of the content. Television engineers have noted that with digital content, "the number of distinct varieties of Metadata is potentially limitless" (EBU/SMPTE Task Force for Harmonized Standards for the Exchange of Program Material as Bitstreams, 1998) and offer such suggestions as copyright information, author(s), and origination date and time and such technical indicators as color correction parameters, time code, and edit decision lists used to produce the video. In the future, the metadata capability may also be used to store information about the content and form, such as characters in the frame, the dialogue being spoken (i.e., the script), and type of shot and transition at each point in time. This type of metadata could pave the way to a fully automatic form of content analysis for the moving image.

Immediate expansion of metadata capabilities is possible with new MPEG[10] standards for the compression and transmission of video and audio signals. The MPEG-7 group is working on standards for a "tool set" that will accommodate a large quantity of metadata.

Streaming Video Applications

Real-time video on the Internet may one day render cable, broadcast, and satellite television obsolete, but for now, the phenomenon is still very much under development (Dupagne, 2000). To establish a streaming source requires advanced knowledge of server and network operation as well as video production expertise. And because streamed video is compressed and therefore not of the same quality as current video systems, special strategies must be developed for its use and analysis. On the positive side, streaming video allows Internet users to play video clips "anytime anywhere, thereby eliminating the spatial and time constraints of traditional media forms" (Dupagne, 2000, p. 11). Once technical deficits have been remedied, future content analysts will very likely do their coding of film and television content and of videotaped communication behaviors streamed directly from online archives. This type of coding will have obvious advantages: the elimination of costly materials, such as videotapes and playback equipment, and the efficiency of multiple coders having immediate access to the same pool of messages.

Sampling

Sampling is the process of selecting a subset of units for study from the larger population. Fink and Gantz (1996) provide a nice capsule description of the options: "For the social science tradition, generalizing from the sample to the population is important. As a result, probability [random] sampling serves as the ideal. When constrained (e.g., by time or money), social scientists turn to nonprobability [nonrandom] samples" (p. 117).

Random Sampling

For a content analysis to be generalizable to some population of messages, the sample for the analysis should be randomly selected. The requirements are identical to those for conducting a random survey of individuals. Randomness may be defined as follows: Every element (unit) in the population must have an equal chance of being selected.[11]

This process typically requires itemizing all units in the population. This list is called a *sampling frame*. Often, such lists can be generated from message archives. Harwood (1999) used Nielsen audience ratings, obtained from trade publications, to create his sampling frame of television programs. Ward (1995) used Nielsen ratings specifically for children aged 2 through 11 in her study of prime time sexuality. Zullow (1991) used the *Billboard* "Hot 100" charts to sample popular songs from the years 1955 to 1989.

If a sampling frame list cannot be generated, as in the case of phone calls coming into a crisis hotline or news stories being broadcast on the radio, then some type of flow of occurrence may be established. Then, systematic random sampling is the logical choice (e.g., choosing every 10th call to the hot line or every 10th news story within randomly selected time periods).

In instances where individuals or groups will be generating messages that will then be analyzed, sampling may require a two-step process: (a) sampling the individuals or groups and (b) sampling messages generated by those individuals or groups. For the first part, the issues are similar to those facing survey and experimental researchers: How does one constitute a representative sample of people in general? Or of employees, or some other target population of people? For the second part, either the sampling frame or flow-of-occurrence technique might be considered, depending on the types of messages to be analyzed (e-mails might be listed and then sampled; arguments might be better sampled as they occur, e.g., recording every third disagreement). It's important to note the importance of executing random sampling from populations at *two stages* for this type of work.

There are several types of random sampling techniques available. All rely on two basic forms, *simple random sampling* and *systematic random sampling*.

Simple Random Sampling

Two types of simple random sampling (SRS) exist: (a) pulling units out of a hat—quite literally, if we cut up a sampling frame into separate slips of paper (one unit per slip) and draw slips from a box, we may achieve SRS; (b) if the sampling frame is numbered, then we may use a table of random numbers (available in any basic methodology book) to pick units.

With SRS, we have the choice of using sampling *with replacement* or *without replacement*. Sampling with replacement would mean that for the "out of a hat" technique, we'd put the selected unit back in the hat, and it might be drawn again. For the numbered-list technique, it would mean that if the same number came up twice in the table of random numbers, we would select the same unit a second time.

Why would we go through such a strange and tedious process? Technically, sampling with replacement better meets the requirement of every unit having an equal chance of being selected. To illustrate, imagine a case in which the population consists of 500 units. On the first pick, each unit has a 1/500 chance of being selected. On the second pick *without replacement,* each unit has a 1/499 chance; on the third pick, a 1/498 chance; and so on. With replacement, every pick carries a 1/500 chance for each unit.

Sampling with replacement does not make sense in many situations—for example, in selecting households to interview by telephone. But it does make a great deal of sense for some content analysis applications. For example, one study of race portrayals in children's TV commercials (Anonymous, 2000) coded commercials as many times as they appeared in a time-based sample, "inasmuch as every exposure to a commercial is an 'impression' " (p. 15) for the viewers. When selecting days of the week and cable or TV channels in a multistage method for randomly selecting TV show episodes (e.g., Lombard et al., 1996), there is obvious "replacement" (e.g., a number of Tuesdays may be selected; the cable network Bravo may be sampled more than once).

Systematic Random Sampling

Systematic random sampling consists of selecting every *xth* unit, either from the sampling frame or in some flow of occurrence over time. For example, a researcher may select every 15th message posted to an Internet discussion group. For systematic sampling to be random, it is assumed that the process begins with a random start, between 1 and *x*.

A couple of considerations are important to this type of sampling. First, a *skip interval* must be established—the "*x*" in "*xth*." If the size of the population is known, then the skip interval is N/n. For example, with a population of 10,000 units and a desired sample size of 500, we would calculate a skip interval of

$$\frac{(population\ N)}{(sample\ n)} = \frac{10,000}{500} = 20$$

So, we would select every 20th unit.

The second consideration has to do with how the skip interval relates to the sampling frame. If there is *periodicity* in the frame or in the flow of occurrence of units that matches up with the skip interval, then the representativeness of the sample is threatened. For example, if the sampling frame is a sequential list of top 50 U.S. box office films for each year and the skip interval just happens to turn out to be 50, then there is the possibility that every film selected may be the very top box office hit of its year. It is certain that the sample will not represent all the top 50 films but only one specific ranking (1st, 25th, 30th, or whatever). If there is some such type of periodicity to a sampling frame, then systematic random sampling is not a good choice.

A clear example of systematic random sampling is Newhagen, Cordes, and Levy's (1995) study of e-mail responses to NBC Nightly News's invitation to respond during a series on new technologies. After screening for irrelevant messages, they chose every sixth message from a population of 3,200, for an *n* of 650.

All the other random sampling options are variations on these two themes. The primary variations follow.

Cluster Sampling

This includes any random sampling in which a group or set of messages are sampled together, usually for logistic reasons. For example, Lin (1997) collected a full week of broadcast network prime time TV commercials, with the month and week randomly selected.

Stratified Sampling

With this type of random sampling, the sampling frame is segmented according to categories on some variable(s) of prime interest to the researcher. This segmentation or stratification ensures appropriate representation for the various groupings when the subsamples are based on the size of the groupings in the population. As Babbie (1995) notes, "you ensure that appropriate numbers of elements are drawn from homogeneous subsets of that population"

(p. 210). Statistically, stratified sampling reduces the sampling error for the stratifying variable to zero.

Smith's (1999) study of women in film is a simple example of stratified sampling. Interested in comparing women's role portrayals during the Golden Age of Hollywood (the 1930s and 1940s) with contemporary images (the 1990s), she stratified according to decade. She first constructed three different sampling frames of the top box office films featuring women, one for each of the target decades, and then conducted a systematic random sample for each.

In *nonproportionate* stratified sampling, the sizes of the sample groupings are not proportionate to their relative sizes in the population. As a result, the sample groupings become like samples of separate populations and may not be pooled for a full-sample analysis unless statistical adjustments are made. But that's not usually a problem, given the goal of stratification. For example, Breen (1997) used a nonproportionate stratified sample of 100 news articles from each of seven different time periods. His goal was to compare the seven periods, not to describe the pooled set, so ensuring a reasonable sample size for each of the seven periods was the proper decision.

Multistage Sampling

This includes any random sampling technique in which two or more sampling steps are used. For example, Hill and Hughes (1997) employed a two-stage sampling technique. They first randomly sampled newsgroups from a sampling frame, a list derived from USENET. Then, they randomly sampled threads of discussion from those newsgroups selected. In another good example, Hale, Fox, and Farmer (1996) sampled senate campaigns from a complete list they generated. Then, they used the Political Commercial Archive at the University of Oklahoma to randomly select ads from each of the selected campaigns.

Combinations of Random Sampling Techniques

Very common in content analysis studies, especially those that examine mass media content, is the use of some combination of random sampling techniques. For example, Danielson and Lasorsa (1997) used a stratified, multistage, cluster sampling technique in their study of symbolic content in sentences on the front pages of the *New York Times* and *Los Angeles Times* over a 100-year period. They stratified by newspaper, randomly selected 10 days per year, and then randomly selected sets of 10 sentences (clusters) from the front page of each day's issue.

The principal scholars who have examined what constitutes the optimal sampling procedure (and sample size) for news media are Riffe, Lacy, and their associates (e.g., Riffe, Lacy, & Fico, 1998). Riffe, Lacy, Nagovan, and Burkum

(1996) studied the efficiency of several sample types (i.e., the degree to which the sample represents the population with a relatively small *n*). They used a known population of ABC and CBS newscasts from the Vanderbilt Archive descriptions and were able to statistically assess the "success" of various samples. They found the most efficient sampling method for weekday TV network news to be stratification by month, then SRS of 2 days per month. This sample type was identified as more efficient than SRSs of various sizes or quarterly composite weeks (i.e., stratified by day of week, such that for each quarter, 7 days are randomly selected—one Sunday, one Monday, and so on).

Similarly, Riffe, Lacy, and Drager (1996) drew a variety of samples from a studied population of 1 year of *Time* magazines (*N* = 52 issues). They found the greatest efficiency for a composite year of 12 issues, one from each month (i.e., stratification by month), over SRSs of 6, 8, 10, 12, 14, and 16 issues. These researcher have also shown the superiority of composite week samples over SRS for daily newspapers (Riffe, Aust, & Lacy, 1993) and the advantage of stratification by month to create a composite year over SRS when studying consumer magazines (Lacy, Riffe, & Randle, 1998).

It seems that for news content, daily and monthly variations in key variables are important to tap so that stratification by day or month might be appropriate. These cyclic variations are important to consider for all cases of sampling. For example, movies are noted for their seasonal shifts (e.g., summer blockbusters, the holiday family films), and therefore a sample of movies should perhaps include films released at different times of the year.

Nonrandom Sampling

Nonrandom, or nonprobability, samples are undesirable and should be used only when no other options exist. We may *not* generalize findings from a nonrandom sample to a population. There are several common types:

Convenience Sampling

This method relies on the selection of readily available units. Kolbe and Burnett (1991) sadly note the prevalence of convenience sampling among consumer behavior content analyses—their review found 80.5% to be based on convenience samples. And Babbie (1998) notes that the technique is used "all too frequently" in survey research. Sometimes, it's unclear as to why the researcher did not use random sampling, as in Simoni's (1996) convenience sample study of 24 psychology textbooks. Sometimes, it's clear that the researchers would have difficulty obtaining the message content from a random sample of sources. For instance, Schneider, Wheeler, and Cox (1992) analyzed interview responses from 97 panel groups in three financial organizations, something that would be difficult to demand of a strictly random sample of people.

Garcia and Milano's (1990) study of erotic videos is a good example of the use of nonrandom sampling when there is difficulty in creating a reasonable sampling frame. Without a master list of erotic videos, they sent each of their 40 coders (students) to video rental establishments. The researchers admit that their technique of instructing the coders to go to the adult section of the shop and "select the first film they saw" (p. 96) was *not* random.

Purposive or Judgment Sampling

This type of sampling involves the researcher making a decision as to what units he or she deems appropriate to include in the sample. For example, Fan and Shaffer (1989) selected handwritten essays for text analysis on the basis of legibility. Graham, Kamins, and Oetomo (1993) selected print ads from three countries on the basis of recency and of whether they advertised "product pairs"—matching German and Japanese products. (For example, an ad for a German auto would be matched with an ad for a Japanese auto.)

Quota Sampling

This technique is rather like a nonrandom stratified sample. Key variable categories are identified, and then a certain number of units from each category are included in the study. A common example of quota sampling in survey research is the mall intercept: Interviewers employed by marketing research firms to interview shoppers are routinely instructed to get a certain number of targeted consumers, such as 20 females with children or 20 males over 40.

Web site research has been plagued by the difficulty in establishing a population and a sampling frame. In a typical case, Ghose and Dou (1998) sampled 101 Internet "presence sites," with half of them expert-reviewed Lycos Top 5% sites and half of them not rated as top sites. Although the sample encompassed "a wide spectrum of product categories" (p. 36), there was no attempt at true random selection, and the results are therefore not generalizable to a larger population of Web sites.

Sample Size

Unfortunately, there is no universally accepted set of criteria for selecting the size of a sample. A too-common practice is to base sample size on work by others in the area (e.g., Beyer et al., 1996; Slattery, Hakanen, & Doremus, 1996). However, better methods for determining a proper sample size exist.

Some research has tested various sample sizes for specific applications of content analysis. Beginning with Stempel's (1952) identification of two systematically selected composite weeks being sufficient to represent a full year of newspaper issues, a number of studies have examined samples from known populations of media messages. Lacy, Robinson, and Riffe (1995) used 320 different samples taken from 52 issues of each of two weekly newspapers. They found samples of 12 (stratified by month) and 14 (SRS) to adequately represent the population in general. However, they caution that acceptable sample size varied by newspaper and by the variable(s) examined.

A more generalized method of determining the desired sample size is to calculate it using formulas for standard error and confidence intervals. The desired n is derived from two things: (a) the desired confidence interval around a given sample mean and (b) the estimated variance for the variable in the population. The technique assumes a random sample. Box 4.1 provides relevant explanations and formulas, and the table below summarizes the needed sample sizes for selected confidence intervals for one particular simple case—a binomial (dichotomous or two-choice) variable, expressed as a percentage. The formula used to develop these sample size examples is shown as (d) in Box 4.1.

Sampling Error	95% Level of Confidence	99% Level of Confidence
± 2%	2,404	4,160
± 3%	1,087	1,852
± 5%	384	665
± 10%	96	167

Let's imagine that our primary variable of interest is whether political ads are negative (i.e., attacking the opposition) or not. From the table above, we see that to have a random sample that will guarantee us a finding on our variable, plus or minus 5% at the 95% level of confidence, we need to analyze at least 384 political ads. Put differently, with a random sample of 384 or more, we can be 95% confident that our statistic may be generalized to the population parameter, plus or minus 5%; we can be 95% confident that the true population percentage is within 5% of what we find in the sample.

Notice that a substantial sample size is needed to ensure a small confidence interval (e.g., plus or minus 2%). And it should be noted that the needed sample size would be even greater for variables that are not simple dichotomies. It's interesting to note that although such large samples present coding challenges for studies that use human coders, computer text analysis programs can make short work of a big sample. Bear in mind that the efficiency of computer analysis may be tempered by the machine's inability to measure a great many things. These trade-offs between human and computer coding will be further discussed in Chapter 6.

Box 4.1   Standard Error and Confidence Intervals

Roughly, a standard error (SE) is a measure of dispersion for a hypothetical distribution of sample means for a given variable (i.e., it is equivalent to a standard deviation for the *sampling distribution*). The SE allows us to calculate a confidence interval around a particular sample mean. This confidence interval tells us how confident or certain we are that the true population mean (μ) falls within a given range. For example, if we report that the results of a content analysis show average length of shot in a U.S. TV commercial to be "2.1 seconds, plus or minus .5 seconds at the 95% confidence level," this also means that we are 95% certain that the true population mean is between 1.6 and 2.6 seconds. This process is based on the idea that many different sample means will cluster normally around the true population mean in the sampling distribution.

A confidence interval is constructed by multiplying the SE by a given weighting (e.g., 1.0, 1.96, 2.58) based on the normal distribution, thus creating what is called a sampling error, and then adding and subtracting this value around the sample mean. Some commonly reported confidence intervals are

Confidence level	Confidence interval [mean ± (sampling error)]
68%	Mean ± (1.0 x SE)
95%	Mean ± (1.96 x SE)
99%	Mean ± (2.58 x SE)

There are two main formulas for the SE, (a) one for interval or ratio data (i.e., continuous, numeric data; see Chapter 6 for a fuller description) and (b) one for binomial (dichotomous or two-category) measures.

(a):   (b):

$$SE = \sqrt{\frac{\sigma^2}{n}} \qquad\qquad \sqrt{\frac{P \times Q}{n}}$$

where σ^2 = the population variance
         n = sample size
         P = proportion "affirmative" for a binomial in the population
         Q = proportion "negative" for a binomial in the population
             and $(P + Q = 1)$

Using these formulas and guidelines, we may construct formulas for desired sample sizes (Kachigan, 1986, pp. 157-158; Voelker & Orton, 1993), again, both for (c) interval or ratio and (d) binomial measures.

(c):   (d):

$$n = \left(\frac{z_c \sigma}{samp.\,error} \right)^2 \qquad\qquad n = (P \times Q)\left(\frac{z_c}{samp.\,error} \right)^2$$

where z_c = the appropriate normal distribution weighting
              (e.g., 1.96 for 95% confidence)
         σ = estimate of population standard deviation(sd)
   samp. error = the sampling error desired
      P × Q = (.5)(.5) = (.25), the most conservative case estimating the

population proportions for P and Q

There is only one difficulty in using these formulas to set a needed sample size *n*. We don't know the population parameters, σ or P and Q.

Therefore, we must make an estimate as to what the population variance might be. In a binomial case (Example d), what is typically used is the most conservative case, in which P = .50 and Q = .50 (this results in the largest possible P x Q and therefore the largest estimate of needed sample size). In a case of a variable measured at the interval or ratio level (Example c), this task is more difficult, and some prior knowledge about the status of the variable in the population is useful. If the measure has been used in a similar sample, then that sample's standard deviation can be used as an estimate of the population sd. (This is typically adjusted by multiplying the sample variance by a coefficient such as $n/[n-1]$.)

As an example, let's imagine that we want to generalize from a sample to the population of newspaper headlines about a political figure, and our variable of interest is a binomial: whether or not a positive descriptor is applied to the politician in the headline. Let's say that we'd like to be able to generalize plus or minus three percentage points at the 95% confidence level. To calculate,

$$n = (P \times Q)\left(\frac{z_c}{samp.\,error}\right)^2$$

$$n = (.5 \times .5)\left(\frac{1.96}{.03}\right)^2$$

$$n = 1{,}067$$

Thus, we would need a sample of 1,067 headlines in order to make a statement such as, "We are 95% certain that the true population proportion of headlines about the mayor that are positive is 50%, plus or minus 3%, that is, between 47% and 53%." For an example of how this would work with a metric (interval or ratio) variable, let's imagine that we've assessed the verbal intensity of interpersonal utterances on a 0-to-10 scale. Let's assume that we wish to have a 99% confidence interval of plus or minus one point on the 0-to-10 scale and that based on past research, we estimate the population standard deviation to be 5.0. To calculate,

$$n = \left(\frac{z_c \, \sigma}{samp.\,error}\right)^2$$

$$n = \left(\frac{2.58 \times 5}{1}\right)^2$$

$$n = 166.4$$

So with a sample size of 167 or more utterances, we would be able to report our mean verbal intensity plus or minus one point at the 99% level of confidence.

Notes

1. The by-clause analysis affords greater variability than if the entire message was used as the unit of data collection. For example, a verbal message may obtain an anxiety score of 20 rather than just 0 or 1—the score can range between 0 and the number of clauses in the message.

2. This n of 10,000 was further reduced to 8,742 by a precision screening process designed to remove irrelevant stories picked up by the search algorithm. The Jasperson et al. (1998) article is a model of full reportage for both the search process and the screening.

3. For example, when I was first hired as a coder on a major grant project in the mid-1970s, our analysis of prime time television content required us to view on videotape. The "least expensive" option at that time was ½-inch reel-to-reel tape, which was in reality very expensive and very cumbersome; each tape held only 1 hour of programming, and the tapes had to be manually threaded on the massive playback machines. There were no real-time counters, which meant that we pretty much had to code an entire 1-hour tape in one sitting, because we could not note where we left off, and we could not unload the machine without rewinding completely. Although operating the system was not rocket science, it did require a modicum of training. And inexperienced coders did manage to destroy the playback heads on one $5,000 machine.

4. However, the user should be cautioned that searches are still not fully "automatic" and are very much creative processes. For example, when searching for terrorist group Web sites on the Internet, Damphouse and Smith (1998) found that few such groups (e.g., the KKK) included the target term, "terrorism" in their sites, and they had to use a variety of less systematic search strategies to locate a suitable number of relevant sites.

5. This convergence of video and computer includes, but is not limited to, the use of computer-based digital postproduction systems in video and film production (e.g., nonlinear editing, digital special effects; Ferraro & Olson, 2000), the production of "interactive" digital content for CD-ROM and DVD, and the advent of digital television in the United States (Atkin, Neuendorf, Jeffres, & Skalski, 2000; Ely & Block, 1997-1998).

6. Although seemingly a ready source of message information, closed-captioning has not proved an attractive source because of frequent inaccuracies. Even classic films often have closed-captioning that is grossly abbreviated or simplified, not accurately representing the spoken dialogue. And so-called real-time captioning is full of errors (Dellinger, 2000); for example, when Meryl Streep won the Academy Award for *Sophie's Choice,* the word "Holocaust" appeared on-screen as "holly cost." My own 10-minute perusal revealed the following: (a) A joke's punchline on the 2000 Tony Awards was heard as "The house specialty is the congealed meatloaf." It was read as "The house specialty is the concealed meatloaf." (b) The Weather Channel's admonition to "Be wary of a Nor'easter with coastal rain" was read by the hearing impaired as "Be weary of a Nor'easter with coastal rain." DVS seems just as inaccurate.

7. See *The Content Analysis Guidebook Online* for links to vendors for the systems identified in this section.

8. See *The Content Analysis Guidebook Online* for links to vendors for the systems identified in this section.

9. *Time code* is a series of digits that provides an exact reference for each video frame. The American SMPTE time code standard is an eight-digit series of clock-type numbers (hours, minutes, seconds, and video fields; Kindem, 1987). Each frame's time code is stored on the vertical interval for the video signal and is displayed on-screen only when a special time code reader is used.

10. MPEG is an acronym for "moving pictures experts group," formed by the International Standards Organization to set standards for audio and video compression and transmission. MPEG and MPEG-2 are currently used for transfer of digital video through the Internet and for encoding of compressed digital video for DVD and other multimedia formats (Watkinson, 1999).

11. In some instances, this may be a *known* but not necessarily equal chance of being selected.

CHAPTER 5

Variables and Predictions

Although the content analyst should consult both scholarly literature and commercial research and use theory as a guide whenever possible, he or she is, in fact, the boss, the final authority on what content needs to be examined and what variables ought to be tapped. This chapter presents a series of alternative approaches for selecting variables that will be well-grounded.

As indicated in Chapter 3, a *variable* is a definable and measurable concept[1] that varies; that is, it holds different values for different individual cases or units. As indicated in Chapter 1, variables may be delineated as *latent or manifest variables* and as *content or form variables*. Strictly speaking, variables to be included in a content analysis must reside in the message rather than the source or receiver (although linking message variables to source or receiver variables is endorsed; see Chapter 3).

As noted earlier, scholarly work generally proceeds from theory, with research questions, hypotheses, or both derived directly from the theory. A discussion of hypotheses and research questions is provided later in this chapter. In actuality, a review of the content analysis literature indicates that most content analyses do not test formal hypotheses or research questions, and those that do rarely provide a real test of theory. More often, they are driven by curiosity or practicality. It is recommended that even such nontheoretic investigations should follow a carefully considered process in the selection of what aspects of the content—what variables—to study. Such a process is presented here.

Identifying Critical Variables

A useful way to approach the selection of content analysis variables is to consider what constitute critical variables—those features that are vital to a com-

Box 5.1   The Critical Variable That Almost Got Away

Camera Technique in Music Videos

In the 1980s, there was much criticism of the way in which women's images were presented in music videos (Vincent, Davis, & Boruszkowski, 1987), at that time, one of the fastest-growing segments in the media industries. Kalis and Neuendorf (1989) undertook a content analysis of a random sample of MTV videos to assess the presence and treatment of aggressive cues—objects and actions with violent or aggressive meaning. Among other things, Kalis and Neuendorf examined each case in which an initiator or recipient of an aggressive action could be identified.

The basic findings of the study were surprising in light of the prevailing wisdom regarding women's roles in music videos. Females were actually more likely to be initiators than recipients of aggressive acts. But an interesting explanation for this discrepancy was in sight. The researchers had included variables that they considered critical to a study of the fast-paced medium. For every shot in which an aggressive act was shown, they measured the focal length of the camera shot (i.e., long shot, medium shot, close-up, or extreme close-up) at the beginning and the end of the shot. They also measured the length of each shot in seconds, as part of their general investigation of pacing (i.e., quickness of editing) of the videos.

The findings relevant to these additional variables provided a possible explanation for the public salience of female-targeted aggression in music videos. When females were the targets of aggression, they were displayed on the screen for a significantly longer period of time (3.1 seconds on average, compared with 2.0 seconds for a shot containing a male victim). Also, females were more likely than males to be shown in close-up or extreme close-up as targets of aggression. This visual emphasis on female victimization may well have contributed to the events becoming more memorable to viewers and hence a subject of popular criticism.

What's important to remember is that without paying close attention to form variables that are critical to the medium, this finding of focal prominence for female victims would never have been discovered.

prehensive understanding of (a) the message pool (b) in the specific medium used. Identifying such critical features is both painstaking and creative. Failure to identify all the form and content variables that distinguish a set of messages can lead to misleading results. For example, the Kalis and Neuendorf (1989) study outlined in Box 5.1 would have resulted in incomplete conclusions without the measurement of two key formal feature variables.

A researcher may frame the search for variables at a very general level or at a much more specific and applied level. The most comprehensive study should do both. At the most general level, one may always consider the possibility of *universal* variables, that is, characteristics that differentiate all stimuli. At the most specific level, the researcher needs to examine the features that distinguish that particular message type as conveyed in that particular medium.

The sections that follow describe four recommended techniques for selecting variables for a content analysis:

1. A consideration of universal variables

2. Using theory and past research for variable collection

3. A grounded or "emergent" process of variable identification

4. Attempting to find medium-specific critical variables

Each of these four techniques is elaborated on in the following sections.[2]

A Consideration of Universal Variables

All stimuli may be described by a variety of factors. The quest for a finite set of universal variables that may be applied to all stimuli (including message units) has been led primarily by cognitive psychologists, linguists, and anthropologists. Their efforts are worth examining.

Osgood, Suci, and Tannenbaum (1957) were among the first to try to discover universal dimensions of "meaning." Their classic three primary dimensions of semantic meaning (i.e., how individuals discriminate among concepts) —evaluation, potency, and activity—have served as the basis for countless social and behavioral science studies. Their "semantic differential"—using paired concepts to measure evaluation (e.g., good ↔ bad), potency (e.g., strong ↔ weak), and activity (e.g., active ↔ passive)—has become a standard in experimental and survey research (Heise, 1965).

The work of Marks (1978) has attempted to establish evidence of a uniformity in the way in which human senses (hearing, sight, taste, smell, touch) operate. In *Unity of the Senses,* he reviews classic considerations of what he terms primary qualities of objects from such sources as Galileo and Locke, and he proceeds to develop a perspective in which human senses all operate in parallel fashion. According to Marks, a stimulus may be perceived by seeing it or by feeling it, for example, but these experiences will have the *same* dimensions.[3] No matter which sense is used, the stimulus is perceived according to certain "analogous sensory attributes." They are as follows (with particular examples of potential content analysis applications in parentheses).

1. Extension: the apparent spatial magnitude of a sensation (e.g., how long a shot in a movie lasts)

2. Intensity: the apparent strength of a sensation (e.g., how close up the shot is)

3. Brightness: the apparent piquancy of a sensation (e.g., the black-white contrast of the shot or the brilliance of the colors)

4. Quality: a term covering a diverse set of attributes, proposed by philosophers of earlier centuries, which Marks generally dismisses as a *universal* characteristic of sensation (e.g., the mise-en-scene, or placement of elements in the shot; p. 52)

In addition, Marks considers *duration* as a fifth attribute (from 19th-century work by Külpe). These features give us a starting point, although Marks and his intellectual forebears were more interested in describing the individual's experience than in finding characteristics of the stimulus itself. However, they provide us with a general template for thinking about critical variables for any content analysis.

Alternatively, Marks (1978) and others have used a grounded approach in discovering how people differentiate among stimuli. By presenting individuals with a range of stimuli and asking them to report perceived distances among the stimuli in multidimensional cognitive space, researchers can look at the resultant dimensions (McIsaac, Mosley, & Story, 1984; Melara, Marks, & Potts, 1993). For example, when randomly selected landscape photographs were presented to 52 subjects, five dimensions of meaning were identified: (a) open versus enclosed, (b) barren versus verdant, (c) land versus water, (d) natural versus human influence, and (e) entry path versus no entry path (Fenton, 1985). These dimensions are clearly more applied (i.e., specific to photography) than truly universal.

In his classic work, *Aesthetics and Psychobiology,* Berlyne (1971) proposes a set of aesthetic universals. After a consideration of features similar to Marks's (1978) analogous sensory attributes (i.e., "psychophysical variables:" intensity, size, color, visual forms, auditory pitch) and "ecological properties" that describe the meaningfulness of the stimulus, Berlyne (1971) adds his "collative" variables, which are the "irreducibly essential ingredients of art and of whatever else is aesthetically appealing" (p. viii). The collative variables do seem to go beyond features that reside entirely within the stimulus (Cupchik & Berlyne, 1979) and might be described as features that reside in an interaction between the stimulus and the individual perceiving the stimulus (so we must be cautious in adapting them to a content analysis). Others have described them as the combining of "two present features of a stimulus" or the "comparison of a stimulus with a prior expectation" (Martindale, Moore, & Borkum, 1990, p. 54). Berlyne's (1971) aesthetically relevant collative variables follow.

1. Novelty

2. Uncertainty and surprisingness

3. [Subjective] Complexity

4. Relationships among 1-3 (notably, a recognized interaction between novelty and perceived complexity)

Although the efforts of these various scholars to identify universal variables give us much food for thought, many of their contributions are aimed at the receiver's *response* to stimuli or messages, rather than at capturing universal features of the messages themselves. It is only by adapting their efforts that universal message variables may emerge. There may indeed be certain variables, perhaps derived from the more philosophical considerations presented earlier, that are critical for all message studies. One of the most likely of such candidates seems to be *message complexity.* Box 5.2 provides a focus on complexity.

Obviously, no master list of universal variables exists. And even if one were proposed, the researcher must make the decision as to the relevance of each variable to the task at hand. That is, even if a variable is deemed measurable and discriminable for all message stimuli, its utility and predictive power may be nil in a given content analysis. And cultural differences in how receivers respond to so-called universal variables raise questions of their meaning. For example, although "color" is proposed by Berlyne (1971) as a universal psychophysical variable, and few would dispute its importance in describing all object stimuli, its meaning has been shown to vary substantially across cultures (Hupka, Zaleski, Otto, Reidl, & Tarabrina, 1997). One study of five nationalities found significant differences, such as which color connotes envy (United States, green; Russia, black) and which color indicates jealousy (United States, red; Russia, black).

Using Theory and Past Research for Variable Collection

Generally speaking, there are three ways in which theory and past research may be employed: (a) by providing predictions about the effects of messages of various types (thus providing a rationale for the study but usually not providing hypotheses that are testable by a content analysis alone), (b) by providing predictions about the origins of messages, and (c) by providing predictions about the relationships among variables *within* a content analysis.

The first type of theory and research application may be seen as a variation on certain types of linkages (Chapter 3), in which evidence of message effects is linked with content analysis findings. Here, theory offers a *prediction* of such effects (and there may or may not be corresponding research evidence). For example, research by Berkowitz (1964, 1973; Berkowitz & LePage, 1967) indicates that general arousal created by one stimulus may have an impact on how the individual responds to another arousing stimulus. And tests of the excitation transfer theory have supported the theory's notion that general physiological arousal can affect one's subsequent likelihood of behaving aggressively (Gardstrom, 1999; Zillmann, 1971; Zillmann, Johnson, & Day, 2000). In this vein, supportive research has found that television pacing (i.e., how quickly the shots are edited) can increase the viewer's overall physiological arousal, which in turn enhances his or her response to violent content within

Box 5.2   Message Complexity

An Example of a Possible Universal Variable for Content Analysis

There exists quite a bit of research in the psychology literature that indicates that people respond to a complex stimulus quite differently than they do to a simpler stimulus (Berlyne, 1971). Complexity of a message seems to be an important moderating variable to consider in studies of persuasion. For example, Saegert and Jellison (1970) found that with simple stimuli, an inverted relationship was found between exposure and affect, whereas with complex stimuli, exposure and positive affect were positively related (see also Brentar, 1990). That is, with simple stimuli, there may be wear out, when the receiver gets tired of the stimulus. With a more complex stimulus, the more you see it, the more you like it.

What exactly is this construct, complexity? Invoking the considerable contribution of information theory to the study of communication and messages, Watt and Welch (1983) have proposed considering "degree of complexity" along a continuum. They draw on the work of Moles (1968) to show that the degree of complexity of a concept may range from simple (ordered, predictable, structured) to complex (disordered, unpredictable, random; Watt & Welch, 1983, p. 78). Thus, complexity seems to include the characteristic of information potential, something that is clearly important in all message studies.

Watt and Welch (1983) further distinguish between *static* and *dynamic* complexity. Static complexity is the level of randomness of the stimulus at a single point in time. Dynamic complexity is the amount of variation of a stimulus over time. For example, a photograph may have high static complexity but will have zero dynamic complexity. A video presentation that consists of a series of very simple images (each with low static complexity) could have high dynamic complexity if it is edited at a very quick pace.

Complexity of the written word has been measured by human and computer coding in a variety of contexts. The most common indexing of complexity is the assessment of "readability," indicating the approximate grade level of a text—quite literally, 6th grade,

the fast-paced form (Jeffres with Perloff, 1997). Thus, the inclusion of a measure of the pacing of video or film editing in a content analysis can provide a partial prediction as to how the viewer will respond.

An example of the informative role of past research is Cutler, Moberg, and Schimmel's (1999) choice of variables for their investigation of attorney advertising on TV. Key variables used in their analysis are derived from the results of several surveys of consumers that identified the most important criteria people use when choosing an attorney (i.e., knowledge, caring, and courtesy). This third-order link between receiver surveys and the content analysis provides a good rationale for the selection of variables.

The second type of application of theory and research also relates to the notion of integrative linkages introduced in Chapter 3. Here, relationships between source characteristics and message attributes are predicted. For example, Dindia (1987) sought to challenge a set of previous studies that seemed to

8th grade, and so forth. The readability level is indexed by looking at such markers as average word length, average sentence length, and perhaps variety of words used (e.g., total number of words in a text divided by the number of unique words in the text). There are a number of standard readability index formulas. For instance, the Flesch-Kincaid formula (RightWriter, 1985, p. 5-3). Also, the integrative, or cognitive, complexity of the source has been assessed via content analyses of political speeches, interviews, personal letters, and diplomatic documents (Lee & Peterson, 1997).

In their studies of children's responses to television, Watt and Welch (1983) have proposed methods of measuring both static and dynamic visual complexity on a video screen, by overlaying a grid and measuring differences in brightness (luminance) or color (chrominance) between adjacent cells in the grid. Their technique has not been picked up for use by social scientists, but that may change. There is great potential for future computer coding of complexity, notably in the age of digital video (where looking for vector movement in MPEG compression could serve as a measure of dynamic visual complexity) and with the new data stream function of metadata (EBU/SMPTE Task Force, 1998).

Watt and Welch's (1983) studies on children and television have shown the utility of segmenting the construct of complexity into different manifest types—audio versus visual, static versus dynamic. They have found, for example, that children's visual attention to TV programming (i.e., *Sesame Street* and *Mr. Rogers' Neighborhood,* in their studies) is related to greater audio static complexity, greater audio dynamic complexity, and greater video dynamic complexity but not to greater video static complexity. Children's recognition of a featured object from the program was found to be related to greater audio dynamic complexity and greater video dynamic complexity. Recall of information from the program was found to be related to greater audio static complexity —and to *lower* levels of audio dynamic complexity, video static complexity, and video complexity. Simply put, the overall construct of complexity has been shown to be important to understanding how children process TV. And some of the very complexity factors that attract kids' attention—i.e., quick variations in sound and in images—seem to result in lower recall of information from the program.

show that men interrupt more than women and women are interrupted more than men. She based her selection of specific variables—and their precise measurements—on the body of interpersonal interaction literature to date.

The third type of theory and research application provides bases for research questions and hypotheses that may be tested from a content analysis alone. For example, deriving their constructs from a theory of relational communication, Rogers and Farace (1975) developed measures of the symmetry, transitory nature, and complementarity of control in human face-to-face interaction. Their conceptual bases included Bateson (1958) and Watzlawick, Beavin, and Jackson (1967). In application, their coding scheme allows for the analysis of the behaviors in individual speakers, the interactions between members of a dyad, and the systemic aspects of the communication process.

Past research can provide other motives for including variables. In a practical sense, it's often useful to replicate measures from past research. For example, as described in Chapter 6, there are quite a few "standard" dictionaries for text analysis, and using them has the advantage of producing findings that have immediate comparative value.

Sometimes, a cross-cultural, cross-media, or over-time comparison is desired. For example, Oerter, Oerter, Agostiani, Kim and Wibowo (1996) applied a coding scheme to transcripts of interviews about the concept of human nature conducted in four nations (the United States, Indonesia, Japan, and Korea). The same analyses had been conducted with subjects in Germany, China, Slovenia, and Croatia, allowing the authors to make more sweeping cross-cultural comparisons.

Sometimes, the researcher may attempt to "translate" variables from a survey or experiment to the content analysis situation. For example, Smith (1999) attempted to take items that had previously been widely used to measure the trait characteristics of extraversion and neuroticism and apply them to characters in feature films. The translation from subjective, self-report measures to objective, content-analytic assessments was rocky—reliabilities were generally low. Coders could not agree on how "sociable" or "tense" a film character was. On the other hand, some translations have been more successful. Kolt's (1996) application of interpersonal initiation strategies to personal ads in newspapers resulted in high reliabilities and a finding of striking similarity between face-to-face and in-print first encounters.

Much as a survey researcher will use focus group or in-depth interviewing (qualitative techniques) to inform his or her questionnaire construction, so may the content analyst use in-depth, often contemplative and incisive observations from the literature of critical scholars. Quantitative researchers have begun to do this with regard to film content. As Salomon (1987) has noted, "film is perhaps one of the most thoroughly analyzed technological media" with a large number of "philosophical, semiotic, historical, and psychological analyses" having been conducted on the medium's content (p. 51). Yet one could count the number of available quantitative content analyses of film on two hands (e.g., Capwell, 1997; Custen, 1992; Ealy, 1991; Pileggi, Grabe, Holderman, & de Montigny, 2000; Powers, Rothman, & Rothman, 1996; Smith, 1999). Generally, these content analyses have drawn on the rich history of critical and qualitative study of film. For example, Smith (1999) relied heavily on the literature on women's films in her examination of role portrayals of the two genders in top-grossing U.S. movies of the 1930s, 1940s, and 1990s. Some of the critical expectations were borne out, and others were not, indicating that content analysis is not redundant with critical analysis.

A Grounded or Emergent
Process of Variable Identification

When existing theory or research literature cannot give a complete picture of the message pool, the researcher may take a more practical approach. The researcher may need to immerse himself or herself in the world of the message pool and conduct a qualitative scrutiny of a representative subset of the content to be examined. In this way, variables emerge from the message pool, and the investigator is well grounded in the reality of the messages. Quite simply, the researcher needs to "go native." For example, if one wants to content analyze relationship development among soap opera characters, one needs to become, at least temporarily, a soap fan. And to analyze nonverbal styles of stand-up comics, one has to nominally become a connoisseur of comedy.

Failure to identify key variables that typical message receivers would consider critical, and failure to develop a full understanding of the variables in their context, can lead to trivial or embarrassing findings. For example, this author once heard a presentation in which the researcher revealed that none of the U.S. TV commercials sampled were spots for hard liquor. At that time, the National Association of Broadcasters Television Code prohibited the broadcast of such spots, something anyone with even a passing familiarity with the broadcasting industry would have known. Content analysts should acquaint themselves with professional standards and guidelines for media content studies (e.g., Gibson, 1991; Kindem, 1987).

To prevent gaffes and more serious problems, the researcher may wish to invite a visiting committee of working professionals to comment on the research effort before the coding scheme is finalized. Often, these pros are pleased to be asked, and the research can only be enhanced by their contributions. And we shouldn't forget the frontline people. A study of intake interviews for battered women may benefit more from the input of the interviewers than from the input of administrators.

However, a potential problem with identifying emergent variables in this fashion is that the researcher may not be able to see all the ways in which the messages vary. For example, if you read every news article in your daily paper, would you be able to identify all the myriad ways in which they varied? And even simple variations may be difficult to sort out. Garner (1978) shows some clear examples of how a small number of very simple variables can result in stimuli that seem complicated and diverse. This is similar to what would later be identified as chaos theory (Gleick, 1987), wherein complex stimuli may arise from simple rules.

An illustration may show how easy—and how difficult—it may be to discern emergent variables from the stimuli themselves. For example, the four images shown in Figure 5.1 are differentiated by two variables, each holding two different values.

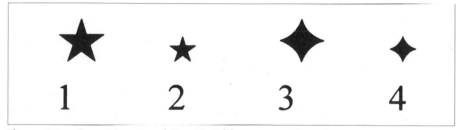

Figure 5.1.   Four Images and Two Variables

If this were our message pool, we'd have no problem identifying all the variables that differentiate the images; they are (a) size (large vs. small) and (b) shape (diamond vs. star).

Now, how about the images in Figure 5.2?

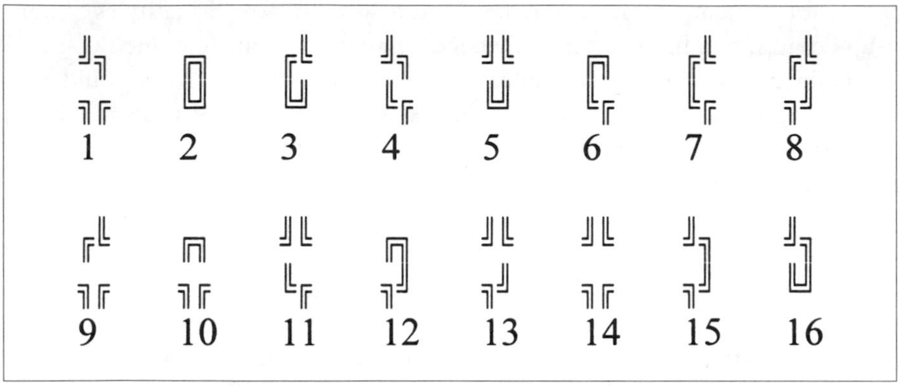

Figure 5.2.   More Images and More Variables

Here, the underlying variables that differentiate the images are not so apparent. Such a challenge can be frustrating, but it may also stimulate the researcher's creativity. It's like a puzzle (and the answer to this one can be found in an endnote[4]). What's important to note is that the diversity shown in the set of images in Figure 5.2 is the result of only *four variables,* each holding only *two values.*

Of course, even if the researcher discovers all the ways in which the messages vary (an unlikely scenario), this does not mean that all those variables need to be included in a study. The researcher still needs to engage in critical thought to decide what variables are essential to the testing of hypotheses or research questions.

Attempting to Find Medium-Specific Critical Variables

Many content analyses examine messages within a medium. Much effort has been expended trying to describe what critical variables distinguish each communication medium, that intermediary device or context through which a message flows from source to receiver. From Bretz's (1971) quaintly precise descriptions of such media as filmstrips and "telewriting" (in which handwriting and voice are both transmitted by telephone lines; p. 117) to contemporary efforts to describe factors that distinguish pages and sites on the Internet (Bauer & Scharl, 2000; Ghose & Dou, 1998), the many efforts to encapsulate each medium have failed to result in standard lists and definitions. This leaves the content analyst with the task of using a combination of the past research and emergent processes, described in the previous two sections, to make a roster of possible medium-specific critical variables.

There are two main issues at hand when trying to establish what medium-specific critical variables are appropriate for a content analysis study: (a) What is the nature of the medium of the messages? And (b) what variables are particular or pertinent to studies of messages found in that medium?

Defining the Medium

This may seem a simple task; it is not. No standard definition of, say, *television* exists. Try to itemize all the charactcristics of television that make it TV. It's tough to do, and no two persons' lists will be identical. Consider media philosopher Marshall McLuhan's (1989) broad-ranging definitions of media. He maintained that media are essentially defined by their *extension of the human senses* and that the medium is the message, as the phrase he made famous states. Yet his definitions of media were quite personal and iconoclastic, with titles such as "tactile television." Although intriguing, his views on the characteristics of media have not become standards.

Several scholars *have* tried to catalog available or even hypothetical media technologies. Bretz (1971) attempted to provide an exhaustive list and classification of media. He argued that "since communication media are all the product of man's [*sic*] inventiveness, there is no natural relationship among them to discover; we must choose some artificial means of classification" (p. 61). His chosen categorization scheme put media into seven categories: (a) audio-motion-visual, (b) audio-still-visual, (c) audio-semi-motion, (d) motion-visual, (e) still-visual, (f) audio, and (g) print. He gave an additional dimension of telemedia versus recording media. Furthermore, he held that individual media may be distinguished from one another by two additional criteria: (a) if they use different combinations of the ways of representing information (sound, picture, line, graphics, print, motion) and (b) if they are based on different hardwares.

Following this, Heeter (1986) developed definitions for 52 "hypothetical media systems," empirically describing them by attributes of function, channel, and interactivity. Neuendorf, Brentar, and Porco (1990) captured respondents' perceptions about 15 media types and 10 sensory concepts, using multidimensional scaling. The three primary dimensions found were (a) level of mediatedness, (b) print versus nonprint, and (c) personal or subjective versus impersonal or objective.

Another aspect one may look at is whether a given medium has characteristics unique to that medium and therefore especially important to tap in a content analysis. In general, media do not have wholly unique characteristics. For example, variables related to graphic design (size and color of font, use of photos, subjects of photos, etc.) are applicable to content in magazines, newspapers, television, film, and the Internet. Variables related to auditory intensity (e.g., use of music, loudness, density and pace of music, paralinguistic aspects of speech) could be applied to studies of audio recordings of speech, CDs, radio, television, and film.[5]

At the very least, these attempts to catalog and differentiate media give us pause to consider what our medium of interest really is and why we might be interested in that medium rather than another.

Finding Critical Variables
Appropriate to the Medium

There may be both form and content variables that are particularly relevant to a study of messages from a particular medium. Although this text recommends that each researcher assess anew the critical variables specific to his or her medium of choice (i.e., there is no catalog worthy of strong endorsement), looking at some past attempts may be fruitful. Generally, attempts at comprehensiveness have focused on form rather than content variables:

Huston and Wright (1983) have identified "salient formal features" for television in their studies of children's viewing behavior. They include physical activity of characters, rapid pace, variability of scenes, visual special effects, loud music, sound effects, and peculiar or nonhuman voices (p. 39). Huston and Wright present a continuum of these formal features, ranging from "purely syntactic" (features that structure the flow of content) to "integrally related to content understanding" (features that provide modes of mental representation, supplanting or eliciting cognitive operations, as when a zoom helps the viewer understand the resulting close-up). They summarize how the formal features of television influence cognitive processing of content, thus providing more than a simple list of variables.

Lombard et al. (1996) have begun the process of documenting such formal features of television, with additions of their own. Their well-developed coding scheme (available at *The Content Analysis Guidebook Online*) includes sections on transitions, pace, camera techniques, object or entity movement, text and graphics, and special effects. Their goal is to conduct a series of large-scale content analyses that benchmark the current and future state of television production.

Gagnard and Morris's (1988) subtitle tells it all—an "analysis of 151 executional variables." Their study of TV commercials that had received CLIO awards was an attempt to exhaustively catalog variables relevant to content and form.

Olsina, Godoy, Lafuente, and Rossi (1999) provide a fairly comprehensive set of variables for the assessment of Web sites. However, their hierarchical approach is criticized by Bauer and Scharl (2000). They measure a host of variables within four categories: functionality, usability, efficiency, and site reliability.

Hypotheses, Predictions, and Research Questions

In a scholarly content analysis, the variables should be linked in the form of research questions or hypotheses. A hypothesis is a *statement* of an expectation about empirical reality, based on a clear theoretic rationale or on prior evidence (Babbie, 1998). Lacking a strong basis for a firmly stated prediction, the researcher can only formulate research questions. A research question is a *query* about empirical reality, typically driven by theory or prior nonscientific observation.

Even in the case of nonscholarly content analysis, it is recommended that careful questions or predictions (or both) be made. This process ensures a logical progression from conceptualization of an issue through measurement and results that address what the researcher has in mind.

Conceptual Definitions

In the process of writing hypotheses, predictions, and research questions, each variable must be carefully defined. This dictionary-type definition is called the *conceptual definition* of the variable. The conceptual definition process is vital to the research process. A conceptual definition is a declaration by the researcher as to exactly what he or she wishes to study. Composing conceptual definitions forces the researcher to think critically about the nature of his or her study. Each conceptual definition is a guide to the subsequent measurement of that variable—the *operationalization* (covered in Chapter 6). The conceptual definition and operationalization need to match; this matching is what many call *internal validity* (Babbie, 1998).

As an illustration, consider the conceptual definition of sex roles adopted by Chu and McIntyre (1995) for their study of children's cartoons in Hong Kong (p. 206; from Durkin, 1985): "The collection of behaviors or activities that a given society deems more appropriate to members of one sex than to members of the other sex." Chu and McIntyre's operationalization of this conceptual variable consisted of no fewer than 39 measures, each of which fit within the conceptual definition (thus providing internal validity). The operationalizations (measures) included 1 occupational role, 17 personality traits (e.g., rough, obedient), 7 appearance traits (e.g., hair length, wearing a dress), 11 activity preferences and skills (e.g., sports), and 3 societal and familial power roles (e.g., final decision maker). Notice that the specifics of the conceptual definition served as a guide to the researchers: "Collection" implied multiple indicators rather than an overall perceptual measure, "behaviors or activities" demanded the measurement of manifest characteristics rather than internal states, "society deems" required that the researchers discover the cultural norms for the society under study, and the nondirectional phrase, "appropriate to members of one sex than to members of the other," indicated that sex roles for both males and females were to be studied.

Additional examples of conceptual definitions appearing in the content analysis literature follow.

1. *Rumination:* "The tendency to think nonproductively about negative affects, situations, and attributions" (Satterfield, 1998, p. 670)

2. *Climate:* "Employee perceptions of one or more strategic imperatives made manifest through work place routines and rewards" (Schneider et al., 1992, p. 705)

3. *Risk information:* "That which links an environmental contaminant to harmful effects on human health (a 'risk linkage')" (Griffin & Dunwoody, 1997, p. 368)

4. *Sexual suggestiveness:* "The Freudian interpretation of 'having or possessing sexual stimuli that triggers or arouses ideas about sex in a person's mind' " (Pokrywczynski, 1988, p. 758)

Each conceptual definition guides the researcher through the process of measurement. In fact, conceptual definitions often appear in whole or in part in codebooks, for the guidance of the coders.

Hypotheses

Formal hypotheses that link variables of interest *should* be based on theory. However, predictive statements are often presented in the content analysis literature based simply on past research. Seven examples of hypotheses follow:

1. "Women who possess predominantly neonate [childlike] facial features will be more preferred during social and economic good times and less preferred during social and economic hard times" (Pettijohn & Tesser, 1999, p. 232; their study examined photographs of popular American film actresses between the years 1932 and 1995).

2. "Girls' advertisements will use more in-home settings; boys' advertisements will use more out-of-home settings" (Smith, 1994, p. 329).

3. "Subjects from different cultures conceptualize similar structures of understanding human nature at different levels of complexity" (Oerter et al., 1996, p. 9).

4. "Mentally ill characters on television are more likely to be violent criminals than are the mentally ill in the U.S. population" (Diefenbach, 1997, p. 292).

5. "Men's graffiti will contain a greater amount of insulting (antiethnic, sexist, and antigay), sexual, and scatological references and women's graffiti will contain a greater amount of romantic content" (Schreer & Strichartz, 1997, p. 1068).

6. "There is a negative relationship between a manager's dominance of the subordinate in their communication and subordinate's perception of decisional involvement" (Fairhurst et al., 1987, p. 399).

7. "Commercials run in the Dominican Republic differ from those run in the United States in the frequency with which music is used" (Murray & Murray, 1996, p. 55).

Notice how the foregoing hypotheses vary in their specificity of the relationships among variables. Some indicate a *directional hypothesis,* predicting either a positive or negative relationship between variables (i.e., Hypotheses 1, 2, 4, 5, and 6). Two state a *nondirectional hypothesis,* where a relationship is specified but not its type (i.e., Hypotheses 3 and 7). That is, Hypotheses 3 and 7 posit differences but not the direction of the differences. Findings that commercials in the Dominican Republic use music more frequently than those in the United States would support Hypothesis 7; so would findings that commercials in the Dominican Republic use music *less* frequently.

Research Questions

When there is no clear theory to drive the research or past studies that have examined the content of interest, research questions may guide the process. Here are some examples from the literature.

1. "What issues do women's and news magazines address concerning breast cancer?" (Andsager & Powers, 1999, p. 535)

2. "Is there an association between physician-patient previous contact and patient domineeringness or dominance?" (Cecil, 1998, p. 131)

3. "What are the effects of community pluralism and contaminator/contaminant location on the framing of news accounts of environmental contamination stemming from institutions?" (Griffin & Dunwoody, 1997, p. 369)

4. "Is there a difference between the types of messages posted during the first half and the second half of the semester?" (Mowrer, 1996, p. 219) (The study was an analysis of student and instructor communication via computer conferencing.)

5. "How widespread is the use of billboards by small businesses?" (Taylor & Taylor, 1994, p. 98)

All variables included in hypotheses and research questions must be measured via one or more indicators. This process of operationalization is discussed in the next chapter.

Notes

1. An explanation of the difference between *concept* and *construct* might be helpful. A concept is anything that can be conceptualized by humans (i.e., practically anything). A construct is a concept that is by nature not directly observable, such as an emotion or an attitude. The special difficulties in measuring unobservable constructs is noteworthy.

2. Smith's (1992) discussion of thematic content analysis to produce psychometric measures notes three ways in which study variables are to be selected: (a) identified in advance on the basis of theoretical or practical considerations, (b) derived by classifying responses after they are produced by finding the descriptive categories into which most responses fit, and (c) identified by determining the effects on responses of theoretically relevant experimental manipulations or differences in naturally occurring groups (whatever is changed by manipulation or varies among groups is what is to be studied; p. 5).

3. How Marks (1978) arrives at his conclusions involves the discussion of something quite fascinating, called *synesthesia*. He reports substantial and long-term evidence of this sensory blending, whereby a stimulus perceived with one sense may result in the activation of a different sense. The most common sort of cross-modal sensing is apparently "colored hearing"—certain individuals (only a minority, according to Marks) quite literally see colors when they hear various sounds. The colors vary in a fashion analogous to the sounds; for instance, a "bright" sound, such as the blare of a trumpet, evokes a "bright" color, such as scarlet. The existence of these analogous variations leads Marks and others to believe that the sensing of a stimulus can be reduced to a very small number of universal features. The study of synesthesia, popular in the 19th century and largely ignored in the 20th, has enjoyed a resurgence in recent years (Baron-Cohen & Harrison, 1997; Cytowic, 1999).

4. The 16 images are created from four variables, each holding only two values. The four variables are the four corners: top left, top right, bottom left, and bottom right. The two values are facing in, and facing out. Image #2 is created from all four corners facing in. Image #14 is generated from all four corners facing out. The 16 images are the set of all possible combinations of the four corners either facing in or out.

oi	ii	io	oi	oo	ii	io	io
oo	ii	ii	io	ii	io	io	oi
io	ii	oo	ii	oo	oo	oi	oi
oo	oo	io	oi	oi	oo	oi	ii

SOURCE: Adapted from Garner, 1978.

5. In a class exercise, my graduate students decided that the medium with the most fully unique characteristics was that of the book—its weight and feel and even smell are as yet unduplicated in other media.

CHAPTER 6

Measurement Techniques

This chapter includes an introduction to measurement theory and to the important measurement standards of validity, precision, and reliability. The practical aspects of measurement in content analysis are discussed, with contrasts between human and computer coding. The construction of dictionaries for text analysis is considered. The chapter elaborates the process of constructing codebooks (i.e., the operational definitions for all variables) and coding forms for human coding (forms created as handy recording formats, corresponding to the codebook). The chapter also presents guidelines for comparing and selecting a text analysis computer program (e.g., Scolari's Diction 5.0, VBPro; also see Resources 3 and 5).

Defining *Measurement*

Perhaps the clearest definition of measurement is provided us by S. S. Stevens's (1951) classic treatment: "Measurement is the assignment of numerals to objects or events according to rules" (p. 1). In content analysis, we simply need to think of objects or events that are message units. The emphasis on numerals and rules is consistent with the goals of content analysis as outlined earlier in this book. This chapter is devoted to the development of the rules by which numerals are assigned.

Measurement theory (or *classical test theory*) assumes that there is a "true" value for each variable on each unit, the value that we are trying to discover. In the measurement process, we are usually unable to discover the exact true value due to a variety of sources of error. This simple idea has often been expressed as a formula.

$$m = t + e$$

that is, a *m*easured score is the result of a *t*rue score and an *e*rror score. Our job in creating measures is to minimize the "e" (error) component.

For example, there is a so-called true number of aggressive acts in a single episode of *ER,* given a precise definition of *aggressive act* in a codebook. The number that is measured will very likely be close to this true number, but it may not be exact. Contributing to this inexactness will be things such as coder misinterpretations (a coder may not have read the codebook carefully and does not realize that he or she should have coded a shove as an aggressive act), coder inattention (e.g., a coder fails to pause the tape when a coworker arrives with lunch, missing one instance of aggression), coder fatigue (e.g., a coder is too tired and just stares at the screen incomprehendingly), and recording errors (e.g., a coder records a "15" when he or she intended to write "13").

Such errors may be either *random error* or *nonrandom error.* Random error consists of errors that are unsystematic. Sometimes, the measurement is too high, and sometimes it's too low, generally summing to zero. This is a threat to reliability. Some of the examples just given would likely be random errors (e.g., recording errors may be as likely to be too high as too low). Nonrandom error is also called *bias* and is a threat to accuracy. It involves a systematic bias to a measuring procedure. For example, if the coder misinterpretation of what counts as aggression is not clarified, the coder may systematically under code acts of aggression.

Validity, Reliability, Accuracy, and Precision

This section covers several key standards for good measurement: reliability, validity, accuracy, and precision.

Reliability

Reliability is the extent to which a measuring procedure yields the same results on repeated trials. The notion relevant to content analysis is that a measure is not valuable if it can be conducted only once or only by one particular person.

Validity

Validity is the extent to which a measuring procedure represents the intended, and only the intended, concept. In thinking about validity, we ask the question, "Are we measuring what we want to measure?"

Accuracy

Accuracy is the extent to which a measuring procedure is free of bias (nonrandom error).

Precision

Precision is the fineness of distinction made between categories or levels of a measure. For example, measuring a character's age in years is more precise than measuring in decades. Precision is generally a good thing, but extreme precision may be counterproductive. That is, measuring age in days is technically more precise than measuring in years but is likely to be too tedious and error prone to be useful. (Could *you* report your own age in days?)

How the Standards Interrelate

In a general sense, validity is the standard of having a "good" measurement. Validity may be seen as encompassing the criteria of reliability, accuracy (freedom from bias—nonrandom error), and precision. That is, a measure cannot be valid if it is not reliable, accurate, and relatively precise. On the other hand, a measure may be reliable, accurate, and precise and still not be valid.

Figure 6.1 shows a graphical way of thinking about these several things that contribute to validity—reliability, accuracy, and precision. The targets are adaptations and extensions of ideas presented by Babbie (1995), Carmines and Zeller (1979), and Fink.[1] Each target shows a model of attempts to measure a variable—to hit the bull's-eye. Each "rifle shot" may be thought of as an attempt to measure the variable for one unit. A shot located far from the center of the bull's-eye indicates a measurement that is inaccurate, missing the true score by a sizeable amount. The caliber of the bullet indicates the measure's precision, with a small hole indicating a more precise measure.

Target A presents what we always hope to achieve—a valid measure, one that is reliable (the shots are closely clustered), accurate (the shots are near the center of the bull's-eye), and precise (the shots are small enough to show fine-grain distinctions). Target B presents good reliability and precision but poor accuracy, and the validity is therefore suspect. Target C shows a case of good precision but low reliability and mixed accuracy, thus threatening the overall validity. Target D displays an instance in which both reliability and accuracy are low, a clearly invalid attempt at measurement.

Last, Target E shows a one-shot attempt (hence, no reliability assessed) in which the measure is very imprecise. The large-caliber bullet does hit the bull's-eye, but it also takes out much of the rest of the target. This undesirable outcome is like, for example, measuring age with two categories—under 60 and over 60. Although we might be very accurate and reliable in our effort, the measure is too gross. There's very little we could do with such an imprecise

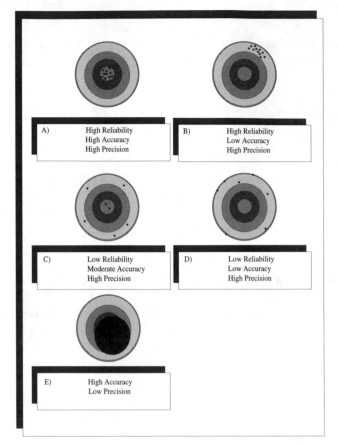

Figure 6.1 Comparing Reliability, Accuracy, and Precision

measure, and the validity is therefore poor. (Did we measure what we wanted to measure? Probably not.)

Types of Validity Assessment

Beyond assessing the reliability of measures (dealt with in detail in Chapter 7) and selecting measures that are as precise as is reasonably possible, there are several other ways of assessing elements of validity for a measure. Some of these go beyond simple accuracy and the targets metaphor shown in Figure 6.1, asking questions such as, "Will my shooting be the same on other targets as well?" "Is this the right target?" And "Does the target cover everything I want to hit?"

External Validity or Generalizability

Some methodologists make a distinction between *external* and *internal* validity. External validity is also referred to as generalizability, and it relates to whether the results of a measure can be extrapolated to other settings, times, and so on. Internal validity, in contrast, is what was previously defined in Chapter 5, the match-up of a conceptual definition and an operational definition (measurement). To assess external validity, we may consider the representativeness of the sample (whether it is a random sample of an identified population; see Chapter 4 for a discussion of random sampling), as well as whether the content analysis measurement process is true to life (what some call *ecological validity,*[2] for instance, coding films on a large screen probably would be more valid than coding from a thumbnail image on a computer screen). And full reportage of all content analysis procedures—dictionaries, complete codebooks, additional protocols for message handling, and so on—is important to ensure *replicability,* the ability of others to repeat the study with a different set of messages. Replicability is highly desirable, and the existence of successful replications supports the measures' external validity.[3]

Face Validity

This is the extent to which a measure, "on the face of things," seems to tap the desired concept. This sounds deceptively simple; in fact, face validity checks can be very informative. This requires that the researcher take a step back, so to speak, and examine the measures freshly and as objectively as possible. He or she may also wish to have others review the measures, with no introduction to the purpose of the study, and have them indicate what they think is being measured, a kind of back translation from operationalization to conceptualization.

It's instructive to take a "WYSIWYG" (what you see is what you get) approach to face validity. If we say we're measuring verbal aggression, then we expect to see measures of yelling, insulting, harassing, and the like. We do not expect to find measures of lying; although a negative verbal behavior, it doesn't seem to fit the "aggression" portion of the concept. (Of course, this will depend on the precise conceptual definition of *verbal aggression.*) Or if we say we're measuring "affection," but our measure counts only the key terms, *affection, love, fondness,* and *devotion,* in a text, we will not capture all the nuances of affection (a content validity issue).

Criterion Validity

This is the extent to which a measure taps an established standard or important behavior that is external to the measure[4] (Carmines & Zeller, 1979; Elder, Pavalko, & Clipp, 1993). This criterion validity may either be concurrent (the standard or behavior exists at the same time as the measure) or predictive (the standard or behavior occurs after the measure).

In an example of a concurrent criterion validity check, Pershad and Verma (1995) used as their standard the clinical diagnoses of schizophrenia for individuals whose open-ended responses to inkblots were content analyzed. In a case of predictive criterion validity assessment, Gottschalk and his colleagues provide good examples—their "hope" content analysis scale, applied to verbal samples collected from individuals, significantly predicted patient follow-through on recommendations to seek psychiatric treatment (Gottschalk, 1995, p. 121). "Hope" scores also predicted survival time of cancer patients.

In total, Gottschalk and colleagues (Gottschalk, 1995; Gottschalk & Bechtel, 1993; Gottschalk & Gleser, 1969) have used four different types of criterion measures to validate their measures of psychological constructs through the content analysis of verbal samples: (a) psychological, (b) physiological, (c) pharmacological, and (d) biochemical. For instance, to validate their anxiety scale, they looked at the relationship between individuals' scores on that scale and (a) their diagnoses by clinical psychologists and (b) their blood pressures and skin temperatures at the times their speech samples were collected. The researchers conducted experiments (c) administering tranquilizers, validating lower anxiety scores for the treatment groups. They also found their content analysis anxiety scale to be validated by (d) the presence of greater plasma-free fatty acids (established by blood tests) for those with higher anxiety scores. It is important that Gottschalk and Gleser reported making revisions as needed in their content analysis scales as the validation process evolved.

Potter and Levine-Donnerstein (1999) draw a distinction between an "expert" standard for coding and a "norm/intersubjectivity" standard.[5] Although using an expert as a criterion validity check may be useful, it should be remembered that according to the definitions and criteria presented in this book, total reliance on expert standard to judge reliability and validity is inconsistent with the goals of content analysis. (Remember that a content analysis scheme needs to be useable by a wide variety of coders, not just a few experts.) The second standard, looking to a norm or an intersubjectively agreed-on standard is highly consistent with the notion of reliability, but it does not inform us about other aspects of validity.

Content Validity

This type of validity is the extent to which the measure reflects the full domain of the concept being measured (Carmines & Zeller, 1979). For example, Smith (1999) tried to tap a wide variety of aspects of female sex-role stereotyping in film characters. She measured 27 characteristics, traits, and behaviors that had been identified in past research as associated primarily with women (e.g., preparing food and drink, shopping, holding clerical and service-oriented occupations, displaying an orientation toward home and family), with a goal of covering all important parts of the construct.

Construct Validity

This is the extent to which a measure is related to other measures (constructs) in a way consistent with hypotheses derived from theory (Carmines & Zeller, 1979). For example, Gottschalk (1995) has developed a number of his psychographic content analytic measures (e.g., depression, hostility) with the thought always in mind as to whether the measures relate as they theoretically should with other variables. All measures that Gottschalk and Bechtel (1993) have attempted with content analysis were first "thoroughly defined," and then a "set of construct-validation studies had to be carried out to ascertain exactly what this verbal behavior analysis procedure was measuring" (Gottschalk, 1995, p. 9).

Although many scholars cite the need for the establishment of construct validity (e.g., Folger et al., 1984; McAdams & Zeldow, 1993), good examples of the process are relatively few. In a content analysis of the news coverage of U.S. senators' initial campaigns for office, Hill, Hanna, and Shafqat (1997) executed a series of construct validity tests of their ideology measure that found it to be related as predicted to national, regional, and state partisan group ideologies and to roll call votes of the senators.

Some interesting attempts have been made to validate several human interaction coding schemes, including Bales's (1950) interaction process analysis system (IPA), Stiles's (1980) taxonomy of verbal response modes (VRM), and Fisher's (1970) decision proposal coding system. Poole and Folger (1981) tested the validity assumption that a coding scheme should relate to the meanings of the utterances as judged by the *interactants,* a variation on construct validity that they call *representational validity.* Using regression procedures on multidimensional spaces for the coding schemes and for the respondents' space, they found good support for the notion that the IPA dimensions and Fisher's (1970) scheme dimensions relate to the dimensions of judgments by interactants.[6] Conversely, Stiles (1980) found no support for validity in his investigation of how dimensions of *overall observer ratings* of speaker behavior relate to dimensions derived from IPA and VRM coding.

For exemplification purposes, there are instances of better-developed validation processes among noncontent analytic measures. Two compilation books from social psychology and communication (Robinson, Shaver, & Wrightsman, 1991; Rubin, Palmgreen, & Sypher, 1994) present excellent documentation for dozens of standard self-report measures. (No comparable source for content analysis coding schemes exists.) For example, the self-report Student Motivation Scale (p. 343) measures motivational states in students via 16 bipolar items. A series of studies have found the measure to be related to other constructs in predictable ways. For example, Beatty, Behnke, and Froelich (1980) found that students offered extra credit scored higher, and that the motivation scale was positively correlated with state anxiety scores. Beatty and Payne (1985) reported a positive correlation between the scale and the length of students' written responses, and Beatty, Forst, and Stewart (1986) a positive correlation between the scale and duration of speeches given by the students. The motivation scale has also been found to be related to teachers' use of power strategies, teacher immediacy, and certain aspects of student learning (Christophel, 1990; Richmond, 1990). This network of relationships conforms to the theoretic expectations for the measure, thus building its construct validity.

The full process of validation must be conducted over a series of studies, testing different relationships between the measure in question and other indicators. Janis (1949) bemoaned the fact that so many content analyses seem to be unique, not using measures that have been used before. Therefore, as he says, with each study, the issue of validation "begins de novo" (begins anew; pp. 74-75). The situation seems to have changed little in 50 years.

Operationalization

Operationalization is the process of developing measures. It's "the construction of actual, concrete measurement techniques" (Babbie, 1995, p. 5).[7] For content analysis, this means the construction of a *coding scheme,* which means either a set of dictionaries (for text analysis) or a set of measures in a codebook (for nontext analysis).

Many of the guidelines for good operationalization in survey and experimental research apply directly to measurement in content analysis as well. Most of the specific applications of the guidelines that follow are particular to the construction of measures for human coding.

In designing the *categories or levels* that will be used for a given measure, the researcher should try to achieve several things: categories or levels that are exhaustive and mutually exclusive and an appropriate level of measurement.

Categories or Levels That Are Exhaustive

There must be an appropriate code for each and every unit coded. This means that the categories "other" and "unable to determine" should frequently be included. For example, the following set of categories are not exhaustive.

Background for magazine article headline:

1	White
2	Photograph
3	Drawing or painting

This measure gives no provision for a solid color background. There also might be other backgrounds that we can't readily think of—an "other" category is an important catchall.

Categories or Levels That Are Mutually Exclusive

There should be only *one* appropriate code for each and every unit coded. If there is the possibility of multiple codes, then these ought to be broken down into separate measures. For example, the coding of Web banner ads' "primary strategy of promotion" in the following manner would result in validity and reliability problems.

Primary strategy of promotion

0   No strategy of promotion

1   More informational than emotional: There is more factual information of products or services than appeals to feelings in advertisement.

2   More emotional than informational: There is more content appealing to emotions than factual information in advertisement.

3   Product shown: The product or service is shown in advertisement to demonstrate its quality and utility.

4   Problem solving: The advertisement poses a problem that could be solved through using the product or accepting the service.

5   Image advertising: The advertisement is designed to enhance prestige of the product or service without giving concrete details about the product or service.

6   Product comparison: The advertisement compares, implicitly or explicitly, the advertised brand with at least one other competing product or service.

The categories are not mutually exclusive; one banner ad may easily be coded as having more than one of the features listed. A more appropriate way to measure these features would be as separate indicators, indeed, separate variables. This checklist approach to coded variables can be useful in many situations.[8]

Informational or emotional appeal

1   More informational than emotional: There is more factual information of products or services than appeals to feelings in advertisement.

2   More emotional than informational: There is more content appealing to emotions than factual information in advertisement.

3   Unable to determine.

Product display

1   Product shown: The product or service is shown in advertisement to demonstrate its quality and utility.

0   Product is not shown.

Problem-solving approach

1   Problem solving: The advertisement poses a problem that could be solved through using the product or accepting the service.

0   No problem-solving approach is used.

Image advertising

1   Image advertising: The advertisement is designed to enhance prestige of the product or service without giving concrete details about the product or service.

0   Image advertising is not used.

Product comparison

1   Product comparison: the advertisement compares, implicitly or explicitly, the advertised brand with at least one other competing product or service.

0   Product comparison is not used.

An Appropriate Level of Measurement

Each variable should be measured with categories that are at the highest level of measurement possible, given the goals of the measure. Stevens (1951) presents the now-classic four levels of measurement, in order of increasing sophistication.

1. The least sophisticated or lowest level of measurement is called *nominal.* A nominal scale consists of a set of categories that are distinct from one another. The use of numbers is for labeling only—words or letters would work just as well. The order of the categories is arbitrary, and reordering the categories makes no difference in the meaning of the scale. Box 6.1 shows an example of a codebook for human-coded content analysis of film or television characters. This codebook includes a number of examples of nominal measures, such as those for gender, sexual preference, accent, marital status, religious affiliation, hair color, baldness, and facial hair. Box 6.2 shows an example of the coding form that matches the codebook. There's more about that later in the chapter.

2. An *ordinal scale* consists of a set of categories that are rank ordered on some continuum. The use of numbers is for maintaining the proper ordering, but the numbers do not signify equal intervals between the groups. The numbers cannot be used as numbers in an ordinary sense—we cannot perform arithmetic manipulations on them. For example, the "social age" variable in the sample codebook in Box 6.1 is measured at the ordinal level. Those characters coded as "5, elderly" are assumed to be older than characters coded as "4, mature adult," who are assumed to be older than characters coded as "3, young adult," and so forth. But we cannot say that the difference between "3, young adult" and "4, mature adult" is the same as the difference between "4, mature adult" and "5, elderly." Nor do we assume a consistent difference between characters coded "3" and those coded "4": Two characters thought by a coder to be about 20 and 64 years of age would be coded "3" and "4" respectively. So would two characters evaluated to be about 39 and 40 years of age. So the intervals between the categories are not equal. Last, we should not calculate an average social

Box 6.1   Sample Codebook

Character Demographics Analysis

Unit of Data Collection: Each individual personality or character who (a) speaks, or (b) performs actions important to the story, or (c) is the subject of a significant amount of conversation.

Episode ID: Fill in the episode's ID number, as indicated on the episode ID list.

Coder ID: Indicate the number of the individual who coded that sheet, according to the coder ID list.

Character Name and Description: Give a brief but discriminating description of each coded character (e.g., "middle-aged man in a shiny blue suit") *and* his or her name if given.

Character ID: Give each character a unique 4-digit number, beginning with 0001 and proceeding upward without duplication across all episodes. If a character appears in more than one episode, code him or her each time, but use the *same* ID number. It is important that these numbers are accurate and nonduplicative.

Role: Indicate whether the character plays a minor, medium, or major part of the episode.
1. *Minor:*   If in an episode a character has 10 or fewer lines (complete sentences or phrases that are part of a dialogue), the character's role will be deemed minor.
2. *Medium:*   If a character speaks more than 10 lines in an episode but is featured (appears, is talked about, or both) in less than 50% of the episode's content, the character's role will be deemed medium.
3. *Major:*   If in an episode a character is featured in 50% or more of an episode's content, the character's role will be deemed major.
9. Unable to determine

Social Age: Estimate the stage at which the character operates in his or her interactions with others.
1. *Child:*   The individual behaves and speaks as one who is 12 years of age or younger.
2. *Adolescent:*   The individual behaves and speaks as one who is 13 to 19 years of age.
3. *Young adult:*   The individual behaves and speaks as one who is 20 to 39 years of age.
4. *Mature adult:*   The individual behaves and speaks as one who is 40 to 64 years of age.
5. *Elderly:*   The individual behaves and speaks as one who is 65 or older.
9. Unable to determine

Chronological Age: Report or estimate the character's chronological age in years (if less than 1 year, code as 0). Indicate below this whether the figure given was explicitly stated in the program or estimated by the coder (1 = explicitly stated, 2 = estimated by coder; if unable to determine, leave blank).

Socioeconomic Status (SES):   Report or estimate the character's SES.
1. *Upper or upper middle class:*   An individual who is well-to-do or moderately well-to-do; this individual typically is independently wealthy or has a high-level job and is not dependent on his or her weekly or monthly income to live.
2. *Middle class:*   An individual who works for a living, has all the necessities and some luxuries, but is dependent on working for his or her livelihood.
3. *Working class or lower class:*   An individual who does not have the necessities of life or just barely has the necessities and no luxuries. He or she may be unemployed or on public assistance.
9. Unable to determine

(continued)

Box 6.1   Continued

Gender: Report the gender of the character.
1. Male
2. Female
9. Unable to determine

Sexual Preference: Report the primary sexual preference of the character, if this is discernable. Indicate whether this was directly stated in the program or estimated by you (1 = explicitly stated, 2 = estimated).
1. *Heterosexual:* An individual whose primary sexual preference is for members of the opposite gender. If a character is married and does not express homosexual orientations, code as heterosexual.
2. *Homosexual:* An individual whose primary sexual preference is for members of the same gender.
3. *Bisexual:* An individual whose sexual orientation includes a desire for members of both genders.
9. Unable to determine

Accent: Report the character's primary mode of speech:
1. U.S. Northern (standard)
2. U.S. Southern
3. U.S. Southwestern (e.g., cowboys)
4. U.S. Eastern (e.g., Boston, New York)
6. Non-U.S. accent
8. Other (specify)
9. Unable to determine

Marital Status: Indicate the character's present marital status. A wedding ring may be used as evidence in coder estimation, except in the case of Roman Catholic priests and nuns. Again, indicate whether the character's marital status was explicitly stated in the program or estimated by the coder (1 = explicitly stated, 2 = estimated by coder).

10. Married, no other information	31. Single, never married
11. Married, first time	32. Single, divorced
12. Remarried after divorce	33. Single, widowed
13. Remarried after widowhood	77. Engaged
20. Separated	88. Other (specify)
30. Single, no other information	99. Unable to determine

Religious Affiliation: Code the character's religious affiliation (if any) and whether it was explicitly stated in the program or estimated by the coder (1 = explicitly stated, 2 = estimated by coder).
1. A member of a specific organized religion
2. Belongs to organized religion but unspecified
3. Definitely does not belong to an organized religion
4. Unable to determine

age, using the ordinal 1-to-5 scale, given that an ordinal measure does not support such arithmetic operations. In addition to social age, the sample codebook contains several other ordinal scale measures: role, socioeconomic status, height, weight, and use of glasses.

Hair Color: Indicate what color hair the character has at the present time.

10. White
20. Gray
30. Blonde
31. Blonde-gray mix
40. Blonde (obviously bleached)
50. Red
51. Red-gray mix

60. Brown
61. Brown-gray mix
70. Black
71. Black-gray mix
80. Completely bald
99. Unable to determine

Baldness: Indicate to what degree the male characters are bald at the present time.
0. Not bald (full head of hair)
1. Receding hair line
2. Bald spot
3. Fringe hair only
4. Totally bald
8. Female character
9. Unable to determine

Facial Hair: Indicate whether the male characters have facial hair (mustache, beard, or both) at the present time.
0. No mustache or beard
1. Mustache only
2. Beard only
3. Mustache and beard
9. Unable to determine

Height: Indicate whether the character is tall, of medium height, or short for his or her gender. This designation would be determined by the following heights: For males: tall = 6′ 0″ or more, medium = 5′ 8″ to 5′ 11″, short = 5′ 7″ or less; For females: tall = 5′ 8″ or more, medium = 5′ 4″ to 5′ 7″, Short = 5′ 3″ or less.
1. Short
2. Medium
3. Tall
9. Unable to determine (including children)

Weight: Indicate whether the character is heavy, of medium build, or thin for his or her height and gender.
1. Thin
2. Medium
3. Heavy
9. Unable to determine

Glasses: Indicate whether the character is shown wearing glasses all the time, some of the time (e.g., for reading only), or never. This does *not* include sunglasses.
0. Never wears glasses
1. Wears glasses intermittently
2. Wears glasses at all times
9. Unable to determine

3. An *interval scale* consists of categories or levels represented by numbers that are quantitative or numeric in the ordinary sense. It differs from an ordinary use of numbers only in that its zero point is arbitrary (zero does not correspond to a total lack of the concept being measured). The dis-

Box 6.2   Sample Coding Form

Character Demographics Analysis

Episode ID _____	Coder ID _____				
Character Name and Description					
Character ID					
Role					
Social Age					
Chronological Age					
Determination for Chronological Age					
SES					
Gender					
Sexual Preference					
Determination for Sexual Preference					
Accent					
Marital Status					
Determination for Marital Status					
Religious Affiliation					
Determination for Religious Affiliation					
Hair Color					
Baldness					
Facial Hair					
Height					
Weight					
Glasses					

tances between the categories (i.e., numbers) are known and typically equal. Purely interval scales are relatively rare. The classic example is the temperature scale of degrees Fahrenheit (Stevens, 1951). Zero is arbitrary, not corresponding to a complete "lack of heat," and indeed, below-zero measurements are possible. Yet the distance between, say, 50° F and 55° F is the same as the difference between 60° F and 65° F. And an average temperature may be calculated. However, because of the lack of a so-called true or meaningful zero point, two Fahrenheit temperatures may not be expressed as a ratio; for instance, 70° F is *not* twice as warm as 35° F. None of the measurements in the Character Demographics codebook (Box 6.1) are interval, and this is typical in content analysis. There seems to be no advantage to creating an interval measure when a ratio measure is possible.[9]

4. The most sophisticated or highest level of measurement is called *ratio*. A ratio scale consists of categories or levels represented by numbers that are quantitative or numeric in the ordinary sense, including a true or meaningful zero point. The differences between the numbers are known and typically equal, and two values on the scale may be expressed as a ratio. For example, one measure from the sample codebook in Box 6.1 is constructed to be ratio: chronological age. There is a true zero (a newborn baby), we may calculate an average age in years, and ratios are possible (such as a 70-year-old who is twice as old as a 35-year-old).

The typical application of dictionaries results in ratio measurement. Using the Diction program, a text may obtain a tenacity score ranging from zero (if no tenacity dictionary words are counted) to a high numeric score (e.g., 55, if many tenacity words are counted).

Novice researchers often make the mistake of believing that the level of measurement is attached to the *variable*, rather than to a particular measure of a variable. This is not the case. A given variable may be measured at different levels. Notice that in the sample codebook in Box 6.1, character age is measured in two ways—one at the ratio level ("estimate the character's chronological age in years") and one at the ordinal level (1 = child, 2 = adolescent, 3 = young adult, 4 = mature adult, 5 = elderly).

An alternative to Stevens's (1951) four levels of measurement that helps the researcher clarify his or her goals is offered by Fink (Edward L. Fink, personal communication, March 26, 1999). His "counts and amounts" approach has the researcher identify, for each variable, whether the goal is to *count* how many cases or units occur in each category or to identify a level or *amount* of a concept with the measure. A single measure may provide the raw materials for category counts, overall amounts, or both. For example, the measure of gender in the sample codebook in Box 6.1 (1 = male, 2 = female, 3 = unable to determine) can provide a count for each of the three categories (e.g., 27 males, 42 females, 5 cases that cannot be determined). The measure of chronological age can provide counts (e.g., three characters are 42 years of age), but this is unlikely to be very useful. Rather, this measure is likely to provide an amount (e.g., average age = 38 years), which might be broken down by another variable (e.g., by gender: average age for females = 28 years, average age for males = 43 years).

Computer Coding

Much effort has been expended developing automatic computer schemes that measure both manifest and latent variables (e.g., Stone et al., 1966). Sections to follow will examine the state of the art for such computer text analysis, which has become so common that it's rare to find a text content analysis today that does *not* use computer analysis. The typical computer coding analysis is limited to text only; conversely, the typical human-coding scheme looks beyond text analysis. Usually, when human coders are asked to engage in text analysis, it's as part of a larger study of static or moving images (e.g., Michelson, 1996) or a study that uses computer text analysis for some measures and supplements them with human coding for content that is more latent (Franke, 2000).

There are several indispensable volumes that have been written about particular applications of computer text content analysis (CATA): Roberts's (1997b) broad-based, edited volume is probably the best starting point. Weber (1990) is useful for the basics of text analysis in general and for a historical perspective. West's (in press) forthcoming book of readings promises to be an invaluable source for computer text content analysis issues and examples. Within that volume, Linderman (in press) provides a clear comparison between human coding and computer coding. Gottschalk (1995), Smith (1992), and Markel (1998) are standards for psychological and psychiatric applications of computer text content analysis.

As detailed in Chapter 4, automatic computer coding of *nontext* message features is relatively undeveloped. The state of the art consists primarily of systems that assist in accessing, storing, retrieving, unitizing, manipulating, annotating, and otherwise preparing the visual content for coding. The future possibilities are limitless, but for now, true automatic systems are very limited in scope and usefulness. At the forefront in the development of automatic systems is William Evans's initiative at Georgia State University. He is attempting to harness existent tools for the manipulation and organizing of content (as described in Chapter 4; e.g., Virage's VideoLogger, OCR technologies) in ways that will make content analysis of the moving image as automatic as the content analysis of text. The title of his recent work articulates his goal: "Teaching Computers to Watch Television" (Evans, 2000).

One exceptional use of computer coding to assess nontext content is Simonton's (1980a, 1980b, 1984, 1987, 1994) computer content analyses of musical melodies. Although only the broader definitions of communication (e.g., Watzlawick et al., 1967) would consider the melodic structure of music to be message content, there's much to be learned from Simonton's systematic, over-time construction of musical dictionaries of melody variations, transitions, keys, instrumentations, and motifs. One important lesson is that coding music is like coding in another language; one must first learn the language before one is able to construct a valid coding scheme. Another is the patience and tenacity required to develop and test a valid and valuable set of dictionaries over a period of years.

Dictionaries for Text Analysis

A dictionary is a set of words, phrases, parts of speech, or other word-based indicators (e.g., word length, number of syllables) that is used as the basis for a search of texts. Usually, a number of dictionaries are used in a single study, each serving as a measure of a different concept. For example, Hart's Diction 5.0 dictionaries measure such variables as rapport, aggression, and embellishment. There are a number of types of dictionaries that may be selected.

Custom Dictionaries

Dictionaries constructed by the researcher are called *custom dictionaries,* as I've mentioned. Following the guidelines of Chapter 5, variables may be selected from theory, past research, researcher immersion in the message pool, and so on. For example, I have used up to 157 different custom word sets (dictionaries) for a single computer content analysis using the computer program VBPro. By using a large number of narrowly defined dictionaries (e.g., "newspaper" and its synonyms; "television" and its synonyms), the researcher has the option of creating a variety of flexible index combinations of the dictionaries. For instance, the "newspaper" and "television" dictionary measures might both contribute to an additive index of "mass media."

Standard Dictionaries

Standard dictionaries and protocols, often developed by the author(s) of the computer program being used, range from simple readability indicators (e.g., Danielson, Lasorsa, & Im, 1992) to complex dictionaries intended to measure very latent, unobservable constructs (e.g., an affiliation motive or an uncertainty orientation; Smith, 1992).

Basic readability was perhaps the first standard mode of measurement for text, originating before computer text analysis.[10] A number of readability indexes have been developed, all intending to measure the complexity of the writing style (a form measure), often reported as the level of education needed to read the text. Even basic word-processing software, such as Microsoft Word, includes a readability analysis. Danielson et al. (1992) used a computer version of the Flesch Reading Ease Score to compare readability of novels and print news stories over a 100-year period. A typical readability measure, the Flesch includes both average sentence length (a syntactic measure) and average word length (a semantic measure). Danielson et al. found a clear divergence in the trends for readability of novels and news—novels have become easier to read, whereas news has become harder to read (due primarily to the use of longer words).

Other standard dictionaries attempt to measure more specific concepts. The earliest, and perhaps most eclectic, collection of standard dictionaries for computer text analysis was the original General Inquirer (see Chapter 3). As described elsewhere, there is a rich tradition of using text content analysis of speech and writing samples to measure psychological traits and states via standard dictionaries and protocols (Gottschalk, 1995; Pennebaker & Francis,

Box 6.3   The Evolution of a Dictionary Set

Political Speech Indexing

Rod Hart's perspective on his Diction (Hart, 1997; 2000b) computer text program is a good framework from which to view all uses of computer content analysis:

> [Diction] is no listener . . . but merely a quick-witted hearer, one who gathers and codifies political sayings but who is without the conceptual apparatus necessary to translate iteration into ideation, hearing into listening. This hearer . . . is thus no better a scholar than the team of scholars it joins, but, equally, it allows that team to hear political sounds that could not have been heard without its assistance. (Hart, 1985, pp. 97-98)

Beginning around 1980, Hart took on the task of "teaching" the computer to "hear" the aspects of political speech in which he was interested. He devised dictionary word lists for four main features of language he deemed highly relevant to the study of political discourse: certainty, realism, activity, and optimism. His dictionaries were an amalgam of previous word lists, drawing on critical perspectives and political philosophy as well as his own expertise.

Each of the four was constituted of a number of subscale dictionaries (e.g., optimism = praise + satisfaction + inspiration – adversity – negation). All told, the 27 subscales encompassed about 3,000 search words. Over the years, the subscale dictionaries evolved—some were dropped, others were combined, some were expanded, and one main dictionary was added (commonality). Today, the collection stands at more than 40 dictionaries and over 10,000 search words.

One important feature of Hart's efforts has been to establish so-called normal ranges of scores on all of the main dictionaries and subscales. For many years, these ranges were based solely on a large collection of political texts. In Diction 5.0, normal ranges are provided for a wider array of text types, including poetry, advertising, and TV scripts. (However, the collection of texts on which these so-called normal ranges are based does not appear to be randomly selected from identified populations. Thus, comparisons with these bases should be made cautiously.)

Hart's prepared dictionaries do not exclude the possibility of custom dictionaries. In their study of the 1996 presidential debates, Hart and Jarvis (1997) supplemented Diction's standard dictionaries with six custom dictionaries: patriotic terms, party references, voter references, leader references, religious terms, and irreligious terms.

1999; Smith, 1992). And Box 6.3 details the history of the development of Diction's 40-plus dictionaries devised over a 20-year period to measure key characteristics of political speech (Hart, 1997).

Work in linguistics (e.g., Litkowski, 1992; Pennebaker & Francis, 1999) uses dictionaries based on lexical categorization of words. For example, the Linguistic Inquiry and Word Count (LIWC) program uses dictionaries totaling 2,290 words and word stems to count words representing a variety of linguistic dimensions (e.g., prepositions, articles) and relativity (references to time, space, and motion). The program also taps a variety of psychological processes (e.g., affective processes, such as anger; cognitive processes, such as inhibition; sensory and perceptual processes, such as hearing; and social processes, such as family) and personal concerns (e.g., religion, sexuality). Another linguistic and psychological analysis tool is the Minnesota Contextual Content Analysis (MCCA) protocol. It places each of 11,000 words into one of 116 categories, ranging from pronoun use (e.g., "I/me") to affect (e.g., "negatives") to semantic usage (e.g., "strive nouns"). It counts the words in each category and compares the frequency profile against that of general English language usage ("Principles and procedures of category development," 2000, p. 3). It includes a disambiguation procedure for assigning a single category when a word falls into more than one.[11]

One caution about using standard dictionaries is the issue of "black box" measurement. Many computer analysis programs do not reveal the precise nature of their measures or how they construct their scales and indexes. The researcher enters his or her text into a veritable black box from which output emerges. This mystery analysis is typically due to the proprietary nature of the commercially available programs (e.g., Gottschalk & Bechtel, 1993; Hart 1997). The Diction program is a bit more forthcoming than most in providing word lists for its dictionaries, but the documentation still does not reveal the algorithms by which the dictionary words are combined for each score. It's the position of this book that the user should be fully informed as to the substance of dictionaries and how they might be combined.

The user should be cautious about using standard dictionaries simply because they are there. It's a very attractive proposition to simply sit back and let the program do its work, with handy prewritten dictionaries. The problem is, these handy dictionaries may have nothing to do with the variables the researcher hopes to measure. The researcher should keep in mind the fact that he or she can always construct custom dictionaries that meet his or her precise needs.

Dictionaries Emergent From the Data

This approach to dictionary construction is to base the lists on actual word frequencies from the message sample. For example, Miller, Andsager, and Riechert (1998) conducted a computer text analysis of news releases and elite newspaper coverage concerning the 1996 Republican presidential primary. They selected for further analyses only those words that appeared high on a frequencies list output from the VBPro program.[12]

Other Word-Based, Nondictionary Outcomes

Some program applications create output that, although based on word occurrences and co-occurrences, does not use dictionaries in the typical sense.

For example, the VBPro program goes beyond dictionary counting to map concepts in multidimensional space, based on their co-occurrence.

The program CATPAC (see Resource 3) is designed to conduct semantic network analysis. Traditional network analysis is a method of connecting nodes (people or groups) on the basis of communication patterns measured by surveys; semantic network analysis is a method of connecting frequently occurring words based on their co-occurrence. Based also on the principles of neural network analysis (modeling the connections within the human brain), CATPAC identifies the most frequently occurring words in a text, ignoring standard and custom "stop words," such as simple articles like "a," "the," and "and." Based on co-occurrences of the frequently occurring words, the program conducts a cluster analysis to produce a dendogram, output that graphically shows the levels of co-occurrence. Like VBPro, it also conducts a multidimensional scaling analysis (MDS) of the co-occurrence matrix (and presents the map in color and 3-D, if you have the glasses).

Selection of a Computer Text Content Analysis Program

The options for computer text content analysis have exploded in the past 10 years. There are now no fewer than two dozen programs, with additions and revisions appearing regularly. For that reason, the reader should consult *The Content Analysis Guidebook Online* for updates.

VBPro is a featured computer text content analysis program for this book. It is simple and straightforward, appropriate to many content analysis tasks, is a good choice for the novice analyst, and is available as a *free* download. Resource 3 presents a brief how-to introduction for VBPro, from preparation of the text (e.g., deleting reserved characters and saving as ASCII), through dictionary construction, to data outcomes suitable for further analysis using such programs as SPSS (Statistical Package for the Social Sciences). *The Content Analysis Guidebook Online* provides links and additional materials relevant to this versatile do-it-yourself program.

A very good way of helping assess whether a program is useful for a particular purpose is to collect a few examples of available publications or Web site reports that detail research projects that have used the program. *The Content Analysis Guidebook Online* contains limited bibliographies for each program that can help in this task.

Resource 3 provides a chart comparing many of the most used and most useful computer programs designed for the content analysis of text. The headers for this chart are good bases on which to compare features:

Number of Cases or Units Analyzed

Some programs are designed to process only one text unit at a time, a very tedious process for large-scale projects. Others will batch the texts and analyze each in turn, providing separate per-unit data from one run.

Frequency Output

The most basic quantitative output available from the programs is a word count, reporting the frequency of each word occurring in a text or a set of texts. Most often, words are also sorted in order of descending frequency. Often, a type/token ratio is reported, indicating the number of unique words divided by the total number of words.

Alphabetical Output

Those programs that provide by-word frequency counts also tend to provide an alphabetized list of all words in the text or set of texts.

Multiple-Unit Data File Output[13]

Some programs analyze a series of message units, creating one data line per unit (with as many entries as there are dictionaries) and providing a full multiple-unit data file with as many lines as there are units in the data set. Many of the programs that analyze only one unit at a time do not concatenate the output in this way, leaving the researcher with a bunch of separate output files.

KWIC or Concordance

KWIC stands for "key word in context." A concordance is essentially the same thing, indicating the searching and identification of all cases of a word or phrase, shown in context. A KWIC output displays the contexts of the located strings. For example, a KWIC search of Charles Dickens's novel *David Copperfield* for the word "tears" would include the following:

. . . I had never before seen Agnes cry. I had seen **tears** in her eyes . . .

. . . Again she repressed the **tears** that had begun to flow . . .

Each KWIC or concordance gives us a better understanding of the use of the search term than would be granted by a raw dictionary count. And notice that a dictionary count would fail to indicate that the second instance of "tears" is one in which the character did *not* cry. But KWIC or concordance output is more qualitative than content analysis and does not provide the by-unit data or summaries that are expected of a quantitative technique.

Standard Dictionaries

As noted earlier, sets of search terms may be provided within the program. The output consists of a numeric score on each unit for each dictionary.

Custom Dictionaries

Most, but not all, programs allow the user to create their own dictionaries. The output consists of a numeric score on each unit for each dictionary.

Specialty Analyses

Some programs provide features not readily categorized, such as VBPro's provision of "VBMap," a routine that uses co-occurrence matrices of concepts (dictionaries) to place concepts in a multidimensional space. Concepts that co-occur frequently are close together in the space, whereas concepts that rarely co-occur in message units are far apart (Miller, 2000). Other specialty analyses include the clustering and mapping provided by CATPAC and the comparative data provided by Diction.

Human Coding

All measures for human content analysis coding need to be fully explicated in a document called a *codebook*. The codebook corresponds to a *coding form,* which provides spaces appropriate for recording the codes for all variables measured. Together, the codebook and coding form should stand alone as a protocol for content analyzing messages. As described earlier, Boxes 6.1 and 6.2 contain simple examples of a paired codebook and coding form for measuring demographic and descriptive information about characters appearing in moving image media.

Codebooks and Coding Forms

The goal in creating codebooks and coding forms is to make the set so complete and unambiguous as to almost eliminate the individual differences among coders. The construction of an original codebook is a rather involved process, with repeated revisions right up until the moment when coding begins. Even the most mundane details need to be spelled out. All instructions should be written out carefully and fully. There should be instructions on what is a codable unit (see the codebook example in Box 6.1), and any other instructions on the coding protocol (e.g., "View the commercial a *second* time to code *characters* within the spot.").

The researcher has some choice on the distribution of measurement details between the codebook and the coding form. Some choose to put many instructions and details in the coding form, leaving little additional information to be contained in the accompanying codebook. Naccarato and Neuendorf (1998) went this route, and it resulted in a 12-page coding form, which was a bit unwieldy. The Naccarato and Neuendorf materials are available for inspection at *The Content Analysis Guidebook Online.*

The more common choice is to include lots of detail in the codebook and to leave the coding form looking like an empty shell, merely a convenient repository for numeric information. Lombard et al. (1996) have chosen this tack, as may be seen in their materials on the book's Web site. Also, the sample codebook and coding form displayed in Boxes 6.1 and 6.2 follow this model. Note how the coding form uses shorthand version for variable names and is rather meaningless without the codebook.

Coder Training

Three words describe good coder preparation: Train, train, and train. As part of the training process, the researcher may need to revise the codebook repeatedly until researcher and coders are all comfortable with the coding scheme. Practice coding, called *pilot* coding, can inform the researchers as to the reliability and overall viability of the coding scheme. Then, revisions may be made before final coding commences.

Coding decisions should be made from information available in the coded message only. For example, when coding behaviors exhibited on television soap operas, coders may not use information they might have from being fans of a show over a period of years (e.g., a character's divorces, paternity, etc.). At the same time, it is common practice to allow coders to review the message units as often as they need to extract the maximum information from the content.

Final coding is to be done by each coder individually; at this stage, it is not a consensus-building process. Consensus is useful only during training, pilot, and revision stages. All arguments leading to consensus at these earlier stages should be documented in the codebook, to enable future efforts to achieve the same level of reliability. Nor is final coding a democratic, majority-rule situation. Rather, it is geared to standardize the coders' techniques. Their coding methods need to be calibrated so that they view the content in the same way, as they code *independently,* without discussion or collaboration.

Blind coding, in which coders do not know the purpose of the study, is desirable, to reduce bias that compromises validity. Of course, the coders clearly need to fully understand the variables and their measures, but preferably they should *not* be aware of the research questions or hypotheses guiding the investigation. This is to avoid the coder equivalent of what is termed *demand characteristic* (Orne, 1975): the tendency of participants in a study to try to give the researcher what he or she wants. Kolbe and Burnett (1991) argue the value of what they call *judge independence,* the freedom of coders to make judgments without input from the researcher. Sparkman (1996) used a blind coder as a check against the primary, informed coder (the principal investigator himself). Banerjee, Capozzoli, McSweeney, & Sinha (1999) point out the biasing effect of coder knowledge of variables extraneous to the content analysis (e.g., being aware of the political party of political speakers at a convention), and offer techniques of statistical control for such confounding influences.

The Processes

The process of coder training is inextricably linked with the process of codebook development, at least for the original development of a codebook.

The process may be long and arduous. What follows would be the extreme scenario, including *all* possible points for codebook revision, in the case of the first development of a coding scheme.

➔ Write codebook, with variable selection following guidelines in Chapter 5 and variable measurement following guidelines in this chapter
  ➔ Coder training, with discussion
    ➔ Coders practice code together, engaging in consensus-building discussion
      ➔ Possible codebook revisions
        ➔ Coder training on revisions
          ➔ Coders practice code independently on a number of units representing the variety of the population
            ➔ Coders discuss results of independent practice coding
              ➔ Possible codebook revisions
                ➔ Coder training on revisions
                  ➔ Coders code pilot subsample for reliability purposes (see Chapter 7)
                    ➔ Researcher checks reliabilities
                      ➔ Possible codebook revisions
                        ➔ Coder training on revisions
                          ➔ Final, independent coding (including final reliability checks)
                            ➔ Coder "debriefing," which asks coders to analyze their experiences (may be written)

The coder debriefing process has proved to be a valuable tool for the long-term evolution of a coding scheme, providing the researcher with possible changes, additions, and deletions based on the experiences of the frontline workers, the coders (e.g., Capwell, 1997; Smith, 1999).

Medium Modality and Coding

The medium in which the messages to be analyzed are stored or transmitted can have implications for the human coding process.

In general, it seems to be appropriate to attempt to code in the *same modality* in which the messages are created and received (thus, maximizing ecological validity). So to code popular music, it makes sense to use an audio playback on tape or CD. To code naturally occurring interpersonal interaction, high-quality videotape rather than audiotape seems to be the logical choice, coming as close to face-to-face as possible. Coding films released after 1952 should be done on letterboxed versions; the pan-and-scan versions actually have an altered editing pace, and entire characters may be missing from scenes.[14]

Above all, the researcher needs to know the capabilities and limitations of his or her delivery system. He or she should test it out before even collecting the message sample. For example, if using VHS format videotape, the researcher will be tempted to use the EP recording option, to save money on tapes (EP allows 6 hours of content on a standard VHS 120 tape, whereas SP accommodates only 2 hours). However, the EP quality is significantly lower, and some playback equipment cannot execute fast scans and freeze-frames in EP, functions essential to coding from videotape.

Some Tips

Research reports and articles usually put the best face possible on a content analysis project and do not report the technical or mundane challenges and failures. So, many of the selected tips that follow are culled from my own experiences and those of my colleagues and students. They are organized by modality.

Text

- Human text coding seems to work better with hard copy (Franke, 2000), especially when some measures are helped by the coders being able to mark up the pages. Sometimes, the old ways are best.

- Many assume that text analysis by computer is intuitive or user-friendly. This is not always the case. Some text analysis programs will run only on certain operating systems. Others have manuals or protocols so complicated that attendance at a training seminar is necessary. Some are proprietary and can be run only by licensed representatives or so intractable and mathematically complex that only their authors use them.

Static Images

- Analyses of static images often borrow variables from the practice of graphic design (e.g., Hendon, 1973; Holbrook & Lehmann, 1980; Reid, Rotfeld, & Barnes, 1984; Standen, 1989). Most of these variables are form variables and depend on accurate physical measurements.

- Any duplication should come as close to the original as possible (e.g., using high-quality color photocopies). The original medium should be used whenever possible, be it magazine, newspaper, textbook, or photograph (Low & Sherrard, 1999).

- It is difficult to code many historical images in their original forms. For example, ads are sometimes excised from magazines and journals before libraries bind them (Michelson, 1996). Some periodicals are available only on microfilm or microfiche, often rendering them completely in black and white.

- Computer display may allow zooming in on small design details for a careful examination (e.g., using a graphics program such as Photo-

Shop). However, some of the beauty of the images is lost when coding on computer (e.g., magazine photographs), accurate measurements of image size may be lost, and load time can be a problem for high-quality images.

Audio Messages

- Few content analysis studies examine audio-only messages. Most often, spoken audio messages are transcribed, and text analysis is applied to the transcriptions (e.g., LaBarge, Von Dras, & Wingbermuehle, 1998; Tunnicliffe & Reiss, 1999). This process misses the paralanguage[15]: other nonverbals, music, and other accompanying sounds that might have implications for how the message is normally received. Even the few studies that have used audio as the coding modality generally have not measured these additional features of the audio media (e.g., Hurtz & Durkin, 1997; Lont, 1990).

- Studies of music typically target the lyrics (Lull, 1987) and ignore the music itself. The exceptions to this rule are the works of musicologists (largely qualitative, not what we would call content analysis) and the unique work of Simonton (1994; see also Chapter 9).

Moving Images

- The quality of the images is an issue for coding. The current state of video as played back on most computers is of inferior quality. The standard VHS tape format is the lowest-quality tape system to be marketed. DVD is compressed, and loss of small details and general ambiance may not fully reflect the original production.

- Obviously, the coding of moving images may include the analysis of text, static images, and audio, as well as measures focusing on the image movement. With that in mind, the delivery system needs to accommodate these possibilities—with monitors large and clear enough to allow the reading of titles, playback allowing a clear and stable freeze-frame function, and good audio quality (with individual headsets if several coding stations are in the same room).

- When using a video system, it's important that the equipment provides a real-time counter (or time code). This helps the coder remain organized and is essential for the measurement of certain dynamic features (e.g., editing pace, number of transitions over a certain period of time).

- The study of the *scripts* of television or film content should be identified as just that. Such an analysis will necessarily miss a great deal of the content of the moving image form. And such a study of scripts should consider carefully what script version(s) to use. Often, the original script is quite different from the shooting script, which in turn is quite different from the final script and what we hear when listening to the production. Many scripts are now available in Internet archives, but they vary as to type. Abstracts of scripts are even farther removed from the original moving image content and should be used with caution (Althaus, Edy, & Phalen, 2000).

Multimedia

- To date, the content analysis coding of multimedia content has borrowed heavily from past work in all the areas from which multimedia draw—text, static images, and moving images. The really significant new work has added measures designed to tap the unique nature of the Internet, CD-ROM, DVD, and other multimedia—dimensions of *interactivity* (e.g., use of hypertext, feedback, and scalability; Ghose & Dou, 1998). Chapter 9 contains a section highlighting the state of content analysis research on Internet content.

- Those coding on the Internet need to be aware of differences in machines and browsers. What one coder sees and hears using Netscape may be rather different from what another encounters on Explorer. Layout may differ, animations may fail to move, and so forth.

Index Construction in Content Analysis

Often, more than one measure is used to tap a concept, especially if that concept is broad; therefore, multiple measures are needed to meet the requirement of content validity. When two or more measures are combined mathematically into a single indicator, that indicator is called a scale or *index*.[16]

Indexes are routinely used in text content analysis, and most standard and custom dictionaries are, in essence, indexes. For example, the "tax" custom dictionary used by Miller et al. (1998) includes measures for the following words: flat, mortgage, mortgages, overtaxed, tax, taxable, taxation, taxed, taxer, taxes, taxing, taxpayer, and taxpayers. The total index is a sum of the frequencies of all the individual word counts.

Standard indexes may be developed for content analysis in the same way scales and indexes are established for survey and experimental purposes (DeVellis, 1991). This involves a series of data collections, which aids in the refinement of the index over time.

In the case of combined measures from a human coding analysis, the measures are sometimes adapted from self-report indexes designed for survey or experiment applications. In this case, it is appropriate to examine the internal consistency of the group of measures, just as one would do for an index in a survey or experiment. This involves using a statistic such as Cronbach's alpha to assess how well the individual measures intercorrelate (Carmines & Zeller,

1979). For example, Smith (1999) adapted Eysenck's (1990) three dimensions of personality—extraversion-introversion, neuroticism, and psychoticism—for her study of women's images in American film. Her 15 individual coded measures (reduced in number from the original indexes due to the challenges of objective coding) were summed together to create the three indexes, and the sets were each examined for intercorrelation, using Cronbach's alpha.

Perhaps the most problematic issue in index construction for human-coded content analysis is whether to restrict an index to individual measures meeting a certain level of intercoder reliability. As will be discussed in Chapter 7, intercoder reliability assessment is vital to human coding, and variables that do not achieve a criterion level are often dropped from subsequent analyses. In the case of an index, is it enough that the full index is reliable across coders, or does every individual measure have to meet the criterion? Obviously, those wishing to hold content analysis to the highest standard will choose the latter. At present, however, the methodological literature does not address this question. It *is* addressed from a reliability standpoint in the next chapter.

Notes

1. This was garnered from my notes from a class lecture given by Edward L. Fink in 1977, Department of Communication, Michigan State University, East Lansing.

2. Some might argue that ecological validity would require that when the content analysis is motivated by concerns over effects on receivers, that coding be similar to "naive" exposure to the content—that all coding of television content be done in real time, without reviewing the material repeatedly and thus discovering nuances of information that would not be noticed the first time. There are several problems with this argument. First, in today's communication environment, most receivers do have control over the speed and repetition of their exposure to messages (with videotape, CD-ROM, DVD, hypertextuality on the Internet, and even the old-fashioned random access of newspaper reading). Second, the content analyst's job seems to be to tap all information that receivers might have access to; although there doesn't seem to be research on the issue, exercises in my classes have revealed an extraordinary variety in what individuals notice the first time they see film content. And of course, things that people don't notice may still have an effect on them. To tap all possible receiver experiences, it may take considerable repetition and effort by an individual coder.

3. It's surprising how few reports of human content analysis make the full set of coding materials available. Some good examples of reports that do are Lange, Baker, and Ball (1969), Gottschalk (1995), and the National Television Violence Study (1997).

4. Janis (1949) phrased it this way: "The validity of a measuring device is usually studied by comparing the results or measures obtained from it with those obtained by another device, the validity of which is already established for measuring the same characteristic" (p. 58).

5. Potter and Levine-Donnerstein (1999) also introduce an expansion on the manifest-latent content dichotomy, splitting *latent* into "pattern" and "projective"

content. Pattern latent content focuses on patterns in the content itself. Potter and Levine-Donnerstein present the example (from Johnston and White, 1994) of a measure of the mode of dress of female political candidates—formal suit, soft feminine suit, dress, casual, or a combination. This measure represents pattern content because it requires the coders to consider various combinations of manifest content (i.e., clothing items, such as jackets, scarves, pants) and evaluate how formal or feminine the combinations are (Potter and Levine-Donnerstein, 1999, pp. 259-260). Projective latent content focuses on coders' interpretations of the meanings of the content. The example used (from Signorielli, McLeod, and Healy, 1994) is a five-point measure of attractiveness for characters on MTV, ranging from very attractive to repulsive or ugly. This measure taps projective latent content because it relies on coders' *individual* mental schema.

6. The assumption that coding schemes should be validated through an examination of sources' perceptions of the messages has been called into question by Rogers and Millar (1982), who note that under the "pragmatic" approach to communication, the researcher is concerned with "how behavior means" rather than "what the performer means" (p. 250).

7. Novice researchers are often confused about the differences among measurement, operationalization, and operational definition (described by Babbie, 1995, p. 116, as "a definition that spells out precisely how the concept will be measured"). For most intents and purposes, *measurement* and *operational definition* mean the same thing. *Operationalization* is simply the process of developing these measurements. Throughout this book, *measurement* will be the primary term used.

8. For a good example of a coding scheme using this approach, see the Brayack (1998) materials on *The Content Analysis Guidebook Online*.

9. The following would be an example of a hypothetical interval measure: "Indicate the ad's use of color on a 0-to-10 scale, with 0 = minimal color and 10 = wide use of color." But there seems to be no reason not to construct the measure as ratio, that is, with a true zero: "Indicate the ad's use of color on a 0-to-10 scale, with 0 = no color in the ad and 10 = wide use of color."

10. For a comprehensive review of measures of readability, see Severin and Tankard (1997).

11. The MCCA computer program is available as part of the DIMAP package, which is described in Resource 3 and in *The Content Analysis Guidebook Online*.

12. The "further analyses" included a sophisticated process of using the VBMap program to place the most frequently occurring words in a multidimensional space based on co-occurrence, then submitting the dimensional coordinates of these words to SPSS for cluster analysis and using the new cluster-based concept sets for a second VBMap analysis. This final analysis resulted in dimensional coordinates that were plotted in 3-D, creating visual representations of the key concept clusters for news releases and elite press coverage.

13. Throughout this chapter and in Resource C, *multiple-unit data file output* is used to designate a frequency output matrix that is *case-by-variable* in format. It is a data file only in the sense that it is typically a numeric matrix that is further submitted to statistical analyses via SPSS or other statistical package.

14. Wide-screen filmmaking began in the United States in 1953, with 20th Century-Fox's release of the CinemaScope epic, *The Robe*. A variety of wide-screen formats exist, and all of their aspect ratios are wider than the 4:3 current U.S. television standard (e.g., CinemaScope's aspect ratio is 2.35 to 1, width to height). There are two op-

tions for the display of wide-screen movies on a U.S. NTSC TV screen. A letterboxed version of a wide-screen film shows the entire original image, with black bands at the top and bottom of the TV screen to fill the unused space. A pan-and-scan version crops off the sides of the wide image to fit it to the nearly square TV screen and typically pans and cuts back and forth across the original wide image to capture the action, thus fundamentally changing the editing and mise-en-scene (shot framing) of the film. For example, a sequence in Stanley Kramer's *Guess Who's Coming to Dinner* (1967) shows the Katharine Hepburn and Spencer Tracy characters taking a drive in their car. In the original version, a long take allows the viewer to see both characters at the same time during their entire meaningful discussion. The pan-and-scan version cuts back and forth between the two to catch only the speaker so that the listener's reactions are lost. In another example, the character played by comedienne Mary Wickes in *The Music Man* (1962) is virtually eliminated from most of her scenes in the pan-and-scan version, because her minor character often stands near the edge of the frame. Her priceless comedic nonverbal reactions are never seen.

15. *Paralanguage* consists of all the elements of speech that are in addition to the words (i.e., oral behaviors that are not verbal). It includes such nonverbals as speech rate, pitch, intonation, and nonfluencies (e.g., "uh . . . ").

16. This book typically uses the term *index* rather than *scale* to designate a simple composite measure, following the terminology of Babbie (1995). By his definitions, a multiple-item scale is a set of measures that vary in intensity, such as Bogardus's (as cited in Babbie, p.176) social distance scale ("Are you willing to permit Swedes to live in your country?"; "Are you willing to permit Swedes to live in your neighborhood?"; "Would you let your child marry a Swede?"). The goal is to locate a respondent's position along a continuum of *items* that make up the scale. An index is a more general construction (usually additive) of multiple items. An additional reason for the use of *index* over *scale* is the confusion that sometimes arises with the concept of *measurement scale*, the set of responses or coding categories for one variable.

CHAPTER 7

Reliability

R*eliability* can be defined as the extent to which a measuring procedure yields the same results on repeated trials (Carmines & Zeller, 1979). When human coders are used in content analysis, this translates to *intercoder reliability* or the amount of agreement or correspondence among two or more coders. Although the concept of reliability has been introduced in earlier chapters, its full discussion warrants an entire chapter. Given that a goal of content analysis is to identify and record relatively objective (or at least intersubjective) characteristics of messages, reliability is paramount. Without the establishment of reliability, content analysis measures are useless. Remember that without reliability, a measure cannot be considered valid. (However, reliability does not ensure validity; i.e., reliability is a necessary but not sufficient condition for validity.)

The discussion in this chapter focuses on human coding techniques, with consideration given to how to achieve high intercoder reliability. The chapter presents a variety of intercoder reliability coefficients, including their formulas, and gives attention to the use of multiple human coders, a widely used technique that is largely ignored in the current methodology literature. Reference is made to the computer program PRAM (Program for Reliability Assessment with Multiple-Coders) for intercoder reliability coefficients and the Resource that documents the program (see Resource 4).

A portion of this chapter deals with procedures for the treatment of variables that do not achieve acceptable levels of reliability. These range from dropping the variables from analysis to integrating noncontent analytic data for particularly subjective, audience-centered variables (e.g., type of humor, emotional impact of a message). The chapter also deals with the rare but very real possibility of needing to drop a *coder* from a study.

Intercoder Reliability Standards and Practices

Achieving an acceptable level of intercoder reliability is important for two reasons:

1. To provide basic validation of a coding scheme: That is, it must be established that more than one individual can use the coding scheme as a measurement tool, with similar results. Put a different way, it must be confirmed that the coding scheme is *not* limited to use by only one individual. (That would be more along the lines of expert analysis and not a true content analysis; Carletta, 1996; Krippendorff, 1980.) As Tinsley and Weiss (1975) note, it is important to demonstrate that the "obtained ratings are not the idiosyncratic results of one rater's subjective judgment" (p. 359). This means that even if the principal investigator does all of the coding, a reliability check with a second coder is needed (Evans, 1996).

2. For the practical advantage of using multiple coders: Splitting up the coding task allows for more messages to be processed, but the two or more coders must be "calibrated" against one another.

For reason number 1, at least two coders need to participate in any human-coding content analysis. For number 2, we may employ up to 30 or 40 different individuals (Potter & Levine-Donnerstein, 1999).

There is growing acknowledgment in the research literature that the establishment of intercoder reliability is essential, a necessary criterion for valid and useful research when human coding is employed. This has followed a period during which many researchers were less than rigorous in their reliability assessment. As Perrault and Leigh (1989) noted, the marketing research literature to date had "no accepted standard for evaluating or reporting the reliability of coded data" (p. 137). In the consumer behavior research, Kolbe and Burnett (1991) found 31% of the content analysis articles reported no reliability coefficients, and an additional 19% had no discernible method of calculation for reliability. A full 36% reported only one so-called overall reliability for the study. Reporting on an analysis of 486 content analysis studies published in *Journalism and Mass Communication Quarterly* from 1971 through 1995, Riffe and Freitag (1997) found that only 56% of the studies reported intercoder reliability figures and that most of these failed to report reliability variable by variable. An analysis of 200 content analyses in the communication literature by Snyder-Duch, Bracken, and Lombard (2001) found that only 69% discussed intercoder reliability, with only 41% reporting reliability for specific variables.

This practice of averaging reliability coefficients across variables is inappropriate. It obviously results in the obscuring of low reliabilities that do not pass muster. For example, in a study of television characters, a variable such as "empathetic or not empathetic" with an agreement reliability of only 20% (obviously unacceptable) could be averaged with such no-brainer variables as gender, race, age category, and marital status and might easily be hidden in an overall average reliability of over 80%. Reliability coefficients must be reported separately for each and every measured variable.

What constitutes an acceptable *level* of intercoder reliability for each variable is open to debate. Unfortunately, common standards are not in place (Krippendorff, 1980; Perrault & Leigh, 1989; Popping, 1988; Riffe, Lacy, & Fico, 1998). Various rules of thumb have been proposed.

- Most basic textbooks on research methods in the social sciences do not offer a specific criterion or cutoff figure, and those that do report a criterion vary somewhat in their recommendations. Ellis (1994, p. 91) indicates a "widely accepted rule of thumb" of correlation coefficients exceeding .75 to .80 indicative of high reliability. Frey, Botan, and Kreps (2000) declare a 70% agreement to be considered reliable.

- Popping (1988) proposes a criterion of .80 or greater for Cohen's *kappa*.

- The following criteria have been proposed for Cohen's *kappa*: .75+ indicating excellent agreement beyond chance; .40 to .75, fair to good agreement beyond chance; and below .40, poor agreement beyond chance (Banerjee et al., 1999).

- Without specifying the *type* of reliability coefficient, Krippendorff (1980, p. 147) proposes the guideline of reporting on variables only if their reliability is above .80, with only "highly tentative and cautious conclusions" made about variables with reliabilities between .67 and .80.

- Riffe, Lacy, and Fico (1998) endorse a relatively high standard; again, without specifying the type of reliability coefficient, they report that studies typically report reliabilities "in the .80 to .90 range" and that "research with reliability assessment below .70 becomes hard to interpret and the method of dubious value to replicate" (p. 131).

It's clear from a review of the work on reliability that reliability coefficients of .90 or greater would be acceptable to all, .80 or greater would be acceptable in most situations, and below that, there exists great disagreement. In general, the beyond-chance statistics, such as Scott's *pi* and Cohen's *kappa,* are afforded a more liberal criterion.

Tests of statistical significance have occasionally been applied to reliability coefficients (e.g., the use of a z-statistic to test the difference between a *kappa* value and zero; Bartko & Carpenter, 1976),[1] but the meaning of such tests is open to debate. There is a difference between inferential statistical significance and substantive significance, or meaningfulness, as when a Pearson correlation coefficient of $r = .12$, with shared variance between the two sets of scores only about 1%, is found to be statistically significant. What this indicates is that a very small relationship (substantively rather unimportant) may confidently be generalized to the population (statistically significant). This problem can be shown in a reliability application with Bartko and Carpenter's (p. 311) report of a *kappa* of .40 (not acceptable by most rules of thumb) that is highly statistically significant. The conclusion is that we may generalize a relatively low reliability to a population.

In the absence of a uniform standard or test of meaningful significance (Popping, 1988), the best we can expect at present is full and clear reporting of at least one reliability coefficient for each variable measured in a human-coded content analysis. Dixon and Linz (2000) provide a model for such reportage, giving reliability coefficients for each of 14 variables, reported separately for each of five message sources.

Lombard et al. (1999) have proposed and are in the process of conducting a large-scale examination of the methodologies and reportage for content analyses in the communication literature. Their analyses will give a quantitative answer to whether reliability reportage has indeed been improving and what new standards may be emerging. Following an analysis of 200 communication content analyses, Snyder-Duch et al. (2001) have put forward a set of recommendations, including a standard of a minimum of two coders, the calculation of an appropriate reliability figure for each variable measured, and the clear reportage of the reliability sample size and its relation to the overall sample.

Issues in the Assessment of Reliability

Before exploring the means of calculating intercoder reliability, a consideration of the main issues inherent in selecting an appropriate process of reliability assessment will be presented.

Agreement Versus Covariation

Two main types of reliability assessment can be used. *Agreement* looks at whether or not coders agree as to the precise values assigned to a variable across a set of units—it looks at hits and misses. *Covariation* assesses whether the scores assigned by coders (rating units on an ordinal, interval, or ratio measure) go up and down together, not necessarily in precise agreement. In communication and business research, researchers seem to report agreement without reporting covariation. In clinical and other applications in psychology, the tendency has been the opposite, to report covariation without agreement (Bartko & Carpenter, 1976). The best situation, of course, would be one in which coded scores are shown to have both high agreement and high covariation (Tinsley & Weiss, 1975). In later sections of this chapter, these two types of reliability assessment will be explained and common coefficients will be shown.

Reliability as a Function of Coder and Unit Subsamples

Although we would like to think of reliability analysis as reflecting the success of the coding scheme, reliability is a function of two other elements as well: the particular units rated and the judges making the ratings. It is for this reason, as Tinsley and Weiss (1975) point out, that it would be inappropriate to report a generalized reliability for a variable extracted from other studies. The representativeness of the message units and of the coders are important considerations. In a later section, reliability subsample selection and assignment procedures that take this notion into account are described.

If we view a reliability test as a sample representative of all possible tests, then it makes sense to apply inferential techniques to indicate what the true population reliability might be. Some researchers have promoted the application of the notion of standard errors and confidence intervals to reliability tests (Kraemer, 1980; Lacy & Riffe, 1996). In other words, each reliability figure may have a confidence interval constructed around it; for example, we could hypothetically say, "the reliability for number of verbal nonfluencies was .92, plus or minus .04 at the 95% confidence level."[2] Confidence intervals are rarely reported in the business and social science literature at present. Some examples of their calculation will be given in an endnote that goes along with calculations in Boxes 7.2 and 7.3.

Threats to Reliability

In practice, there are several key threats to reliability that should be taken into account:

1. A poorly executed coding scheme: This could mean a poorly worded set of instructions in a codebook, the failure of the researcher to make changes in the coding scheme after a pilot test, or both.

2. Inadequate coder training: As outlined in Chapter 6, coder training typically involves several sessions and practice codings to establish a good initial reliability for the pilot test.

3. Coder fatigue: The coding schedule should be reasonable and not overtax the energies of the coders. This refers both to the length of the codebook and the number of units to be coded in a given time period.

4. The presence of a rogue coder: Although rarely encountered, there is always the possibility of the appearance of a coder who simply cannot—or will not—be trained to achieve reliability (e.g., Capwell, 1997). The coder may have to be removed from the study, but this should be done

only after repeated attempts at training and the examination of that coder's reliability performance against several other coders across a wide variety of variables (e.g., *National Television Violence Study,* 1997).

Reliability for Manifest Versus Latent Content

"With manifest content, the coding task is one of clerical recording," note Potter and Levine-Donnerstein (1999, p. 265). Although this might be an oversimplification, it does clarify the distinction between coding manifest and latent content. Objectivity is a much tougher criterion to achieve with latent than with manifest variables, and for this reason, we expect variables measuring latent content to receive generally lower reliability scores. Obviously, this indicates a need for greater coder training efforts in instances of latent-content coding. And there may exist certain constructs that are problematic because of their latency; for example, Box 7.1 discusses the problems inherent in attempted measurements of the construct "humor."

Reliability and Unitizing

As described in Chapter 4, clear agreement on the identification of codable units in the message pool is of utmost importance. Krippendorff (1995) has extended his *alpha* intercoder reliability coefficient to apply to differences in coders' unitizing of continuous records, such as transcripts and video presentations. At present, the use of his coefficient in this way is quite unwieldy, but the issue is an important one for future consideration.

Pilot and Final Reliabilities

Reliability should always be assessed at two points in a content analysis: *pilot* and *final*. The pilot reliability assessment should be done on a randomly selected subsample of the total sample message pool *before* the study begins in earnest. If the pilot test reveals serious problems, then the coding scheme may need to be changed. In that case, the pilot test data should *not* be included in the final data analysis; the pilot subsample message units should be recoded with the revised scheme. The final reliability assessment should be done on another randomly selected subsample during the full data collection, to fairly represent the coders' performance throughout the study. These final reliability figures are the ones to be reported with the study's results.

Reliability assessment in a pilot study of the content under investigation is essential to the development of a valid, reliable, and useful coding scheme. It addresses all four threats to reliability outlined earlier, by allowing the following three *diagnostic* measures:

Box 7.1   Humor, A Problematic Construct

**Partitioning a Construct on the Basis
of Reliability-Imposed Constraints**

Humor, so ubiquitous in messages of so many kinds (Zillmann, 1977), can be difficult to conceptualize and to operationalize. It's a popular construct for students trying to content analyze messages; their typical "I know it when I see it" attitude often results in unacceptable reliabilities (e.g., Naccarato, 1990; Wongthongsri, 1993). Virtually all attempts to isolate individual instances of humor in messages and then code each with a scheme of mutually exclusive and exhaustive humor type categories have failed to produce reliable outcomes.

There are several challenges to the concept of humor: It's subjective, so much so that some scholars say it resides in the receiver rather than the message (Eshleman & Neuendorf, 1989; Neuendorf & Skalski, 2000; Ziv, 1984). It's multidimensional, and multiple senses of humor (i.e., abilities to identify and appreciate humor types) may exist (Crawford & Gressley, 1991; McGoun, 1991; Neuendorf & Skalski, 2000; Ziv, 1984). It's primarily latent in nature rather than manifest, with the typical challenges that go along with latent content.

Two divergent tactics have been used by researchers to try to reliably measure humor in messages. First, some have gone with very specific aspects of humor. They have defined manifest characteristics related to portions of the overall humor construct and have achieved reliability for particular components—for instance, blunt versus refined humor (Zillmann, 1977), disparagement humor (Stocking, Sapolsky, & Zillmann, as cited in Zillmann, 1977), tendentiousness (Cantor, 1977), nonsense humor (Bryant, Hezel, & Zillmann, 1979), incongruity humor (Alden, Hoyer, & Lee, 1993), aggressive-sexual humor (McCullough, 1993), and level of brutality in humor (Zillmann, Bryant, & Cantor, 1974).

The second tactic is quite the opposite, taking a macroscopic approach by examining the simple humorous intent of the message without judging the nature of the humor or how it is received. This general approach seems to facilitate reliability (Potter & Warren, 1998; Weinberger, Spotts, Campbell, & Parson, 1995). But it fails to tap humor type(s) and may therefore result in poor predictive ability; in other words, its validity is suspect. For example, there are highly mixed findings with regard to the effectiveness of humor in advertising (Markiewicz, 1974; Weinberger et al., 1995) due to the highly divergent ways in which humor has been operationalized in those studies. As Weinberger et al. note, "Generalizations about its effects are difficult to come by because of its diverse nature" (p. 54).

Humor is a highly attractive construct, which many practitioners and scholars would agree is an important mediating variable for the reception of messages (Alden, Hoyer, & Lee, 1993). But it means so many things to so many people, it must be partitioned carefully to develop measures that are reliable.

1. Identification of problematic measures: When a variable with poor reliability is identified in a pilot test, remedies include (a) further training and rechecking reliability, (b) rewriting coding instructions to clarify the mea-

surement of the variable, (c) changing the categories of the variable (e.g., collapsing categories), and (d) splitting the variable into two or more simpler or more concrete (more manifest) variables.

2. The identification of problematic categories or values within a variable (Krippendorff, 1980): By looking at a Coder-A-by-Coder-B matrix of coded values, we see key confusions that indicate what categories within a variable are not clearly differentiated in the coding scheme. This confusion matrix allows us to dig deeper than simply looking at an overall reliability figure. For example, we may see that where Coder A is coding certain verbal utterances as "attacking," Coder B tends to systematically code the same utterances as "opposing." Further training or codebook revisions (or both) are needed to eliminate this systematic source of measurement error.

3. The identification of problematic coders: By examining pairwise reliabilities for individual coders, we may see whether one coder simply doesn't match up with the others. Additional training for that coder may help, before the unpleasant decision to drop the coder is reached.

Intercoder Reliability Coefficients: Issues and Comparisons

A variety of coefficients are available for reporting the level of agreement or correspondence between coders' assessments. The most popular coefficients in business and the social and behavioral sciences seem to be raw percent agreement (the "measure of crude association"), Scott's *pi,* Cohen's *kappa,* Krippendorff's *alpha,* Spearman *rho,* and Pearson *r.* Only Cohen's *kappa* and Krippendorff's *alpha* accommodate more than two coders at a time, an issue to be addressed later. There are dozens of other options for calculating intercoder reliability, and some particularly unique and innovative coefficients will be presented later.

All of these intercoder reliability coefficients are distinct in nature from internal-consistency reliability applications, which typically rely on such coefficients as Cronbach's *alpha* and the Spearman-Brown formula (Carmines & Zeller, 1979; Traub, 1994) to assess how well a set of variables fits together. These internal-consistency statistics examine interitem correlations to see if they warrant combining a set of variables in a scale or index (Babbie, 1998). Both types of reliability coefficient—intercoder and internal consistency—are based on the same notions of reliability as dependability, reproducibility, or consistency (Traub, 1994), but they usually have quite different applications.[3]

The intercoder reliability coefficients do not assess internal consistency among a variety of measures. Rather, they are concerned with the assessment, one measure at a time, of one or more of the following criteria: agreement,

agreement beyond chance, and covariation. In the discussion that follows, it is assumed that we are looking at only two coders. The case of three-plus coders will be taken up later. Also, note that the discussion includes conceptual formulas when appropriate but does not include calculation formulas for the coefficients (those can be found in Boxes 7.2 and 7.3, presented later).

Agreement

This criterion is concerned with whether coders agree as to the precise values assigned to a given variable. This is particularly appropriate to measures that are categorical (i.e., nominal), wherein each pair of coded measures is either a hit or a miss. There are two ways to calculate simple agreement.

1. Percent agreement (sometimes called "crude agreement"): This is a simple percentage, representing number of agreements divided by total number of measures. A conceptual formula for percent agreement could be written as follows:

$$PA_O = A/n$$

where PA_O stands for "proportion agreement, observed," A is the number of agreements between two coders, and n is the total number of units the two coders have coded for the test (also, the maximum agreement they could achieve). This statistic ranges from .00 (no agreement) to 1.00 (perfect agreement).

2. Holsti's method (1969): In cases in which two coders code the same units (which is the recommended method), this is equal to percent agreement. The formula differs only a little:

$$PA_O = 2A/(n_A + n_B)$$

where PA_O stands for "proportion agreement, observed," A is the number of agreements between two coders, and n_A and n_B are the number of units coded by coders A and B, respectively. This statistic also ranges from .00 (no agreement) to 1.00 (perfect agreement).

Simple agreement is one of the most popular coefficients. For example, Hughes and Garrett (1990) found that 65% of the reported reliability coefficients in their sample of marketing research articles were simple percent agreement. However, simple agreement has important drawbacks, such as the failure to account for chance agreement and the rigid requirement of the precise matching of coders' scores.

In applying simple agreement assessment to variables that are ordinal, interval, or ratio, some researchers have expanded the notion of precise agreement to what we might call *range agreement*—counting a hit any time two coders come within a certain distance of one another. Tinsley and Weiss (1975) report on the Lawlis and Lu method of setting up a decision rule for ±1-point or ±2-point agreement. In an application of a similar technique, Dominick (1999) defined an agreement as ratings that were within one point of one another on a 1-to-10 scale. Notably, in his study of personal Web sites, the measure in question tapped a rather subjective concept—whether the coders felt they "knew" the person from the content in his or her home page.

For interval or ratio measures, some researchers have proposed *standardizing* each coder's values (Tinsley & Weiss, 1975) before applying agreement assessment procedures so that the coders are statistically calibrated. It is debatable as to whether this forced calibration is desirable over an alternative of more extensive coder training for calibration.

Agreement Controlling for the Impact of Chance Agreement

Some portion of coders' agreement must be considered to be due to chance. That is, if two coders are assessing whether videotaped speakers are male or female, they will agree 50% of the time just by chance alone—if they flip coins instead of watching the screen or code with their eyes shut, they'll agree about 50% of the time. Researchers are often interested in accounting for this chance component, and several popular agreement-based coefficients do just that, providing beyond-chance indicators.

3. Scott's *pi* (π):[4] In correcting for the role of chance agreement, this statistic uses a *joint distribution* across two coders. This takes into account not just the number of categories but how these categories are used by the coders. The statistic's normal range is from .00 (agreement at chance level) to 1.00 (perfect agreement), and a value of less than .00 indicates agreement less than chance. The statistic assumes nominal-level data and ignores differences in how the two coders distribute their evaluations across coding categories for that variable (Scott, 1955).

4. Cohen's *kappa* (κ): This statistic was planned as an improvement over *pi*, taking into account the differences in coders' distributions by using a multiplicative term instead of an additive one (Cohen, 1960). Since its introduction, numerous adaptations of this agreement coefficient have been proposed (Banerjee et al., 1999; Kraemer, 1980).[5] A number of sources report *kappa* to be the most widely used reliability coefficient (Perrault & Leigh, 1989; Zwick, 1988). Like *pi*, it assumes nominal-level data and has a normal range from .00 (agreement at chance level) to 1.00 (perfect agreement), and a value of less than .00 indicates agreement less than chance.

Cohen (1968) also took into account the differing importances of misses in his adaptation of *kappa*, the "weighted *kappa* coefficient." In this application, not all misses are treated equally. For example, Bartko and Carpenter (1976) give an example in which psychiatric diagnoses are made by raters (coders):

> If two raters diagnose a patient as manic-depressive and reactive psychotic depression . . . this disagreement might be weighted 2, while a manic-depression—schizophrenic disagreement might be weighted 4. The more serious the disagreement, the larger the weight (p. 311).

Both Scott's *pi* and Cohen's *kappa* are derived from the same conceptual formula (as are a number of other coefficients, e.g., the *S* coefficient [Zwick, 1988]):

$$Pi \text{ or } Kappa = \frac{PA_O - PA_E}{1 - PA_E}$$

where PA_O stands for "proportion agreement, observed," and PA_E stands for "proportion agreement, expected by chance."

Both *pi* and *kappa* have been criticized as being overly conservative, giving credit only to agreement beyond chance, a tough challenge in the case of extreme distributions (Perrault & Leigh, 1989; Potter & Levine-Donnerstein, 1999). For example, when two categories are joint coded at 90% and 10%, chance agreement would be .82, and even 90% raw agreement would net a beyond-chance *pi* of only .44. This undesirable influence of prevalence of certain coding categories has been identified as an important disadvantage, and alternatives have been presented in the literature (Feinstein & Cicchetti, 1990), although none have yet won popular support.

5. Krippendorff's *alpha* (α): This statistic takes into account chance agreement and, in addition, the magnitude of the misses, adjusting for whether the variable is measured as nominal, ordinal, interval, or ratio (Krippendorff, 1980). This is a highly attractive coefficient but has rarely been used because of the tedium of its calculation.
   Its conceptual formula is as follows:

$$alpha = 1 - \frac{D_O}{D_E}$$

where D_O = observed disagreement and D_E = expected disagreement.

Covariation

For measures that are metric (measured at the interval or ratio level), researchers are often interested in the level of covariation of coders' scores, particularly in instances where precise agreement is unlikely. For example, if two coders are scoring television characters' estimated ages in years, it's unlikely that they will score a precise hit very often. But reliability may be shown in the covariation of their scores—quite literally, whether their age estimates "co-vary," that is, when one is high, the other is high, and when one is low, the other is low. Thus, the following pairs of age scores would show high covariation:

| Coder A: | 25 | 55 | 68 | 35 | 34 | 58 | 72 | 18 |
| Coder B: | 27 | 58 | 70 | 33 | 30 | 57 | 75 | 17 |

Notice that the two coders' level of agreement would be 0% (unless we use some sort of range agreement). Yet we would agree that the two coders display at least an acceptable level of reliability and therefore might prefer to use a reliability statistic that gives credit for covariation. Coefficients that take covariation into account include two statistics that are used more commonly for testing relationships between two variables:

6. Spearman *rho* (ρ): This statistic assumes *rank order* ordinal data, and its calculation will result in strange, inflated values if the data are not rank orderings. It ranges from −1.00 (perfect negative relationship, or disagreement) through .00 (no relationship between the two coders' rankings) to 1.00 (perfect agreement on rankings).

7. Pearson correlation coefficient (r): This statistic assesses the degree of linear (i.e., straight-line) correspondence between two sets of interval or ratio numbers. The more tightly clustered the data points are around a line, the higher the absolute value of r. It should be noted that some prefer the reporting of r-squared (the coefficient of determination), in that this represents the *proportion* of shared variance between the two sets of coder scores and is therefore closer in form to such reliability coefficients as percent agreement and Scott's *pi*. In the foregoing age score example, the Pearson r is .995 and r^2 is .99. That is, 99% of the variance of Coder A's age scores is shared with the variance of Coder B's age scores. The r statistic ranges from −1.00 (perfect negative linear relationship) through .00 (no linear relationship) to 1.00 (perfect positive linear relationship).

There are criticisms that coefficients such as r overestimate reliability. Because the Pearson r inherently standardizes the coders' scores, covariation is assessed, but level of agreement is completely ignored. That is, envision a case in which Coder A always reports a character age that is exactly 10 years older than Coder B's estimate (i.e., 40 & 30 years, 70 & 60 years, 25 & 15 years). The Pearson r for these values would be 1.0—a perfect linear relationship, with an r^2 of 1.0 (100%). This is for two sets of values with *zero* agreement, even within a reasonable range, which prompts us to question the validity of the measures. Some adjustment for this coder bias might be advisable.

For example, in comparing human and computer scoring of verbal samples for level of anxiety, Gottschalk and Bechtel (1993) reported that the computer scoring was *significantly lower* than the human coding scores. They reported a correlation between the two sets of scores of $r = .85$, which seems reasonably reliable. However, the strong covariation notwithstanding, a significant difference would remain, without some type of statistical correction (Gottschalk and Bechtel *did* employ a correction for their computer-scored data).

8. Lin's concordance correlation coefficient (r_c): This is an alternative to r for measuring covariation of interval or ratio data that takes systematic coding errors into account (Lin, 1989). It assesses the linear relationship between two sets of metric scores under the constraints that the correlation line passes through the origin and has a slope of one (Chinchilli, Martel, Kumanyika, & Lloyd, 1996). So in a case such as that described earlier, in which one coder always rates age higher than the other coder, the concordance correlation coefficient would be *lower* than the Pearson correlation r, having taken the coder bias into account. Like the Pearson r, this statistic ranges from -1.00 (perfect negative linear relationship) through $.00$ (no linear relationship) to 1.00 (perfect positive linear relationship).

This statistic shows great promise for rectifying problems with other covariation statistics used for reliability but has not been used outside of the medical research literature and is not yet well established.[6]

Calculating Intercoder Reliability Coefficients

In Box 7.2, formulas for the more popular agreement coefficients are presented, and sample calculations are given. For each case, the 95% confidence interval is also reported in an endnote.[7] In Box 7.3, the two featured covariation coefficients are presented, with calculations.

These statistics are included in the PRAM program (see Resource 4), which accommodates both two-coder and multiple-coder situations. Earlier attempts at automating reliability calculations include Kang, Kara, Laskey, and Seaton's (1993) SAS macro for several nominal statistics for multiple coders, including Cohen's *kappa,* Berry and Mielke's (1997) Fortran subroutine to calculate *kappa* for multiple coders, Popping's (1984) AGREE, a computer program for the calculation of *kappa* and related coefficients for nominal scale agreement (which included certain category and coder diagnostics), and the SimStat statistical package's application of *pi, kappa,* and several other statistics to two-coder cases.

Box 7.2   Popular Agreement Coefficients

Calculating Percent Agreement, Scott's *pi*, Cohen's *kappa*, and Krippendorff's *alpha* (nominal data only)

In the following example, two coders have coded one nominal (categorical) variable for 10 units (cases). They have assessed Web banner ads for type, with three categories: 1 = product ad, 2 = corporate ad, and 3 = other. Both Coder A and Coder B have coded the same 10 banner ads. The outcome of this coding is as follows:

Unit	Coder A	Coder B	Agree or Disagree
Ad 1	1	1	A
Ad 2	2	2	A
Ad 3	2	3	D
Ad 4	1	3	D
Ad 5	3	3	A
Ad 6	1	1	A
Ad 7	2	2	A
Ad 8	3	3	A
Ad 9	2	1	D
Ad 10	2	2	A

$$\text{Total A's} = 7 \atop \text{Total D's} = 3 \Big\} \text{ total } n = 10$$

First, we can calculate simple **percent agreement**:

$$PA_O = \frac{Total\ A's}{n} = \frac{7}{10} = .70\ (\textbf{70\% agreement})$$

Another way we could look for agreements (hits) and disagreements (misses) is by generating a cross-tabulation table. The **bold** numbers are the hits, the numbers of units for which the coders agree.

		CODER A			
		1	*2*	*3*	TOTAL
C					
O	1	**2**	1	0	3
D					
E	2	0	**3**	0	3
R					
	3	1	1	**2**	4
B					
	TOTAL	3	5	2	10

Using the marginals (totals) for each coder, we can multiply and add to produce the bits of information we'll need for Scott's *pi* and Cohen's *kappa*.

| Category | Marginals | | Product of marginals: | Sum of marginals: | Joint marginal proportions: |
	n for Coder A	n for Coder B	A x B	A + B	p_i
1 (product ad)	3	3	9	6	6/20 = .30
2 (corporate ad)	5	3	15	8	8/20 = .40
3 (other)	2	4	8	6	6/20 = .30
	10	10		20	1.00

Scott's *pi* $= \dfrac{PA_O - PA_E}{1 - PA_E}$ where $PA_E = \sum p_i^2$

p_i = each joint marginal proportion

So $PA_E = \sum p_i^2$

$= (.30)^2 + (.40)^2 + (.30)^2$

$= .09 + .16 + .09$

$= .34$

And Scott's *pi* $= \dfrac{PA_O - PA_E}{1 - PA_E}$

$= \dfrac{.70 - .34}{1 - .34}$

$= \dfrac{.36}{.66}$

$= \mathbf{.545}$

Cohen's *kappa* $= \dfrac{PA_O - PA_E}{1 - PA_E}$ where $PA_E = (1/n^2)(\sum pm_i)$

n = number of units coded in common by coders

pm_i = each product of marginals

So $PA_E = (1/n^2)(\sum pm_i)$

$= (1/10^2)(9 + 15 + 8)$

$= (1/100)(32)$

$= .32$

And Cohen's *kappa* $= \dfrac{PA_O - PA_E}{1 - PA_E}$

$= \dfrac{.70 - .32}{1 - .32}$

$= \dfrac{.38}{.68}$

$= \mathbf{.56}$

Box 7.2   Continued

For Krippendorff's *alpha* (nominal data only; other forms of data require weightings of products of marginals with various coefficients, beyond the scope of this example), the data must be reconfigured in yet another way.

			Frequencies for Both Coders		
Unit	Coder A	Coder B	Category 1	Category 2	Category 3
Ad 1	1	1	2	0	0
Ad 2	2	2	0	2	0
Ad 3	2	3	0	1	1
Ad 4	1	3	1	0	1
Ad 5	3	3	0	0	2
Ad 6	1	1	2	0	0
Ad 7	2	2	0	2	0
Ad 8	3	3	0	0	2
Ad 9	2	1	1	1	0
Ad 10	2	2	0	2	0
			$\Sigma = 6$	8	6

Krippendorff's *alpha* (nominal) $= 1 - \dfrac{nm-1}{m-1}\left(\dfrac{\Sigma pfu}{\Sigma pmt}\right)$

where $\quad$ *pfu* = product of any frequencies for a given unit that are different (i.e., show disagreement)

$\qquad$ *pmt* = each product of total marginals

$\qquad$ *n* = number of units coded in common by coders

$\qquad$ *m* = number of coders

So $\qquad$ *pfu* $= (1 \times 1) + (1 \times 1) + (1 \times 1)$ [disagreements for units 3, 4, and 9]

$\qquad\qquad = 3$

And $\qquad$ *pmt* $= (6 \times 8) + (6 \times 6) + (8 \times 6)$ [all pairings are added]

$\qquad\qquad = 48 + 36 + 48$

$\qquad\qquad = 132$

Alpha $\qquad = 1 - \dfrac{nm-1}{m-1}\left(\dfrac{\Sigma pfu}{\Sigma pmt}\right)$

$\qquad\qquad = 1 - \dfrac{(10)(2)-1}{2-1}\left(\dfrac{3}{132}\right)$

$\qquad\qquad = 1 - \dfrac{19}{1}\left(\dfrac{3}{132}\right)$

$\qquad\qquad = 1 - 19\,(.023) \quad = 1 - .43 \quad = .57$

Box 7.3   Popular Covariation Coefficients

Calculating Spearman *rho* and Pearson Correlation (r)

In this example, two coders have coded 10 Web banner ads for one ordinal, rank-ordering variable, such as vibrancy of the colors in the ad.

Unit	Coder A	Coder B	Coding discrepancy (d)
Ad 1	2	3	−1
Ad 2	6	8	−2
Ad 3	9	10	−1
Ad 4	1	1	0
Ad 5	8	6	2
Ad 6	3	2	1
Ad 7	10	9	1
Ad 8	4	4	0
Ad 9	5	5	0
Ad 10	7	7	0

$$\text{Spearman } rho = 1 - \frac{6 \times \Sigma d^2}{n^3 - n}$$

where n = number of units coded in common by coders
  d = each coding discrepancy (Coder A ranking minus Coder B ranking)

$$\text{So Spearman } rho = 1 - \frac{6 \times \Sigma d^2}{n^3 - n}$$

$$= 1 - \frac{6 \times [(-1)^2 + (-2)^2 + (-1)^2 + 0^2 + 2^2 + 1^2 + 1^2 + 0^2 + 0^2 + 0^2]}{10^3 - 10}$$

$$= 1 - \frac{6 \times 12}{1000 - 10}$$

$$= 1 - 72/990$$

$$= 1 - .073$$

$$= .927$$

In this example, two coders have coded 10 Web banner ads for a ratio-level variable, number of identifiable human characters shown. In the table to follow, the coders' scores are also shown squared and cross-multiplied in preparation for calculating the Pearson r.

Unit	Coder A	Coder B	A^2	B^2	$A \times B$
Ad 1	3	3	9	9	9
Ad 2	2	1	4	1	4
Ad 3	7	8	49	64	56
Ad 4	0	0	0	0	0
Ad 5	0	1	0	1	0
Ad 6	5	5	25	25	25
Ad 7	3	3	9	9	9
Ad 8	12	10	144	100	120
Ad 9	1	1	1	1	1
Ad 10	2	2	4	4	4
$\Sigma =$	35	34	245	214	226

(continued)

Box 7.3   Continued

A variety of formulas exist for the Pearson r. A good conceptual formula would be as follows:

$$r_{AB} = \frac{\Sigma ab}{\sqrt{(\Sigma a^2)(\Sigma b^2)}}$$

where a = each deviation score (Coder A score minus mean for A)
b = each deviation score (Coder B score minus mean for B)

Roughly, this is the ratio between the *covariation* of A and B's deviation scores and the product of their individual variations.

For hand calculations, a better formula would be as follows:

$$r = \frac{n\Sigma AB - (\Sigma A)(\Sigma B)}{\sqrt{[n\Sigma A^2 - (\Sigma A)^2][n\Sigma B^2 - (\Sigma B)^2]}}$$

$$= \frac{10 \times 226 - 35 \times 34}{\sqrt{[10 \times 245 - 35^2][10 \times 214 - 34^2]}}$$

$$= \frac{2260 - 1190}{\sqrt{[2450 - 1225][2140 - 1156]}}$$

$$= \frac{1070}{\sqrt{1225 \times 984}}$$

$$= .97$$

The Reliability Subsample

There are several key decisions to make in selecting and using reliability subsamples, both for the pilot reliability assessment and for final reliability. They have to do with subsample size, sampling type, and assignment of units to coders.

Subsample Size

How many units should be used in each reliability assessment? A certain proportion or percentage of the total sample or a certain n? Unfortunately, there is no set standard for this decision. General textbooks on social science research methods present rough guidelines, such as 10% to 20% of the total sample (Wimmer & Dominick, 1997). In a selective review of recent content analyses, Potter and Levine-Donnerstein (1999) found the reliability subsample size to range from 10% to 100% of the full sample. Lacy and Riffe (1996) have proposed a systematic method of determining subsample size based on the desired sampling error, but so far, their statistical work-up for this method has been limited to the case of simple percent agreement, with two coders and a binary (two-choice) nominal variable. Despite the current limitations of their technique, it does point to future developments needed for reliability subsampling. Browsing through their tables, we readily learn that there is no set subsample size or proportion that will guarantee a level of representativeness of the reliability tests. For example, for an assumed population agreement of 90%, one would need a subsample of 100 if the total sample size is 10,000 and a subsample of 51 if the total sample size is 100 (the percentages are 1% and 51%, respectively).

If one could attempt to make a general statement from the accumulated knowledge so far, it would be that the reliability subsample should probably never be smaller than 50 and should rarely need to be larger than about 300. The factors that would indicate the need for a subsample to be at the high end of this range are (a) a large population (i.e., full sample) size and (b) a lower assumed level of reliability in the population (i.e., full sample; Lacy & Riffe, 1996).

Sampling Type

For the reliability subsample to accurately reflect the full sample, sampling units from the full sample for reliability purposes should follow the same guidelines for randomness as extracting the full sample of message units. As outlined in Chapter 4, this probability sampling will be either SRS or systematic random sampling. In this case, the sampling frame is the list of all elements in the full sample.

Researchers have given some thought to purposively including certain units in the reliability subsample to ensure the occurrence of key characteristics in the reliability check. For example, the incidence of sex appeals in Thai commercials might be quite low (Wongthongsri, 1993), and a reliability subsample is therefore unlikely to include any. This may result in a misleading 100% agreement between coders who uniformly code the total absence of the appeal. Only by making sure that some ads that include sex appeals are in the subsample will the researcher be able to see whether coders can agree on its presence versus absence. Whether such a nonrandom, purposive inclusion of odd units in the reliability subsample is appropriate is under debate (Krippendorff, 1980; Riffe, Lacy, & Fico, 1998).

Assignment of Units to Coders

The typical situation is for all coders to receive the same units to code for reliability purposes. When all coders do not code the same units from the subsample, the assignment of units to coders should be random. (This applies to coder assignments for the full sample as well, as indicated in Chapter 4.)

Treatment of Variables That Do Not Achieve an Acceptable Level of Reliability

Assuming that reliability testing has been completed, called-for changes have been made in the coding scheme, and rigorous training of the coders has been conducted, there should be few variables that do not achieve an acceptable level of reliability in the final reliability check. But there probably will be a few.
The options are several.

1. Drop the variable from all analyses (e.g., Naccarato, 1990).

2. Reconfigure the variable with fewer and better-defined categories (e.g., Fink & Gantz, 1996). Of course, this should be done during the pilot coding process, prior to the final data collection.

3. Use the variable only as a component in a multimeasure index, which itself has been shown to be reliable (e.g., Schulman, Castellon & Seligman, 1989; Smith, 1999). This is a questionable practice at present in that it obscures unacceptable reliabilities for individual aspects of the index. On the other hand, a pragmatic approach would focus on what the original intent was; if it was to measure extraversion, then perhaps the reliability coefficient that counts should be the one for extraversion rather than the ones for its several individual components.[8] (See Chapter 6 for a discussion of index construction in content analysis.)

4. Use noncontent analysis data (e.g., survey data) for that particular variable, and integrate the data into the study with other content analysis variables. For example, Kalis and Neuendorf (1989) used survey response data for the variable "perceived level of aggressiveness" for cues present in music videos. And Sweeney and Whissell (1984, following the work of Heise, 1965) created a dictionary of affect in language by presenting subjects with individual words that the subjects were asked to rate along the dimensions of pleasantness and activation. Ratings were obtained by adults for 4,300 words, and these ratings have been used in conjunction with subsequent content analyses, both human coded and computer coded (Whissell, 1994a, 1994b; Whissell, Fournier, Pelland, Weir, & Makarec, 1986). Based on survey work using a large sample of words ($n = 15,761$), Whissell (2000) was also able to identify distinct emotional characteristics of phonemes, the basic sound units of a language. This allowed her to create profiles for texts in terms of their preferential use of different types of phonemes and therefore their phonoemotional tone. Note that for such research, perceptual ratings may be closer to the researcher's con-

ceptual definitions of the variables and therefore preferred over traditional content analytic measures.

The Use of Multiple Coders

Most content analyses involve the use of more than two coders. How to conduct reliability analyses in these cases has not been well discussed in the literature. There are several possibilities.

1. Use reliability statistics designed to accommodate multiple-coder statistics—most prominently, Cohen's *kappa* (adapted for multiple coders; see Fleiss, 1971) and Krippendorff's *alpha*. This will provide a single reliability coefficient for each variable across all coders simultaneously, which is quite useful for the reporting of final reliabilities. However, it is problematic for pilot reliability analyses, in that the coefficients obscure pairwise intercoder differences, making it impossible to identify coders who might need extra training or the odd rogue coder.

2. Use two-coder reliability statistics in a pairwise fashion, creating a matrix of reliabilities for each variable. This is highly useful as a diagnostic for the pilot reliabilities but very cumbersome for reporting of final reliabilities.

3. Average reliability coefficients across all pairs of coders. This is routinely done for simple percent agreement coefficients but has not been widely used for the other statistics (the reporting of reliability protocols is so often obscure or incomplete, it is possible that this practice is more common than we might think). Weighting the average by the number of cases per coder pair seems like a logical extension of this practice. Alternatively, a Cronbach's *alpha* coefficient, more typically used as an internal consistency reliability statistic for multiple items in an index measure, may serve as an averaged r, with a correction for number of coders (Schulman et al., 1989).[9] The adaptation of the Spearman-Brown formula presented by Rosenthal (1987), which calculates "effective reliability" from the mean intercoder correlation coefficient, shows a formula that is identical to that for Cronbach's *alpha*. In the case of the use of Cronbach's *alpha* or Rosenthal's effective reliability, the assumption is that the researcher is attempting to generalize from a set of coders to a population of potential coders, not something that is currently widely endorsed as a principal goal of reliability. Simply adding coders without increasing average intercoder reliability will result in greatly inflated apparent reliability coefficients. This seeming advantage to adding coders should be viewed critically.

4. There is also the possibility of establishing a *distribution* for the reliability coefficient across the coders to examine its shape and look for outliers for possible exclusion.

The PRAM computer program does most of the foregoing. It provides both of the discussed multicoder reliability statistics, reports all statistics pairwise for all coders, and averages the two-coder statistics across all pairs.

Advanced and Specialty Issues in Reliability Coefficient Selection

Beyond Basic Coefficients

There are dozens of alternative reliability coefficients, used either for very specialized applications or not yet established or widely used.

Janson and Vegelius (1979) have developed "*C*" and "*S*" coefficients, alternatives to *kappa*. Perrault and Leigh (1989) introduced their reliability coefficient "*I*," which does not contrast observed agreement with chance agreement but rather takes into account the notion of a true population level of agreement. The sample coefficient "*I*" is an *estimate* of that population value, and as such, we may calculate a confidence interval around it. (Thus, Perrault and Leigh take a *parametric or inferential* statistical approach, as opposed to the more common *nonparametric* approach to intercoder reliability.)

Popping (1988) has considered no fewer than 39 different agreement indices for coding nominal categories with a predetermined coding scheme.[10] Using 13 evaluative criteria (many highly particular in focus or mathematical in nature or both), he concludes that Cohen's *kappa* is optimal.

Tinsley and Weiss (1975) reviewed a number of alternative reliability coefficients, including Finn's *r* for ordinal ratings, the intraclass correlation (*ICC*) for interval measures, and the Lawlis-Lu *chi-square*,[11] and they considered cases when composite ratings of a group of coders are to be used. Hughes and Garrett (1990) considered Winer's dependability index and the G-theory framework, which uses analysis of variance (ANOVA) to estimate variance components, allowing the isolation of that component which can be attributed to intercoder variation. Banerjee et al. (1999) looked at a variety of agreement coefficients in specialized applications in the health sciences, such as the tetrachoric correlation coefficient. They presented a compelling argument for using advanced statistical methods (e.g., log linear models) that can model the structure of agreement rather than summarize it with a single number. This might prove to be useful in assessing the confusion matrix between coders.

Bartko and Carpenter (1976) evaluated "the best and/or most commonly used reliability statistics" (p. 308), including *kappa*, weighted *kappa*, and the *ICC*. They note that the Pearson *chi-square* statistic is "often used" as an indicator of agreement deviating from chance, but they point out how it is inappropriate (i.e., *disagreement* deviating from chance may also make the *chi-square* significant).

The Possibility of "Consistency"
Intracoder Reliability Assessment

Tinsley and Weiss (1975) reviewed the use of rate-rerate methods as another indication of reliability. Similar to the test-retest method for assessing consistency reliability of a set of measures (Carmines & Zeller, 1979), this procedure requires a coder to recode a set of units at a second point in time. Tinsley and Weiss (1975) dismiss this rate-rerate technique as inappropriate; Krippendorff (1980) criticizes the use of this type of reliability (using Weber's [1990] term, "stability reliability") and cautions that it is the "weakest form of reliability" (p. 130).

Controlling for Covariates

An advanced form of diagnostics for reliability analyses involves comparing reliability coefficients across values of a control variable. For example, Kacmar and Hochwarter (1996) used ANOVA to compare intercoder agreement scores across three combinations of medium types—transcripts-audio, audio-video, and transcripts-video. They found no significant differences between the three types, showing that this potential covariate was not significantly related to reliability outcomes.

Sequential Overlapping
Reliability Coding

Researchers have begun to consider the possibility of using sequential overlapping coding for reliability testing. For example, Coder A codes units 1 through 20, Coder B codes units 11 through 30, Coder C codes units 21 through 40, and so on so that every unit in the reliability subsample is coded by precisely two coders, but there are multiple coders used. This overlapping of coder assignments is used to maximize the reliability subsample size and to better meet the second goal of intercoder reliability (the practical advantage of more coders and more units coded). This technique is questionable at present, and more research is needed to establish the utility of this option. Potter and Levine-Donnerstein (1999) do not support its use, but they also do not present a statistical argument against it. The practice of having different units rated by different coders does have some precedent; Fleiss (1971) and Kraemer (1980) have developed extensions of *kappa* in which units are rated by different sets of judges.

Reliability is the bare bones of acceptability for the reportage of findings —that is, variables that do not achieve reliability should not be included in subsequent analyses. How measures that make the cut are analyzed and the results reported are the province of the next chapter.

Notes

1. Noting that there have been several variations on the calculation of *kappa*'s standard deviation, Bartko and Carpenter (1976, p. 310) present this pair of formulas for testing the size of a *kappa* coefficient with a *z*-test:

$$\sigma_\kappa = \sqrt{PA_O(1-PA_O)/n(1-PA_E)^2}$$
$$z = kappa/\sigma_\kappa$$

where σ_κ is the estimate of the standard deviation of *kappa*, PA_O is the proportion agreement, observed, PA_E is the proportion agreement, expected by chance, and *n* is the total number of units the coders have assessed.

The value of *z* is assessed in a table of normal curve probabilities, found in any basic statistics book. A statistically significant *z* indicates that the *kappa* coefficient is significantly different from zero.

2. Stated differently, we could say, "We are 95% confident that the true population reliability for this variable, number of verbal nonfluencies, is between .88 and .96."

3. Occasionally, an internal consistency reliability coefficient is used in content analysis when an index is constructed. For example, Peterson, Bettes, and Seligman (1985) combined the ratings of four judges and properly reported Cronbach's *alpha* for the composite index.

4. In this text, repeated use of Greek letters will be avoided to minimize the glazing over of the readers' eyes.

5. The most sophisticated and particularized applications of *all* the reliability coefficients appear in the medical literature, wherein rater or coder decisions can have life-and-death implications. Banerjee et al.'s (1999) fine review of agreement coefficients was partly funded by the National Cancer Institute.

6. A citation check shows 133 cites to Lin (1989), *all* of which are in the science citation index.

The formula for Lin's concordance correlation coefficient is as follows:

$$\text{estimated } r_c = \frac{2(\frac{\Sigma ab}{n})}{\frac{\Sigma a^2}{n} + \frac{\Sigma b^2}{n} + (\text{Mean}_A - \text{Mean}_B)^2}$$

where   *a* = each deviation score (Coder A score minus mean for A)
          b = each deviation score (Coder B score minus mean for B)
          n = number of units coded in common by coders.

Using the same data used for the Pearson *r* in Box 7.3, the concordance correlation coefficient would be .968, very similar to the obtained .97 Pearson *r*. However, in a hypothetical case in which Coder C always codes two points higher than Coder A (from Box 7.3), the Pearson *r* and the concordance r_c would show a wider discrepancy —*r* = 1.0 and r_c = .86. The concordance r_c successfully takes note of the imperfect correspondence between the two coders.

7. To show the application of confidence intervals to the reportage of reliability coefficients, the confidence intervals (CIs) for the percent agreement, Scott's *pi*, and Cohen's *kappa* from Box 7.2 are calculated as follows.

For percent agreement:

$$95\% \text{ CI} = \text{percent agreement} \pm 1.96 \text{ SE}$$

$$\text{where } SE = \frac{(PA_0)(1 - PA_0)}{n - 1}$$

$$SE = (.7)(.3)/9$$
$$= .02$$

$$95\% \text{ CI} = .70 \pm (1.96)(.02)$$
$$= .70 \pm .04$$
$$= .66 - .74$$

For Scott's *pi:*

$$95\% \text{ CI} = pi \pm (1.96)\,\sigma_\pi$$

$$\text{where } \sigma_\pi^2 = \left(\frac{1}{1 - PA_E}\right)^2 \left(\frac{PA_0(1 - PA_0)}{n - 1}\right)$$

$$= \left(\frac{1}{1 - .34}\right)^2 \left(\frac{.70(.30)}{9}\right)$$
$$= 2.30 \times .023$$
$$= .054$$
$$\text{so } \sigma_\pi = .23$$

$$95\% \text{ CI} = .545 \pm (1.96)(.23)$$
$$= .545 \pm .45$$
$$= .095 - .995$$

For Cohen's *kappa:*

$$95\% \text{ CI} = kappa \pm (1.96)\,\sigma_\kappa$$

$$\text{where } \sigma_\kappa^2 = \frac{PA_O(1 - PA_O)}{n\,(1 - PA_E)^2}$$

$$= \frac{.70(1 - .70)}{10(1 - .32)^2}$$

$$= \frac{.70(.30)}{10(.46)}$$

$$= .046$$

$$\text{so } \sigma_\kappa = .21$$

$$95\% \text{ CI} = .56 \pm (1.96)(.21)$$
$$= .56 \pm .41$$
$$= .15 - .97$$

Notice how *large* the CIs are for *pi* and *kappa*—we are 95% confident that the population (i.e., full sample) Scott's *pi* reliability for banner ad type is between .095 and .995, and we are 95% confident that the population Cohen's *kappa* reliability for banner ad type is between .15 and .97. These unacceptably huge intervals are a result of the very small reliability subsample size ($n = 10$), chosen to facilitate the by-hand calculations. With a subsample of 100, the CIs would instead be .405 ↔ .685 and .42 ↔ .70, respectively.

8. On the other hand, using the approach of retaining only the reliable individual indicators may be seen as capitalizing on chance. That is, if 50 items measuring masculinity are attempted and only 5 items achieve an acceptable level of reliability of .90, the reliability of the total set may be seen as not exceeding chance. Controls, comparable to the Bonferroni adjustment for multiple statistical tests, might be employed in future efforts.

9. This use of Cronbach's *alpha* to assess multiple-coder reliability for a variable that is measured at the interval or ratio level is not often conducted. However, it seems to be an overly advantageous adjustment to an average intercoder correlation, as shown by Carmines and Zeller (1979, p. 46). For example, in the case of six coders who have an average correlation of only .40, the Cronbach's *alpha* adjusts upward to .80. For 10 coders and an average correlation of .40, the Cronbach's *alpha* is .87. Notice that given a consistent reliability among pairs of coders, increasing the number of coders inevitably results in the inflation of R, the effective reliability.

This adjustment for number of coders can be seen in the following formula:

$$\text{Cronbach's } alpha = m(\text{Mean}_r)/[1 + (\text{Mean}_r)(m - 1)]$$

where Mean_r = the mean of all intercoder correlations for a given variable and
m = the number of coders.

However, Carmines and Zeller's (1979) interpretation of Cronbach's *alpha* does not translate well from the multiple-measures case to the multiple-coders case. They note that *alpha* can be considered a "unique estimate of the expected correlation of one test with an alternative form containing the same number of items" or "the expected correlation between an actual test and a *hypothetical* alternative form of the same length, one that may never be constructed." (p. 45)

Translated, this might be "an estimate of the expected correlation between a composite measure of all m coders with another, *hypothetical* composite measure from a different set of m coders, who may never actually code."

10. Popping (1988) identifies the use of a predetermined (or what this book has termed an *a priori*) coding scheme as *a posteriori* coding.

11. The formula for the Lawlis-Lu chi-square is given by Tinsley and Weiss (1975, p. 367) as follows:

$$\chi^2 = \frac{(n_1 - nP - .5)^2}{nP} + \frac{(n_2 - n(1 - P) - .5)^2}{n(1 - P)}$$

where n_1 = number of agreements, n_2 = number of disagreements, and P = probability of chance agreement.

CHAPTER 8

Results and Reporting

This chapter presents options for the reporting of content analysis findings. It clarifies the point that the most common form of presentation—simple descriptive frequencies—is not the only option. For certain analyses, time lines may be appropriate. Relationships among variables may be examined, and so long as random sampling from a known population of messages has been achieved, inferential statistics may be used. Relationships between content analysis variables and noncontent analysis variables may be explored in first-order and second-order links, as defined in Chapter 3.

Data Handling and Transformations

Clearly, how the data that have been collected are treated prior to analyses will affect what statistics may be used and what conclusions may be reached. For example, collapsing categories so that the level of measurement is reduced from interval or ratio to ordinal will curtail the range of statistics that can be applied (e.g., collapsing age in years to categories of ages). In addition, many statistical procedures make assumptions about the distribution of the variable being analyzed, assuming a normal distribution, for example. Hair et al. (1998) provide good advice on how to handle violations of assumptions. The reader should be prepared to deal with nonlinear transformations; a positive skew, for example, may be remedied with a log or natural log transformation. It should be remembered that the variable is now one step removed from its original form and that linear relationships found between the transformed variable and other measures are essentially nonlinear.

Hypothesis Testing

Hypotheses and Research Questions—A Reminder

In Chapter 5, we explored the generation of hypotheses and research questions. Remember that a hypothesis is a predictive statement about the relationship among two or more variables. To make such a firm prediction, there needs to be theory or past research evidence to justify it. If no clear prediction is possible, then a research question may be forwarded. When the data have been gathered, the findings must be presented in a way that directly addresses the hypotheses or research questions. Although additional findings may be reported, the top priority is the testing of the hypotheses and the answering of the research questions.

Also, remember the difference between directional and nondirectional hypotheses. When a statistic used to test a hypothesis has both one-tailed and two-tailed versions, the one-tailed test is appropriate for testing a directional hypothesis, whereas the two-tailed version is appropriate for a nondirectional hypothesis.

Generally speaking, to test a hypothesis, some type of statistical test of significance is used. If the test is statistically significant, we say we have achieved support for our hypothesis. If it is not significant, we say that we failed to find support. With a research question, the situation is a bit more ambiguous. Many research questions demand a statistical test; for example, the research question, "Are texts written by schizophrenics different in their level of pessimism than texts written by nonschizophrenics?" is properly addressed with a statistical test that compares the levels of pessimism for two groups. This could be achieved with a t-test, which indicates whether two means and distributions (of pessimism, in this case) are different enough to indicate two different populations and not a chance difference. On the other hand, the research question, "What are the most common conflict themes in discussions between married partners?" would probably best be addressed with simple frequencies of occurrence and no test of statistical significance.

Inferential Versus Nonparametric Statistics

There are two types of statistics—*inferential* and noninferential or *nonparametric*. Inferential statistics allow us to establish how certain we are that our findings may be generalized to the population from which our sample was drawn. Notice that if a census study has been conducted, there is no need for inferential statistics. Nonparametric statistics do not attempt to gauge the certainty of generalizing a finding to a population (i.e., no parameter is estimated). They may be entirely descriptive in nature, such as a mean or median; they may serve a data-reduction role, as a factor analysis does; or they may statistically compare a finding to some criterion other than a population parameter, as the chi-square statistic compares a found distribution with a hypothetical chance distribution.

Although when we achieve statistical significance, we like to say that the strength of a relationship between or among variables is well established, inferential statistics are really telling us something else. They're telling us, based on the size of the relationship and the degrees of freedom (usually strongly determined by the sample size), whether our sample's findings may be generalized to the population. For example, students are often amazed that a correlation coefficient they have obtained is statistically significant—"It's only an r of .12. That's a shared variance of only 1.4%. How can that be statistically significant?" (See Box 7.3 for more on the Pearson correlation coefficient.) Well, there is a difference between statistical significance and the substantive importance of a relationship. With a sample size of 300 or more, that small correlation figure is statistically significant at the .05 level.[1] What this significant inferential test indicates is that the small relationship (only 1.4% shared variance) may clearly be generalized to the population. We're 95% confident that this small relationship exists in the population.

Selecting the Appropriate Statistical Tests

Statistics are also categorized according to how many variables are analyzed. With a single variable, the statistics available are called univariate. With two variables—one independent variable and one dependent variable—the appropriate statistics are called *bivariate*. And when there are more than two variables in a hypothesized model, the statistics appropriate to the task are called *multivariate*.

Teaching the reader all about statistics, their calculations, and all their applications is beyond the scope of this book; however, many excellent statistical sources exist.[2] Box 8.1 provides a guide to basic decision making regarding appropriate statistics.[3] The statistics are organized into the three types: univariate, bivariate, and multivariate. They are identified by whether they are inferential or nonparametric, how many independent and dependent variables are accommodated by the test, and what level(s) of measurement are assumed for these variables.

Also, there is a model shown for each statistical procedure, indicating the structure of the predicted relationships among the variables. For example, for all bivariate statistics, the predictive model is X→ Y: One dependent variable Y predicted by one independent variable X. For multivariate statistics, the models vary. A common theme, however, is that many tests assume a single dependent variable.

The researcher needs to match up his or her hypothesis or research question with the sample models and other information about the statistics. For example, if a research question asks, "What formal features of print ads are

Box 8.1   Selecting Appropriate Statistics

	$U/B/M^a$	IVs^b	DVs^c	I/N^d	Model
Mode	U	1: N		N	X
Median	U	1: O		N	X
Mean	U	1: I/R		N	X
Range & interquartile range	U	1: O		N	X
Standard deviation & variance (sd^2)	U	1: I/R		N	X
Standard error (SE) & confidence interval (CI)	U	1: I/R		I	X
Chi-square	B	1: N	1: N	N	X $\longrightarrow$ Y
Single factor analysis of variance ("ANOVA")					
t-test	B	1: N$_{(2\ group)}$	1: I/R	I	X $\longrightarrow$ Y
F-test	B	1: N$_{(3+group)}$	1: I/R	I	X $\longrightarrow$ Y
Spearman rank-order coefficient (rho)	B	1: O	1: O	N	X $\longrightarrow$ Y
Pearson correlation	B	1: I/R	1: I/R	I	X $\longrightarrow$ Y
Bivariate regression	B	1: I/R	1: I/R	I	X $\longrightarrow$ Y
Multiple-factor ANOVA	M	2+: N	1: I/R	I	$X_1, X_2, X_3, X_4 \longrightarrow Y$
Multivariate ANOVA (MANOVA)	M	2+: N	2+: I/R	I	$X_1, X_2, X_3, X_4 \longrightarrow [Y_1, Y_2, Y_3]$
Discriminant Analysis	M	2+: I/R	1: N	I	$[X_1, X_2, X_3, X_4] \longrightarrow Y$
Factor Analysis	M	2+: I/R	None (factors emerge)	N/I	$[X_1, X_2, X_3, X_4] \longrightarrow F_1, F_2$
Multiple Regression	M	2+: I/R	1: I/R	I	$X_1, X_2, X_3, X_4 \longrightarrow Y$

	a	b	c	d	
Logistic Regression	M	2+: I/R	1: N(2-cat.)	I	X_1 X_2 X_3 X_4 → Y
Canonical Correlation	M	2+: I/R	2+: I/R	I	X_1 X_2 X_3 X_4 ↔ Y_1 Y_2 Y_3
Cluster Analysis	M	2+: I/R	None (clusters emerge)	I	X_1 X_2 X_3 X_4 → C_1 C_2
Multidimensional Scaling	M	2+: I/R	None (dims.are extracted)	I	X_1 X_2 X_3 X_4 → D_1, etc.
Structural Equation Modeling	M	2+: I/R	1+: I/R	N/I	X_1 → Y_1 ← Y_2; X_2 → Y_3 → Y_4

a. Univariate, Bivariate or Multivariate
b. Independent Variable(s), number and assumed level of measurement (N = nominal, O = ordinal, I/R = interval/ratio)
c. Dependent variable(s), number and assumed level of measurement
d. Inferential or nonparametric statistic

strongly related to content features?" a canonical correlation might be in order, so long as all the variables are measured at the interval or ratio level.[4] The canonical correlation will reveal patterns of linear relationships between a set of multiple independent variables (the formal features) and a set of multiple dependent variables (content features).

Imagine that a hypothesis states, "A soap opera character's physical attractiveness, age, and apparent social status will relate to whether the character's verbal orders are frequently obeyed by others." If all four variables are measured at the ratio level, then multiple regression is appropriate (three independent variables, physical attractiveness, age, and social status, lead to a single dependent variable, frequency of successful ordering). If the hypothesis is "Fear of failure, fear of rejection, and avoidance of uncertainty will all be greater for unmarried individuals than for married individuals," it sounds like a job for MANOVA, in that a single independent, nominal variable (marital status) predicts three dependent variables, all measured at the interval or ratio level (fear of failure, fear of rejection, and avoidance of uncertainty, all psychographic content analysis measures).

This is an obvious simplification. Each statistical test has additional assumptions and features. For example, in the case of MANOVA, the dependent variables are assumed to be related to one another (otherwise, there would be no need for an overall MANOVA test, in that each dependent variable could be assessed separately, a clearer and simpler process). This chapter will not be able to present all the ins and outs of statistical analysis. Box 8.1 and these examples are provided to steer the reader in the right direction, but he or she needs to know a great deal more about the chosen statistical tests than can be conveyed here.

The sections that follow are designed to acquaint the reader with a variety of statistical and graphical presentations for content analysis findings. In each case, an attempt is made to link the findings back to a motivating hypothesis or research question.[5]

Frequencies

For basic univariate frequencies, several main options are available: numeric frequencies, pie charts, and bar graphs. Table 8.1 shows basic numeric frequencies from a study by Olson (1994), a content analysis of sexual activity in 105 hours of network daytime soap opera programming, setting those findings side by side with the findings from an earlier study by Lowry and Towles (1989). Frequencies are reported for 11 variables, with most expressed as hourly rates (number of occurrences divided by number of hours in the sample). These findings would answer a research question such as, "What are the types and frequencies of sexual behaviors (physical, implied, and verbal) and their consequences as depicted on daytime soap operas?" No specific hypotheses are being tested, and correspondingly, there are no tests of statistical significance.

What tests *could* have been used? If a hypothesis predicted that the hourly rate of erotic touching was significantly greater than zero, a one-sample z-test could be used. To address a research question or hypothesis comparing the Olson (1994) results with the Lowry and Towles (1989) results, bivariate tests—*t*-tests and difference-of-proportions tests—could be used[6] (Voelker & Orton, 1993). And if the Olson results are to be generalized to a population of soap opera episodes, then confidence intervals would need to be reported for each of the figures in the 1989-1990 column in Table 8.1 (see Box 4.1).

Figure 8.1 gives an example of a frequency pie chart. Using the relational coding scheme developed by Rogers and Farace (1975), Fairhurst et al. (1987) analyzed messages exchanged in conversations between managers and subordinates at two Midwestern manufacturing plants. Nearly 12,000 messages from 45 manager-subordinate dyads were analyzed. One element of the coding scheme examines the control direction of each message: "Messages asserting definitional rights are coded one up (↑), accepting or requesting

Table 8.1   Rate Results With Comparison to 1987 Sample

	Rate[a]	
	1987	*1989-1990*
1A. Frequency & type of sexual behaviors		
Intercourse, physical	0	0
Implied	.3	.10
Verbal references	1.3	1.50
Erotic touching	4.1	.15
Discouraged acts (aggressive sexual contact & prostitution)	.2	.16
1B. Character portrayals of implied and verbal depictions of sexual intercourse		
Unmarried partners	1.50	1.12
Married partners	.10	.50
Age 30 to 40 years old	47%[b]	68%
1C. Consequences		
Pregnancy prevention	0	.04
STDs	0	0
AIDS	0	.04

SOURCE: Reprinted by permission from *Journalism Quarterly,* Vol. 71, p. 846 (Olson, 1994).
a. Rate per hour
b. Sample from 1982

other's definition of the relationship are coded one down (↓), and non-demanding, nonaccepting, leveling movements are coded one across (→)" (pp. 401-402). The analysis revealed a preponderance of messages that were one across for both managers and subordinates. About 65% of all messages were one across, 18% were one down, and 17% were one up. For messages generated by subordinates, the figures were 66% one across, 16% one down, and 18% one up. Messages generated by managers were 63% one across, 22% one down, and 15% one up, as displayed in Figure 8.1. The findings reported in the figure are an appropriate answer to a research question such as, "What are the relative frequencies of occurrence of the different types of control directions for messages generated by managers and conveyed to subordinates?" No statistical tests are employed and no hypotheses are addressed by this descriptive portion of the findings.[7]

A third option for presenting basic frequencies is shown in Figure 8.2, showing some of the results from Sengupta's (1996) study of television commercials in the United States and India. The chart indicates what percentage of the two samples contained each of four types of "hedonistic" appeals—modernity, straight hedonism, image, and variety. In this bivariate analysis, the independent variable is the country, and the dependent variables are the four hedo-

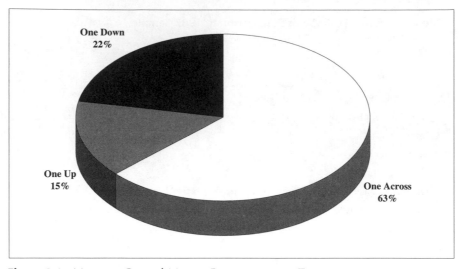

Figure 8.1. Manager Control Moves: Percentages per Type
SOURCE: Adapted from results reported in Fairhurst et al. (1987).

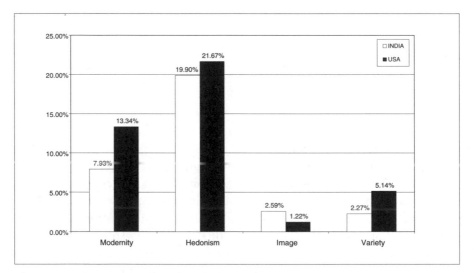

Figure 8.2. Percentage of Hedonistic Appeals
SOURCE: Reprinted from Sengupta, Subir. (1996). Understanding consumption related values from advertising: A content analysis of television commercials from India and the United States. *Gazette, 57,* 81-96. Copyright © 1996, with kind permission from Kluwer Academic Publishers.

nistic appeals. In his text, Sengupta provides ANOVA tests comparing the two countries, and all four are statistically significant. Thus, we can see how a visual presentation can help with bivariate as well as univariate analysis, in this case, helping the reader understand the comparative use of the different hedonistic appeals. The results as presented in Figure 8.2 would answer research questions such as, "How frequently do the four hedonistic appeals appear in U.S. TV commercials? . . . in Indian commercials?"

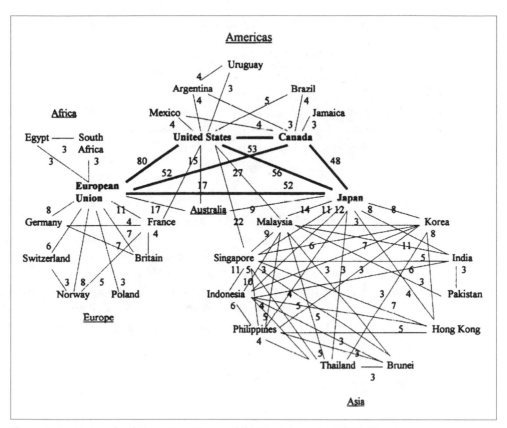

Figure 8.3. Network of Countries Covered by Reuters at the WTO Meeting

SOURCE: Reprinted from Chang, Tsan-Kuo. (1998). All countries not created equal to be news: World system and international communication. *Communication Research, 25,* 528-563, copyright © 1998 by Sage Publications, Inc. Reprinted by Permission of Sage Publications, Inc.

NOTE: WTO = World Trade Organization. Entries represent frequencies of WTO countries in the same region co-covered by Reuters in at least three different stories from Day 1 through Day 4 (December 9-12, 1996, n = 116). Based on multiple coding, each pair was counted only once in the same story. Frequencies of co-coverage between the United States and other countries were as follows: India, 16; Indonesia, 16; South Korea, 11; Norway, 10; United Kingdom, 8; Germany, 8; Hong Kong, 7; Pakistan, 5; Switzerland, 5; Thailand, 5; and Brunei, 3. Other cross-zone linkages are not shown.

Co-Occurrences and In-Context Occurrences

Chang (1998) provides a visually appealing way of presenting simple co-occurrences of concepts in a study of international news coverage. His graphical display is shown in Figure 8.3. Focusing on coverage of the first World Trade Organization (WTO) conference in 1996, he content analyzed Reuters's news service coverage of countries attending the conference. He diagramed the key co-occurrences. He concluded that among the 28 nations diagramed, four core countries and regions—the United States, the European Union, Japan, and Canada—dominated the coverage. This provides an answer to the research question, "Will the pattern of network coverage of the WTO conference center around the core countries?"

Table 8.2   KWIC Analysis of *Fear* in Coleridge's *The Ancient Mariner*

Line 233	I	fear	thee, ancyent Marinere!
Line 234	"I	fear	thy skinny hand;
Line 237		Fear	not, fear not, thou wedding guest!
Line 237	Fear not,	fear	not, thou wedding guest!
Line 305	Doth walk in	fear	and dread,
Line 348	I turned my head in	fear	and dread

"Key word in context" (KWIC) findings are rather microscopic and idiographic, not truly in the spirit of the *summarizing* nature of content analysis. However, they are very much a part of the content analysis literature. A sample presentation of a KWIC analysis is shown in Table 8.2. This example is the result of a search for the word *fear* in Coleridge's *The Rime of the Ancient Mariner*. These findings would answer a research question such as, "In what ways is the concept of fear used by Coleridge?"

Time Lines

Some of the more interesting content analyses have collected longitudinal data and are able to present findings along a time line. The statistical tests of such time lines are sophisticated, typically involving lagged correlations or time-series analysis (Collins & Horn, 1991; Cryer, 1986; Hamilton, 1994; Hogenraad, McKenzie, & Martindale, 1997; Poole, Van de Ven, Dooley, & Holmes, 2000). Such analyses allow the discovery not only of cross-sectional relationships but also over-time impacts of message content on social habits and behaviors. Studies have looked at such relationships as that between news coverage and various types of public opinion (Brosius & Kepplinger, 1992; Gonzenbach, 1992; Hertog & Fan, 1995; Jasperson et al., 1998; Jenkins, 1999; Watt, Mazza, & Snyder, 1993) and the relationship between news content and the seeking of health care by individuals (Yanovitzky & Blitz, 2000).[8]

Pileggi, Grabe, Holderman, and de Montigny (2000) studied the plot structures of top-grossing Hollywood films about business released between 1933 and 1993, developing a multifaceted "myth index" that measured prevalence of a pro-American dream message. They found that the correlation between an index of national economic well-being (based on unemployment and federal deficit figures) and their myth index was maximized with a 2-year lag, that is, when the economic index was matched with the myth index 2 years later. They interpreted these findings as suggesting that "Hollywood films

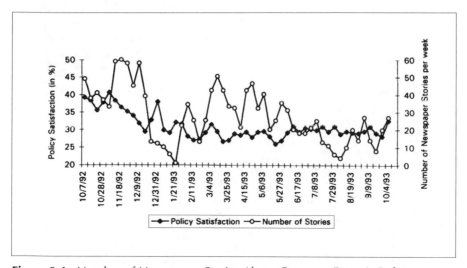

Figure 8.4. Number of Newspaper Stories About Governor Patten's Reform Proposal and Satisfaction With Patten's Reform Policy
SOURCE: Copyright 1996 from *Political Communication* by Lars Willnat and Jian-Hua Zhu. Reproduced by permission of Taylor & Francis, Inc., http://www.routledge-ny.com

tend to replicate existing economic conditions rather than promote changes in economic conditions" (p. 221).

Figures 8.4 and 8.5 present two time lines. Figure 8.4 shows a portion of Willnat and Zhu's (1996) time-series analysis of newspaper coverage and public opinion regarding Governor Patten's democratization plan for Hong Kong. Using an agenda-setting perspective, they predicted a first-order link relationship between Hong Kong newspaper coverage and public approval of Patten's reform proposal, as measured via a weekly public opinion poll. Figure 8.4 shows the trends for the two variables graphically. Using an ARIMA time-series model, the researchers found a significant prediction of public policy satisfaction from news coverage, with a 1-week delay. The statistically significant results confirm the agenda-setting hypothesis, "Greater newspaper coverage of the governor's proposal will lead to greater approval by the public."

Figure 8.5 shows Finkel and Geer's (1998) analysis of political advertising tone, operationally defined as the percentage of positive issue and trait appeals, in TV commercials run by the two major party candidates for the U.S. presidential elections from 1960 through 1992. The graph also charts figures for national voter turnout during this period. The graph shows an overall trend toward more negative political advertising, with a positive swell in the 1970s. This graph would answer a research question such as, "Has political television advertising tone in U.S. presidential races changed in the past three decades?" In addition to displaying the graph, Finkel and Geer also used logistic regression to test whether voter turnout was affected by overall advertising

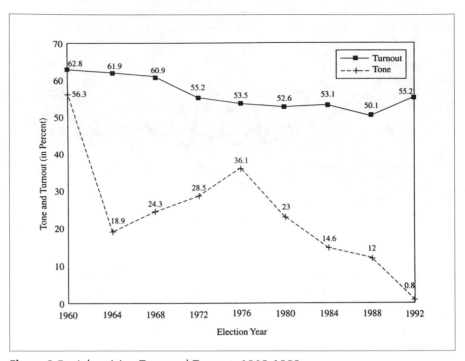

Figure 8.5. Advertising Tone and Turnout, 1960-1992

SOURCE: Reprinted from Finkel, Steven E., & Geer, John G. (1998). A spot check: Casting doubt on the demobilizing effect of attack advertising. *American Journal of Political Science, 42,* 573-595, © 1998.

tone over the 1960-1992 period, concluding that it was not a significant factor.[9]

Bivariate Relationships

Formal tests of relationships between two variables (one independent, one dependent) may be conducted with bivariate statistics. Table 8.3 shows a tabular presentation of a couple of two-variable relationships. Schreer and Strichartz (1997) conducted a content analysis of 428 pieces of restroom graffiti from two U.S. campuses (one college and one university). Each "graffito" was coded into one of 19 categories (as shown in Table 8.3, ranging from ethnic insult to other/miscellaneous). In their table, Schreer and Strichartz cross-tabulated the 19-category graffiti type variable with two other variables (gender and type of campus). In their text, the researchers collapsed categories and conducted a series of chi-square tests, concluding that men and women differ only in their use of insults, and the two types of campus differ only in the occurrence of insults and the display of political issues in the graffiti. The results answer a general research question: "Do gender of the writer and type of college or university campus relate to the type of graffiti found on restroom walls?"

Table 8.3   Number and Percentage of Graffiti for Each Category by
Sex of Writer and by College Campus

Category	Men n	Men %	Women n	Women %	College n	College %	University n	University %
Insults								
Ethnic	10	3	0	0	2	1	8	4
Sexist	3	1	1	1	1	0	3	2
Homophobic	14	4	0	0	7	3	7	3
General	30	9	8	9	20	9	18	9
Total	57	17	9	11	30	13	36	18
Sexual								
Heterosexual	9	3	4	5	10	4	3	2
Homosexual	39	11	5	6	24	10	20	10
Odd sexual	6	2	0	0	4	2	2	1
Total	54	16	9	11	38	16	25	13
Humor								
Scatological	18	5	0	0	12	5	6	3
Sexual	21	6	2	2	8	3	15	8
General	11	3	7	8	6	3	12	6
Total	50	15	9	11	26	11	33	17
Social Issues								
Political	17	5	17	20	8	3	26	13
Philosophy	8	2	2	2	3	1	7	3
Fraternity, sorority	20	6	1	1	15	7	6	3
Religion	4	1	0	0	1	1	3	2
Drugs	15	4	2	2	8	3	9	5
Music	15	4	1	1	9	4	7	3
Sports	9	3	0	0	8	3	1	1
Romantic	2	1	4	5	3	1	3	2
Total	90	26	27	31	55	23	62	32
Other								
Miscellaneous	91	27	32	37	82	36	41	21
Overall Total ($N = 428$)	342		86		231		197	

SOURCE: Reproduced with permission of authors and publisher from Schreer, George E., & Strichartz, Jeremy M. (1997). Private restroom graffiti: An analysis of controversial social issues on two college campuses. *Psychological Reports, 81,* 1067-1074, © *Psychological Reports* 1997.

In Table 8.4, we see a classic example of a cross-tabulation table with a chi-square test. Taylor and Taylor (1994) conducted a content analysis of over 700 Michigan highway billboards in both rural and urban areas, with an eye to identifying the prevalence of ads for alcohol and tobacco products, which have come under criticism by legislators. The table indicates that although alcohol

Table 8.4   Urban Versus Rural Billboard Location by Alcohol/Cigarette Product
Category Versus All Others

	Alcohol and Tobacco Billboards	All Other Billboards	
Urban	42 11.7% 76.4%	31 88.3% 48.9%	360 51.1%
Rural	13 3.8% 23.6%	332 96.2% 51.1%	345 48.9%
	55 7.8%	650 92.2%	705 100.0%

$$(\chi^2 = 14.20, p < .001)$$

SOURCE: Reprinted with permission from *Journal of Public Policy & Marketing*, published by the American Marketing Association, Charles R. Taylor & John C. Taylor, 1994, Vol. 13, p. 104.
NOTES: This table indicates the number of alcohol or tobacco billboards by urban and rural areas. Urban areas contained more than three times the number of such billboards as rural areas. Overall, 7.8% of all billboards were for alcohol or cigarette products. The first percentage figure in each cell is a row percentage. The second percentage is the column percentage.

and tobacco billboards were relatively uncommon (constituting only 7.8% of the entire sample), they were significantly more common along urban highways (11.7% of urban billboards, compared with 3.8% of rural billboards). The significant chi-square of 14.20 ($p < .001$) indicates that this pattern of difference between urban and rural is significantly different from a chance distribution. The finding would support a hypothesis of "Alcohol and tobacco billboards will be more commonly found along urban highways than along rural highways."

Table 8.5 presents results from Cutler and Javalgi (1992), in which 21 bivariate relationships are compactly summarized in one table. The 21 dependent variables—a variety of form and content variables for ads in women's, business, and general-interest magazines—were each broken down by the main independent variable, country of origin (United States, U.K., France). When the dependent variable was nominal, the chi-square statistic was used. When the dependent was ratio, ANOVA was used (*F* test). The table indicates whether each of the 21 hypotheses was supported. For example, H1c, "The frequency of usage of black-and-white visuals will differ significantly by country," was supported with a statistically significant chi-square. And H1a, "The size of the visual will differ significantly by country," received support with a statistically significant *F* test, indicating that the difference in the three country means (with French visuals the largest, U.S. visuals the next largest, and

Table 8.5   Component Differences by Country by Product

Hypothesis Number	U.S.	U.K.	France	Significance Level	Support for Hypothesis
Not product specific					
1c black and white	5.7%	11.3%	13.2%	$\chi^2 = 10.1, n = 795, p = .01$	supported
2b comparison	10.0%	4.7%	1.0%	$\chi^2 = 19.7, n = 800, p = .00$	supported
3a minority race*	6.8%	4.8%	7.1%	small cells	
3b elderly person*	2.7%	2.4%	1.4%	small cells	
3c children*	15.5%	3.6%	5.7%	$\chi^2 = 10.4, n = 302, p = .01$	supported
Durables product line					
1a size	336cm	315cm	390cm	$F = 4.8, n = 277, p = .01$	supported
1b photograph	72.9%	74.7%	48.5%	$\chi^2 = 17.9, n = 278, p = .00$	supported
1d product shown	57.3%	60.2%	49.0%	$\chi^2 = 2.6, n = 277, p = .28$	
1e product size	117cm	124cm	157cm	$F = 3.1, n = 288, p = .05$	supported
1f price shown	16.7%	24.1%	16.3%	$\chi^2 = 2.2, n = 277, p = .33$	
2a description	68.8%	67.5%	72.7%	$\chi^2 = 0.7, n = 278, p = .72$	
2c association	51.0%	37.3%	42.4%	$\chi^2 = 3.5, n = 278, p = .17$	
2d symbolic	10.4%	16.9%	37.4%	$\chi^2 = 22.5, n = 278, p = .00$	supported
Nondurables product line					
1a size	362cm	389cm	431cm	$F = 4.6, n = 521, p = .01$	supported
1b photograph	82.3%	68.4%	60.0%	$\chi^2 = 21.6, n = 522, p = .00$	supported
1d product shown	41.6%	49.1%	37.5%	$\chi^2 = 4.1, n = 520, p = .13$	
1e product size	88cm	96cm	126cm	$F = 3.9, n = 536, p = .02$	supported
1f price shown	6.2%	8.6%	15.2%	$\chi^2 = 7.4, n = 521, p = .02$	supported
2a description	43.2%	42.0%	39.0%	$\chi^2 = 0.5, n = 522, p = .77$	
2c association	65.0%	43.7%	51.4%	$\chi^2 = 19.4, n = 522, p = .00$	supported
2d symbolic	6.2%	23.6%	20.0%	$\chi^2 = 27.3, n = 522, p = .00$	supported

SOURCE: Reprinted from Cutler, Bob D., & Javalgi, Rakshekhar G. (1992). A cross-cultural analysis of the visual components of print advertising: The United States and the European community. *Journal of Advertising Research, 32*(1), 71-80.

*Percentage of ads containing a person rather than percentage of all ads (38% of ads contained at least one person).

U.K. visuals the smallest) may be generalized to the populations from which the ads were drawn.[10]

Figure 8.6 shows correlational results from Smith's (1999) analysis of women's images in female-focused films of the 1930s, 1940s, and 1990s. Examining the 307 principal characters in the 60 randomly selected films, she measured a wide range of descriptive and psychologically based variables (see Chapter 1 for more information). Her summative scales measuring female sex-role traits and psychoticism were found to be linearly related ($r = -.698, p < .001$). That relationship is graphed in Figure 8.6.[11] This negative correlation

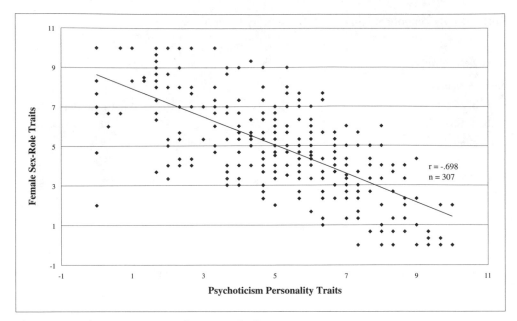

Figure 8.6. Characters in Female-Focused Films
SOURCE: Adapted from results reported in Smith (1999).

would support a hypothesis of "The more psychotic a character is portrayed, the fewer female sex-role traits that character is likely to exhibit." The statistical significance of $p < .001$ indicates that we are more than 99.9% confident in generalizing the finding to all characters in the population of films from which the sample was drawn.

Multivariate Relationships

In Table 8.6, we see the results of a stepwise multiple regression[12] from Naccarato and Neuendorf's (1998) study of business-to-business magazine ads (also see Box 3.2). In a first-order, unit-by-unit linking of content analysis variables and a noncontent analysis dependent variable, the researchers explored the relationship between form and content attributes of the ads and the ads' success in generating recall among readers. Their table indicates that a model of seven significant predictors (independent variables) was successful in significantly predicting recall, with 58% of the variance in recall explained ($F = 37.83$, p = .0001). The beta coefficients show the relative size and direction of the individual, unique (partial) contributions of the seven independent variables—presentation as a tabloid spread, use of color, having copy in the bottom half of the ad, having larger subvisuals, and advertising a service rather than a product are all positive predictors of recall, whereas presentation as a

Table 8.6　Stepwise Prediction of Aided Advertisement Recall

Independent Variable	Pearson r	Reliability (% or r)	Frequency (%)	Final Beta	Sig.
Form variables					
Fractional page	−.53	96%	19.4%	−.47	< .0001*
Junior page	−.15	96%	47.4%	−.34	< .0001*
Tabloid spread	.36	96%	6.9%	.31	< .0001*
Color	.48	.92 (r)	NA	.24	< .0001*
Copy in bottom half	.10	78%	49.8%	.18	.0002*
Copy in right half	−.04	78%	14.2%	−.16	.0005*
Major visual chart/graph	−.12	75%	1.6%	−.10	.0140
Average size of subvisuals	.18	85-100%	NA	.09	.0336
Content variables					
Service advertised	.18	84%	20.6%	.12	.0059

Total R^2 = .59; Adjusted R^2 = .58

$F_{(9,2330)}$ = 37.83; Sig. = .0001

SOURCE: From Naccarato, John L., & Neuendorf, Kimberly A. (1998). Reprinted with permission.

*Sig. holds at $< p$ .05 using Bonferroni test (criterion = .0007) for the final 75 independent variables entered in the multiple regression.

NOTE: NA indicates the reliability or frequency is not applicable because variables in this table have been combined, averaged, or otherwise manipulated from the original measures(s).

fractional page or junior page, having copy in the right half of the ad, and having a chart or graph as the major visual are all negative predictors of recall. Overall, the multiple regression findings answer the research question, "To what extent do form and content attributes predict recall for business-to-business print ads?"[13] The statistical significance of the regression means that the results may be generalized to the population of ads from which the sample was randomly drawn.

In their study of magazines' coverage of breast cancer issues, Andsager and Powers (1999) used cluster analysis to combine sets of frequently co-occurring concepts. Then, they used an MDS (using VBMap) to discover dimensions of discrimination among the concept clusters and to illustrate the relationships among clusters. This is a form of semantic mapping similar to that employed by the CATPAC program. In Figure 8.7, their MDS map for news magazines is shown. Each labeled circle represents a cluster of concepts. Clusters that are close to one another occur together frequently in the sample of news stories. For example, "biopsy" and "early detection" are close together, indicating that stories that included biopsy-related words are likely to also include early-detection-related terms. And the closeness of *Newsweek* to the two clusters indicates that the stories in *Newsweek* are likely to include concepts from the two clusters. Although sophisticated, the researchers' analyses would have to be classified as nonparametric—no statistics are available to assess

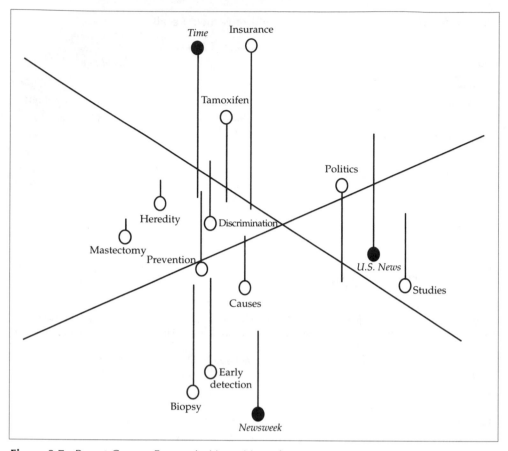

Figure 8.7. Breast Cancer Frames in News Magazines

SOURCE: Reprinted with permission from Andsager, Julie L., & Powers, Angela. (1999). Social or economic concerns: How news and women's magazines framed breast cancer in the 1990s. *Journalism and Mass Communication Quarterly, 76,* 531-550.

whether the results are generalizable to the population of news magazine stories. They would properly address a research question such as "How do news magazines differ in their framing of stories about breast cancer?"

Figure 8.8 presents a simple semantic map, from Carley (1994). This type of research uses text content analysis to discover patterns of usage and co-occurrence of linguistic concepts in messages, coupled with map analysis as a method of displaying the contexts of occurrence of key concepts. Carley's work has examined the efficacy of using such language analysis techniques to draw conclusions about cultural differences, similarities, and change (e.g., Carley, 1994; Palmquist, Carley, & Dale, 1997). One of several examples in Carley (1994) is that of the representation of robots in science fiction. The researcher conducted an analysis of passages from science fiction books that described individual robots during three different time periods—pre-1950s, the 1950s and 1960s, and the 1970s and 1980s. Figure 8.8 presents linkages that

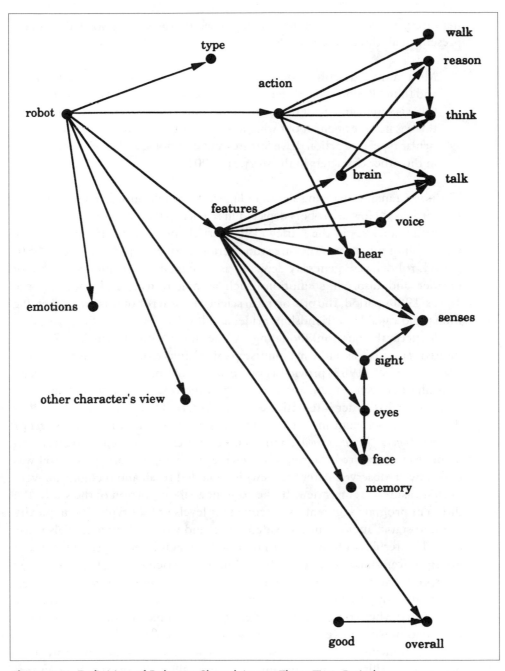

Figure 8.8. Definition of Robot as Shared Across Three Time Periods
SOURCE: Reprinted from *Poetics, 22,* Carley, Kathleen, Extracting culture through textual analysis, 291-312, copyright 1994, with permission from Elsevier Science.

are apparent in the literature of all three periods. In the figure, we see a wide variety of frequently occurring coded descriptors within five general classes of discourse about robots (e.g., emotions, features, action). As Carley notes in her interpretation of the figure, "a map based on the social knowledge that is present in all three time periods,"

> Most authors described robots as being able to walk, talk, hear, reason and think. Robots typically have a face and eyes, and memory. In general there is some agreement that something about robots is good (although there is no agreement about what it is). In addition, robots are of a particular type, take action, have features and emotions, and evoke feelings in the other characters in the story. (p. 300)

The nonparametric mapping shown in Figure 8.8 would answer a research question such as, "How are robots depicted in science fiction literature?"

Other analyses in the Carley (1994) article point out differences in the treatment of robots over the three time periods. For example, in the pre-1950s period, robots were generally depicted as nonmetallic humanoids capable of murder and displaying emotions such as anger, fear, and pain. By the 1970s-1980s period, the prototypical science fiction robot was now a metallic humanoid capable of friendship, pride, and loyalty.

Structural equation modeling is the most comprehensive form of multivariate analysis, allowing multistep causal links to be specified and tested. Watt and Welch (1983) provide a good example of a path model that tests relationships between content analytic variables and receiver responses, a nice example of a first-order integrative link (see Figure 8.9). The researchers conducted an experiment in which children viewed episodes of *Sesame Street* or *Mister Rogers' Neighborhood,* and their responses to different program segments were measured. During the viewing, the subject's attention level was coded by an observer. After the viewing, unaided recall and recognition were both measured via interview. In the content analysis portion of the study, the different program segments were coded for levels of four types of complexity —audio static, audio dynamic, video static, and video dynamic (see also Box 5.2). The result is the model in Figure 8.9, which indicates significant and nonsignificant links among variables. With such a rich model, there are many interpretive statements that could be made. For example, a significant negative relationship is shown between video dynamic complexity and recall; we can say that when controlling for other types of complexity, the more complex the video movement (e.g., fast editing, lots of motion in shots), the less the child can remember. This would support a hypothesis of "Video dynamic complexity will result in lower program segment recall for children, when controlling for other types of complexity."

The output examples presented in this chapter are not intended to be exhaustive—many other models exist. Some methods of presentation cannot be anticipated and are unique to the pieces of research. For example, in Figure 8.10, we may examine Whissell's (1996) construction of what she calls her "Emotion Clock," a descriptive application of emotional stylometrics. Based on norms established by 50 different text sources, a new message may be plot-

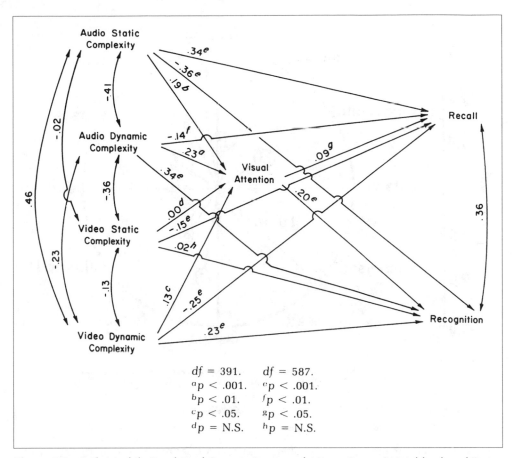

Figure 8.9. Path Model, Combined *Sesame Street* and *Mister Rogers' Neighborhood* Data
SOURCE: Reprinted with permission from Watt, James H. Jr., & Welch, Alicia J. (1983). Effects of static and dynamic complexity on children's attention and recall of televised instruction. In Jennings Bryant & Daniel R. Anderson (Eds.), *Children's understanding of television: Research on attention and comprehension* (pp. 69-102). New York: Academic Press.

ted by its ratings on two content analysis indexes, pleasantness (evaluation) and activation. In Figure 8.10, we see the results of Whissell's content analysis of 15 Beatles songs written by Lennon-McCartney. The 12 words around the perimeter of the "clock" aid in the interpretation of the songs' placements.

It should be clear by now that the range of options for the presentation of content analysis findings is as great as the range for presenting *any* quantitative findings. The content analyst needs to be as well versed in statistical methods and modes of presentation as any survey researcher or experimentalist.

Several practical guidelines could be summarized from the material in this chapter:

1. The researcher should be sure that results directly address hypotheses or research questions.

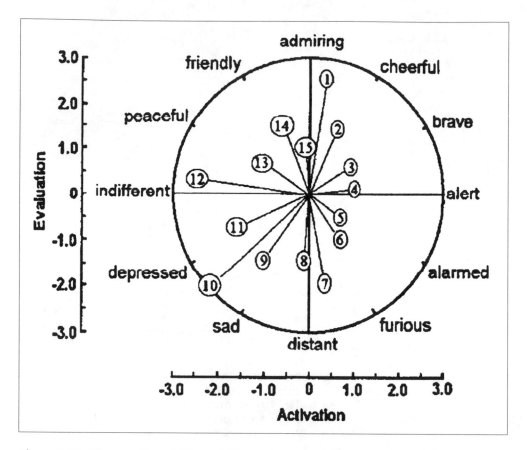

Figure 8.10. The Location of Fifteen Different Lennon-McCartney Songs on the Emotion Clock.

SOURCE: Whissell, Cynthia. (1996). Traditional and emotional stylometric analysis of the songs of Beatles Paul McCartney and John Lennon. *Computers and the Humanities, 30,* 257-265. Figure 2, copyright © 1996, *Computers and the Humanities,* with kind permission from Kluwer Academic Publishers.
Legend: 1. I'll Follow the Sun, 2. Getting Better, 3. Sgt. Pepper's Lonely Hearts Club Band, 4. Run For Your Life, 5. Not a Second Time, 6. We Can Work It Out, 7. Magical Mystery Tour, 8. Mean Mr. Mustard, 9. Yer Blues, 10. Nowhere Man, 11. For No One, 12. I'm Only Sleeping, 13. Another Girl, 14. Yellow Submarine, 15. Martha My Dear

2. Statistics should be selected that are appropriate to the levels of measurement, sampling method, and model to be tested.

3. Visual presentations may clarify and enhance purely statistical findings.

Notes

1. The .05 level indicates a Type I error of 5%; that is, there is a 5% chance of concluding that there is a relationship when in fact there is none.

2. Every quantitative researcher has his or her own preferred statistics texts. Based on many years of experience teaching research methods and statistics, I offer my own recommendations:

For univariate and bivariate statistics,
Kachigan, 1986; Voelker & Orton, 1993; Williams, 1992
For general coverage of multivariate statistics,
Hair, Anderson, Tatham, & Black, 1998; Kachigan, 1986
For multiple regression,
Cohen & Cohen, 1983
For discriminant analysis,
Klecka, 1980
For ANOVA/MANOVA techniques,
Bray & Maxwell, 1985; Keppel, 1991; Winer, 1971
For canonical correlation,
Thompson, 1984
For cluster analysis,
Aldenderfer & Blashfield, 1984
For multidimensional scaling,
Kruskal & Wish, 1978
For structural equation modeling,
Maruyama, 1998

3. Andrews, Klem, Davidson, O'Malley, and Rodgers (1981) present a highly useful, even more comprehensive programmatic guide for selecting appropriate statistics.

4. It should be noted that many multivariate tests that assume interval or ratio-level measurement also accommodate "dummy coding," a method of representing a nominal, categorical variable with zeros and ones, allowing the dummied variables to be treated as interval or ratio. For example, gender may be coded as 0 = male, 1 = female, and then the variable (a 0/1 measure of "femaleness") may be used in such analyses as multiple regression. A three-category variable would require two dummy variables to represent its information. For a more complete discussion, see Cohen and Cohen (1983).

5. The research questions and hypotheses presented are in most cases *hypothetical,* not those presented by the researchers. This is due to several reasons, most prominently the fact that the various results are presented here *out of context.* In addition, some research articles lack research questions, and others do not present an appropriate test of hypotheses.

6. Another mode of comparison sometimes used in content analyses of fictional media content is the contrast between the fictional and true-to-life worlds. For example, Gerbner et al. (1979) have used a "TV world/real world" comparison in their work on violent television. And Dixon and Linz (2000) found key differences between TV portrayals of perpetrators of crimes and real-world crime statistics.

7. Fairhurst et al. (1987) addressed five hypotheses and one research question in their article, using multiple regression and correlational analyses.

8. Although many of the content analyses that use time-series analysis study media content over time, the application of time-series methods to other message types is also to be found, as in Langs, Badalamenti, and Bryant's (1991) study of interactions in therapeutic consultations.

9. Notice that the researchers are linking their content analysis findings with noncontent analysis findings, voter turnout. This by-time linkage is what Chapter 3 would identify as a first-order link, with year as the linking unit of analysis.

10. As always, generalization is dependent on having a representative sample, typically a random sample.

11. Another striking example of correlational findings and graphical presentation may be found in Pettijohn and Tesser (1999), who conducted a content analysis of photographs of female film stars and then, in a first-order integrative link based on year as the unit of analysis, attempted to relate their measures to a noncontent analysis indicator, General Hard Times. First, based on the Annual Quigley Publications Poll, they identified the top American actresses from 1932 through 1995. Suitable photos for 57 of the 85 actresses were available, and they were coded for a variety of facialmetric assessments (from Cunningham's [1986] model of facial feature measurement). And they constructed their General Hard Times Measure as a standardized index of seven archival social and economic indicators, such as consumer price index and marriage rate. They identified seven statistically significant linear correlations between particular facial features and the Hard Times index across the 63-year period. They found that during hard economic and social times, actresses with thin cheeks, wide chins, and large chins are preferred, while actresses with large and high-placed eyes and prominent cheekbones are eschewed.

12. In *stepwise* regression, only the variables that contribute significantly to the prediction of the dependent measure are retained in the model.

13. The statistical procedure would also be an appropriate test of a hypothesis such as, "Form and content features will relate significantly to whether or not an ad is recalled."

CHAPTER 9

Contexts

T he intent of this chapter is to provide the reader with capsule descriptions of the status of research in many of the main areas of content analysis. The summaries are intended to hit the highlights of common applications and major trends and to refer the reader to optimal resources for learning about the use of content analysis in a variety of contexts.

The term *context* is used flexibly here. There are substantive contexts, such as the study of gender roles in human interaction and in the media. There are form contexts, such as the emerging research on the nature of the Internet. And there are ideological contexts, such as the semantic-network approach to the study of linguistics. These are all ways in which people have framed content analysis and therefore categories in which bodies of research have accumulated. Framing involves selection and salience and generally transcends the particular medium (Jeffres, 1997). That is, the context of minority images, for example, is composed of research in a variety of disciplines, looking at images in many different media.[1]

Generally, the frames or contexts presented in this chapter are scholarly, but the chapter also includes a section on known applied and commercial applications of content analysis. These are harder to find than one might think, due to the proprietary nature of much of the commercial work. Some of the contexts of study require a specialized knowledge base for the researcher—linguistic analyses, psychological diagnoses, and musicological analyses of melody, for example. The references given should point the reader in the right direction for learning more about such specialized bodies of knowledge. Taken together, the various sections of this chapter present a snapshot of the state of the art in content analysis today. In a final box, predictions for the future are presented.

Psychometric Applications of Content Analysis

The goal of some content analysis work is to discover psychological character-istics about the individuals or groups who created the messages. A typical sce-nario is one in which a social researcher wants to make attributions about[2] psy-chological traits or states from written or spoken messages created by a series of individuals. Obviously, consideration of both psychology and linguistics is involved. It's no wonder that the two areas are often linked in the content anal-ysis literature. When the goal is to measure these psychological characteristics, content analysis becomes a form of psychometrics (measures intended to tap internal, psychological constructs).

There are two main approaches to psychometric content analysis, both of which have been introduced in part elsewhere in this book: (a) thematic con-tent analysis and (b) clinical content analysis. The two approaches overlap somewhat (e.g., both have measures of personality and mood factors), and they also share characteristics with studies from the literatures on open-ended coding, linguistic analyses, semantic networks, and stylometrics, as reviewed in the discussion to follow.

Thematic Content Analysis

This type of content analysis attempts to measure psychological character-istics of individuals, generally for survey or experimental purposes. The mea-sures of the subjects' messages essentially stand in for other, alternative mea-sures, such as self-report scales and indexes. The definitive early work on the use of computers to conduct this type of content analysis is Stone et al.'s (1966) edited volume, *The General Inquirer: A Computer Approach to Con-tent Analysis.*[3] The essential contemporary source for this technique is *Motiva-tion and Personality: Handbook of Thematic Content Analysis* (Smith, 1992), a fascinating and highly inclusive volume presenting no fewer than 80 different content analysis measurement schemes. Although the inclusiveness of the work means that some newer measures might be less well validated than oth-ers, the book is invaluable.

From Smith's (1992) perspective, thematic content analysis is the scoring of messages for content, style, or both for the purpose of assessing the charac-teristics or experiences of persons, groups, or historical periods (p. 1). This purpose is different than the goal of clinical work, where the outcome is a diag-nosis of a psychological pathology. Here, the researcher is simply trying to measure person-based variables in an alternative fashion—without having the individuals fill out questionnaires. According to Smith, all the content analysis measures in the volume are oriented toward the use of previously validated in-dividual-differences measures of "particular person variables" (p. 4). For ex-ample, the book includes such adapted measures as

Fear of success	(Fleming)
Leadership	(Veroff)
Helplessness	(Peterson)
The Protestant ethic	(McClelland & Koestner)
Job satisfaction	(McAdams)
Responsibility	(Winter)
Self-definition	(Stewart)

Although impressive, the Smith compilation is not absolute. Newer and alternative schemes are available. Schneider et al. (1992) used their own thematic analysis scheme to analyze employees' descriptions of the service climate in their organization. Approaching the task from a more qualitative, semiotic (i.e., analysing the meaning of symbols) standpoint, Markel (1998) provides important bases for the in-depth study of speech as an indicator of emotions and attitudes. He presents both idiographic and nomothetic paradigms and, using the latter, has developed an application of a coding scheme for verbal utterances (from Soskin & John, 1963).

One well-used coding scheme for verbal samples (oral or written) is CAVE—content analysis of verbatim explanations (Peterson, Luborsky, & Seligman, 1983). Its goal is to assess each subject's causal attributions, measuring whether they tend to find explanations for events that are internal versus external, stable versus unstable, and global versus specific (Peterson et al., 1988; Schulman et al., 1989). A related coding method is for pessimistic rumination, a measure of the frequency and intensity of pessimistic attributions, emotions, and events (Satterfield, 1998; Zullow, 1991).

Criteria-based content analysis, part of statement validity assessment, is most often used to establish the truth of children's allegations of sexual abuse (Tully, 1998). The technique looks for key criteria that would indicate lying (e.g., certain references, attributions, and expressed motivations; Horowitz et al., 1997). This application has attracted critics who claim that its validity has not yet been established (e.g., Shearer, 1999).

Clinical Applications

Perhaps beginning with Freud's notion of "symptomatic texts" (Christie, 1999), psychologists and psychiatrists have been interested in tapping the inner workings of the troubled mind in an unobtrusive fashion, particularly by analyzing messages generated by that mind. With the diagnosis of psychological problems a goal, some researchers and clinicians have worked to develop appropriate content analytic techniques.

Lee and Peterson (1997) note that content analysis may be more than just an alternative to clinical diagnosis procedures, that in fact it may have advantages because it follows the scientific method:

What makes content analysis more than just a clinical impression from text is the explicit specification by the researcher of the rules used to make inferences. Content analysis requires that the researcher obtain suitable material, develop a coding protocol, and ascertain the reliability and validity of actual coding. In this sense, content analysis is no different in principle from other research methods. (p. 960)

Probably the most published analyst with regard to the clinical application of psychological content analysis is Louis Gottschalk, who diagnosed Unabomber Ted Kaczynski as "not mentally impaired" based on the text of his manifesto ("Assessing cognitive impairment," 1999) and President Reagan as experiencing a "significant increase" in cognitive impairment between the 1980 and 1984 presidential debates (although he held the release of the findings until 1987; "Acclaimed neuroscientist pledges," 1997). Gottschalk's (1995) book, *Content Analysis of Verbal Behavior: New Findings and Clinical Applications,* is a comprehensive source of information on the use and validation of the 20 measurement schemes he and his colleagues developed first for human coding and, later, for computer coding. The Gottschalk-Gleser Scales include measures for anxiety, hostility, cognitive impairment, depression, hope, sociality, narcissism, achievement strivings, and positive affect.

Enthusiasm for Gottschalk's approach is tempered by Lee and Peterson (1997), who indicate skepticism toward Gottschalk and others using similar so-called microscopic approaches (i.e., Gottschalk uses the grammatical clause as his unit of data collection). They present as an alternative Luborsky's (1996) much more macroscopic approach, analyzing therapy transcripts before and after the onset of a symptom.

Open-Ended Written and Pictorial Responses

Both human and computer coding may be applied to the analysis of open-ended responses (Mohler & Zuell, in press). In either case, there are two types of approaches to coding individuals' written and pictorial responses to questions and stimulus materials. One approach uses any of a variety of *pre-set coding* (a priori) schemes. When the goal is the measurement of psychological constructs, it essentially follows the thematic content analysis procedures described earlier (perhaps the only difference is that the measures in this section are typically applied to communicative responses to *specific* questions or tasks rather than analyses of fairly generic or naturally occurring speech or writing). The second approach uses *emergent coding* of the content, in which a coding scheme is established after all responses are collected; then, systematic content analysis is conducted applying this scheme to the responses, with appropriate reliability assessment.

Some of the earliest devised and still popular pre-set open-ended coding applications are for thematic apperceptive measures (the best known is the TAT, or Thematic Apperception Test) and inkblot tests (such as the Rorschach). Thematic apperceptive measures require individuals to respond by making up stories to go along with a standard set of pictures representing personal and interpersonal situations. Pre-set coding options include measures of need achievement, need affiliation, and need power (Chusmir, 1985). Inkblot tests ask the subjects to report what they see in each of a series of symmetrical, abstract inkblots. The responses may be scored with standard classifications for location (which portions of the blots are used), determinants (the form, or structural, characteristics commented on), and content (the substance of what is seen, such as animal or human referents). Additional coding options have been proposed, such as Urist's application of a mutuality-of-autonomy measure (measuring perceived psychological autonomy of others; Urist, 1977; Urist & Shill, 1982).

Both types of measures were originally devised as projective tools for psychoanalysis, and some critics maintain that they cannot meet the standards of psychometric measurement; rather, they maintain, the techniques are idiographic and provide stimuli that will drive the clinical psychoanalytical process between analyst and subject (Aronow, Reznikoff, & Moreland, 1994; Gregory, 1987; Te'eni, 1998).

Focusing on *drawings* rather than written responses to questions, the Human Figure Drawing literature in psychology seeks to use evaluations of drawings as psychological diagnostic tests (Koppitz, 1984). Similarly, the Goodenough-Harris Drawing Test is a psychographic technique for assessing the intellectual maturity of young people (Harris & Pinder, 1974). Others have used pre-set coding schemes to categorize drawings. Stiles, Gibbons, and Schnellmann (1987) used a standard 10-variable coding scheme to establish significant gender differences between ninth-graders' drawings of the "ideal man" and the "ideal woman." And DiCarlo, Gibbons, Kaminsky, Wright, and Stiles (2000), studying street children in Honduras, found both age and gender differences for an adapted "ideal person" coding scheme.

The second approach to open-ended responses, that of emergent coding, obviously uses coding schemes that are more idiosyncratic and less well validated but in many instances may be the required technique. When no useful standard classification or coding scheme exists, or when the researcher wishes to begin the development of a new scheme, the emergent option is employed. Crawford and Gressley (1991) faced just such a situation in their study of humor preferences and practices for men and women. Their study participants were asked to write a paragraph about a specific individual with an "outstanding sense of humor" (p. 222). Respondents' answers were transcribed and examined by the researchers, who discerned five theme dimensions: hostility, jokes, real-life humor, creativity, and caring. These five were used as separate variables, and each original written narrative was coded for the presence or absence of each. A high level of intercoder agreement was reached.

An alternative to the researchers' inspection and derivation of the five dimensions would be for volunteers, blind to the purpose of the research, to derive the dimensions. All unique responses could be typed on cards, and then volunteers could each perform a card sort,[4] placing the cards in the smallest number of piles possible, based on perceived similarity. The patterns emerging from different volunteers would be compared, and important commonalities used to create the dimensions that would be used for final coding of the open-ended responses.

Linguistics and Semantic Networks

Linguistics is the study of the structure and nature of human speech. There is a range of emphases, from the structural, "form-al," study of syntax to the more semantically focused study of language meaning (Markel, 1998). The latter overlaps with other areas of message study, particularly thematic content analysis for psychographic purposes.

Quantitative content analysis is only one of many approaches used in linguistics. Many cross-language comparisons and searches for universal characteristics of languages (Goldberg, 1981) use qualitative participant observation, critical methodologies, or both. However, with computer advances, there has been a growing interest in quantitative linguistics (Kohler & Rieger, 1993), particularly in computational linguistics (Litkowski, 1992, 1999), and the general study of semantic grammars (systems that codify statements' unique meanings-as-intended as opposed to surface-level, superficial, ambiguous syntax grammars; Roberts, 1997a).

Although technically a part of linguistics, the study of messages using semantic networks has its own distinct literature and adherents. An ultimate goal of this approach is to map the network of interrelationships among concepts. Carley (1993) has contrasted the typical use of text content analysis (focusing on the extraction of concepts from texts) with the use of semantic networks (or map analysis, focusing on both concepts and the relationships among them). Dictionaries may (or may not) be used for semantic network content analysis; the goal is to discover patterns of co-occurrence of words or phrases in a text. Often, these patterns are displayed via 2-D or 3-D maps (e.g., using such programs as MECA or CATPAC; see Figure 8.8 for an example of a graphical display of a semantic network), in a method similar to that of multidimensional scaling (Barnett & Woelfel, 1988; Kruskal & Wish, 1978; Woelfel & Fink, 1980).

Like neural networks that represent cognitive structures and processes, semantic networks represent systems of concepts with "meaning-full" relationships (Litkowski, 1999). These relationships are based on word usage by individuals, groups, organizations, or societies (Carley, 1997a; Doerfel & Barnett, 1999). As Carley (1997b) notes, "Language can be represented as a network of concepts and the relationships among them. This network can be thought of as the social structure of language or, equivalently, the representation of extant social knowledge" (p. 79).

Mapping semantic networks from the content analysis of speech or text might have had conceptual appeal for decades; however, it's only in recent years that computer processing power and speed have made the various networking procedures viable and widely accessible (Young, 1996). And the Internet has made text archives (corpora) available for the execution of both specialized and standard-usage language studies (see Resource 1 for examples).

Stylometrics and Computer Literary Analysis

Stylometrics refers to the analysis of the *style* of language. The technique is used to identify a language style that is distinctive, with the aim of describing, distinguishing, and sometimes establishing authorship. Tweedie, Singh, and Holmes (1996) define style as "a set of measurable patterns which may be unique to an author" (p. 401), including the identification of the number of nouns or other parts of speech used, the number of unique words, and the most common words. As with semantic mapping, these sophisticated quantitative linguistic analyses have been made possible by advances in computer text analysis software and the ready availability of texts in electronic form.

Stylometrics is most commonly used in literary studies. One popular application has been to attempt to establish the authorship of texts or settle disputes about authorship. Shakespeare has received much attention, due to questions surrounding the true authorship of works bearing his name. Elliott and Valenza (1996) helped to develop more than 50 computer tests to compare writings attributed to Shakespeare to the writings of Shakespeare claimants—"nobler" authors who could have conceivably been the real Shakespeare. They compared textual features, such as preferred words, rare words, new words, grade level, contractions, intensifiers, prefixes, and suffixes, and concluded that *none* of the claimants matched Shakespeare. Another related application of stylometrics has been to *compare* the styles of authors. Sigelman and Jacoby (1996), for example, used computer analysis techniques to distinguish the works of mystery writer Raymond Chandler from his imitators, based on four main stylistic elements: simplicity, action, dialogue, and vivid language. They found Chandler's work to be consistent in style and concluded that the imitators failed to successfully replicate that style. Potter (1991) offers a fairly comprehensive review and critique of stylometric and other content analyses of literature appearing in the journal *Computers and the Humanities* from 1966 through 1990.

In addition to its applications to literature, stylometrics has also been used in other humanities contexts. Whissell (1996) employed traditional stylometric procedures along with new measures of emotionality to compare the songs of Beatles members Paul McCartney and John Lennon, discovering that Lennon was the less pleasant and sadder lyricist of the two. In a bizarre but intriguing application of stylometrics, Bucklow (1998) analyzed craquelure (the pattern of cracks that forms on paintings as they age) as a means of establishing authorship of works of art.

In sum, computers give literary, linguistic, and other scholars the opportunity to shed fresh light on the formal and stylistic features of important works. As mentioned, electronic versions of texts are now more common and accessible than ever. Project Gutenberg, for example, is a free, online electronic archive of important works of fiction (see Resource 1 for more information). Even more works will be available in the future: The Text Encoding Initiative project, for one, seeks to develop standards for the preparation and interchange of computer text for scholarly research purposes (Ide & Sperberg-McQueen, 1995). With the continued growth and development of archives and computer text analysis sources, the future possibilities for the content analysis of literature and other works should be extraordinary.

Interaction Analysis

The systematic analysis of human verbal interactions is a small but important part of the content analysis literature. Most studies of interactive discourse are *not* content analyses but rather more qualitative and ideographic in nature. However, a number of quantitative coding schemes have been developed. Notably, these schemes are typically called *interaction analysis* in the literature rather than *content analysis*.

In the communication field, the most prominent system is Rogers and Farace's (1975) relational coding scheme. Owing a debt to the theoretic notions of anthropologist Gregory Bateson (1958) and to earlier classification systems, such as those by Bales (1950), Borke (1967, 1969), and Mark (1971), the Rogers and Farace (1975) scheme takes a relational communication perspective: It is concerned with the *control* or dominance aspects of message exchange in dyads. Each utterance in a verbal exchange is the unit of data collection. The scheme assumes that relational control is based on both the grammatical form of the message (the codes are *assertion, question, talk-over, noncomplete,* and *other*) and the metacommunicative response of the message relative to the statement that came before it (the codes are *support, nonsupport, extension, answer, order, disconfirmation, topic change, initiation-termination,* and *other*). These codes are used to create control codes (*one-up, one-down,* and *one-across*), indicating movement by a speaker with regard to relational control.

The Rogers and Farace (1975) scheme has been used to analyze interactions between husbands and wives (Courtright, Millar, & Rogers-Millar, 1979; Rogers-Millar & Millar, 1978), employees and employers (Fairhurst et al., 1987), physicians and patients (Cecil, 1998; O'Hair, 1989), and parents and children (Seklemian, as cited in Cecil, 1998). An adapted system has even been applied to television character interactions (Greenberg & Neuendorf, 1980; Neuendorf & Abelman, 1987).[5]

The validity of the Rogers and Farace (1975) scheme has been questioned (Folger & Poole, 1982), and alternative schemes for the analysis of verbal interactions have been presented. They include Ellis's (1979) RELCOM system, which uses more control categories than the Rogers and Farace (1975) scheme but does not measure grammatical form. Others are Tracey and Ray's (1984) topic-based coding scheme and Patterson's (1982) Family Interaction Coding Scheme, designed specifically to tap aversive interactions in families with an antisocial child. The SYMLOG system for analyzing group interactions has many elements that are similar to quantitative content analysis, but ultimately, the measures rely on observers' subjective evaluations rather than objective, reliable estimates (Bales & Cohen, 1979).

MacWhinney's (1996) CHILDES project (the Child Language Data Exchange System; see also the CHILDES archive, linked at *The Content Analysis Guidebook Online*), dedicated to the study of language learning, includes CHAT, a system for discourse notation and coding. This scheme calls for the separate coding of each utterance for phonology, speech acts, speech errors, morphology, and syntax. The Roter Interaction Analysis System (Roter, Lipkin, & Dorsgaard, 1991), designed for the coding of interactions between doctors and patients, codes each statement or complete thought into one of 34 categories (e.g., agreement, worry, procedural instructions, persuasive attempts regarding therapeutic regimen). The Marital Interaction Coding System (Heyman, Weiss, & Eddy, 1995) and the Dyadic Parent-Child Interaction Coding System (Eyberg & Robinson, 1983) are both designed to analyze family interactions for family therapy purposes.

A number of other interaction analysis schemes have been proposed (see Gunawardena, Lowe, & Anderson, 1997; Hirokawa, 1988; Jones, Gallois, Callan, & Barker, 1999; Tardy, 1988; Witt, 1990). Generally, the coding schemes have been applied to specific domains of interaction, such as group decision making, negotiation, family communication, and classroom interaction, with measures designed to provide in-depth understanding of the nuances of communication within a given context.[6]

Other Interpersonal Behaviors

Similarly, a number of rigorous and sound coding schemes have been developed for the systematic analysis of other interpersonal communication behaviors, not generally applied to a representative sample of realistic interactions but used for measuring actions in experimental settings. In addition, the coding of human behaviors in the study of psychological processes might also be deemed content analytic, and that literature can inform us with regard to unitizing and intercoder reliability (Bakeman, 2000).

The study of nonverbal behaviors has produced primarily qualitative, idiographic, and gestalt-type investigations. However, taxonomies (category schemes) for the study of nonverbals are quite well developed (Ekman & Rosenberg, 1997; Messing & Campbell, 1999). And some researchers have used systematic and objective coding schemes looking at paralanguage (e.g., speech rate: Beaumont, 1995; Feyereisen & Harvard, 1999; Kelly & Conture, 1992), body positioning (e.g., Newtson, Engquist, & Bois, 1977), facial expressions (Lagerspetz, Wahlroos, & Wendelin, 1978), and gestures (e.g., Feyereisen & Harvard, 1999; Guerrero & Burgoon, 1996; see also the *Journal of Nonverbal Behavior*). A number of studies have looked at nonverbal behaviors for such mediated persons as characters in commercials aimed at children (Browne, 1998), candidates in political commercials (Hacker & Swan, 1992), televangelists (Neuendorf & Abelman, 1986), and the film roles of a durable screen actress (Ealy, 1991).

Self-disclosure, the sharing of personal information with another, has been studied, with age and gender differences a main focus. Although the evidence on age is mixed (Capwell, 1997; Collins & Gould, 1994), the evidence with regard to gender seems clear—women are more likely to disclose than are men, especially when discussing intimate topics (Cozby, 1973; Hacker, 1981; Shaffer, Pegalis, & Cornell, 1991).

Interrupting behaviors have been studied by a number of content analysts. Researchers have found conversation interruptions to occur more often when one is speaking to someone of the opposite sex rather than someone of one's own sex (Dindia, 1987) and to be more frequently committed by adolescent girls than their mothers (Beaumont, 1995). The long-held belief that males interrupt more than do females has been refuted by a number of contemporary studies (e.g., Dindia, 1987; Marche & Peterson, 1993).

Violence in the Media

When we try to explain content analysis to a layperson, we often fall back on the example of television violence: "You know, those studies that find more aggressive acts on Saturday morning cartoons than anywhere else . . . " (i.e., between 20 and 25 violent acts per hour; Jeffres, 1997). This is the application of content analysis that has received the most public attention, from the early Payne Fund Studies of motion pictures and youth in the 1930s (Dale, 1935), through the flurry of attention to aggressive TV content and its effects on children in the 1960s and 1970s (Lange et al., 1969; Comstock & Rubinstein, 1969), to current ongoing efforts to track the level of violence on TV (*National Television Violence Study* (Vol. 1), 1997). Hundreds of studies have examined some aspect of violent or aggressive behavior in media content or its effects on adult and child audiences. Chapter 2 highlights several of the major initiatives that not only addressed the problem of violence in American society but also contributed in meaningful ways to the repertoire of content analysis methods (Gerbner, Signorielli, & Morgan, 1995; Greenberg, 1980).

The research on violent media content may be seen as progressing from raw number counts (Dale, 1935) to a consideration of a variety of types of aggressive behavior, including verbal aggression (Lange et al., 1969; Greenberg, 1980, who found about half of all aggressive behaviors to be verbal) to an extension to cable and other new content delivery systems as well as broadcasting and a careful consideration of the context of the aggression (Kunkel et al., 1995, Potter & Ware, 1987).[7] As Kunkel et al. (1995) point out, industry executives argue that "the meaning and impact of violence in a film such as *Schindler's List* is quite different from that of *Terminator II*" (p. 285). Their multiyear content analysis includes such contextual variables as the nature of the perpetrator and of the target (e.g., human vs. animal, gender, age, ethnicity, "good" vs. "bad"), the reasons for the violence (e.g., personal gain, anger, retaliation), the means or method of violence (e.g., firearms, so-called natural means), the extent of the violence (how many behavioral acts in a violent interaction), the graphicness of the violence (e.g., presence of blood and gore, long shot vs. close-up), the realism of the violence (fantasy, fiction, reality), rewards and punishments associated with the violence, consequences of the violence (amount of harm), and presence or absence of humor in the violent scene.

The recent findings by the National Television Violence Study (1997) group indicate the highest level of violence to be on premium cable and independent broadcast channels and in movies and reality-based programs. The vast majority of violence is not punished at the time of the act, and "good" characters engaging in violence are rarely punished at all. About half of all violent interactions do not show harm or pain to the target, and a quarter include the use of a gun. Blood and gore are rarely shown on television, and 39% of all violent scenes contain humor (p. 137).

More detailed reviews of the many past content analyses of violent media content may be found in several good sources: the 1995 article by Kunkel et al.; a report by that same group in the first volume of the *National Television Violence Study* (1997); and John Murray's (1998) call for a more applied research agenda for the 21st century.

Gender Roles

Perhaps no substantive area has been more frequently studied across all the mass media than that of the roles of males and females. A limited number of content analyses have looked at gender role behaviors among real people—comparing males and females with regard to dreams, memories, perceptions of the world, interrupting behaviors, and explanatory style, for example (Barrett & Lally, 1999; Buchanan & Seligman, 1995; Domhoff, 1999; Greener & Crick, 1999; Lance, 1998; Marche & Peterson, 1993). This leaves the many media-focused content analyses with relatively few bases for real-world comparisons.

An amazing variety of media form and content types have been examined for their gender role portrayals. Studies have compared male and female roles and behaviors for domestic or international content in television, film, news coverage, magazines, radio talk, textbooks, children's books, advertising of all types, comics, video games, software, rock and roll music, music videos, slasher films, birth congratulatory cards, and even postage stamps. Generally, the findings confirm a message environment of androcentrism (i.e., with males heavily overrepresented in sheer numbers and routinely given more important roles) and sex stereotyping (i.e., with significant and often predictable differences between male and female characterizations; Barner, 1999; Chappell, 1996; Drewniany, 1996; Greenberg, 1980; Kalis & Neuendorf, 1989; Lemish & Tidhar, 1999; Low & Sherrard, 1999; Michelson, 1996; Ogletree, Merritt, & Roberts, 1994; Watkins, 1996; Weaver, 1991). Busby's (1975) review of female images is an excellent, comprehensive source but in need of an update.[8] More recent studies continue to find sex stereotyping. When compared to females, males are characterized as more active on birth cards (Bridges, 1993), less argumentative on radio talk shows (Brinson & Winn, 1997), less likely to be portrayed as sex objects in video games (Dietz, 1998), and older in films of the 1930s, 1940s, and 1990s (Smith, 1999), for example. However, Signorielli and Bacue (1999) found some changes in occupational depictions for women from the 1960s through the 1990s. Extending their examination beyond content alone (using an integrative approach), Lauzen, Dozier, and Hicks (2001) found involvement of female TV executives and creative personnel to be predictive of the use of powerful language patterns by female characters.

One very particular application of gender-based content analysis has been the examination of face-ism, the tendency of a photo to reveal more of the subject's face or head than body. Associated with audience perceptions of dominance and positive affect (Levesque & Lowe, 1999; Zuckerman, 1986), higher face-ism has been generally granted to males over females in the mass media (Copeland, 1989; Sparks & Fehlner, 1986).

Recent attention has focused on body image (weight and shape) as a potentially strong influence on young female audience members (Botta, 2000). Research has found low-weight female characters to be overrepresented and highly praised by other characters on television situation comedies (Fouts & Burggraf, 1999).

Minority Portrayals

A sizeable amount of research has been devoted to the systematic content analysis of the images of racial and ethnic minorities in the media. *The Howard*

Journal of Communications is a prominent outlet for research on racial differences in both real-life communication behaviors and mediated portrayals. Also, a large number of unpublished theses and dissertations have focused on U.S. racial and ethnic minority images as their focus.

Some investigations have done comparative analyses of media images of several racial groups (e.g., Dixon & Linz, 2000; Taylor, Lee, & Stern, 1996; Taylor & Stern, 1997). Of those studies focusing on a single minority group, the vast majority have examined African American portrayals, and they include several important reports and volumes that provide an excellent first look at some of the landmark content analyses in this area (Dates & Barlow, 1990; MacDonald, 1992; Poindexter & Stroman, 1981; Stroman, Merritt, & Matabane, 1989-1990; U.S. Commission on Civil Rights, 1977, 1979). Prior to 1970, images of Black Americans emphasized domestic and submissive roles (MacDonald, 1992). Even as gains were made in entertainment television portrayals (e.g., *The Cosby Show*), news images still emphasized a menacing African American criminal element (Atkin & Fife, 1993-1994; Barber & Gandy, 1990; Dates & Barlow, 1990; Dixon & Linz, 2000; Entman, 1992). Contemporary content analyses tend to find that advertising and entertainment images of African Americans do not underrepresent Blacks in terms of numbers but still present relatively homogenous, stereotypical role portrayals (e.g., Keenan, 1996b; Matabane & Merritt, 1996; Plous & Neptune, 1997; Wilkes & Valencia, 1989).

Few studies have examined the status of Hispanics, Asian Americans, or Native Americans in entertainment, commercial, or news media content (e.g., Greenberg, Burgoon, Burgoon, & Korzenny, 1983; Singer, 1982, 1997; Wilkes & Valencia, 1989). The evidence that exists points toward underrepresentation and stereotypical portrayals, even when those portrayals are generally positive (e.g., the Asian American as the hard-working model minority; Taylor & Stern, 1997).

Like the research on women's roles in the media, studies on racial or ethnic minorities encompass a variety of media, including textbooks, news coverage, magazines, pornography, reality-based crime shows, direct mail advertising, and jokes (Cowan & Campbell, 1994; Oliver, 1994; Spencer, 1989; Stevenson & Swayne, 1999).

Advertising

There are two divergent approaches to the content analysis of advertising—the marketing-advertising professional approach and the social effects approach. The professional approach seeks to understand the content and form of advertising in order to produce more effective ads (e.g., Gagnard & Morris, 1988; James & VandenBergh, 1990; Naccarato & Neuendorf, 1998; Stewart & Furse, 1986; also see Boxes 3.2 and 3.3). Articles demonstrating this approach are likely to be found in such journals as *Journal of Advertising, Journal of Advertising Research,* and *Journal of Marketing.*

The social effects approach is motivated by concern over the impact of advertising on individuals and societies. A number of prominent areas of study have emerged. The role of women in advertising has received quite a bit of attention (e.g., Riffe, Place, & Mayo, 1993; Signorielli et al.; Smith, 1994), including a 15-year trend analysis of the role of women in TV ads (Ferrante, Haynes, & Kingsley, 1988). International comparisons of advertising styles and substance have been an important part of the literature (e.g., Cheng & Schweitzer, 1996; Murray & Murray, 1996; Tak, Kaid, & Lee, 1997; Wongthongsri, 1993). The analysis of minorities in advertising (e.g., Taylor & Bang, 1997), the tracking of advertising for potentially hazardous products, such as tobacco and alcohol (e.g., Finn & Strickland, 1982; Lee & Callcott, 1994; Neuendorf, 1985, 1990a), and the critical examination of political advertising, notably negative ads (e.g., Tak, Kaid, & Lee, 1997), have all continued to be viable areas of study.

A special focus has been on advertising aimed at children, from the exclusive viewpoint of the social effects scholar (e.g., Smith, 1994). For example, Rajecki et al. (1994) found a number of attractive but dubious themes in TV ads for food for kids—64% of the sample ads included some combination of violence, conflict, and trickery.

News

A tremendous number of studies have examined news content, with most using text analysis, either human coded or, more often today, CATA (Riffe et al. 1998; Shoemaker & Reese, 1996). The availability of news stories online from NEXIS (see Resource 2) has spurred the expansion of work in this area. A major outlet for content analyses of news coverage is *Journalism & Mass Communication Quarterly.*

The range of topics studied is large, overlapping with other context headings in this chapter, such as the treatment of minorities and women. The coverage of science issues is a popular topic (Dunwoody & Peters, 1992), with an eye to establishing whether scientific findings are reported accurately. There are scores of studies tracking international news flow, generally finding that developing nations are well supplied with information about Western nations, whereas Western nations find little in their news about the rest of the world (Chang, 1998; Stevenson, 1994). In a study of general news and social trends in the United States, Danielson and Lasorsa (1997) studied 100 years of front-page content in the *New York Times* and the *Los Angeles Times,* identifying such shifts as a decrease in emphasis on the individual and an increase in emphasis on the group and a move away from religion and local governmental power to expert authority and central government (p. 114).

Some of the most sophisticated analyses in content analysis have been executed with a news focus. The news framing approach, used by Miller, Andsager, and others (Andsager & Powers, 1999; Miller et al., 1998; Miller & Riechert, in press), clusters concepts according to how often the concepts occur together and then places the concepts in a three-dimensional map to allow interpretation of the frames used to cover the issue by different sources. For example, Andsager and Powers (1999) found that *Newsweek* framed breast cancer stories with regard to causes and treatments, whereas *Time* more often used an economic framing (e.g., insurance concepts), and *U.S. News and World Report* presented breast cancer news with a research focus (also see Figure 8.7). Fan's ideodynamic mathematical model (Fan, 1988, 1997; Fan, Brosius, & Esser, in press) has proved useful in accurately predicting public opinions over time from news coverage patterns. Notably, many of these advances in the analysis of news coverage have extended to legal, governmental, and commercial applications (Fan & Bengston, 1997).

Perhaps the best-developed literature examining news coverage is that focused on political issues. This is developed a bit farther in the next section.

Political Communication

Chapter 2 delineated the important early contributions to content analysis methodology by researchers in the political arena (e.g., Lasswell et al., 1949). Systematic studies continue to be conducted on politicians' speeches, debates, news releases, and even Web sites (Kaid & Bystrom, 1999; Laver & Garry, 2000; Musso, Weare, & Hale, 2000; Owen, Davis, & Strickler, 1999). Other content analyses have looked at the communication strategies of reform candidates and parties (Gibson & Ward, 1998; Jenkins, 1999; Ziblatt, 1998). An increasing number have examined news coverage and political advertising in a range of countries around the world.

News coverage of political issues has often been studied from the agenda-setting perspective. This theoretic perspective proposes that media content doesn't so much tell the audience *what* to think as it tells the audience what to think *about*. The news sets the public opinion agenda, bringing some issues to the forefront and minimizing others. This theory has motivated researchers to combine content analyses with public opinion survey data, either at the aggregate level (e.g., Fan, 1997; McCombs, Llamas, Lopez-Escobar, & Rey, 1997; Pfau et al., 1998) or the individual level (e.g., Roessler, 1999). Some studies have also examined so-called intermedia agenda setting, in which news coverage by one medium or media institution is followed by similar coverage by another medium or institution at a later date (Lopez-Escobar, Llamas, McCombs, & Lennon, 1998; Roberts & McCombs, 1994). Generally, the bulk of the evidence supports a news-media-stimulated agenda-setting effect.

A major focus of the content analyses of political advertising has been that of negative, or "attack," ads (Kaid & Bystrom, 1999). Motivated by effects research that has shown both negative and positive shifts in opinions toward the negative ad target as a result of exposure (Haddock & Zanna, 1997; Lin, 1996; Merritt, 1984; Schenck-Hamlin, Procter, & Rumsey, 2000), content analyses have looked at the frequency of the appearance of negative political ads (Finkel & Geer, 1998) as well as the news coverage of the controversial ads (Kaid, Tedesco, & McKinnon, 1996).

Web Analyses

The Internet emerged in the 1990s as an important new source of mediated messages. Shortly thereafter, the World Wide Web combined characteristics of existing media (e.g., print, audio, video) with a number of new critical attributes, including hypertextuality and interactivity (Newhagen & Rafaeli, 1996). This complex mix of old and new features has made the medium a challenge for would-be content analysts. McMillan (1999) reviewed 16 of the first studies that attempted to content analyze messages on the Internet. She discovered a lack of a clear unit of measurement across studies (perhaps due to the medium's many content forms) and little information about coder training and reliability. Potter (1999) addressed the difficulty of sampling from the Web, given its size and "chaotic design structure" (p. 12). He suggested using lists generated for commercial purposes (e.g., Yahoo and Web 21) as sampling frames. Clearly, the complexity of the Web can be overcome through creativity backed by careful adherence to sound content analytic principles.

Examples of sound Web content analyses include Ghose and Dou (1998), who identified a nearly exhaustive list of interactivity variables and used them to code business sites as to level of interactivity, and Bucy, Lang, Potter, and Grabe's (1999) study of the formal features of 496 Web sites, which showed significant relationships between site traffic and page structure. The latter study points to the potential of using Web content analysis as part of an integrative content analysis model along with source or receiver data or both (in this case, unobtrusive measures obtained from reports of the number of visitors or "hits" for each site).

One exciting prospect for Web content analysis comes from the development of automated computer site analysis programs. Bauer and Scharl (2000) describe their use of a program called WebAnalyzer, which parses a site's HTML code and computes frequency information about a host of site features, including the number of images and external links. Because many Web sites contain thousands of pages (which would be difficult to human code), computer content analysis techniques will allow researchers to analyze whole sites instead of the often-cited home page unit of analysis (e.g., Bates & Lu, 1997; Ha & James, 1998). A number of computer Web text analysis programs are currently in development (one by M. Mark Miller and another by Harald

Klein, the creators of the computer text analysis programs VBPro and TextQuest, respectively; see *The Content Analysis Guidebook Online*). Future automated programs may have to incorporate audio and video analysis functions (instead of simply text) to fully deal with the rich media mix on the Web.

The Web gives researchers a world of content (currently, millions of sites and many more pages). This sheer enormity can be overwhelming, but it can also be exciting, especially to the careful, well-prepared content analyst. For example, there are currently many underexplored or unexplored novel genres of Web content, ranging from personal home pages to online auctions. These all deserve attention, given the promise of expanding online communication. The Web is "the new kid on the block" who content analysts should definitely try to get to know.

Other Applied Contexts

There are many other, less-well-established contexts or framings that could be considered. For the sake of presenting a variety of applications, a few examples are highlighted:

Electronic Messaging: A small set of literature reports the studies of the substance of e-mail, voice mail, and other personal and organizational technologies. Just a few studies have examined the content of voice mail (e.g., Rice & Danowski, 1991) and computer conferencing (e.g., Rosenbaum & Snyder, 1991). A greater number of studies have looked at e-mail content generated in educational and business contexts (Danowski & Edison-Swift, 1985; Hill, Camden, & Clair, 1988; Kot, 1999; Marttunen, 1997; McCormick & McCormick, 1992). Generally, these e-mail studies have identified social support communication networks that link together individuals based on interests rather than physical location, sometimes creating links and relationships that did not exist before the introduction of e-mail. They have also identified communication strategies used in e-mail that are different than those used in face-to-face interaction (e.g., Pratt, Wiseman, Cody, & Wendt, 1999).

Health Images in the Media: Increasingly, media treatments of health topics have come under the scrutiny of content analysts, both academic and private sector. The studies that examine body image as a method of better understanding eating disorders, especially among young girls, have already been mentioned. So has the sizeable literature on the advertising of health-hazardous substances, such as alcohol and tobacco. An impressive current initiative by the Kaiser Foundation examines the health-related sexual behaviors of TV characters (see the sections that follow). Other research has focused on images of mental illness (e.g., Fruth & Padderud, 1985), the incidence of substance use and abuse (Greenberg, Fernandez-Collado, Graef, Korzenny, & Atkin, 1980; Roberts & Christenson, 2000), images of persons with disabilities (Gilbert, MacCauley, & Smale, 1997), and portrayals of health professionals (e.g., Gerbner, Morgan, & Signorielli, 1982). Neuendorf (1990b) provides a review of health-related content analyses through 1990.

Music: The lyrics of popular songs have been the subject of content analyses over the years (e.g., Rothbaum & Tsang, 1998; Rothbaum & Xu, 1995; Zullow, 1991), as indicators of societal trends and for cross-cultural comparisons. Less often, the nature of the music itself has been content analyzed (e.g., Narmour, 1996; Simonton, 1994). But the greatest number of investigations relevant to popular music have been content analyses of music videos, generally addressing a concern over violent and sexist images (e.g., Baxter, de Riemer, Landini, Leslie, & Singletary, 1985; Jones, 1997; Kalis & Neuendorf, 1989; Sherman & Dominick, 1986).

Commercial and Other Client-Based Applications of Content Analysis

As the popularity of content analysis as an academic research tool has grown, there has been a corresponding developing interest in applying content analysis to business and other real-world issues. These include instances of the public-sector and private-sector funding of content analysis research conducted by academics, the strictly-for-hire content analysis work of academic researchers, and the use of content analysis by private institutions.

Both Lindenmann (1983) and Stone (1997) report numerous examples of public relations, advertising, marketing, and public opinion polling firms that include content analysis as one of the services they offer to clients. And Lindenmann describes the in-house research efforts of AT&T, which in the 1970s began a program of content analysis of newspaper coverage of the corporation to gauge PR effectiveness.

Unfortunately, many of the purely commercial applications of content analysis are proprietary and unavailable for us to learn from.[9] There *is* anecdotal evidence that commercial content analysis studies do not routinely follow the good-science guidelines presented in this book. Industry standards, such as those established for polling by the American Association for Public Opinion Research, are not yet in place. There is a need for the establishment of self-monitoring standards for commercial content analysis, and these should include a call for open reportage of methods.

Funded Research Conducted by Academics

Sponsorship of academically conducted content analysis research by governmental, nonprofit, or for-profit granting agencies may be regarded as a form of client-based research. Certainly, the funding organization typically has explicit goals for the content analysis research. The early, groundbreaking Payne Fund Studies of movie content and effects would be a good example of this type of research. Sponsored by a grant from The Payne Fund and motivated by the Motion Picture Research Council's concern over the effects popular movies were having on the youth of America, the project included research initiatives by researchers at seven universities, including the primary content analysis group at Ohio State University (see Box 2.2). The following are some additional examples of projects executed at universities but with real-world goals of discovery motivating the granting agencies:

Project CASTLE (Children and Social Television Learning): Funded in the 1970s by the U.S. Office of Child Development of the Department of Health, Education, and Welfare, this Michigan State University project looked at the content and effects of television viewed by children and included a set of large-scale, 3-year content analyses of entertainment television. The results were disseminated in government reports and published in book form (Greenberg, 1980).

The Content and Effects of Alcohol Advertising: Funded in the 1970s by the U.S. Bureau of Alcohol, Tobacco, and Firearms, the multipronged Michigan State study included content analyses of alcohol advertising in a variety of media. The results were published in government reports and a number of academic outlets (e.g., Atkin et al., 1983).

RIB (Religion in Broadcasting): Funded in the 1980s by UNDA-USA, a nonprofit organization of Roman Catholic broadcasters, the Cleveland State University project encompassed six major content analyses of religious television broadcasting. The results were made public through client reports and academic publications (see Box 1.3).

The National Television Violence Study: Funded in the 1990s by the National Cable Television Association, this large-scale project continues to look at violence in cable and television programming. Executed by researchers at four United States universities (University of California at Santa Barbara, University of Texas at Austin, University of Wisconsin at Madison, and University of North Carolina at Chapel Hill), the project's results are published by Sage Publications (e.g., *National Television Violence Study,* Volume 1, 1997). Roberts (1998), in a discussion of media content labeling systems (i.e., rating systems), summarizes the real-world implications of the findings that examined the contexts of violent portrayals:

> The contextual factors characteristic of much . . . U.S. television programming are just those that *increase* the likelihood of negative consequences among youthful viewers. Indeed, the results of the NTVS content analysis read like a primer on how *not* to produce programming for children. (p. 359)

Sex on TV: Funded in the 1990s by the Kaiser Foundation, the ongoing project at the University of California, Santa Barbara, looks at the frequency and type of sexual behavior on television, with particular interest in the responsibilities and health risks associated with sex. The results of the studies are published online (e.g., Kunkel et al., 1999; Kunkel et al., 2001).

Commercial Applications of Text Analysis

Text analysis procedures are attractive to commercial clients. Both thematic (Stone, 1997) and linguistic (Camden & Verba, 1986) content analyses of recordings or transcripts of focus groups have been conducted by advertising, marketing, and public opinion firms. The text content analysis of news coverage is another popular application. For example, Stone (1997) describes the subscriber service, Trend Report, developed by Naisbitt (1984) to follow news reportage of national trends (it also formed the basis for Naisbitt's best-selling *Megatrends*). Commercial research projects have tracked news coverage for legal cases in which a change of venue may need to be requested (McCarty, 2001).[10] Fan and Bengston's (1997) use of the InfoTrend computer text analysis program to track the amount and tone of news coverage for the U.S. Forest Service is another example.

Obviously, psychological diagnostic content analysis techniques are often used by practitioners in a commercial context. For a fee, a client can even get a computer text diagnosis online, from text sent via e-mail (see the Psychological Testing section of *The Content Analysis Guidebook Online*). The CATPAC semantic network computer program has been used extensively for consulting purposes (Salisbury, in press). Unable to share the details of these proprietary studies, Salisbury provides a demonstration of CATPAC's use in assessing corporate image in a study of Visa International's external communication. In his analysis of the most salient terminology in the message pool, he identified two major areas: a product development area (attempting to convey an image of Visa as a "state of the art" banking provider) and a state-of-the-business area (identifying Visa as the world's largest banking services provider).

Content Analysis for Standards and Practices

In some cases, content analysis is used by media institutions for self-monitoring their own messages. Basic readability measures are used to set and check writing standards by newspapers, magazines, and wire services (Danielson et al., 1992; Severin & Tankard, 1997). And in a rare disclosure of the inner workings of a broadcast network's standards and practices department, Wurtzel and Lometti (1984) described the then-current ICAF system at ABC. This system involved human coding of their own prime-time programming—with careful coder training and true reliability checks—to identify and categorize violent acts. Violence was tracked over time, norms were established for different types of programming, and significant deviations were therefore identifiable.

Applied Web Analyses

The hot new area in real-world content analysis is the emerging trend of offering automatic analyses of Web sites. Although some of these Web-based services analyze only the technical parameters of Web sites and the servers where they are resident (e.g., Webperf, from the Standard Performance Evaluation Corporation; TPC-W, from the Transaction Processing Performance Council), others have begun to analyze the message form and content with a diagnostic eye. In essence, both Web search engines and Web filtering devices are basic commercial Web content analysis protocols. Probably the most comprehensive analysis system is the Web Site Garage, which offers a "free one page tune up" that includes a load time check, a dead-link check, a spell check, an HTML check, an analysis of browser compatibility, a link popularity check, and an optimization of images ("GIF Lube"). A not-for-profit analysis service with a much more specific goal, "Bobby" analyzes Web pages for their accessibility to people with disabilities. And PICS is a system of labeling Web content with metadata that can be used to screen Web sites for objectionable content. Bauer and Scharl (2000) is the current definitive source for further information about these new analysis systems. (Also see *The Content Analysis Guidebook Online* for current links to such service sites.)

Future Directions

West (in press) concludes his edited volume with 10 predictions for the immediate future of CATA, including growing roles for artificial intelligence, automated data screening, applications of computer analysis to nontext-nondata messages, and warehoused large-scale data archives. His predictions are well backed by data and other evidence. Going beyond this, I engage in a flight of fancy in Box 9.1, extrapolating from current technological developments to predict the future. I've always wanted to be a futurist, and this is my chance.

This is not to mean that I endorse the predictions in Box 9.1. Quite the contrary. The changes in the world's information order and the advancing technologies that support the changes are actually both humbling and frightening. If there is one message for the future that I hope readers will take with them, it would be a recommendation for higher, and more widely accepted, *standards* for the execution of content analysis, both academic and commercial. This includes a call for full reportage of methods, for purposes of replicability and comparative analyses. Only through full disclosure and healthy debate can we fully understand the implications of our proliferating methods and tools for message analysis.

Box 9.1   Content Analysis in the Year 2100

Based on current advances in content analysis methodologies and in media tech-nologies, we might be able to estimate where content analysis might be in about a hundred years. These are just my predictions; I could be wrong.

In the year 2100, content analyses that are most concerned with describing the source will engage in real-time, cumulative analyses of every individual's and every media source's messages and behaviors. Any message that someone wants to keep private will have to be heavily encrypted. All messages will be archived and indexed automatically. There will be few text messages; the future equivalents of cameras will be everywhere. Individuals will have personal recorders following their every move. Whether this will be achieved via anatomically embedded chips, satellite surveillance, or an "Internet 12" with expanded capability is hard to gauge at this time. As digital visual recordings are made, metadata tags will automatically attach to the stream of information.

With psychological diagnoses already available online in the year 2000 and current e-mail generated or received at work the property of the employer, are unobtrusive diagnoses far away? In the year 2100, each individual's psychological states and moods will be followed in time-series fashion.

For receiver-based content analyses, those concerned with the effects of messages, there will be individualized, not aggregated, analyses. Each individual's precise commu-nication exposure patterns will be documented, and the content of the interpersonal and mass messages he or she receives will be automatically computer content analyzed. Computers will not only know how to read text and watch TV, they'll also know how to listen to music and interpret visual imagery.

This predicted world of an automated "Big Sibling" approaches M.I.T. scientist Ed Fredkin's notion of reality as composed of information and the universe as a giant data processor (Wright, 1988). In this universe of information, there will be no such thing as sampling and inferential statistics. All information will be kept and analyzed. It will be an all-census, longitudinal data world.

In 2100, will the content analysis of thoughts and dreams be the cutting edge? With the human genome completely mapped, cognition might be the next uncharted scien-tific territory, one for which content analysis may be uniquely suited.

Notes

1. See Chapter 5 for a consideration of the challenges of medium-specific analyses.

2. A reminder that although this book does not endorse the use of unbacked, in-validated inference from message to source, the literature on psychological measure-ment using content analysis has a strong history of validation studies. "Make attribu-tions about," as used here, means to make conclusions about a message source after comparisons with standards established over many investigations.

3. See also Philip Stone's update and recommendations for future directions in Roberts's (1997b) edited book on text analysis.

4. This is a variation on the Q-sort, a time-honored method for dealing with disparate responses (Selltiz, Jahoda, Deutsch, & Cook, 1967; Vogt, 1993).

5. The final coding scheme, which owes much to the influence of Bales (1950), Borke (1969), and Greenberg (1980), is available at *The Content Analysis Guidebook Online*.

6. As a result of this context specificity and the fact that such coding schemes have been applied most often to small, nonrandom samples of interactants, often in artificially induced interactions, no generic, noncontextual body of evidence of how people naturally interact with one another has been developed. This has caused consternation for media researchers who have tried to compare, for example, human interaction in the TV world and a real-world standard (e.g., Greenberg, 1980).

7. Although Kunkel et al. (1995) claim that context has been largely ignored by the Gerbner research group, an early content analysis codebook devised by Gerbner and found in Lange et al.'s (1969) report includes many context variables, including use of firearms, consequences of the violence to source and receiver, use of humor, and a wider array of source and receiver characteristics than those used by Kunkel et al. in the *National Television Violence Study* (1997).

8. However, the reader is referred to the journal, *Sex Roles,* for its many articles on the portrayals of women in media.

9. In fact, both the author and Resource author Paul Skalski have been involved in a number of commercial content analyses—none of which they are at liberty to discuss.

10. As a result of the precedent-setting Sam Sheppard murder trial, excessively negative pretrial publicity may be legal cause for a change of venue (i.e., location for the trial) when it is deemed impossible to find an unbiased jury capable of rendering a fair verdict.

Message Archives
Paul D. Skalski

Listed in this Resource are some popular and interesting message archives, arranged according to message type, with a brief description of the content available from each. For a more complete list of archives and additional information, check out *The Content Analysis Guidebook Online*, located at **http://academic.csuohio.edu/kneuendorf/content.** Links to online indexes, databases, and archives/corpora are also provided.

General Collections

LEXIS-NEXIS: This online, searchable database includes full-text archives of most popular newspapers and magazines, plus court materials, financial and market reports, legislative materials, and transcripts. For more on LEXIS-NEXIS, see Resource 2.

National Archives and Records Administration: This collection includes billions of textual materials from the three branches of the federal government, nearly 300,000 reels of motion picture film, more than 200,000 sound and video recordings, and nearly 14 million still pictures and posters. Some materials are available online.

Mass Communication History Collection at Wisconsin: This collection holds the papers of hundreds of important individuals, corporations, and professional organizations in the fields of journalism, broadcasting, advertising, and public relations.

Popular Culture Library at Bowling Green State University: This collection includes popular fiction (e.g., in the mystery-detective, science fiction-fantasy, and historical fiction genres) as well as materials documenting the performing arts and the entertainment industry, graphic arts, recreation and leisure, and popular religion.

Film, Television, and Radio Archives

American Archives of the Factual Film at Iowa State University: These archives collect 16 mm, nontheatrical business, educational, and documentary films, including 4,500 educational films shown in classrooms and 1,000 government-produced films.

American Archive of Broadcasting: This archive collects manuscripts and personal papers of television and radio personalities and more than 20,000 radio and television scripts.

Annenberg Television Script Archive: This collection includes more than 29,000 television scripts, including the TV Guide Collection and ABC Soap Opera Collection.

Archives of Labor and Urban Affairs: These archives collect and preserve records of the American labor movement, with special emphasis on industrial unionism and related social, economic, and political organizations in the United States and also historical records related to urban affairs.

bfi Collections (The British Film Institute National Film and Television Archive): These collections include animated, avant garde, and gay and lesbian works, plus documentaries, early and silent films, and materials related to film and television, such as stills, posters, and designs.

CNN World Report Television Archive (Texas Tech University): This archive collects all episodes of the weekend CNN World Report television program.

Drew's Script-O-Rama: This collection contains full-text screenplays from motion pictures. The screenplays can be downloaded for free in electronic text form.

George Eastman House Motion Picture Collection: This collection contains more than 17,000 films produced from 1894 to present, including a silent film collection, the MGM Studio Collection, shorts, documentaries, and newsreels.

Human Studies Film Archives: These archives include a broad range of ethnographic and anthropological moving image materials and also related documentation including audio tapes, stills, manuscripts and other associated texts, field notes, camera and sound logs, and production logs.

Library of Congress Motion Picture, Broadcasting and Recorded Sound Division: This collection includes films produced from 1918 to 1955 for Black audiences, cartoons produced by Warner Brothers before 1949, and a large collection of works shot by anthropologist Margaret Mead, plus the NBC Television Collection of more than 18,000 programs aired from 1948 to 1977 and also 30,000 videotapes of PBS shows.

Television News Archive (Vanderbilt University): This archive has all network news broadcasts from 1968 to the present plus more than 9,000 hours of special news-related programming, such as coverage of special national and international events. Indexes and abstracts are available online.

UCLA Film and Television Archive: This archive contains 220,000 films, 27 million feet of newsreel footage, and television programs, including the ABC Collection of nearly all prime time programs airing on the network from the 1950s to the 1970s and nearly 10,000 TV commercials dating from 1948 to the 1980s.

USC Cinema Television Library and Archives of the Performing Arts: These archives include books and periodicals on all aspects of film and television, along with clipping files, recorded interviews, scripts, stills, pressbooks, scrapbooks, video cassettes, and discs of feature films, as well as audiotapes.

Literary and General Corpora

Corpus Linguistics: This online source has a list of links to sites with corpora, including literary corpora and transcripts and samples of ordinary spoken language representing a variety of dialects and eras.

Project Gutenberg: This collection archives thousands of free electronic texts, ranging from light literature (e.g., the Sherlock Holmes and Tarzan books) to more serious works (e.g., The Bible, works of Shakespeare, Poe, and Dante) to reference works (e.g., Roget's Thesaurus, various almanacs).

Other Archives

The Political Communication Center (University of Oklahoma): This collection contains more than 56,000 radio and television commercials representing candidates running for offices from the U. S. Presidency all the way down to school boards, commercials by political action committees, ads sponsored by corporations and special interest groups on public issues, and commercials done for foreign elections.

Murray Research Center: This center collects data extracted from many types of subjects through a variety of research methods. Also included in the archive are videotaped data of over 1,200 hours of human interaction plus some audiotaped data.

Using NEXIS for Text Acquisition for Content Analysis

In the 1960s, the Ohio State Bar Association (OSBA) wanted to build a centralized computer database containing the case law of Ohio and other states. They contracted with a small Ohio company, Data Corporation, to build this system, but before the project got underway, Data Corporation was purchased by the Mead Corporation, a large manufacturer of paper and printing products headquartered in Dayton, Ohio. At first unaware of the OSBA contract, Mead eventually rose to the challenge, establishing a special division for the development of the project, Mead Data Central. Its creation, the LEXIS legal database, contained case law of only two states (Ohio and New York), federal case law, and federal statutes, on its debut in 1973 (Emanuel, 1997).

By the time Mead sold the system to Reed Elsevier Inc. in 1994, it had developed perhaps the most comprehensive and well-constructed message archive on earth. To the legal holdings (LEXIS), they added news sources (NEXIS). With 10,200 different databases, the bundle of services adds nearly 15 million documents each week. There are approximately 2.5 billion documents online. All databases are "full text searchable," meaning that the user may specify any word or string of characters, and due to the unique organizing patterns of the system, all documents containing that string will be located almost instantly. The selected documents may be downloaded in their entireties and saved in text format, compatible with virtually all word-processing programs. (See *The Content Analysis Guidebook Online* for current information and links.)

Today, the NEXIS side of the system includes all stories from most major and many minor newspapers, many magazines and trade journals, transcripts of TV and cable news programs, and transcripts of radio news (e.g., from NPR and BBC). The LEXIS-NEXIS services are not—nor were they ever—intended to meet the needs of a content analyst. It is only by virtue of its extensive and systematic database storage, search, and download capabilities that NEXIS has unintentionally become a vital resource for media content analysts.

The content analysis user should be wary of LEXIS-NEXIS Academic Universe, what some call "LEXIS-NEXIS Lite," a partial application of the services that is widely available at public and nonlaw college libraries. This abbreviated version is insufficient for content analysis research, in that the user cannot always control precisely which publications are being searched, many of the publications available on the full LEXIS-NEXIS system are not included in this limited database, and articles may not be downloaded and may be printed only one at a time (Quinn, 2000).

The full LEXIS-NEXIS bundle of services is expensive and not available at all libraries. The user may need to acquire access through a law school, law firm, or other business that subscribes to the service. When access is acquired, the user will probably have access to some type of manual or documentation. However, these reference sources are generally oriented to the legal user rather than the scientific user. Thus, the user will find no reference to random sampling, sampling frames, or any other scientific terminology.

With that in mind, here are some tips for the content analyst using NEXIS.

- The user should acquaint himself or herself with all the NEXIS holdings by exploring all the "source" databases online (click on each "I" button for "information"). New publications are added to the databases regularly, so published lists are likely to be inaccurate.

- The user should be cautious about using grouped sources, such as "News Group File" or "Major Newspapers" for any longitudinal (over-time) study, because of the changing lists of included publications. For example, practically *any* search on a given topic from 1990 to 2000 will show exponential growth in the number of articles—due to added publications, rather than heavier news coverage.

- By clicking the "By Individual Publication" folder and then the "I" button for an individual publication, the user may view a "Source Information" page that includes valuable background information about the publication and the methods of NEXIS annotation for an article from that publication. The Source Information page often includes a Sample Document from that publication. It is important that the Source Information page also includes the date of first NEXIS coverage for that publication. Which leads us to . . .

- It's surprising how late some publications were to join the NEXIS database. Even some major newspapers were slow to switch to computer technologies allowing digital uploads to the NEXIS databases. For example, the *Cleveland Plain Dealer* went online with NEXIS on November 1, 1992, so no stories prior to that date are in the NEXIS system. When planning a study, the user should check the "Coverage" information on each publication's Source Information page, to determine the earliest coverage date.

- Instead of having to deal with the shifting sands of the grouped sources, the content analyst will probably prefer to search specified individual publications or a set of combined sources that he or she selects. However, there are some serious limitations to the process of combining sources, such as the requirement in the typical Web interface (vs. the alternative dial-up interface) that combined files all be on the Web page the user is currently viewing (which is usually a list of publications beginning with the same letter of the alphabet).

- The selection of publications available in the NEXIS databases is rather unpredictable (e.g., it has *Entertainment Weekly* but not *TV Guide*). It seems somewhat biased toward U.S. sources (except for international wire services, the international sources are spotty) and business publications and, in general interest magazines, away from publications aimed at special audiences, some of which may be of interest to a content analyst. For example, most of the traditional women's magazines are not included—*Ladies Home Journal, Women's Day, Good Housekeeping*. Nor is the popular publication of the AARP, *Modern Maturity*. However, NEXIS does cover some amazingly specialized trade publications, such as *Beverage World, Coal Week*, and *Ice Cream Reporter*.

- For searching, LEXIS-NEXIS uses *Boolean searching*, a relatively common system of logical operators. The user should consult an in-depth source for more details (e.g., Emanuel, 1997), but the following examples provide some of the basics of Boolean searching for LEXIS-NEXIS:

The command	*will find any article containing*
cat AND *dog*	both *cat* and *dog* in it
cat OR *dog*	*cat* alone, *dog* alone, or both *cat* and *dog* in it
cat AND NOT *dog*	*cat* in it, but not *dog*
cat W/S *dog*	*cat* within the same sentence as *dog*
cat W/P *dog*	*cat* within the same paragraph as *dog*
cat W/N 5 *dog*	*cat* within 5 words either direction of *dog*
cat PRE/N 5 *dog*	*cat* within the 5 words preceding *dog*

The system uses two types of wild-card characters: ! for multiple unspecified characters and * for a single unspecified character. For example,

The command	will find any article containing
electrocut!	any word that begins with "electrocut," including "electrocute," "electrocution," and "electrocutions"
electrocut*	any word that begins with "electrocut" and has only one more character, including "electrocute," but not including "electrocution" or "electrocutions"

Of course, the user may string Boolean language together to formulate complex search commands. The order of operation is such that all ORs are executed first, then all other commands in the order they appear. The use of parentheses can change the order in which connectors operate. For example,

The command	will find any article containing
execut! OR electrocut! OR (capital W/N 3 punishment) OR death penalty	any word that begins with "execut," any word that begins with "electrocut," any phrase in which the words "capital" and "punishment" appear within 3 words of one another (e.g., "capital punishment"), or the precise phrase "death penalty"

- In addition to Boolean searching for text strings, LEXIS-NEXIS also allows searches by author, dateline, and, depending on the publication, a variety of other segments. For example, in the *New York Times,* 40 different searchable segments are available, such as organization, person, state, industry, length of article, and geographic location. The user is also able to restrict the search to certain dates or ranges of dates.

- The search protocol has some idiosyncracies to be aware of: It treats singular and plural forms of a word as the same, which is not always desirable from a scientific standpoint (e.g., a search for the sports team the "Browns" will also find every use of the word *brown*). There are a number of automatic equivalents (e.g., "18th" and "eighteenth" are treated as the same thing). It does not recognize hyphenated words. And there are certain common usage "noise words" that cannot be searched for (e.g., *who, then*).

- The Boolean search language must be *precisely* what the researcher wants (a good validity check, actually). A slight difference in the search wording can make a big difference in the results. For example, a search of the *Cleveland Plain Dealer* for the years 1992 through 2000 for "Taiwan's presidential election" netted 6 hits, while the similar "Taiwan AND presidential election" netted 69 hits.

- Each search is limited to 1,000 hits. This often requires multiple searches segmented by years. (This limitation does not apply to the dial-up interface.)

- Each download is limited to 200 articles, which can make the downloading process quite tedious. In addition, if the user is downloading to floppy disk, he or she should be aware that there is no notification given if the disk fills before all 200 articles are downloaded.

- Once a search is complete, the user may obtain a cite list, which lists and numbers all the hits, giving each article's title, date, and publication. At this point, the user may download *all* entries on the cite list or may sample by typing in the numbers of the desired articles. Thus, the user may engage in systematic random sampling (e.g., downloading articles 3, 13, 23, 33, etc.) or SRS (using random numbers from a table to select, e.g., downloading articles 32,17, 06, 29, 51, etc.).

- The articles *must* be screened for relevance. Even the best-designed search criteria will result in some nonsensical hits. For example, in a search for stories about the Cleveland Browns football team, the search term "browns" generated a fair number of "hits" that were obituaries for people named Brown, stories about food (e.g., "hash browns"), and nature and garden stories (e.g., "the autumn golds and browns").

- And of course, before submitting the text to a computer text content analysis program, each story needs to be cleaned up, by deleting header, footers, and other annotations not part of the original story as it appeared in the publication. The user should be aware that *photos* are not part of the NEXIS databases, although cutlines for the photos are.

Computer Content Analysis Software

Paul D. Skalski

This appendix provides information about quantitative computer text analysis software. Table R3.1 lists quantitative text analysis programs and highlights key features of each. Additional information about each program is included in Part I, which follows. This list owes much to the work of Popping (1997), Evans (1996), Alexa and Zuell (1999), and numerous Web site authors who have previously compiled lists of quantitative text analysis software. Part II of this Resource focuses on one basic text analysis software program, VBPro.

Although Table R3.1 contains a sample of some of the best programs currently available, it is not comprehensive; for an exhaustive list of quantitative text analysis programs, we recommend visiting Harald Klein's text analysis resources page, which can be accessed through *The Content Analysis Guidebook Online*. This companion site to the book also contains a more up-to-date list of programs, including qualitative and audio and video content analysis programs and links to the program Web sites whenever possible. The site can be accessed at the following URL: **http://academic.csuohio.edu/kneuendorf/ content**.

Part I. Quantitative Computer Text Analysis Programs

The programs listed in Table R3.1 were identified in a search of published sources and Web sites. The table presents the following information about each program (numbers correspond to table columns, from left):

Table R3.1 Computer Text Analysis Software

Program	Operating System	Freeware	Demo[a]	Cases Analyzed	Frequency Output	Alphabetical Output	Multiunit Output	KWIC or Concordance	Standard Dictionary	Custom Dictionary	Special Analyses
CATPAC	Windows	No	No	Single	Yes	Yes	No	No	No	Yes	Yes
CPTA	DOS	NS	No	NS	Yes	Yes	NS	Yes	NS	NS	Yes
Concordance 2.0	Windows	No	Yes	Multiple	Yes	Yes	No	Yes	No	No	No
Diction 5.0	Windows	No	Yes	Multiple	Yes	Yes	Yes	No	Yes	Yes	Yes
DIMAP-3	Windows	No	Yes	Multiple	Yes	Yes	Yes	Yes	Yes	Yes	Yes
Gen. Inquirer	Internet	Yes	NA	Single	Yes	No	No	No	Yes	No	No
INTEXT 4.1	DOS	No	Yes	Multiple	Yes	Yes	NS	Yes	No	Yes	No
Lexa	DOS	NS	Yes	Multiple	Yes	NS	NS	NS	NS	NS	Yes
LIWC	Windows and Mac.	No	No	Multiple	No	No	NS	No	Yes	Yes	No
MCCAlite	Windows	No	Yes	Multiple	Yes	Yes	Yes	Yes	Yes	No	Yes
MECA	DOS	NS	No	Multiple	No	No	No	No	No	Yes	Yes
PCAD 2000	Windows	No	No	Multiple	No	No	Yes	No	Yes	No	Yes
SALT	Windows and Mac.	No	Yes	Single	Yes	Yes	Yes	No	Yes	Yes	No
SWIFT 3.0	DOS	Yes	NA	Multiple	Yes	Yes	NS	Yes	No	Yes	Yes
TextAnalyst	Windows	No	Yes	NS	No	No	NS	No	No	Yes	Yes
TEXTPACK 7.0	Windows	No	Yes	Multiple	Yes	Yes	Yes	Yes	No	Yes	Yes
TextQuest 1.05	Windows	No	Yes	Multiple	Yes	Yes	NS	Yes	No	Yes	No
TextSmart	Windows	No	No	Multiple	Yes	Yes	NS	Yes	No	Yes	Yes
VBPro	DOS	Yes	NA	Multiple	Yes	Yes	Yes	Yes	No	Yes	Yes
WordStat 3.03	Windows	No	Yes	Multiple	Yes	Yes	Yes	Yes	No	Yes	Yes

a. Some demos allow for program testing with any user-provided data, whereas others allow testing using only data provided by the authors.
NS = not specified; NA = not applicable.

1. Program name

2. Operating system

3. Freeware (yes or no)

4. Demo availability (yes or no)

5. Cases analyzed at once (single or multiple)

The table also indicates (yes or no) whether the programs can perform the following common text analysis functions:

6. Frequency list

7. Alphabetical list

8. Multi-unit data file output (in case-by-variable form)

9. Key word in context (KWIC) or concordance

10. Coding with a built-in (standard) dictionary

11. Coding with a user-created (custom) dictionary

12. Specialty analyses

The functions are explained in the VBPro section to follow. An elaboration on each column in Table R3.1 can be found in Chapter 6.

The annotated list to follow provides a capsule description for each program listed in Table R3.1. The list contains (a) the name of the program, (b) a brief description, and (c) at least one published reference (if available), either reporting on the program or about research in which the program was used. Following the reference(s), the designation **"Web site"** indicates that there is a program Web site from which additional information can be obtained; visit *The Content Analysis Guidebook Online* for a link to the site.

A research team also evaluated several of the programs from Table R3.1. The results of our tests, along with sample output from each program, can also be viewed at *The Content Analysis Guidebook Online*.

The VBPro program receives special attention in this Resource for several reasons. First, it performs all key computer text analysis functions, making it a good vehicle through which to explain the typical process and principal functions of a computer text analysis. Second, the program is available free online. If you are a beginner to computer text analysis, we recommend trying VBPro first to get a feel for the technique. Our step-by-step guide in Part II of this Resource is designed to make the process of using VBPro as simple as possible.

VBPro

Description: VBPro outputs frequency and alphabetical word lists, key words in context (KWIC), and coded strings of word-occurrence data based on user-defined dictionaries. In addition, it includes a multidimensional concept-mapping sub-program called VBMap that measures the degree to which words co-occur in a text or series of texts. Miller, Andsager and Riechert (1998) used the program to compare the press releases sent by 1996 GOP presidential candidates to the coverage the candidates received in the press. The program helped the researchers (a) generate a list of key words appearing in the text and (b) generate a map showing the relative positions of candidates, in both press releases and media coverage, to each other and on key issues in the election (e.g., family values, education). The program runs under DOS and is available for free from the software author's Web site.

Criteria From Table

Unit of Analysis: VBPro can analyze sentences, paragraphs or cases. Users can combine all of their text into a single text file to simplify the analysis process.

Frequency and Alphabetical Output: Alphabetical output includes the name of the word and frequency of occurrence (e.g., *conservative, 12*). Word frequency output (listed from most frequent to least occurring) includes the word name, number of occurrences, and percentage of tokens (or total words) that the word represents (e.g., *liberal, 11, 0.750*).The frequency command also produces a type/token frequency and ratio and the occurrence rates of tokens.

Multi-Unit Data File Output: Refers to grid-like frequency output suitable for import into a statistical analysis package (e.g., SPSS), typically with case or unit numbers on the vertical axis and dictionary terms on the horizontal, as in this partial example.

	Dictionary Counts by Term			
Case	*Liberal*	*Political*	*Blame*	*Other*
1	5	12	3	—
2	2	5	4	—
and so on . . .	—	—	—	—

Through the CODE command, VBPro can give multiunit data file output, displaying frequency information about each dictionary category for each case (e.g., each news story in a text file of 100 stories).

KWIC or Concordance: KWIC can be generated through the SEARCH function of VBPro. Each time a dictionary term occurs, the entire unit of analysis (e.g., sentence) will appear in the SEARCH output with the key word designated by marks (e.g., . . . due to the leftist principles of . . .). After the KWIC analyses, the SEARCH command outputs summary information, including number of cases, sentences, and paragraphs containing the dictionary terms.

Coding With Dictionary: Once a dictionary is prepared, the VBPro CODE command can code a text file based on the dictionary terms. This type of coding is done on a case-by-case basis within a single text file. The comma-delimited text output file from CODE can then be imported into a statistics program (e.g., SPSS) for further analysis.

Specialty Analyses: VBPro can also perform concept mapping through a subprogram called VBMap (see earlier "Description" section and Chapter 6 for more information).

Developer: M. Mark Miller

References: Dyer (1994a, 1994b); Dyer, Miller, and Boone (1991); Miller et al. (1992); Miller et al. (1998); Miller and Denham (1994); Web site

CATPAC

Description: CATPAC reads text files and produces a variety of outputs ranging from simple diagnostics (e.g., word and alphabetical frequencies) to a summary of the main ideas in a text. It uncovers patterns of word usage and performs analyses such as simple word counts, cluster analysis (with icicle plots), and interactive neural cluster analysis. A nifty add-on program, called Thought View, can generate two and three-dimensional concept maps based on the results of CATPAC analyses. One especially neat feature of Thought View allows users to look at the results through 3-D glasses and experience MDS-style output like never before!

Developer: Joseph Woelfel

References: Doerfel and Barnett (1999), Salisbury (in press); Web site

Computer Programs for Text Analysis

Description: This is not a single computer program but rather a series of separate programs. Each performs one or two basic functions, including analyzing appearances of characters in a play (ACTORS program), getting KWIC (CONCORD program), computing the amount of quotation in texts (DIALOG program), and comparing the vocabulary of two texts (IDENT program). The programs seem ideal for literary-type analyses.

Developer: Eric Johnson

Reference: Web site

Concordance 2.0

Description: This program allows users to make concordances on texts of any size. Program functions include (a) making one concordance from multiple input files; (b) sorting output according to length, frequency, alphabetical listing, and other criteria; and (c) making Web concordances, which allow users (and Web surfers) to point to a word in an online text and retrieve concordance information instantly, through the magic of hypertextuality. A demo of Web concordances can be found on the program Web site.

Developer: R. J. C. Watt

Reference: Web site

In addition to the Concordance, several other programs are available, primarily for KWIC analyses, such as MonoConc and ParaConc. Information on these programs can be found at *The Content Analysis Guidebook Online.*

Diction 5.0

Description: Diction 5.0 contains a series of built-in dictionaries that search text documents for five main semantic features (activity, optimism, certainty, realism and commonality) and 35 subfeatures (including tenacity, blame, ambivalence, motion, and communication). After the user's text is analyzed, Diction compares the results for each of the 40 dictionary categories to a provided normal range of scores established by running more than 20,000 texts through the program. Users can compare their text to either a general normative profile of all 20,000-plus texts or to any of six specific subcategories of texts (business, daily life, entertainment, journalism, literature, politics, and scholarship) that can be further divided into 36 distinct types (e.g., financial reports, computer chat lines, music lyrics, newspaper editorials, novels and short stories, political debates, social science scholarship). In addition, Diction outputs raw frequencies (in alphabetical order), percentages, and standardized scores; custom dictionaries can be created for additional analyses.

Developer: Roderick P. Hart

References: Hart (1985, 2000a); Hart and Jarvis (1997); Web site

DIMAP-3

Description: DIMAP stands for DIctionary MAintenance Programs, and its primary purpose is text content analysis dictionary development. The program includes a variety of tools for lexicon building rooted in computational linguistics and natural language processing (Litkowski, 1992). With DIMAP, users can build, manage, edit, maintain, search, and compare custom and established dictionaries. The program also includes a text analysis module called MCCA (the "lite" version of which is described later), providing printing of output, additional co-occurrence analyses, and multidimensional scaling of matrices measuring the distance of texts. A new version of the program, DIMAP-4, is now available in a beta version.

Developer: Ken Litkowski

References: Litkowski (1978); Litkowski (1992); Web site

General Inquirer (Internet version)

Description: This venerable, still widely used program has found new life on the World Wide Web. The online version of the General Inquirer gets our vote for the simplest and quickest way to do a small-scale computer text analysis—simply visit the Internet General Inquirer site, type or paste some text into a box, click "submit," and your text will be analyzed. The Internet General Inquirer codes and classifies text using the Harvard IV-4 dictionary, which assesses such features as valence, Osgood's three semantic dimensions, language reflecting particular institutions, emotion-laden words, cognitive orientation, and more. The program also returns cumulative statistics (e.g., simple frequencies for words appearing in the text) at the end of each analysis. A stand-alone computer-based version of the program, which can process multiple cases, is now available free to academics and nonprofit organizations. See the program Web site for more information.

Developers: Phillip J. Stone, The Gallup Organization, and Vanja Buvac (Web version)

References: Kelly and Stone (1975); Stone et al. (1966); Web site

INTEXT 4.1

Description: INTEXT is a program designed for the analysis of texts in the humanities and the social sciences. It performs content analysis, text analysis, indexing, concordance, KWIC, KWOC (key word out of context), readability analysis, personality structure analysis, word lists, word sequence, word permutation, stylistics, and more. The content analysis module allows interactive coding and can handle ambiguous or negated search patterns. In dictionaries, search patterns can be single words, phrases, or co-occurences.

Developer: Harald Klein

References: Klein (1991); Web site

Lexa (Version 7)

Description: Designed with linguists in mind, Lexa Corpus Processing Software is a suite of programs for tagging, lemmatization, providing type/token frequency counts, and conducting several other forms of computer text analysis.

Developer: Raymond Hickey

Reference: Web site

LIWC (Lingustic Inquiry and Word Count)

Description: LIWC was developed for researchers interested in emotional, cognitive, social, or other psychological processes. Using internal dictionaries, the program analyzes individual or multiple text samples along 72 dimensions, including psychological constructs (e.g, affect and cognition), personal-concern categories (e.g, work, home, and leisure activities), and standard linguistic dimensions (e.g., percentages of pronouns and articles). The various dictionaries have good psychometric properties. LIWC can also analyze up to 100 dimensions with custom dictionaries. Individual files can be automatically divided and analyzed in units set by the user.

Developers: James W. Pennebaker and Martha E. Francis

References: Gunsch, Brownlow, Haynes, and Mabe (2000); Pennebaker and Francis (1999); Pennebaker, Francis, and Booth (2001); Web site

MCCALite

Description: Though somewhat hampered by quirks such as limited function availability, the "lite" version of MCCA analyzes text by producing frequencies, alphabetical lists, KWIC, and coding with built-in dictionaries. The built-in dictionaries search for traditional, practical, emotional, and analytic contextual dimensions and emphases among 116 idea categories, such as physical descriptions; role, time, emotion, traditional and analytic nouns; positive and negative adjectives; control, analysis, deviance, activity, pressure, and negative and positive reaction verbs. The program's window-driven output makes sorting and switching between results easy. MCCALite also includes a multiple-person transcript analysis function suitable for examining plays, focus groups, interviews, hearings, TV scripts, and other such texts.

Developers: Donald G. McTavish and Ellen B. Pirro

References: McTavish and Pirro (1990); Web site

MECA

Description: MECA, which stands for Map Extraction Comparison and Analysis, contains 15 routines for text analysis. Many of these routines are for doing cognitive mapping and focus on both concepts and the relations between them. There are also routines for doing more classic content analyses, including a multiunit data file output routine that shows the number of times each concept appears in each map.

Developer: Kathleen Carley

References: Carley (1993, 1997a, 1997b)

PCAD 2000

Description: PCAD 2000 applies the Gottschalk-Gleser content analysis scales, which measure the magnitude of clearly defined and categorized mental or emotional states, to transcriptions of speech samples and other machine-readable texts. In addition to deriving scores on a variety of scales, including anxiety, hostility, social alienation, cognitive impairment, hope, and depression, the program compares scores on each scale to norms for the demographic groups of subjects. It can also explain the significance and clinical implications of scores and place subjects into clinical diagnostic classifications derived from the Diagnostic and Statistical Manual of Mental Disorders, Fourth Edition (DSM-IV), developed by the American Psychiatric Association.

Developers: Louis Gottschalk and Bob Bechtel

References: Gottschalk (1995); Gottschalk & Bechtel (1993); Gottschalk & Gleser (1969); Gottschalk, Stein, & Shapiro (1997); Web site

SALT (Systematic Analysis of Language Transcripts)

Description: This program is mainly designed to help clinicians identify and document specific language use problems. It executes myriad analyses, including types of utterances (e.g., incomplete, unintelligible, nonverbal), mean length of utterances, number and length of pauses and rate of speaking, and frequencies for sets of words (e.g., negatives, conjunctions, and custom dictionaries). The Salt Reference Database, described online, allows users to compare the results of their SALT analyses to normative language measures collected via a sample of more than 250 children of various ages, economic backgrounds, and abilities in the Madison, Wisconsin area plus rural northern Wisconsin.

Developers: Jon F. Miller, Robin S. Chapman, and Ann Nockerts

Reference: Web site

SWIFT 3.0

Description: SWIFT (Structured Word Identification and Frequency Table) is a program designed for the analysis of many short passages of text (e.g., abstracts, open-ended questionnaire responses). The program outputs word occurrence frequencies based on user-defined dictionary terms and the output can be imported into statistical software for further analysis. According to the program Web site, SWIFT now

> serves mainly as a introductory-level program that does a few things very well but is not up to snuff as a general purpose CATA program. . . . It is still very good (the best in the author's humble opinion) for analyzing a large set of short responses to open-ended questions.

Developer: Ronald B. Heady

Reference: Web site

TextAnalyst

Description: TextAnalyst seems to be designed primarily for managing texts, but it has some functions of use to content analysts. It contains neural network technology for the structural processing of texts. This technology helps manage large amounts of textual information and can be applied effectively to perform the following tasks: creation of knowledge bases expressed in a natural language; creation of hypertext, searchable, and expert systems; and automated indexing, topic assignment, and abstracting of texts.

Developer: Megaputer Intelligence Inc.

Reference: Web site

TEXTPACK 7.0

Description: The TEXTPACK program, which was originally designed for the analysis of open-ended survey responses, has been broadened in recent years to include many aspects of CATA and most of content analysis. It produces word frequencies, alphabetical lists, KWIC and KWOC searches, cross-references, word comparisons between two texts, and automatic coding based on user-created dictionaries. This multiunit data file output can be imported in statistical analysis software. A Windows version of the program is now available.

Developers: Peter Ph. Mohler and Cornelia Zuell

References: Olsen (1989); Web site

TextQuest 1.05

Description: This is the Windows version of Intext, described earlier. It performs most of the Intext analyses in the current version but through an easier-to-use

Windows interface. A new add-on program, TextGrab, captures whole Web sites, copies them to a hard drive, and formats them for TextQuest analyses.

Developer: Harald Klein

Reference: Web site

TextSmart by SPSS

Description: This software, designed primarily for the analysis of open-ended survey responses, uses cluster analysis and multidimensional scaling techniques to automatically analyze key words and group texts into categories. Thus, it can code, so to speak, without the use of a user-created dictionary. TextSmart has a pleasant, easy-to-use Windows interface that allows for quick sorting of words into frequency and alphabetical lists. It also produces colorful, rich-looking graphics, such as bar charts and two-dimensional MDS plots.

Developer: SPSS

Reference: Web site

WordStat v3.03

Description: This add-on to the SimStat statistical analysis program includes several exploratory tools, such as cluster analysis and multidimensional scaling, for the analysis of open-ended survey responses and other texts. It also codes based on user-supplied dictionaries and generates word frequency and alphabetical lists, KWIC, multi-unit data file output, and bivariate comparisons between subgroups. The differences between subgroups can be displayed visually in high-resolution line and bar charts and through 2-D and 3-D correspondence analysis biplots. One particularly noteworthy feature of the program is a dictionary-building tool that uses the WordNet lexical database and other dictionaries (in English and five other languages) to help users build a comprehensive categorization system.

Developer: Provalis Research

Reference: Web site

Part II: VBPro How-To Guide and Executional Flowchart

This how-to guide takes you through a typical VBPro session. (See also the flowchart that follows.) For information about how to get a free copy of

VBPro, visit *The Content Analysis Guidebook Online*. The VBPro program includes a copy of the official, complete VBPro User's Guide, which contains in-depth information on all of the topics mentioned here.

Preparation: Before starting VBPro, there are a few preparatory steps that may need to be taken. First, if you plan to analyze several cases of data (e.g., single news stories in a file of news stories), each case should be identified (ID'd) with a "#" sign followed by numbers, as in "#001." Second, if you plan to code with a set of custom dictionaries, they should be created at this point. A user-created dictionary file in VBPro consists of search categories of interest (i.e., dictionaries) separated by >><< marks above each entry (e.g., >> colors <<, with red, blue, green, etc., on their own separate lines underneath).

Tips: Here are some additional preparatory steps that we've come up with, based on our own experience with the program:

1. Delete all # signs before adding IDs to your text file.

2. Make sure all IDs are left justified and each is located on its *own* line.

3. Bracket all material that you do *not* wish to have included in your analysis, using the characters [and]. All other brackets should be removed, as the material enclosed by them will be ignored by VBPro.

4. Change ellipses with embedded spaces to strings with no spaces (" . . . " becomes "...").

5. Change hyphens to spaces ("ticket-holder" becomes "ticket holder").

Note that most of these changes can easily be done with the "Find and Replace" tool on popular word-processing packages.

Step 1: Save your text and dictionary (if used) in the VBPro program directory (e.g., C:\VBPro) in ASCII-DOS format. If done properly, both files should now have an .asc extension (e.g., JOKES.ASC, DICT.ASC). As you move through the process of using VBPro, you will notice that the dictionary file (DICT.ASC) is required for several functions: CODE, SEARCH, and MAP. Your dictionary file should be the *same* for all three applications in any given text analysis.

Step 2: Open VBPro and *format* your ASCII text using the FORMAT function. Note that VBPro does not support the use of a mouse. All commands must be executed with a keyboard. To select functions from the main screen, press the control (Ctrl) key and the first letter of the function simultaneously (e.g., "Ctrl + F" for FORMAT). Follow the directions in the format menu. After you do so, the format window should say "Formatted File Saved: [filename].frm" (e.g., JOKES.FRM).

Once your text is formatted, you have three immediate choices:

Step 3a: One choice is to have the text words sorted in *alphabetical order* along with each word's frequency of occurrence (e.g., *conservative, 12*). The ALPHABETIZE function does this. Enter the ALPHABETIZE menu and follow the instructions. The alphabetical words file will be saved in your VBPro directory with an .alf extension (e.g., JOKES.ALF).

Step 3b: Another choice is to *code* your text using custom dictionaries. The VBPro CODE command produces multiunit data file output (illustrated earlier in this Resource) based on user-created dictionaries. To run CODE, enter the code menu and follow the instructions. Say "yes" to "Ignore Caps?" and be sure to input the name of your dictionary file (e.g., DICT.ASC)and output file. The coded data file will be saved in your VBPro directory with the name and extension of your choice (e.g., JOKES.COD).

Step 3c: A third choice is to have VBPro perform a KWIC analysis of your text. The SEARCH command does this. Like CODE, SEARCH requires user-created dictionaries. KWIC output will be returned for all dictionary terms. To run SEARCH, enter the menu and follow the on-screen instructions. Be sure to input the dictionary name and an output file name of your choice. The KWIC analysis will be saved in the VBPro directory with the name you specify (although again, we recommend a standard .src extension, e.g., JOKES.SRC).

Step 4:   The saved alphabetical file can be used to create a *frequency* output file. Though the ALPHABETIZE command gives a simple frequency figure, the RANK command gives some additional statistics, including percentage of occurrence for each term compared to all terms and a variety of type/token measures. To produce frequency information, select RANK from the main VBPro menu and simply indicate the name of your alphabetical file. The frequency file will be saved in the VBPro directory with an .frq extension (e.g., JOKES.FRQ).

Step 5:   Using a separate, optional program available at the developer's Web site, the SELECT function compares two different alphabetized lists (i.e., two alf. files). The top 200 word frequency differences between the lists are identified and analyzed using a chi-square test. The output of this analysis is written to a file with a .sct extension (e.g., JOKES.SCT).

Step 6:   A final option, *concept mapping,* can be performed through the VBMap subprogram (vbmap.exe in your VBPro directory). Concept mapping generates a matrix of dimensional coordinates that can be used to construct a three-dimensional map of concepts (dictionaries), in which the proximities between terms are indicative of the degree to which they tend to co-occur. To run VBMap, you first need coded output, which can be obtained through the CODE function. The coded output must then be entered into VBMap, which, using the dictionary files (e.g., DICT.ASC), produces the dimensional coordinates—but *not* the actual three-dimensional representation of concepts. The dimensional coordinates alone are written to a file with a .uns extension automatically provided (e.g., JOKES.UNS), and output, including eigenvalues, coordinates, percentage total variance per eigenvector, and cumulative percentage total variance, are provided in a file with a .map automatic extension (e.g., JOKES.MAP). To subsequently obtain a visual map of the results, you need to import the output from VBMap into a program with graphics capabilities (e.g., SPSS or Thought View). If SPSS is used, the concepts can be visually mapped with the "Scatterplot" selection under the "Interactive graphs" menu. See Figure 8.7 for an example of a VBPro 3-D concept map.

Figure R3.1 presents a flowchart indicating the range of analyses that VBPro performs and the steps that must be taken to execute and access each type of analysis. The file name JOKES.ASC refers to a sample file of jokes, and the file name DICT.ASC refers to a multiconcept dictionary file. Examples of dictionary files and VBPro output can be found at *The Content Analysis Guidebook Online*.

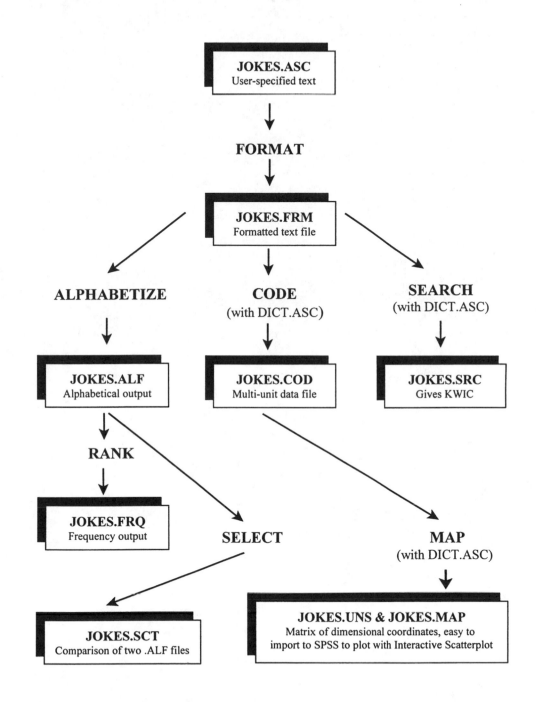

Figure R3.1. VBPro Flowchart

An Introduction to PRAM—
A Program for Reliability
Assessment With Multiple Coders

The PRAM computer program is a new Windows-based application for the PC, designed to simplify the calculation of intercoder reliability coefficients when more than two coders are used. An academic version of the program is available free of charge to readers of *The Content Analysis Guidebook*. This version provides the full complement of intercoder reliability statistics (see the discussion to follow) but is limited as to file size. The professional version of the program is available for purchase from the program's authors (see *The Content Analysis Guidebook Online*). PRAM requires an input data file that is formatted for Excel (with an .xls extension; the SPSS program has the capability of saving data files as .xls).

The file must be structured in the following way: (a) The first column must contain the coder IDs in numeric form, (b) the second column must contain the unit (case) IDs in numeric form, and (c) all other columns may contain numerically coded variables, with variable names on the header line. All reliability cases may be included in a single file; the main feature of the program is its ability to organize data lines by coder IDs and unit IDs and to calculate reliability coefficients for all pairs of coders as well as for all coders taken together.

The program provides the following reliability statistics (see Chapter 7 for explanations and formulas).

For Coder Pairs	Assumed Level of Measurement
Percent agreement	Nominal
Scott's *pi*	Nominal
Cohen's *kappa*	Nominal
Spearman *rho*	Ordinal (rank-order)
Pearson correlation coefficient (r)	Interval or ratio
Lin's corcordance correlation coefficient (r_c)	Interval or ratio

For Multiple Coders	Assumed Level of Measurement
Cohen's *kappa* for multiple coders	Nominal
Krippendorff's *alpha*	Any (user selects)

In a Windows environment, the PRAM user may select the following for each analysis conducted:

- The ID numbers of the coders to be included

- The variable names of the measures to be assessed

- The statistic to be calculated

The output of PRAM is displayed on-screen and is savable to disk or drive. If a coder pair coefficient is selected, the output presents (a) the selected reliability coefficient for each and every variable specified for each pair of coders *separately* and (b) the average of the selected reliability coefficient across all pairs of coders. If a multiple-coders coefficient is selected, the output presents the overall statistic for each and every variable specified.

In conducting analyses for all coder pairs separately, the program provides a diagnostic tool for identifying coders whose performance may be substandard. The program also accommodates instances in which not all coders analyze exactly the same units. For each coder pair, PRAM matches all common units by unit IDs and calculates the coder pair reliability coefficients on the basis of that common set.

The Content Analysis Guidebook Online

T*he Content Analysis Guidebook Online* supplements materials available in this text with an extensive array of content analytic resources. The site is divided into the following sections.

Content Analysis Resources

This section of the site contains general information about *The Content Analysis Guidebook,* including an annotated guide to each chapter. Links to other content analysis resources (e.g., other Web sites, articles, and manuscripts) are also provided.

- Table of Contents for *The Content Analysis Guidebook*
  - Annotations for each chapter, with links
- Content analysis flowchart (from the *Guidebook*)
- Links to other content analysis sites
- Links to articles and manuscripts on content analysis

Bibliographies

This section includes several bibliographies of content analysis studies and articles. The main bibliography lists all research materials collected for this book (including articles not cited herein). A "keyword search" function allows users to retrieve citations for articles addressing particular interests, ranging from television to psychology to content analysis methods. This section serves as a good starting point for any content analysis research endeavor or literature review.

- Bibliography for the *Guidebook*
- Bibliography for content analysis citations from *Communication Abstracts,* 1990-1997

Message Archives and Corpora

This section of the site contains links to archive Web sites, arranged according to interest area (with an emphasis on media archives). Archive sites with downloadable messages (i.e., electronic text) are listed first, followed by "information only" Web sites.

- Links by category

Reliability

This section provides options for the computer-based calculation of intercoder reliability.

- Description of PRAM, the *P*rogram for *R*eliability *A*ssessment for *M*ultiple Coders(with link).
- Using SimStat to calculate reliability (with link)

Human Coding Sample Materials

This section contains sample coding materials from past studies on a variety of topics, including television, film, and advertising. The coding materials for several studies mentioned in this text (e.g., Smith, 1999) are listed here. The codebooks and coding forms are arranged by author name and project title in a printer-friendly format (either HTML or pdf).

- List of content analysis projects (name and title only)
  - Individual project pages with abstracts
    - Sample codebook(s)
    - Sample coding form(s)

Computer Content Analysis

This section contains information on computer content analysis software. All of the programs from Resource 3 are described here—further information and demos can be obtained through links to the official program Web sites, which are included. In addition, the information on the quantitative computer text analysis software is augmented with evaluation results from tests conducted on selected programs by a research team as well as sample dictionaries, runs, and output.

- Evaluation page for computer text analysis programs
  - Links to text analysis sites
  - Sample runs and output
  - Sample dictionaries (custom and standard)
- Links to audio-visual software supporting content analysis tasks
- Links to psychological and linguistic testing
- Introduction to VBPro (extension from Resource 3)

Full details on each section of *The Content Analysis Guidebook Online* can be found on the site itself, located at http://academic.csuohio.edu/ kneuendorf/content. The site will be updated as more information becomes available. Submissions of additional materials (e.g., coding schemes) are welcomed.

References

Abelman, Robert I., & Neuendorf, Kimberly A. (1984a, May). *The demography of religious television programming.* Paper presented to the Mass Communication Division at the annual meeting of the International Communication Association, San Francisco, CA.

Abelman, Robert I., & Neuendorf, Kimberly A. (1984b). *The type and quantity of physical contact on religious television programming.* Report to UNDA-USA, Washington, DC.

Abelman, Robert, & Neuendorf, Kimberly. (1985a). The cost of membership in the electronic church. *Religious Communication Today, 8,* 63-67.

Abelman, Robert, & Neuendorf, Kimberly. (1985b). How religious is religious television programming? *Journal of Communication, 35*(1), 98-110.

Abelman, Robert, & Neuendorf, Kimberly. (1987). Themes and topics in religious television programming. *Review of Religious Research, 29,* 152-174.

Acclaimed neuroscientist pledges $1.5 million to UCI College of Medicine. (1997, Jan. 7). UCI News Press Release. http://www.communications.uci.edu/releases/001tc97.html. [May 8, 2000].

Alden, Dana L., Hoyer, Wayne D., & Lee, Chol. (1993). Identifying global and culture-specific dimensions of humor in advertising: A multinational analysis. *Journal of Advertising, 57*(2), 64-75.

Aldenderfer, Mark S., & Blashfield, Roger K. (1984). *Cluster analysis.* Beverly Hills, CA: Sage.

Alexa, Melina, & Zuell, Cornelia. (1999). A review of software for text analysis. *ZUMA Nachrichten Spezial 5.* Mannheim, Germany: ZUMA.

Allport, Gordon W. (1942). *The use of personal documents in psychological science.* New York: Social Science Research Council.

Allport, Gordon W. (Ed.). (1965). *Letters from Jenny.* New York: Harcourt, Brace & World.

Alonge, Antonietta, Calzolari, Nicoletta, Vossen, Pick, Bloksma, Laura, Castellon, Irene, Marti, Maria Antonia, & Peters, Wim. (1998). The linguistic design of the EuroWordNet database. *Computers and the Humanities, 32,* 91-115.

Althaus, Scott L., Edy, Jill A., & Phalen, Patricia F. (2000, June). *Using the Vanderbilt Television Abstracts to track broadcast news content: Possibilities and pitfalls.* Paper presented to the annual meeting of the International Communication Association, Acapulco, Mexico.

Andrews, Frank M., Klem, Laura, Davidson, Terrence N., O'Malley, Patrick M., & Rodgers, Willard L. (1981). *A guide for selecting statistical techniques for analyzing social science data* (2nd ed.). Ann Arbor: University of Michigan, Institute for Social Research, Survey Research Center.

Andsager, Julie L., & Miller, M. Mark. (1992, November). *Exploring patterns of controversy: Newspaper coverage of RU-486.* Paper presented at the annual meeting of the Midwest Association for Public Opinion Research, Chicago, IL.

Andsager, Julie L., & Powers, Angela. (1999). Social or economic concerns: How news and women's magazines framed breast cancer in the 1990s. *Journalism and Mass Communication Quarterly, 76,* 531-550.

Anheier, Helmut K., Neidhardt, Friedhelm, & Vortkamp, Wolfgang. (1998). Movement cycles and the Nazi party: Activities of the Munich NSDAP, 1925-1930. *American Behavioral Scientist, 41*(9), 1262-1281.

Anonymous. (2000). Discourse about race and interracial relationships in children's television commercials. Manuscript submitted to *Journal of Broadcasting & Electronic Media.*

Aristotle. (1991). *Aristotle on rhetoric: A theory of civic discourse* (George A. Kennedy, Trans.). New York: Oxford University Press.

Aronow, Edward, Reznikoff, Marvin, & Moreland, Kevin. (1994). *The Rorschach technique: Perceptual basics, content interpretation, and applications.* Boston: Allyn & Bacon.

Assessing cognitive impairment. (1999, Winter). *UCI Journal. http://www.communications.uci.edu/journal/winter99/ip/05.html*(accessed May 8, 2000).

Atkin, Charles K., Neuendorf, Kimberly A., & McDermott, Steven. (1983). The role of alcohol advertising in excessive and hazardous drinking. *Journal of Drug Education, 13,* 313-325.

Atkin, David, & Fife, Marilyn. (1993-1994). The role of race and gender as determinants of local TV news coverage. *Howard Journal of Communications, 5,* 123-137.

Atkin, David, Neuendorf, Kimberly, Jeffres, Leo, & Skalski, Paul. (2000, June). *Predictors of audience interest in adopting digital television.* Paper presented to the Communication and Technology Division at the annual meeting of the International Communication Association, Acapulco, Mexico.

Auld, Frank Jr., & Murray, Edward J. (1955). Content-analysis studies of psychotherapy. *Psychological Bulletin, 52*(5), 377-395.

Babbie, Earl. (1986). *Observing ourselves: Essays in social research.* Belmont, CA: Wadsworth.

Babbie, Earl. (1995). *The practice of social research* (7th ed.). Belmont, CA: Wadsworth.

Babbie, Earl. (1998). *The practice of social research* (8th ed.). Belmont, CA: Wadsworth.

Bakeman, Roger. (2000). Behavioral observation and coding. In Harry T. Reis & Charles M. Judd (Eds.), *Handbook of research methods in social and personality psychology* (pp. 138-159). Cambridge, UK: Cambridge University Press.

Baldwin, Thomas F., & Lewis, Colby. (1972). Violence in television: The industry looks at itself. In George A. Comstock & Eli A. Rubinstein (Eds.), *Television and social behavior, reports and papers, volume I: Media content and control. A technical report to the Surgeon General's Scientific Advisory Committee on Television and Social Behavior* (pp. 290-373). Rockville, MD: National Institute of Mental Health.

Bales, Robert F. (1950). *Interaction process analysis: A method for the study of small groups.* Cambridge, MA: Addison-Wesley.

Bales, Robert F., & Cohen, Stephen P., with the assistance of Williamson, Stephen A. (1979). *SYMLOG: A system for the multiple level observation of groups.* New York: Free Press.

Bales, Robert F., Strodtbeck, Fred L., Mills, Theodore M., & Roseborough, Mary E. (1951). Channels of communication in small groups. *American Sociological Review, 16,* 461-468.

Banerjee, Mousumi, Capozzoli, Michelle, McSweeney, Laura, & Sinha, Debajyoti. (1999). Beyond kappa: A review of interrater agreement measures. *Canadian Journal of Statistics, 27*(1), 3-23.

Baran, Stanley J., & Davis, Dennis K. (1995). *Mass communication theory: Foundations, ferment, and future.* Belmont, CA: Wadsworth.

Barber, John T., & Gandy, Oscar H., Jr. (1990). Press portrayal of African American and white U.S. representatives. *Howard Journal of Communications, 2,* 213-225.

Barner, Mark R. (1999). Sex-role stereotyping in FCC-mandated children's educational television. *Journal of Broadcasting & Electronic Media, 43,* 551-564.

Barnett, George A., & Woelfel, Joseph J. (Eds.). (1988). *Readings in the Galileo system: Theory, methods and applications.* Dubuque, IA: Kendall/Hunt.

Baron-Cohen, Simon, & Harrison, John E. (Eds.). (1997). *Synaesthesia: Classic and contemporary readings.* Oxford, UK: Blackwell.

Barrett, E., & Lally, V. (1999). Gender differences in an on-line learning environment. *Journal of Computer Assisted Learning, 15*(1), 48-60.

Bartko, John J., & Carpenter, William T., Jr. (1976). On the methods and theory of reliability. *Journal of Nervous and Mental Disease, 163,* 307-317.

Bates, Marcia J., & Lu, Shaojun. (1997). An exploratory profile of personal home pages: Content, design, metaphors. *Online and CDROM Review, 21*(6), 331-340.

Bateson, Gregory. (1958). *Naven* (2nd ed.). Stanford, CA: Stanford University Press.

Bauer, Christian, & Scharl, Arno. (2000). Quantitative evaluation of Web site content and structure. *Internet Research: Electronic Networking Applications and Policy, 10,* 31-43.

Baxter, Richard L., de Riemer, Cynthia, Landini, Ann, Leslie, Larry, & Singletary, Michael. (1985). A content analysis of music videos. *Journal of Broadcasting & Electronic Media, 29,* 333-340.

Beatty, Michael J., Behnke, Ralph R., & Froelich, Deidre L. (1980). Effects of achievement incentive and presentation rate on listening comprehension. *Quarterly Journal of Speech, 66,* 193-200.

Beatty, Michael J., Forst, Edmund C., & Stewart, Robert A. (1986). Communication apprehension and motivation as predictors of public speaking duration. *Communication Education, 35,* 143-146.

Beatty, Michael J., & Payne, Steven K. (1985). Is construct differentiation loquacity? A motivational perspective. *Human Communication Research, 11,* 605-612.

Beaumont, Sherry L. (1995). Adolescent girls' conversations with mothers and friends: A matter of style. *Discourse Processes, 20,* 109-132.

Berelson, Bernard. (1952). *Content analysis in communication research.* New York: Hafner.

Berger, Arthur Asa. (1982). *Media analysis techniques.* Beverly Hills, CA: Sage.

Berger, Arthur Asa. (1991). *Media research techniques.* Newbury Park, CA: Sage.

Berger, Peter L., & Luckman, Thomas. (1966). *The social construction of reality: A treatise in the sociology of knowledge.* New York: Anchor.

Beriker, Nimet, & Druckman, Daniel. (1996). Simulating the Lausanne peace negotiations, 1922-1923: Power asymmetries in bargaining. *Simulation & Gaming, 27*(2), 162-183.

Berkowitz, Leonard. (1964). Aggressive cues in aggressive behavior and hostility catharsis. *Psychological Review, 71*(2), 104-122.

Berkowitz, Leonard. (1973). Word and symbols as stimuli to aggressive responses. In John F. Knutson (Ed.), *The control of aggression: Implications from basic research* (pp. 113-143). Chicago: Aldine.

Berkowitz, Leonard, & LePage, Anthony. (1967). Weapons as aggression-eliciting stimuli. *Journal of Personality and Social Psychology, 7*(2), 202-207.

Berlin Ray, Eileen, & Donohew, Lewis. (1990). *Communication and health: Systems and applications.* Hillsdale, NJ: Lawrence Erlbaum.

Berlyne, D. E. (1971). *Aesthetics and psychobiology.* New York: Appleton-Century-Crofts.

Berry, John W. (1990). Imposed etics, emics, and derived etics: Their conceptual and operational status in cross-cultural psychology. In Thomas N. Headland, Kenneth L. Pike, & Marvin Harris (Eds.), *Emics and etics: The insider/outsider debate* (pp. 84-99). Newbury Park, CA: Sage.

Berry, Kenneth J., & Mielke, Paul W., Jr. (1997). Measuring the joint agreement between multiple raters and a standard. *Educational and Psychological Measurement, 57*(3), 527-530.

Beyer, Christine E., Ogletree, Roberta J., Ritzel, Dale O., Drolet, Judy C., Gilbert, Sharon L., & Brown, Dale. (1996). Gender representation in illustrations, text, and topic areas in sexuality education curricula. *Journal of School Health, 66*(10), 361-364.

Bird, Alexander. (1998). *Philosophy of science.* Montreal: McGill-Queen's University Press.

Boiarsky, Greg, Long, Marilee, & Thayer, Greg. (1999). Formal features in children's science television: Sound effects, visual pace, and topic shifts. *Communication Research Reports, 16*(2), 185-192.

Borke, Helene. (1967). The communication of intent: A systematic approach to the observation of family interaction. *Human Relations, 20,* 13-28.

Borke, Helene. (1969). The communication of intent: A revised procedure for analyzing family interaction from video tapes. *Journal of Marriage and Family, 31,* 541-544.

Botta, Renée. (2000). *Body image on prime-time television.* Unpublished manuscript. Cleveland, OH: Cleveland State University.

Boykin, Stanley, & Merlino, Andrew. (2000). Machine learning of event segmentation for news on demand. *Communications of the ACM, 43*(2), 35-41.

Bray, James H., & Maxwell, Scott E. (1985). *Multivariate analysis of variance.* Beverly Hills, CA: Sage.

Brayack, Barbara. (1998). *A content analysis of housing messages targeting the elderly.* Unpublished master's thesis, Cleveland State University, Cleveland, OH.

Breen, Michael J. (1997). A cook, a cardinal, his priests, and the press: Deviance as a trigger for intermedia agenda setting. *Journalism and Mass Communication Quarterly, 74,* 348-356.

Brentar, James E. (1990). *Exposure effects and affective responses to music.* Unpublished master's thesis, Cleveland State University, Cleveland, OH.

Bretz, Rudy. (1971). *A taxonomy of communication media*. Englewood Cliffs, NJ: Educational Technology.

Bridges, Judith S. (1993). Pink or blue: Gender-stereotypic perceptions of infants as conveyed by birth congratulations cards. *Psychology of Women Quarterly, 17*(2), 193-205.

Brinson, Susan L., & Winn, J. Emmett. (1997). Talk shows' representations of interpersonal conflicts. *Journal of Broadcasting & Electronic Media, 41*, 25-39.

Broehl, Wayne G., Jr., & McGee, Victor E. (1981). Content analysis in psychohistory: A study of three lieutenants in the Indian mutiny, 1857-1858. *Journal of Psychohistory, 8*(3), 281-306.

Brooks, Tim, & Marsh, Earle. (1999). *The complete directory of prime time network and cable TV shows, 1946-present* (7th ed.). New York: Ballantine.

Brosius, Hans-Bernd, & Kepplinger, Hans Mathias. (1992). Linear and nonlinear models of agenda-setting in television. *Journal of Broadcasting & Electronic Media, 36*, 5-23.

Browne, Beverly A. (1998). Gender stereotypes in advertising on children's television in the 1990s: A cross-national analysis. *Journal of Advertising, 27*(1), 83-96.

Bryant, Jennings, Hezel, Richard, & Zillmann, Dolf. (1979). Humor in children's educational television. *Communication Education, 28*, 49-59.

Buchanan, Gregory McClellan, & Seligman, Martin E. P. (Eds.). (1995). *Explanatory style*. Hillsdale, NJ: Lawrence Erlbaum.

Bucklow, Spike L. (1998). A stylometric analysis of craquelure. *Computers and the Humanities, 31*, 503-521.

Bucy, Erik P., Lang, Annie, Potter, Robert F., & Grabe, Maria Elizabeth. (1999). Formal features of cyberspace: Relationships between web page complexity and site traffic. *Journal of the American Society for Information Science, 50*, 1246-1256.

Budd, Richard W., Thorp, Robert K., & Donohew, Lewis. (1967). *Content analysis of communications*. New York: Macmillan.

Budge, Ian, & Hofferbert, Richard I. (1996). Comparative textual analyses of government and party activity: The work of the Manifesto Research Group. In Louis M. Imbeau & Robert D. McKinlay (Eds.), *Comparing government activity* (pp. 82-100). New York: St. Martin's.

Busby, Linda J. (1975). Sex-role research on the mass media. *Journal of Communication, 25*(4), 107-131.

Buston, K. (1997). NUD*IST in action: Its use and its usefulness in a study of chronic illness in young people. *Sociological Research Online, 2*(3). http://www.socsresonline.org.uk/socresonline/2/3/6.html [May 5, 2001].

Camden, Carl, & Verba, Steve. (1986). Communication and consciousness: Applications in marketing. *Western Journal of Speech Communication, 50*, 64-73.

Cantor, Joanne R. (1977). Tendentious humour in the mass media. In Antony J. Chapman & Hugh C. Foot (Eds.), *It's a funny thing, humour* (pp. 303-310). Oxford, UK: Pergamon.

Capwell, Amy. (1997). *Chick flicks: An analysis of self-disclosure in friendships*. Unpublished master's thesis, Cleveland State University, Cleveland, OH.

Carletta, Jean. (1996). Assessing agreement on classification tasks: The kappa statistic. *Computational Linguistics, 22*(2), 249-254.

Carley, Kathleen. (1993). Coding choices for textual analysis: A comparison of content analysis and map analysis. In Peter V. Marsden (Ed.), *Sociological Methodology, Vol. 23* (pp. 75-126). Oxford, UK: Blackwell.

Carley, Kathleen. (1994). Extracting culture through textual analysis. *Poetics, 22,* 291-312.

Carley, Kathleen M. (1997a). Extracting team mental models through textual analysis. *Journal of Organizational Behavior, 18,* 533-558.

Carley, Kathleen M. (1997b). Network text analysis: The network position of concepts. In Carl W. Roberts (Ed.), *Text analysis for the social sciences: Methods for drawing statistical inferences from texts and transcripts* (pp. 79-100). Mahwah, NJ: Lawrence Erlbaum.

Carmines, Edward G., & Zeller, Richard A. (1979). *Reliability and validity assessment.* Beverly Hills, CA: Sage.

Carney, T. F. (1971). Content analysis: A review essay. *Historical Methods Newsletter, 4*(2), 52-61.

Cecil, Denise Wigginton. (1998). Relational control patterns in physician-patient clinical encounters: Continuing the conversation. *Health Communication, 10*(2), 125-149.

Chamblee, Robert, Gilmore, Robert, Thomas, Gloria, & Soldow, Gary. (1993). When copy complexity can help ad readership. *Journal of Advertising Research, 33*(3), 23-28.

Chang, Tsan-Kuo. (1998). All countries not created equal to be news: World system and international communication. *Communication Research, 25,* 528-563.

Chappell, Kelly K. (1996). Mathematics computer software characteristics with possible gender-specific impact: A content analysis. *Journal of Educational Computing Research, 15*(1), 25-35.

Charters, W. W. (1933). *Motion pictures and youth: A summary.* New York: Arno & the *New York Times.*

Chen, Chaomei, & Rada, Roy. (1996). Interacting with hypertext: A meta-analysis of experimental studies. *Human-Computer Interaction, 11,* 125-156.

Cheng, Hong, & Schweitzer, John C. (1996). Cultural values reflected in Chinese and U.S. television commercials. *Journal of Advertising Research, 36*(3), 27-45.

Chinchilli, Vernon M., Martel, Juliann, K., Kumanyika, Shiriki, & Lloyd, Tom. (1996). A weighted concordance correlation coefficient for repeated measurement designs. *Biometrics, 52,* 341-353.

Christenfeld, Nicholas, Glynn, Laura M., Phillips, David P., & Shrira, Ilan. (1999). Exposure to New York City as a risk factor for heart attack mortality. *Psychosomatic Medicine, 61,* 740-743.

Christenfeld, Nicholas, Phillips, David P., & Glynn, Laura M. (1999). What's in a name: Mortality and the power of symbols. *Journal of Psychosomatic Research, 47*(3), 241-254.

Christie, Ian. (1999). Commentary for "The Red Shoes." Audio recording accompanying DVD. Criterion Collection, http://www.criterionco.com.

Christophel, Diane M. (1990). The relationships among teacher immediacy behaviors, student motivation, and learning. *Communication Education, 39,* 323-340.

Chu, Donna, & McIntyre, Bryce T. (1995). Sex role stereotypes on children's TV in Asia: A content analysis of gender role portrayals in children's cartoons in Hong Kong. *Communication Research Reports, 12,* 206-219.

Chusmir, Leonard H. (1985). Short-form scoring for McClelland's version of the TAT. *Perceptual and Motor Skills, 61,* 1047-1052.

Cohen, Jacob. (1960). A coefficient of agreement for nominal scales. *Educational and Psychological Measurement, 20*(1), 37-46.

Cohen, Jacob. (1968). Weighted kappa: Nominal scale agreement with provision for scaled disagreement of partial credit. *Psychological Bulletin, 70*(4), 213-220.

Cohen, Jacob, & Cohen, Patricia. (1983). *Applied multiple regression/correlation analysis for the social sciences* (2nd ed.). Hillsdale, NJ: Lawrence Erlbaum.

Collins, Caroline L., & Gould, Odelle N. (1994). Getting to know you: How own age and other's age relate to self-disclosure. *International Journal of Aging and Human Development, 39,* 55-66.

Collins, Linda M., & Horn, John L. (Eds.). (1991). *Best methods for the analysis of change: Recent advances, unanswered questions, future directions.* Washington, DC: American Psychological Association.

Comstock, George A., & Rubinstein, Eli A. (Eds.). (1972). *Television and social behavior, reports and papers, volume I: Media content and control. A technical report to the Surgeon General's Scientific Advisory Committee on Television and Social Behavior.* Rockville, MD: National Institute of Mental Health.

Copeland, Gary A. (1989). Face-ism and primetime television. *Journal of Broadcasting & Electronic Media, 33,* 209-214.

Council on Interracial Books for Children. (1977). *Stereotypes, distortions and omissions in U.S. history textbooks.* New York: Racism and sexism resource center for educators.

Courtright, John A., Millar, Frank E., & Rogers-Millar, Edna. (1979). Domineeringness and dominance: Replication and expansion. *Communication Monographs, 46,* 179-192.

Cowan, Gloria, & Campbell, Robin R. (1994). Racism and sexism in interracial pornography: A content analysis. *Psychology of Women Quarterly, 18,* 323-338.

Cozby, Paul C. (1973). Self-disclosure: A literature review. *Psychological Bulletin, 79,* 73-91.

Crawford, Mary, & Gressley, Diane. (1991). Creativity, caring, and context: Women's and men's accounts of humor preferences and practices. *Psychology of Women Quarterly, 15*(2), 217-231.

Cryer, Jonathan D. (1986). *Time series analysis.* Boston: Duxbury.

Cunningham, Michael R. (1986). Measuring the physical in physical attractiveness: Quasi-experiments on the sociobiology of female facial beauty. *Journal of Personality and Social Psychology, 50,* 925-935.

Cupchik, Gerald C., & Berlyne, Daniel E. (1979). The perception of collative properties in visual stimuli. *Scandinavian Journal of Psychology, 20*(2), 93-104.

Custen, George F. (1992). *Bio/pics: How Hollywood constructed public history.* New Brunswick, NJ: Rutgers University Press.

Cutler, Bob D., & Javalgi, Rakshekhar G. (1992). A cross-cultural analysis of the visual components of print advertising: The United States and the European community. *Journal of Advertising Research, 32*(1), 71-80.

Cutler, Bob D., Moberg, Chris, & Schimmel, Kurt. (1999). Attorney advertising: The link between ad cues and consumer search criteria. *Journal of Professional Services Marketing, 19*(1), 1-14.

Cytowic, Richard E. (1999). *The man who tasted shapes.* Cambridge: MIT Press.

Dale, Edgar. (1935). *The content of motion pictures.* New York: Macmillan.

Damphouse, Kelly R., & Smith, Brent L. (1998). The Internet: A terrorist medium for the 21st century. In Harvey W. Kushner (Ed.), *The future of terrorism: Violence in the new millennium* (pp. 208-225). Thousand Oaks, CA: Sage.

Danielson, Wayne A., & Lasorsa, Dominic L. (1997). Perceptions of social change: 100 years of front-page content in the *New York Times* and the *Los Angeles Times*. In Carl W. Roberts (Ed.), *Text analysis for the social sciences: Methods for drawing statistical inferences from texts and transcripts* (pp. 103-115). Mahwah, NJ: Lawrence Erlbaum.

Danielson, Wayne A., Lasorsa, Dominic L., & Im, Dae S. (1992). Journalists and novelists: A study of diverging styles. *Journalism Quarterly, 69,* 436-446.

Danowski, James A., & Edison-Swift, Paul. (1985). Crisis effects on intraorganizational computer-based communication. *Communication Research, 12,* 251-270.

Dates, Jannette L., & Barlow, William. (Eds.). (1990). *Split image: African Americans in the mass media.* Washington, DC: Howard University Press.

Dejong, William, & Atkin, Charles K. (1995). A review of national television PSA campaigns for preventing alcohol-impaired driving, 1987-1992. *Journal of Public Health Policy, 16,* 59-80.

Delia, Jesse G. (1987). Communication research: A history. In Charles R. Berger & Steven H. Chaffee (Eds.), *Handbook of communication science* (pp. 20-98). Newbury Park, CA: Sage.

Dellinger, Matt. (2000, March 27). Steno dept. meets Oscar's transcriber. *New Yorker,* p. 39.

DeVellis, Robert F. (1991). *Scale development: Theory and applications.* Newbury Park, CA: Sage.

DiCarlo, Margaret A., Gibbons, Judith L., Kaminsky, Donald C., Wright, James D., & Stiles, Deborah A. (2000). Street children's drawings: Windows into their life circumstances and aspirations. *International Social Work, 43*(1), 107-120.

Diefenbach, Donald L. (1997). The portrayal of mental illness on prime-time television. *Journal of Community Psychology, 25*(3), 289-302.

Diefenbach, Donald L. (in press). Historical foundations of computer-assisted content analysis. In Mark D. West (Ed.), *Theory, method, and practice in computer content analysis* (pp. 13-42). Westport, CT: Ablex.

Dietz, Tracy L. (1998). An examination of violence and gender role portrayals in video games: Implications for gender socialization and aggressive behavior. *Sex Roles, 38,* 425-442.

Dindia, Kathryn. (1987). The effects of sex of subject and sex of partner on interruptions. *Human Communication Research, 13,* 345-371.

DiSanza, James R., & Bullis, Connie. (1999). "Everybody identifies with Smokey the Bear": Employee responses to newsletter identification inducements at the U.S. Forest Service. *Management Communication Quarterly, 12,* 347-399.

Dixon, Travis L., & Linz, Daniel. (2000). Overrepresentation and underrepresentation of African Americans and Latinos as lawbreakers on television news. *Journal of Communication, 50*(2), 131-154.

Doerfel, Marya L., & Barnett, George A. (1999). A semantic network analysis of the International Communication Association. *Human Communication Research, 25,* 589-603.

Dollar, Charles M., & Jensen, Richard J. (1971). *Historian's guide to statistics: Quantitative analysis and historical research.* New York: Holt, Rinehart & Winston.

Dollard, John, & Mowrer, O. Hobart. (1947). A method of measuring tension in written documents. *Journal of Abnormal and Social Psychology, 42,* 3-32.

Domhoff, G. William. (1999). New directions in the study of dream content using the Hall and Van de Castle coding system. *Dreaming: Journal of the Association for the Study of Dreams, 9*(2-3), 115-137.

Dominick, Joseph R. (1990). *The dynamics of mass communication* (3rd ed.). New York: McGraw-Hill.

Dominick, Joseph R. (1999). Who do you think you are? Personal home pages and self-presentation on the World Wide Web. *Journalism and Mass Communication Quarterly, 76,* 646-658.

Domke, David, Fan, David P., Fibison, Michael, Shah, Dhavan V., Smith, Steven S., & Watts, Mark D. (1997). News media, candidates and issues, and public opinion in the 1996 presidential campaign. *Journalism and Mass Communication Quarterly, 74,* 718-737.

Donath, Bob. (1982, August). Ad copy clinic: Q: What makes the perfect ad? A: It depends. *Industrial Marketing, 67,* 89-92.

Donohue, William A. (1991). *Communication, marital dispute, and divorce mediation.* Hillsdale, NJ: Lawrence Erlbaum.

Doris, John. (1994). Commentary on criteria-based content analysis. *Journal of Applied Developmental Psychology, 15,* 281-285.

Drewniany, Bonnie. (1996). Super Bowl commercials: The best a man can get (or is it?). In Paul Martin Lester (Ed.), *Images that injure: Pictorial stereotypes in the media* (pp. 87-92). Westport, CN: Praeger.

Duncan, Judith. (1996). "For the sake of the children" as the worth of the teacher? The gendered discourses of the New Zealand national kindergarten teachers' employment negotiations. *Gender and Education, 8*(2), 159-170.

Dunwoody, Sharon, & Peters, Hans. (1992). Mass media coverage of technological and environmental risks: A survey of research in the United States and Germany. *Public Understanding of Science, 1,* 199-230.

Dupagne, Michel. (2000). How to set up a video streaming operation: Lessons from a University of Miami project. *Feedback, 41*(2), 11-21.

Durkin, Kevin. (1985). *Television, sex roles and children: A developmental social psychological account.* Milton Keynes, UK: Open University Press.

Dyer, Sam C. (1994a). A newsflow analysis of the sale of a public asset. *Australian Journal of Political Science, 29,* 172-178.

Dyer, Sam C. (1994b). Using newsflow analysis to evaluate media coverage. *Public Relations Quarterly, 38,* 35-39.

Dyer, Sam C., Miller, M. Mark, & Boone, Jeff. (1991). Wire service coverage of the Exxon Valdez crises. *Public Relations Review, 17*(1), 27-36.

Ealy, James Allen. (1991). *Nonverbal communication on film: The career of Bette Davis.* Unpublished master's thesis, Cleveland State University, Cleveland, OH.

EBU/SMPTE Task Force for Harmonized Standards for the Exchange of Program Material as Bitstreams. (1998, September). Final report: Analyses and results, July 1998. *SMPTE Journal, 107*(9), 603-815.

Eco, Umberto. (1976). *A theory of semiotics.* Bloomington, IN: Indiana University Press.

Ekman, Paul, & Rosenberg, Erika L. (Eds.). (1997). *What the face reveals: Basic and applied studies of spontaneous expression using the facial action coding system (FACS).* New York: Oxford University Press.

Elder, Glen H., Jr., Pavalko, Eliza K., & Clipp, Elizabeth C. (1993). *Working with archival data: Studying lives.* Newbury Park, CA: Sage.

Elliott, Ward E. Y., & Valenza, Robert J. (1996). And then there were none: Winnowing the Shakespeare claimants. *Computers and the Humanities, 30,* 191-245.

Ellis, Donald G. (1979). Relational control in two group systems. *Communication Monographs, 46,* 153-166.

Ellis, Lee. (1994). *Research methods in the social sciences.* Madison, WI: WCB Brown & Benchmark.

Ely, Mark, & Block, Dave. (1997-1998). *Publishing in the age of DVD* (2nd ed.). Sonic Solutions: http://www.sonic.com.

Emanuel, Steven L. (1997). *LEXIS-NEXIS for law students* (3rd ed.). Larchmont, NY: Emanuel.

Entman, Robert M. (1992). Blacks in the news: Television, modern racism, and cultural change. *Journalism Quarterly, 69,* 341-361

Eshleman, Joseph G., & Neuendorf, Kimberly A. (1989, August). *Perspectives on humor and their application to mass media comedy.* Paper presented to the Mass Communication and Society Division at the annual meeting of the Association for Education in Journalism and Mass Communication, Washington, DC. (Also available as ERIC document.)

Evans, William. (1996). Computer-supported content analysis: Trends, tools, and techniques. *Social Science Computer Review, 14*(3), 269-279.

Evans, William. (2000). Teaching computers to watch television: Content-based image retrieval for content analysis. *Social Science Computer Review, 18,* 246-257.

Eyberg, Sheila M., & Robinson, Elizabeth A. (1983, December). Dyadic parent-child interaction coding system (DPICS): A manual. *Psychological Documents, 13*(2), 24.

Eysenck, Hans J. (1990). Biological dimensions of personality. In Lawrence A. Pervin (Ed.), *Handbook of personality theory and research* (pp. 244-276). New York: Guilford.

Fairhurst, Gail T., Rogers, L. Edna, & Sarr, Robert A. (1987). Manager-subordinate control patterns and judgments about the relationship. In Margaret L. McLaughlin (Ed.), *Communication yearbook 10* (pp. 395-415). Newbury Park, CA: Sage.

Fan, David P. (1988). *Predictions of public opinion from the mass media: Computer content analysis and mathematical modeling.* New York: Greenwood.

Fan, David P. (1997). Computer content analysis of press coverage and prediction of public opinion for the 1995 sovereignty referendum in Quebec. *Social Science Computer Review, 15*(15), 351-366.

Fan, David, & Bengston, David. (1997). *Attitudes toward roads on the National Forests: An analysis of the news media.* Report prepared for the USDA Forest Service, Office of Communications, Washington, DC. http://www.fs.fed.us/news/roads/DOCSattitudes.html [May 10, 2000].

Fan, David P., Brosius, Hans-Bernd, & Esser, Frank. (in press). Computer and human coding of German text on attacks on foreigners. In Mark D. West (Ed.), *Practice in computer content analysis.* Norwood, NJ: Ablex.

Fan, David P., & Shaffer, Carol L. (1989, November). *Opinion survey using open ended essays and computer content analysis: College students' knowledge of AIDS.* Paper presented at the annual meeting of the Midwest Association for Public Opinion Research, Chicago, IL.

Farley, Jennie. (1978). Women's magazines and the Equal Rights Amendment: Friend or foe? *Journal of Communication, 28*(1), 187-192.

Feinstein, Alvan R., & Cicchetti, Domenic V. (1990). High agreement but low kappa: I. The problems of two paradoxes. *Journal of Clinical Epidemiology, 43,* 543-549.

Fellbaum, Christiane. (1998). A semantic network of English: The mother of all WordNets. *Computers and the Humanities, 32,* 209-220.

Fenton, D. Mark. (1985). Dimensions of meaning in the perception of natural settings and their relationship to aesthetic response. *Australian Journal of Psychology, 37,* 325-339.

Ferrante, Carol L., Haynes, Andrew M., & Kingsley, Sarah M. (1988). Image of women in television advertising. *Journal of Broadcasting & Electronic Media, 32,* 231-237.

Ferraro, Carl David, & Olson, Beth. (2000). Revisiting attitudes toward use of the computer in video production. *Feedback, 41*(2), 22-27.

Feyereisen, Pierre, & Harvard, Isabelle. (1999). Mental imagery and production of hand gestures while speaking in younger and older adults. *Journal of Nonverbal Behavior, 23*(2), 153-171.

Fink, Edward, & Gantz, Walter. (1996). A content analysis of three mass communication research traditions: Social science, interpretive studies and critical analysis. *Journalism and Mass Communication Quarterly, 73,* 114-134.

Finkel, Steven E., & Geer, John G. (1998). A spot check: Casting doubt on the demobilizing effect of attack advertising. *American Journal of Political Science, 42,* 573-595.

Finn, T. Andrew, & Strickland, Donald E. (1982). A content-analysis of beverage alcohol advertising. 2. Television advertising. *Journal of Studies on Alcohol, 43,* 964-989.

Fisher, B. Aubrey. (1970). Decision emergence: Phases in group decision-making. *Speech Monographs, 31,* 53-66.

Fleiss, Joseph L. (1971). Measuring nominal scale agreement among many raters. *Psychological Bulletin, 76,* 378-382.

Floud, Roderick. (1977). Quantitative history: Evolution of methods and techniques. *Journal of the Society of Archivists, 5,* 407-417.

Fogel, Robert William, & Engerman, Stanley L. (1974a). *Time on the cross: Evidence and methods.* Boston: Little, Brown.

Fogel, Robert William, & Engerman, Stanley L. (1974b). *Time on the cross: The economics of American Negro slavery.* Boston: Little, Brown.

Folger, Joseph P., Hewes, Dean E., & Poole, Marshall Scott. (1984). Coding social interaction. In Brenda Dervin & Melvin J. Voigt (Eds.), *Progress in communication sciences* (pp. 115-161). Norwood, NJ: Ablex.

Folger, Joseph P., & Poole, Marshall Scott. (1982). Relational coding schemes: The question of validity. In Michael Burgoon (Ed.), *Communication yearbook 5* (pp. 235-247). New Brunswick, NJ: Transaction.

Fouts, Gregory, & Burggraf, Kimberley. (1999). Television situation comedies: Female body images and verbal reinforcements. *Sex Roles, 40,* 473-481.

Fowler, Gilbert L., Jr. (1986). Content and teacher characteristics for master's level research course. *Journalism Quarterly, 63,* 594-599.

Franke, Michael. (2000). *Social perception and attribution of responsibility in news magazine coverage of the Manson family.* Unpublished manuscript, Department of Communication, Cleveland State University, Cleveland, OH.

Frankl, Razelle. (1987). *Televangelism: The marketing of popular religion.* Carbondale: Southern Illinois University Press.

Frey, Lawrence R., Botan, Carl H., & Kreps, Gary L. (2000). *Investigating communication: An introduction to research methods* (2nd ed.). Boston: Allyn & Bacon.

Fruth, Laurel, & Padderud, Allan. (1985). Portrayals of mental illness in daytime television serials. *Journalism Quarterly, 62,* 384-387, 449.

Furui, Sadaoki, Ohtsuki, Katsutoshi, & Zhang, Zhi-Peng. (2000). Japanese broadcast news transcription and information extraction. *Communications of the ACM, 43*(2), 71-73.

Gagnard, Alice, & Morris, Jim R. (1988). CLIO commercials from 1975-1985: Analysis of 151 executional variables. *Journalism Quarterly, 65,* 859-869.

Garcia, Luis T., & Milano, Laureen. (1990). A content analysis of erotic videos. *Journal of Psychology & Human Sexuality, 3*(2), 95-103.

Gardstrom, Susan C. (1999). Music exposure and criminal behavior: Perceptions of juvenile offenders. *Journal of Music Therapy, 36*(3), 207-221.

Garner, W. R. (1978). Aspects of a stimulus: Features, dimensions, and configurations. In Eleanor Rosch & Barbara B. Lloyd (Eds.), *Cognition and categorization* (pp. 99-133). Hillsdale, NJ: Lawrence Erlbaum.

Gauvain, Jean-Luc, Lamel, Lori, & Adda, Gilles. (2000). Transcribing broadcast news for audio and video indexing. *Communications of the ACM, 43*(2), 64-70.

Gerbner, George. (1972). Violence in television drama: Trends and symbolic functions. In George A. Comstock & Eli A. Rubinstein (Eds.), *Television and social behavior, reports and papers, volume I: Media content and control. A technical report to the Surgeon General's Scientific Advisory Committee on Television and Social Behavior* (pp. 28-187). Rockville, MD: National Institute of Mental Health.

Gerbner, George, & Gross, Larry. (1976). Living with television: The violence profile. *Journal of Communication, 26*(2), 173-197.

Gerbner, George, Gross, Larry, Morgan, Michael, & Signorielli, Nancy. (1980). The mainstreaming of America: Violence profile number 11. *Journal of Communication, 30*(3), 10-29.

Gerbner, George, Gross, Larry, Morgan, Michael, & Signorielli, Nancy. (1986). Living with television: The dynamics of the cultivation process. In Jennings Bryant & Dolf Zillmann (Eds.), *Perspectives on media effects* (pp. 17-40). Hillsdale, NJ: Lawrence Erlbaum.

Gerbner, George, Gross, Larry, Morgan, Michael, & Signorielli, Nancy. (1994). Growing up with television: The cultivation perspective. In Jennings Bryant & Dolf Zillmann (Eds.), *Media effects: Advances in theory and research* (pp. 17-41). Hillsdale, NJ: Lawrence Erlbaum.

Gerbner, George, Gross, Larry, Signorielli, Nancy, Morgan, Michael, & Jackson-Beeck, Marilyn. (1979). The demonstration of power: Violence profile number 10. *Journal of Communication, 29*(3), 177-196.

Gerbner, George, Holsti, Ole R., Krippendorff, Klaus, Paisley, William J., & Stone, Philip J. (1969). *Analysis of communication content: Developments in scientific theories and computer techniques.* New York: John Wiley.

Gerbner, George, Morgan, Michael, & Signorielli, Nancy. (1982). Programming health portrayals: What viewers see, say, and do. In David Pearl, Lorraine Bouthilet, & Joyce Lazar (Eds.), *Television and behavior: Ten years of scientific progress and implications for the eighties, Vol. II, Technical reviews* (pp. 291-307). Rockville, MD: U.S. Department of Health and Human Services.

Gerbner, George, Signorielli, Nancy, & Morgan, Michael. (1995). Violence on television: The Cultural Indicators Project. *Journal of Broadcasting & Electronic Media, 39,* 278-283.

Ghose, Sanjoy, & Dou, Wenyu. (1998). Interactive functions and their impacts on the appeal of Internet presence sites. *Journal of Advertising Research, 38*(2), 29-43.

Gibson, Martin L. (1991). *Editing in the electronic era* (3rd ed.). Ames: Iowa State University Press.

Gibson, Rachel K., & Ward, Stephen J. (1998). U.K. political parties and the Internet: "Politics as usual" in the new media? *Harvard International Journal of Press/Politics, 3*(3), 14-38.

Gilbert, Adrienne, MacCauley, Marilyn I., & Smale, Bryan J. A. (1997). Newspaper portrayal of persons with disabilities over a decade. *Therapeutic Recreation Journal, 31*(2), 108-120.

Gleick, James. (1987). *Chaos: Making a new science.* New York: Penguin.

Goble, John F. (1997). A qualitative content analysis of case studies presenting the therapist's conceptualization and treatment of sexual desire disorders. *Dissertation Abstracts International, A: The Humanities and Social Sciences, 58*(2), 596-A.

Godfrey, Donald G. (1992). *Reruns on file: A guide to electronic media archives.* Hillsdale, NJ: Lawrence Erlbaum.

Goldberg, Lewis R. (1981). Language and individual differences: The search for universals in personality lexicons. In Ladd Wheeler (Ed.), *Review of personality and social psychology, 2* (pp. 141-165). Beverly Hills, CA: Sage.

Golden, Frederic. (1999, April 5). Lying faces unmasked. *Time,* pp. 52-53.

Gonzenbach, William J. (1992). A time-series analysis of the drug issue, 1985-1990: The press, the president and public-opinion. *International Journal of Public Opinion Research, 4*(2), 126-147.

Gordy, Laurie L., & Pritchard, Alice M. (1995). Redirecting our voyage through history: A content analysis of social studies textbooks. *Urban Education, 30*(2), 195-218.

Gottschalk, Louis A. (1995). *Content analysis of verbal behavior: New findings and clinical applications.* Hillsdale, NJ: Lawrence Erlbaum.

Gottschalk, Louis A., & Bechtel, Robert. (1993). *Psychological and neuropsychiatric assessment survey: Computerized content analysis of natural language or verbal texts.* Redwood City, CA: Mind Garden.

Gottschalk, Louis A., Fronczek, Janny, & Buchsbaum, Monte S. (1993). The cerebral neurobiology of hope and hopelessness. *Psychiatry, 56,* 270-281.

Gottschalk, Louis A., & Gleser, Goldine, C. (1969). *The measurement of psychological states through the content analysis of verbal behavior.* Berkeley: University of California Press.

Gottschalk, Louis A., Stein, Marsha K., & Shapiro, Deane H. (1997). The application of computerized content analysis of speech to the diagnostic process in a psychiatric outpatient clinic. *Journal of Clinical Psychology, 53,* 427-441.

Graham, John L., Kamins, Michael A., & Oetomo, Djoko S. (1993). Content analysis of German and Japanese advertising in print media from Indonesia, Spain, and the United States. *Journal of Advertising, 22*(2), 5-15.

Gray, Judy H., & Densten, Iain L. (1998). Integrating quantitative and qualitative analysis using latent and manifest variables. *Quality & Quantity, 32,* 419-431.

Greenberg, Bradley S. (1980). *Life on television: A content analysis of U.S. TV drama.* Norwood, NJ: Ablex.

Greenberg, Bradley S., Burgoon, Michael, Burgoon, Judee K., & Korzenny, Felipe. (1983). *Mexican Americans and the mass media.* Norwood, NJ: Ablex.

Greenberg, Bradley S., Fernandez-Collado, Carlos, Graef, David, Korzenny, Felipe, & Atkin, Charles K. (1980). Trends in the use of alcohol and other substances on television. In Bradley S. Greenberg, *Life on television: Content analyses of U.S. TV drama* (pp. 137-146). Norwood, NJ: Ablex.

Greenberg, Bradley S., & Neuendorf, Kimberly. (1980). Black family interactions on television. In Bradley S. Greenberg, *Life on television: Content analyses of U.S. TV drama* (pp. 173-181). Norwood, NJ: Ablex.

Greener, Susan, & Crick, Nicki R. (1999). Normative beliefs about prosocial behavior in middle childhood: What does it mean to be nice? *Social Development, 8,* 349-363.

Gregory, Richard L., with the assistance of Zangwill, O. L. (Eds.). (1987). *The Oxford companion to the mind.* Oxford, UK: Oxford University Press.

Griffin, Robert J., & Dunwoody, Sharon. (1997). Community structure and science framing of news about local environmental risks. *Science Communication, 18,* 362-384.

Grossman, Lev. (2001, February 12). Welcome to the Snooper Bowl. *Time,* p. 72.

Guerrero, Laura K., & Burgoon, Judee K. (1996). Attachment styles and reactions to nonverbal involvement change in romantic dyads: Patterns of reciprocity and compensation. *Human Communication Research, 22,* 335-370.

Gunawardena, Charlotte N., Lowe, Constance A., & Anderson, Terry. (1997). Analysis of a global online debate and the development of an interaction analysis model for examining social construction of knowledge in computer conferencing. *Journal of Educational Computing Research, 17,* 397-431.

Gunsch, Mark A., Brownlow, Sheila, Haynes, Sarah E., & Mabe, Zachary. (2000). Differential linguistic content of various forms of political advertising. *Journal of Broadcasting & Electronic Media, 44,* 27-42.

Gunter, Barrie. (2000). *Media research methods: Measuring audiences, reactions and impact.* London: Sage.

Ha, Louisa, & James, E. Lincoln. (1998). *Interactivity in business Web sites: A content analysis.* Paper presented at the annual meeting of the American Academy of Advertising, Lexington, KY.

Hacker, Helen M. (1981). Blabbermouths and clams: Sex differences in self-disclosure in same-sex and cross-sex friendship dyads. *Psychology of Women Quarterly, 5,* 385-401.

Hacker, Kenneth L., & Swan, William O. (1992). Content analysis of the Bush and Dukakis 1988 presidential election campaign television commercials. *Journal of Social Behavior and Personality, 7,* 367-374.

Hadden, Jeffrey K., & Swann, Charles E. (1981). *Prime time preachers: The rising power of televangelism.* Reading, MA: Addison-Wesley.

Haddock, Geoffrey, & Zanna, Mark P. (1997). Impact of negative advertising on evaluations of political candidates: The 1993 Canadian federal election. *Basic and Applied Social Psychology, 19*(2), 205-223.

Hair, Joseph F., Anderson, Rolph E., Tatham, Ronald L., & Black, William C. (1998). *Multivariate data analysis* (5th ed.). Upper Saddle River, NJ: Prentice Hall.

Hale, Jon F., Fox, Jeffrey C., & Farmer, Rick. (1996). Negative advertisements in U.S. senate campaigns: The influence of campaign context. *Social Science Quarterly, 77,* 329-343.

Hamilton, James D. (1994). *Time series analysis.* Princeton, NJ: Princeton University Press.

Harris, Dale B., & Pinder, Glenn D. (1974). *The Goodenough-Harris Drawing Test as a measure of intellectual maturity of youths.* Rockville, MD: U.S. Department of Health, Education, and Welfare.

Hart, Roderick P. (1985). Systematic analysis of political discourse: The development of Diction. In Keith R. Sanders, Lynda Lee Kaid, & Dan Nimmo (Eds.), *Political communication yearbook 1984* (pp. 97-134). Carbondale: Southern Illinois University Press.

Hart, Roderick P. (1997). *Diction 4.0: The text-analysis program.* Thousand Oaks, CA: Scolari.

Hart, Roderick P. (2000a). *Campaign talk: Why elections are good for us.* Princeton, NJ: Princeton University Press.

Hart, Roderick P. (2000b). *The text-analysis program: Diction 5.0.* Austin, TX: Digitext.

Hart, Roderick P., & Jarvis, Sharon E. (1997). Political debate: Forms, styles and media. *American Behavioral Scientist, 40,* 1095-1122.

Harwood, Jake. (1999). Viewing age: The age distribution of television characters across the viewer lifespan. Available: http://falcon.cc.ukans.edu/~harwood/crr.htm [7/14/99].

Haskell, Molly. (1987). *From reverence to rape* (2nd ed.). Chicago, IL: University of Chicago Press.

Headland, Thomas N., Pike, Kenneth L., & Harris, Marvin. (Eds.). (1990). *Emics and etics: The insider/outsider debate.* Newbury Park, CA: Sage.

Heeter, Carrie Jill. (1986). *Perspectives for the development of research on media systems.* Unpublished Ph.D. dissertation, Michigan State University, East Lansing, MI.

Heise, David R. (1965). Semantic differential profiles for 1,000 most frequent English words. *Psychological Monographs, 79*(8).

Hendon, Donald Wayne. (1973). How mechanical factors affect ad perception. *Journal of Advertising Research, 13*(4), 39-45.

Hertog, James K., & Fan, David P. (1995). The impact of press coverage on social beliefs: The case of HIV transmission. *Communication Research, 22,* 545-574.

Hesse-Biber, Sharlene, Dupuis, Paul R., & Kinder, T. Scott. (1997). Anthropology: New developments in video ethnography and visual sociology—Analyzing multimedia data qualitatively. *Social Science Computer Review, 15*(1), 5-12.

Heyman, Richard E., Weiss, Robert L., & Eddy, J. Mark. (1995). Marital interaction coding system: Revision and empirical evaluation. *Behaviour Research and Therapy, 33,* 737-746.

Hicks, Jeffrey Alan. (1992). Television theme songs: A content analysis. *Popular Music and Society, 16*(1), 13-20.

Hijmans, Ellen. (1996). The logic of qualitative media content analysis: A typology. *Communications, 21,* 93-109.

Hill, Kevin A., & Hughes, John E. (1997). Computer-mediated political communication: The Usenet and political communities. *Political Communication, 14*(3), 3-27.

Hill, Kim Quaile, Hanna, Stephen, & Shafqat, Sahar. (1997). The liberal-conservative ideology of U.S. Senators: A new measure. *American Journal of Political Science, 41,* 1395-1413.

Hill, Susan E. Kogler, Camden, Carl, & Clair, Robyn. (1988). Computer office systems and organizational communication: A case study. *Office Systems Research Journal, 7*(1), 5-12.

Hirokawa, Randy Y. (1988). Group communication research: Considerations for the use of interaction analysis. In Charles H. Tardy (Ed.), *A handbook for the study of human communication: Methods and instruments for observing, measuring, and assessing communication processes* (pp. 229-245). Norwood, NJ: Ablex.

Hogenraad, Robert, & McKenzie, Dean P. (1999). Replicating text: The cumulation of knowledge in social science. *Quality and Quantity, 33,* 97-116.

Hogenraad, Robert, McKenzie, Dean P., & Martindale, Colin. (1997). The enemy within: Autocorrelation bias in content analysis of narratives. *Computers and the Humanities, 30,* 433-439.

Holbrook, Morris B., & Lehmann, Donald R. (1980). Form versus content in predicting Starch scores. *Journal of Advertising Research, 20*(4), 53-62.

Holman, Rebecca H., & Hecker, Sid. (1983). Advertising impact: Creative elements affecting brand saliency. In James H. Leigh & Claude R. Martin, Jr. (Eds.), *Current issues and research in advertising 1983* (pp. 157-172). Ann Arbor: University of Michigan, Graduate School of Business Administration.

Holsti, Ole R. (1969). *Content analysis for the social sciences and humanities.* Reading, MA: Addison-Wesley.

Holt, Thomas C. (1995). Reconstruction in United States history textbooks. *Journal of American History, 81,* 1641-1651.

Horowitz, Steven W. (1998). Reliability of criteria-based content analysis of child witness statements: Response to Tully. *Legal and Criminology Psychology, 3,* 189-191.

Horowitz, Steven W., Lamb, Michael E., Esplin, Phillip W., Boychuk, Tascha D., Krispin, Orit, & Reiter-Lavery, Lisa. (1997). Reliability of criteria-based content analysis of child witness statements. *Legal and Criminology Psychology, 2,* 11-21.

Hughes, Marie Adele, & Garrett, Dennis E. (1990). Intercoder reliability estimation approaches in marketing: A generalizability theory framework for quantitative data. *Journal of Marketing Research, 27,* 185-195.

Hupka, Ralph B., Zaleski, Zbigniew, Otto, Jurgen, Reidl, Lucy, & Tarabrina, Nadia V. (1997). The colors of anger, envy, fear, and jealousy: A cross-cultural study. *Journal of Cross-Cultural Psychology, 28*(2), 156-171.

Hurtz, Wilhelm, & Durkin, Kevin. (1997). Gender role stereotyping in Australian radio commercials. *Sex Roles, 36,* 103-114.

Huston, Aletha C., & Wright, John C. (1983). Children's processing of television: The informative functions of formal features. In Jennings Bryant & Daniel R. Anderson (Eds.), *Children's understanding of television: Research on attention and comprehension* (pp. 35-68). New York : Academic Press.

Ide, Nancy M., & Sperberg-McQueen, C. M. (1995). The TEI: History, goals, and future. *Computers and the Humanities, 29,* 5-15.

Iyengar, Shanto, & Simon, Adam. (1993). News coverage of the Gulf crisis and public opinion: A study of agenda setting, priming, and framing. *Communication Research, 20,* 365-383.

James, E. Lincoln, & VandenBergh, Bruce G. (1990). An information content comparison of magazine ads across a response continuum from direct response to institutional advertising. *Journal of Advertising, 19*(2), 23-29.

Janis, Irving L. (1949). The problem of validating content analysis. In Harold D. Lasswell, Nathan Leites, & Associates (Eds.), *Language of politics: Studies in quantitative semantics* (pp. 55-82). New York: George W. Stewart.

Janson, Svante, & Vegelius, Jan. (1979). On generalizations of the g index and the phi coefficient to nominal scales. *Multivariate Behavioral Research, 14,* 255-269.

Jarausch, Konrad H., & Hardy, Kenneth A. (1991). *Quantitative methods for historians: A guide to research, data, and statistics.* Chapel Hill: University of North Carolina Press.

Jasperson, Amy E., Shah, Dhavan V., Watts, Mark, Faber, Ronald J., & Fan, David P. (1998). Framing and the public agenda: Media effects on the importance of the federal budget deficit. *Political Communication, 15,* 205-224.

Jeffres, Leo W., with Perloff, Richard M. (1997). *Mass media effects* (2nd ed.). Prospect Heights, IL: Waveland.

Jenkins, Richard W. (1999). How much is too much? Media attention and popular support for an insurgent party. *Political Communication, 16,* 429-445.

John, A. Meredith. (1988). *The plantation slaves of Trinidad, 1783-1816: A mathematical and demographic enquiry.* New York: Cambridge University Press.

Johnson, Gerald F. (1987). A clinical study of Porky Pig cartoons. *Journal of Fluency Disorders, 12,* 235-238.

Johnston, Anne, & White, Anne Barton. (1994). Communication styles and female candidates: A study of the political advertising during the 1986 Senate elections. *Journalism Quarterly, 71,* 321-329.

Jones, Elizabeth, Gallois, Cynthia, Callan, Victor, & Barker, Michelle. (1999). Strategies of accommodation: Development of a coding system for conversational interaction. *Journal of Language and Social Psychology, 18*(2), 123-152.

Jones, Kenneth. (1997). Are rap videos more violent? Style differences and the prevalence of sex and violence in the age of MTV. *Howard Journal of Communications, 8,* 343-356.

Kachigan, Sam Kash. (1986). *Statistical analysis: An interdisciplinary introduction to univariate and multivariate methods.* New York: Radius.

Kacmar, K. Michelle, & Hochwarter, Wayne A. (1996). Rater agreement across multiple data collection media. *Journal of Social Psychology, 16,* 469-475.

Kaid, Lynda Lee, & Bystrom, Dianne G. (Eds.). (1999). *The electronic election: Perspectives on the 1996 campaign communication.* Mahwah, NJ: Lawrence Erlbaum.

Kaid, Lynda Lee, Tedesco, John C., & McKinnon, Lori Melton. (1996). Presidential ads as nightly news: A content analysis of 1988 and 1992 televised adwatches. *Journal of Broadcasting & Electronic Media, 40,* 297-308.

Kalis, Pamela, & Neuendorf, Kimberly A. (1989). Aggressive cue prominence and gender participation in MTV. *Journalism Quarterly, 66,* 148-154, 229.

Kang, Namjun, Kara, Ali, Laskey, H. A., & Seaton, F. B. (1993). A SAS macro for calculating intercoder agreement in content analysis. *Journal of Advertising, 22*(2), 17-29.

Keenan, Kevin L. (1996a). Network television news coverage of public relations: An exploratory census of content. *Public Relations Review, 22*(3), 215-231.

Keenan, Kevin L. (1996b). Skin tones and physical features of blacks in magazine advertisements. *Journalism and Mass Communication Quarterly, 73,* 905-912.

Kelly, Edward F., & Stone, Philip J. (1975). *Computer recognition of English word senses.* Amsterdam: North-Holland.

Kelly, Ellen M., & Conture, Edward G. (1992). Speaking rates, response time latencies, and interrupting behaviors of young stutterers, nonstutterers, and their mothers. *Journal of Speech and Hearing Research, 35,* 1256-1267.

Keppel, Geoffrey. (1991). *Design and analysis: A researcher's handbook* (3rd ed.). Englewood Cliffs, NJ: Prentice Hall.

Kindem, Gorham. (1987). *The moving image: Production principles and practices.* Glenview, IL: Scott, Foresman

Klecka, William R. (1980). *Discriminant analysis.* Beverly Hills, CA: Sage.

Klee, Robert. (1997). *Introduction to the philosophy of science: Cutting nature at its seams.* New York: Oxford University Press.

Klein, Harald. (1991). INTEXT/PC: A program package for the analysis of texts in the humanities and social sciences. *Literary and Linguistic Computing, 6,* 108-111.

Knapp, Mark L. (1978). *Nonverbal communication in human interaction.* New York: Holt, Rinehart & Winston.

Köhler, Reinhard, & Rieger, Burghard B. (Eds.). (1993). *Contributions to quantitative linguistics: Proceedings of the First International Conference on Quantitative Linguistics, QUALICO, Trier.* Dordrecht, Germany: Kluwer.

Kohn, Stanislas. (1973). *The cost of the war to Russia: The vital statistics of European Russia during the World War 1914-1917.* New York: Howard Fertig.

Kolbe, Richard H., & Burnett, Melissa S. (1991). Content-analysis research: An examination of application with directives for improving research reliability and objectivity. *Journal of Consumer Research, 18,* 243-250.

Kolt, Jeremy. (1996). *Relationship initiation strategies: Interpersonal communication in personal advertisements.* Unpublished master's thesis, Cleveland State University, Cleveland, OH.

Koppitz, Elizabeth Munsterberg. (1984). *Psychological evaluation of human figure drawings by middle school pupils.* Orlando, FL: Grune & Stratton.

Kot, Eva Marie. (1999, January). Psychological sense of community and electronic mail. *Dissertation Abstracts International: Section B: The Sciences & Engineering, 59*(7-B), 3699.

Kottler, Amanda E., & Swartz, Sally. (1993). Conversation analysis: What is it, can psychologists use it? *South African Journal of Psychology, 23*(3), 103-110.

Kracauer, Siegfried. (1947). *From Caligari to Hitler.* New York: Princeton.

Kraemer, Helena Chmura. (1980). Extension of the kappa coefficient. *Biometrics, 36,* 207-216.

Krippendorff, Klaus. (1980). *Content analysis: An introduction to its methodology.* Beverly Hills, CA: Sage.

Krippendorff, Klaus. (1995). On the reliability of unitizing continuous data. *Sociological Methodology, 25,* 47-76.

Kruskal, Joseph B., & Wish, Myron. (1978). *Multidimensional scaling.* Beverly Hills, CA: Sage.

Kubala, Francis, Colbath, Sean, Liu, Daben, Srivastava, Amit, & Makhoul, John. (2000). Integrated technologies for indexing spoken language. *Communications of the ACM, 43*(2), 48-56.

Kuhn, Thomas S. (1970). *The structure of scientific revolutions* (2nd ed.). Chicago: University of Chicago Press.

Kunkel, Dale, Cope, Kirstie M., Farinola, Wendy Jo Maynard, Biely, Erica, Rollin, Emma, & Donnerstein, Edward. (1999). *Sex on TV: Executive Summary.* http://www.kff.org/topics.cgi?/topic=tv/. [March 15, 2000].

Kunkel, Dale, Cope-Farrar, Kirstie, Biely, Erica, Maynard Farinola, Wendy Jo, & Donnerstein, Edward. (2001). *Sex on TV: A Biennial Report to the Kaiser Family Foundation.* http://www.kff.org/content/2001/3087. [February 17, 2001].

Kunkel, Dale, Wilson, Barbara, Donnerstein, Edward, Linz, Daniel, Smith, Stacy, Gray, Timothy, Blumenthal, Eva, & Potter, W. James. (1995). Measuring television violence: The importance of context. *Journal of Broadcasting & Electronic Media, 39,* 284-291.

LaBarge, Emily, Von Dras, Dean, & Wingbermuehle, Cheryl. (1998). An analysis of themes and feelings from a support group for people with Alzheimer's disease. *Psychotherapy, 35,* 537-544.

Lacy, Stephen R., & Riffe, Daniel. (1996). Sampling error and selecting intercoder reliability samples for nominal content categories. *Journalism and Mass Communication Quarterly, 7,* 963-973.

Lacy, Stephen R., Riffe, Daniel, & Randle, Quint. (1998). Sample size in multi-year content analysis of monthly consumer magazines. *Journalism and Mass Communication Quarterly, 75,* 408-417.

Lacy, Stephen R., Robinson, Kay, & Riffe, Daniel. (1995). Sample size in content analysis of weekly newspapers. *Journalism and Mass Communication Quarterly, 72,* 336-345.

Lagerspetz, Kirsti M. J., Wahlroos, Carita, & Wendelin, Carola. (1978). Facial expressions of pre-school children while watching televised violence. *Scandinavian Journal of Psychology, 19,* 213-222.

Lance, Larry M. (1998). Gender differences in heterosexual dating: A content analysis of personal ads. *Journal of Men's Studies, 6*(3), 297-305.

Lange, David L., Baker, Robert K., & Ball, Sandra J. (1969). *Mass media and violence: A report to the National Commission on the Causes and Prevention of Violence.* Washington, DC: Government Printing Office.

Langs, Robert, Badalamenti, Anthony, & Bryant, Robin. (1991). A measure of linear influence between patient and therapist. *Psychological Reports, 69,* 355-368.

Larey, Timothy S., & Paulus, Paul B. (1999). Group preference and convergent tendencies in small groups: A content analysis of group brainstorming performance. *Creativity Research Journal, 12*(3), 175-184.

Lasswell, Harold D. (1935). Collective autism as a consequence of culture contact: Notes on religious training and the peyote cult at Taos. *Zeitschrift fur Sozialforschung, 4,* 232-246.

Lasswell, Harold D., Leites, Nathan, & Associates. (1949). *Language of politics: Studies in quantitative semantics.* New York: George W. Stewart, Publisher.

Lasswell, Harold D., Lerner, Daniel, & Pool, Ithiel de Sola. (1952). *The comparative study of symbols: An introduction.* Stanford: Stanford University Press, Hoover Institute and Library on War, Revolution, and Peace.

Lauzen, Martha, Dozier, David M., & Hicks, Manda V. (2001). Prime-time players and powerful prose: The role of women in the 1997-1998 television season. *Mass Communication and Society, 4,* 39-59.

Laver, Michael, & Garry, John. (2000). Estimating policy positions from political texts. *American Journal of Political Science, 44,* 619-634.

Lee, Alfred McClung, & Lee, Elizabeth Briant. (Eds.). (1939). *The fine art of propaganda: A study of Father Coughlin's speeches.* New York: Harcourt, Brace.

Lee, Fiona, & Peterson, Christopher. (1997). Content analysis of archival data. *Journal of Consulting and Clinical Psychology, 65,* 959-969.

Lee, Tien-tsung, & Hwang, Hsiao-Fang. (1997, May). *The feminist movement and female gender roles in movie advertisements: 1963 to 1993.* Paper presented to the Visual Communication Interest Group at the annual meeting of the International Communication Association, Montreal, Canada.

Lee, Wei-Na, & Callcott, Margaret F. (1994). Billboard advertising—A comparison of vice products across ethnic groups. *Journal of Business Research, 30*(1), 85-94.

Legg, Pamela P. Mitchell. (1996). Contemporary films and religious exploration: An opportunity for religious education. Part I: Foundational questions. *Religious Education, 91,* 397-406.

Lemish, Dafna, & Tidhar, Chava E. (1999). Still marginal: Women in Israel's 1996 television election campaign. *Sex Roles, 41,* 389-412.

Levesque, Maurice J., & Lowe, Charles A. (1999). Face-ism as a determinant of interpersonal perceptions: The influence of context on facial prominence effects. *Sex Roles, 41,* 241-259.

Lin, Carolyn A. (1997). Beefcake versus cheesecake in the 1990s: Sexist portrayals of both genders in television commercials. *Howard Journal of Communications, 8,* 237-249.

Lin, Lawrence I-Kuei. (1989). A concordance correlation coefficient to evaluate reproducibility. *Biometrics, 45,* 255-268.

Lin, Yang. (1996). Empirical studies of negative political advertising: A quantitative review using a method of combined citation and content analysis. *Scientometrics, 37,* 385-399.

Lindenmann, Walter K. (1983, July). Content analysis: A resurgent communication research technique that represents a wave of the future: The move toward a second dimension of interpretation and analysis. *Public Relations Journal,* pp. 24-27.

Linderman, Alf. (in press). Computer content analysis and manual coding techniques: A comparative analysis. In Mark D. West (Ed.), *Theory, method, and practice in computer content analysis* (pp. 97-110). Westport, CT: Ablex.

Lindlof, Thomas. (1995). *Qualitative communication research methods.* Thousand Oaks, CA: Sage.

Litkowski, Kenneth C. (1978). Models of the semantic structure of dictionaries. *American Journal of Computational Linguistics,* Microfiche 81, Frames 25-74.

Litkowski, Kenneth C. (1992). *A primer on computational lexicology. http://www.clres.com* (accessed February 24, 2000).

Litkowski, Kenneth C. (1999). *Towards a meaning-full comparison of lexical resources* (Proceeding of the Association for Computational Linguistics Special Interest Group on the Lexicon). College Park, MD: Association for Computational Linguistics.

Lombard, Matthew, Snyder-Duch, Jennifer, Bracken, Cheryl Campanella, Ditton, Theresa B., Kaynak, Selcan, Linder-Radosh, Jodi, & Pemrick, Janine. (1999, May). *Structural features of U.S. television: Primary results of a large scale content analysis.* Presentation to the Mass Communication Division of the International Communication Association, San Francisco, CA.

Lombard, Matthew, Campanella, Cheryl, Linder, Jodi, & Snyder, Jennifer, with Ditton, Theresa Bolmarcich, Kaynak, Selcan, Pemrick, Janine, & Steward, Gina. (1996, May). *The state of the medium: A content analysis of television form.* Paper presented to the Information Systems Division at the annual meeting of the International Communication Association, Chicago, IL.

Lont, Cynthia M. (1990). The roles assigned to females and males in non-music radio programming. *Sex Roles, 22,* 661-668.

Lopez-Escobar, Esteban, Llamas, Juan Pablo, McCombs, Maxwell, & Lennon, Federico Rey. (1998). Two levels of agenda setting among advertising and news in the 1995 Spanish elections. *Political Communication, 15,* 225-238.

Low, Jason, & Sherrard, Peter. (1999). Portrayal of women in sexuality and marriage and family textbooks: A content analysis of photographs from the 1970s to the 1990s. *Sex Roles, 40,* 309-318.

Lowe, David, & Matthews, Robert. (1995). Shakespeare vs. Fletcher: A stylometric analysis by radial basis functions. *Computers and the Humanities, 29,* 449-461.

Lowery, Shearon A., & DeFleur, Melvin L. (1995). *Milestones in mass communication research: Media effects* (3rd ed.). White Plains, NY: Longman.

Lowry, Dennis T., & Towles, David E. (1989). Prime-time TV portrayals of sex, contraception and venereal diseases. *Journalism Quarterly, 66,* 347-352.

Luborsky, Lester. (1996). *The symptom-context method: Symptoms as opportunities in psychotherapy.* Washington, DC: American Psychological Association.

Lull, James. (Ed.). (1987). *Popular music and communication.* Newbury Park, CA: Sage.

Lyman, Stanford M. (1997). Cinematic ideologies and societal dystopias in the United States, Japan, Germany and the Soviet Union: 1900-1996. *International Journal of Politics, Culture and Society, 10,* 497-542.

MacDonald, J. Fred. (1992). *Blacks and White TV: African Americans in television since 1948* (2nd ed.). Chicago: Nelson-Hall.

MacWhinney, Brian. (1996). The CHILDES system. *American Journal of Speech-Language Pathology, 5,* 5-14.

Manning, Philip, & Ray, George. (2000). *Setting the agenda in clinical interviews: An analysis of accommodation strategies.* Unpublished manuscript. Cleveland, OH: Cleveland State University.

Marche, Tammy A., & Peterson, Carole. (1993). The development and sex-related use of interruption behavior. *Human Communication Research, 19,* 388-408.

Mark, Robert A. (1971). Coding communication at the relational level. *Journal of Communication, 21,* 221-232.

Markel, Norman. (1998). *Semiotic psychology: Speech as an index of emotions and attitudes.* New York: Peter Lang.

Markiewicz, Dorothy. (1974). Effects of humor on persuasion. *Sociometry, 37,* 407-422.

Marks, Lawrence E. (1978). *The unity of the senses: Interrelations among the modalities.* New York: Academic Press.

Martindale, Colin, & McKenzie, Dean. (1995). On the utility of content analysis in author attribution: The Federalist. *Computers and the Humanities, 29,* 259-270.

Martindale, Colin, Moore, Kathleen, & Borkum, Jonathan. (1990). Aesthetic preference: Anomalous findings for Berlyne's psychobiological theory. *American Journal of Psychology, 103*(1), 53-80.

Marttunen, Miika. (1997). Electronic mail as a pedagogical delivery system: An analysis of the learning of argumentation. *Research in Higher Education, 38,* 345-363.

Maruyama, Geoffrey M. (1998). *Basics of structural equation modeling.* Thousand Oaks, CA: Sage.

Matabane, Paula, & Merritt, Bishetta. (1996). African Americans on television: Twenty-five years after Kerner. *Howard Journal of Communications, 7,* 329-337.

Matcha, Duane A. (1994-1995). Obituary analysis of early 20th-century marriage and family patterns in northwest Ohio. *Omega, 30*(2), 121-130.

McAdams, Dan P., & Zeldow, Peter B. (1993). Construct validity and content analysis. *Journal of Personality Assessment, 61,* 243-245.

McCarty, James F. (2001, January 24). Modell itching to skip town again. *The Plain Dealer*, pp. 1-A, 9-A.

McCombs, Maxwell, Llamas, Juan Pablo, Lopez-Escobar, Esteban, & Rey, Federico. (1997). Candidate images in Spanish elections: Second-level agenda-setting effects. *Journalism and Mass Communication Quarterly, 74,* 703-717.

McCormick, Naomi B., & McCormick, John W. (1992). Computer friends and foes: Content of undergraduates' electronic mail. *Computers in Human Behavior, 8,* 379-405.

McCroskey, James C. (1993). *An introduction to rhetorical communication* (6th ed.). Englewood Cliffs, NJ: Prentice Hall.

McCullough, Lynette S. (1993). A cross-cultural test of the two-part typology of humor. *Perceptual and Motor Skills, 76,* 1275-1281.

McGoun, Michael J. (1991). *The effects of extroversion and neuroticism upon humor enjoyment: The Cosby Show vs. Married with Children.* Unpublished master's thesis, Cleveland State University, Cleveland, OH.

McIsaac, Marina Stock, Mosley, Mary Lou, & Story, Naomi. (1984). Identification of visual dimensions in photographs using multidimensional scaling techniques. *Educational Communication and Technology Journal, 32*(3), 169-179.

McLuhan, Marshall. (1989). The role of new media in social change. In George Sanderson & Frank MacDonald (Eds.), *Marshall McLuhan: The man and his message* (pp. 34-40). Golden, CO: Fulcrum.

McLuhan, Marshall, & Powers, Bruce R. (1989). *The global village: Transformations in world life and media in the 21st century.* New York: Oxford University Press.

McMillan, Sally J. (1999, May). *The microscope and the moving target: The challenge of applying a stable research technique to a dynamic communication environment.* Paper presented to the Mass Communication Division at the annual meeting of the International Communication Association, San Francisco, CA.

McTavish, Donald G., & Pirro, Ellen B. (1990). Contextual content analysis. *Quality and Quantity, 24,* 245-265.

Mehtre, Babu M., Kankanhalli, Mohan S., & Lee, Wing Foon. (1997). Shape measures for content based image retrieval: A comparison. *Information Processing and Management, 33,* 319-337.

Melara, Robert D., Marks, Lawrence E., & Potts, Bonnie C. (1993). Early-holistic processing or dimensional similarity? *Journal of Experimental Psychology: Human Perception and Performance, 19,* 1114-1120.

Merritt, Sharyne. (1984). Negative political advertising: Some empirical findings. *Journal of Advertising, 13*(3), 27-38.

Messing, Lynn S., & Campbell, Ruth. (Eds.). (1999). *Gesture, speech, and sign.* Oxford, UK: Oxford University Press.

Metz, Christian. (1974). *Film language: A semiotics of the cinema.* Chicago: University of Chicago Press.

Metz, Rainer, Van Cauwenberghe, Eddy, & van der Voort, Roel. (Eds.). (1990). *Historical information systems.* Leuven, Belgium: Leuven University Press.

Michelson, Jean. (1996). *Visual imagery in medical journal advertising.* Unpublished master's thesis, Cleveland State University, Cleveland, OH.

Milic, Louis T. (1995). The century of prose corpus: A half-million word historical data base. *Computers and the Humanities, 29,* 327-337.

Miller, Gerald R. (1987). Persuasion. In Charles R. Berger & Steven H. Chaffee (Eds.), *Handbook of communication science* (pp. 446-483). Newbury Park, CA: Sage.

Miller, Kevin J., Fullmer, Steven L., & Walls, Richard T. (1996). A dozen years of mainstreaming literature: A content analysis. *Exceptionality, 6*(2), 99-109.

Miller, M. Mark. (2000, June). *Counting words and building mass communication theory.* Paper presented to the Information Systems Division at the annual meeting of the International Communication Association, Acapulco, Mexico.

Miller, M. Mark, Andsager, Julie L., & Riechert, Bonnie P. (1998). Framing the candidates in presidential primaries: Issues and images in press releases and news coverage. *Journalism and Mass Communication Quarterly, 75,* 312-324.

Miller, M. Mark, Boone, Jeff, & Fowler, David. (1992, November). *The emergence of greenhouse effect on the issue agenda: A news stream analysis.* Paper presented at the annual meeting of the Midwest Association for Public Opinion Research, Chicago, IL.

Miller, M. Mark, & Denham, Bryan. (1994). Reporting presidential election polls in 1988 and 1992: Horserace and issue coverage in prestige newspapers. *Newspaper Research Journal, 15*(4), 20-28.

Miller, Mark, & Riechert, Bonnie Parnell. (in press). Frame mapping: A quantitative method for investigating issues in the public sphere. In Mark D. West (Ed.). *Theory, method, and practice in computer content analysis* (pp. 61-76). Westport, CT: Ablex.

Miller, Peggy J., Wiley, Angela R., Fung, Heidi, & Liang, Chung-Hui. (1997). Personal storytelling as a medium of socialization in Chinese and American families. *Child Development, 68,* 557-568.

Mohler, Peter, & Zuell, Cornelia. (in press). Applied text theory: Quantitative analysis of answers to open-ended questions. In Mark D. West (Ed.), *Practice in computer content analysis.* Norwood, NJ: Ablex.

Moles, Abraham A. (1968). *Information theory and esthetic perception* (Joel F. Cohen, Trans.). Urbana: University of Illinois Press.

Mowrer, Donald E. (1996). A content analysis of student/instructor communication via computer conferencing. *Higher Education, 32,* 217-241.

Murray, Henry A., and the staff of the Harvard Psychological Clinic. (1943). *Thematic Apperception Test manual.* Cambridge, MA: Harvard University Press.

Murray, John P. (1998). Studying television violence: A research agenda for the 21st century. In Joy Keiko Asamen & Gordon L. Berry (Eds.), *Research paradigms, television, and social behavior* (pp. 369-410). Thousand Oaks, CA: Sage.

Murray, Noel M., & Murray, Sandra B. (1996). Music and lyrics in commercials: A cross-cultural comparison between commercials run in the Dominican Republic and in the United States. *Journal of Advertising, 25*(2), 51-63.

Musso, Juliet, Weare, Christopher, & Hale, Matt. (2000). Designing Web technologies for local governance reform: Good management or good democracy? *Political Communication, 17,* 1-19.

Naccarato, John. (1990). *Predictors of readership and recall: A content analysis of industrial ads.* Unpublished master's thesis, Cleveland State University, Cleveland, OH.

Naccarato, John L., & Neuendorf, Kimberly A. (1998). Content analysis as a predictive methodology: Recall, readership, and evaluations of business-to-business print advertising. *Journal of Advertising Research, 38*(3), 19-33.

Naisbitt, John. (1984). *Megatrends.* New York: Warner.

Narmour, Eugene. (1996). Analyzing form and measuring perceptual content in Mozart's sonata K.282: A new theory of parametric analogues. *Music Perception, 13,* 265-318.

National Television Violence Study (Volume 1). (1997). Thousand Oaks, CA: Sage.

Neuendorf, Kimberly. (1985). Alcohol advertising and media portrayals. *Journal of the Institute for Socioeconomic Studies, X*(2), 67-78.

Neuendorf, Kimberly. (1990a). Alcohol advertising: Regulation can help. In Ruth C. Engs (Ed.), *Controversies in the addictions field: Volume I* (pp. 119-129). Dubuque, IA: Kendall-Hunt.

Neuendorf, Kimberly. (1990b). Health images in the mass media. In Eileen Berlin Ray & Lewis Donohew (Eds.), *Communication and health: Systems and applications* (pp. 111-135). Hillsdale, NJ: Lawrence Erlbaum.

Neuendorf, Kimberly, & Abelman, Robert. (1986). Televangelism: A look at communicator style. *Journal of Religious Studies, 13*(1), 41-59.

Neuendorf, Kimberly A., & Abelman, Robert. (1987). An interaction analysis of religious television programming. *Review of Religious Research, 29*(2), 175-198.

Neuendorf, Kimberly A., Brentar, James E., & Porco, James. (1990). Media technology hardware and human sensory channels: Cognitive structures in multidimensional space. *Communication Research Reports, 7,* 100-106.

Neuendorf, Kimberly A., & Skalski, Paul. (2000, June). *Senses of humor: The development of a multi-factor scale in relationship to moving image utility.* Paper presented to the Mass Communication Division at the annual meeting of the International Communication Association, Acapulco, Mexico.

Newcomb, Horace. (Ed.). (1987). *Television: The critical view* (4th ed.). New York: Oxford University Press.

Newhagen, John E., Cordes, John W., & Levy, Mark R. (1995). Nightly@nbc.com: Audience scope and perception of interactivity in viewer mail on the Internet. *Journal of Communication, 45*(3), 164-175.

Newhagen, John, & Rafaeli, Sheizaf. (1996). Why communication researchers should study the Internet: A dialogue. *Journal of Communication, 46*(1), 4-13.

Newtson, Darren, Engquist, Gretchen, & Bois, Joyce. (1977). The objective basis of behavior units. *Personality and Social Psychology, 35,* 847-862.

Nofsinger, Robert E. (1988/1989). "Let's talk about the record": Contending over topic redirection in the Rather/Bush interview. *Research on Language and Social Interaction, 22,* 273-292.

Norton, Robert. (1983). *Communicator style: Theory, applications, and measures.* Beverly Hills, CA: Sage.

Oerter, Rolf, Oerter, Rosemarie, Agostiani, Hendriati, Kim, Hye-On, & Wibowo, Sutji. (1996). The concept of human nature in East Asia: Etic and emic characteristics. *Culture and Psychology, 2,* 9-51.

Ogletree, Shirley Matile, Merritt, Sara, & Roberts, John. (1994). Female/male portrayals on U.S. postage stamps of the twentieth century. *Communication Research Reports, 11,* 77-85.

O'Hair, Dan. (1989). Dimensions of relational communication and control during physician-patient interactions. *Health Communication, 1*(2), 97-115.

Oliver, Mary Beth. (1994). Portrayals of crime, race, and aggression in "reality-based" police shows: A content analysis. *Journal of Broadcasting & Electronic Media, 38,* 179-192.

Olsen, Mark. (1989). TextPack V: Text analysis utilities for the personal computer. *Computers and the Humanities, 23,* 155-160.

Olsen, Mark. (1993). Signs, symbols and discourses: A new direction for computer-aided literature studies. *Computers and the Humanities, 27,* 309-314.

Olsina, L., Godoy, D., Lafuente, G. J., & Rossi, G. (1999). *Specifying quality characteristics and attributes for websites.* Paper presented at the First ICSE Workshop on Web Engineering.

Olson, Beth. (1994). Sex and the soaps: A comparative content analysis of health issues. *Journalism Quarterly, 71,* 840-850.

Orne, Martin T. (1975). On the social psychology experiment: With particular reference to demand characteristics and their implications. In George H. Lewis (Ed.), *Fist-fights in the kitchen* (pp. 183-195). Pacific Palisades, CA: Goodyear.

Osgood, Charles E., Suci, George J., & Tannenbaum, Percy H. (1957). *The measurement of meaning.* Urbana: University of Illinois Press.

Owen, Diana, Davis, Richard, & Strickler, Vincent James. (1999). Congress and the Internet. *Harvard International Journal of Press-Politics, 4*(2), 10-29.

Padilla, Peter A. (1997). A content analysis of United States Army recruiting: 1915-1990. *Dissertation Abstracts International, A: The Humanities and Social Sciences, 58*(3), 1121-A-1122-A.

Palmquist, Michael E., Carley, Kathleen M., & Dale, Thomas A. (1997). Applications of computer-aided text analysis: Analyzing literary and nonliterary texts. In Carl W. Roberts (Ed.), *Text analysis for the social sciences: Methods for drawing statistical inferences from texts and transcripts* (pp. 171-189). Mahwah, NJ: Lawrence Erlbaum.

Pasadeos, Yorgo, & Renfro, Paula. (1988). Rupert Murdoch's style: The *New York Post. Newspaper Research Journal, 9*(4), 25-34.

Patterson, Gerald R. (1982). *A social learning approach: Vol. 3. Coercive family processes.* Eugene, OR: Castalia.

Pennebaker, James W., & Francis, Martha E. (1999). *Linguistic inquiry and word count (LIWC).* Mahwah, NJ: Lawrence Erlbaum.

Pennebaker, James W., Francis, Martha E., & Booth, R. J. (2001). *Linguistic inquiry and wordcount: LIWC 2001.* Mahwah, NJ: Erlbaum.

Perreault, William D., Jr., & Leigh, Laurence E. (1989, May). Reliability of nominal data based on qualitative judgments. *Journal of Marketing Research, 26,* pp. 135-148.

Pershad, Dwarka, & Verma, S. K. (1995). Diagnostic significance of content analysis of SIS-II. *Journal of Projective Psychology and Mental Health, 2*(2), 139-144.

Peterson, Christopher, Bettes, Barbara A., & Seligman, Martin E. P. (1985). Depressive symptoms and unprompted causal attributions: Content analysis. *Behavior Research and Therapy, 23,* 379-382.

Peterson, Christopher, Luborsky, Lester, & Seligman, Martin E. P. (1983). Attributions and depressive mood shifts: A case study using the symptom-context method. *Journal of Abnormal Psychology, 92,* 96-103.

Peterson, Christopher, Seligman, Martin E. P., & Vaillant, George E. (1988). Pessimistic explanatory style is a risk factor for physical illness: A thirty-five-year longitudinal study. *Journal of Personality and Social Psychology, 55,* 23-27.

Pettijohn, Terry F., II., & Tesser, Abraham. (1999). Popularity in environmental context: Facial feature assessment of American movie actresses. *Media Psychology, 1,* 229-247.

Pfau, Michael, Moy, Patricia, Holbert, R. Lance, Szabo, Erin A., Lin, Wei-Kuo, & Zhang, Weiwu. (1998). The influence of political talk radio on confidence in democratic institutions. *Journalism and Mass Communication Quarterly, 75,* 730-745.

Phillips, David P. (1974). The influence of suggestion on suicide: Substantive and theoretical implications of the Werther effect. *American Sociological Review, 39,* 340-354.

Phillips, David P. (1982). The impact of fictional television stories on U.S. adult fatalities: New evidence on the effect of the mass media on violence. *American Journal of Sociology, 87,* 1340-1359.

Phillips, David P. (1983). The impact of mass media violence on U.S. homicides. *American Sociological Review, 48,* 560-568.

Phillips, David P., & Hensley, John E. (1984). When violence is rewarded or punished: The impact of mass media stories on homicide. *Journal of Communication, 34*(3), 101-116.

Phillips, David P., & Paight, Daniel J. (1987). The impact of televised movies about suicide: A replicative study. *New England Journal of Medicine, 317,* 809-811.

Phillips, David P., Van Voorhees, Camilla A., & Ruth, Todd E. (1992). The birthday: Lifeline or deadline? *Psychosomatic Medicine, 54,* 532-542.

Pileggi, Mary S., Grabe, Maria Elizabeth, Holderman, Lisa B., & de Montigny, Michelle. (2000). Business as usual: The American dream in Hollywood business films. *Mass Communication and Society, 3,* 207-228.

Plous, S., & Neptune, Dominique. (1997). Racial and gender biases in magazine advertising: A content-analytic study. *Psychology of Women Quarterly, 21,* 627-644.

Poindexter, Paula M., & Stroman, Carolyn A. (1981). Blacks and television: A review of the research literature. *Journal of Broadcasting, 25,* 103-122.

Pokrywczynski, James V. (1988). Sex in ads targeted to black and white readers. *Journalism Quarterly, 65,* 756-760.

Pool, Ithiel de Sola. (Ed.). (1959). *Trends in content analysis.* Urbana: University of Illinois Press.

Poole, Marshall Scott, & Folger, Joseph P. (1981). A method for establishing the representational validity of interaction coding systems: Do we see what they see? *Human Communication Research, 8,* 26-42.

Poole, Marshall Scott, Van de Ven, Andrew H., Dooley, Kevin, & Holmes, Michael E. (2000). *Organizational change and innovation processes: Theory and methods for research.* Oxford, UK: Oxford University Press.

Popping, Roel. (1984). AGREE, a package for computing nominal scale agreement. *Computational Statistics and Data Analysis, 2,* 182-185.

Popping, Roel. (1988). On agreement indices for nominal data. In Willem E. Saris & Irmtraud N. Gallhofer (Eds.), *Sociometric research: Volume 1, data collection and scaling* (pp. 90-105). New York: St. Martin's.

Popping, Roel. (1997). Computer programs for the analysis of texts and transcripts. In Carl W. Roberts (Ed.), *Text analysis for the social sciences: Methods for drawing statistical inferences from texts and transcripts* (pp. 209-221). Mahwah, NJ: Lawrence Erlbaum.

Potter, Robert F. (1999). *Measuring the bells and whistles of a new medium: Using content analysis to describe the structural features of cyberspace.* Paper presented to the Mass Communication Division at the annual meeting of the International Communication Association, San Francisco, CA.

Potter, Rosanne G. (1991). Statistical analysis of literature: A retrospective on computers and the humanities, 1966-1990. *Computers and the Humanities, 25,* 401-429.

Potter, W. James, & Levine-Donnerstein, Deborah. (1999). Rethinking validity and reliability in content analysis. *Journal of Applied Communication Research, 27,* 258-284.

Potter, W. James, & Ware, William. (1987). An analysis of the contexts of antisocial acts on prime-time television. *Communication Research, 14,* 664-686.

Potter, W. James, & Warren, Ron. (1998). Humor as camouflage of televised violence. *Journal of Communication, 48*(2), 40-57.

Powers, Stephen, Rothman, David J., & Rothman, Stanley. (1996). *Hollywood's America: Social and political themes in motion pictures.* Boulder, CO: Westview.

Pratt, Laurie, Wiseman, Richard L., Cody, Michael J., & Wendt, Pamela F. (1999). Interrogative strategies and information exchange in computer-mediated communication. *Communication Quarterly, 47*(1), 46-66.

"Principles and procedures of category development." (2000). http://www.clres.com/catprocs.html [February 24, 2000].

Propp, Vladimir. (1968). *Morphology of the folk tale* (Laurence Scott, Trans.). Austin, TX: University of Texas Press.

Quinn, Ellen. (2000, Mar. 1). Class lecture. COM 533, Department of Communication, Cleveland State University, Cleveland OH.

Raimy, Victor C. (1948). Self reference in counseling interviews. *Journal of Consulting Psychology, 12,* 153-163.

Rajecki, D. W., McTavish, Donald G., Rasmussen, Jeffrey Lee, Schreuders, Madelon, Byers, Diane C., & Jessup, K. Sean. (1994). Violence, conflict, trickery, and other story themes in TV ads for food for children. *Journal of Applied Social Psychology, 24,* 1685-1700.

Reid, Leonard N., Rotfeld, Herbert R., & Barnes, James H. (1984). Attention to magazine ads as function of layout design. *Journalism Quarterly, 61,* 439-441.

Rice, Ronald E., & Danowski, James. (1991). Comparing comments and semantic networks about voice mail. *ASIS '91: Proceedings of the 54th ASIS annual meeting, 28,* 134-138.

Richmond, Virginia P. (1990). Communication in the classroom: Power and motivation. *Communication Education, 39,* 181-195.

Riffe, Daniel, Aust, Charles F., & Lacy, Stephen R. (1993). The effectiveness of random, consecutive day and constructed week samplings in newspaper content analysis. *Journalism Quarterly, 70,* 133-139.

Riffe, Daniel, & Freitag, Alan. (1997). A content analysis of content analyses: Twenty-five years of *Journalism Quarterly. Journalism and Mass Communication Quarterly, 74,* 873-882.

Riffe, Daniel, Lacy, Stephen, & Drager, Michael W. (1996). Sample size in content analysis of weekly news magazines. *Journalism and Mass Communication Quarterly, 73,* 635-644.

Riffe, Daniel, Lacy, Stephen, & Fico, Frederick G. (1998). *Analyzing media messages: Using quantitative content analysis in research.* Mahwah, NJ: Lawrence Erlbaum.

Riffe, Daniel, Lacy, Stephen, Nagovan, Jason, & Burkum, Larry. (1996). The effectiveness of simple and stratified random sampling in broadcast news content analysis. *Journalism and Mass Communication Quarterly, 73,* 159-168.

Riffe, Daniel, Place, Patricia C., & Mayo, Charles M. (1993). Game time, soap time and prime time of ads: Treatment of women in Sunday football and rest-of-week advertising. *Journalism Quarterly, 70,* 437-446.

RightWriter the intelligent grammar and style checker, user's manual. (1985). Sarasota, FL: Decisionware.

Robb, David. (2000, February 29). Blacks get lots of prime-time roles, but half are in sitcoms, study finds. *Cleveland Plain Dealer,* p. 6E.

Roberts, Carl W. (1997a). Semantic text analysis: On the structure of linguistic ambiguity in ordinary discourse. In Carl W. Roberts (Ed.), *Text analysis for the social sciences: Methods for drawing statistical inferences from texts and transcripts* (pp. 55-78). Mahwah, NJ: Lawrence Erlbaum.

Roberts, Carl W. (Ed.). (1997b). *Text analysis for the social sciences: Methods for drawing statistical inferences from texts and transcripts.* Mahwah, NJ: Lawrence Erlbaum.

Roberts, Donald F. (1998). Media content labeling systems. In Roger G. Noll & Monroe E. Price (Eds.), *A communication cornucopia: Markle Foundation essays on information policy* (pp. 350-375). Washington, DC: Brookings Institution Press.

Roberts, Donald F., & Christenson, Peter G. (2000, February). "Here's looking at you, kid": Alcohol, drugs and tobacco in entertainment media. A literature review prepared for the National Center on Addiction and Substance Abuse at Columbia University. http://www.kff.org/topics.cgi?topic=tv. [March 15, 2000].

Roberts, Marilyn, & McCombs, Maxwell. (1994). Agenda-setting and political advertising—Origins of the news agenda. *Political Communication, 11,* 249-262.

Robinson, John P., Shaver, Phillip R., & Wrightsman, Lawrence S. (1991). *Measures of personality and social psychological attitudes.* San Diego, CA: Academic Press.

Roessler, Patrick. (1999). The individual agenda-designing process: How interpersonal communication, egocentric networks, and mass media shape the perception of political issues by individuals. *Communication Research, 26,* 666-700.

Rogan, Randall G., & Hammer, Mitchell R. (1995). Assessing message affect in crisis negotiations: An exploratory study. *Human Communication Research, 21,* 553-574.

Rogers, Everett M. (1994). *A history of communication study: A biographical approach.* New York: Free Press.

Rogers, L. Edna, & Farace, Richard V. (1975). Analysis of relational communication in dyads: New measurement procedures. *Human Communication Research, 1,* 222-239.

Rogers, L. Edna, & Millar, Frank. (1982). The question of validity: A pragmatic response. In Michael Burgoon (Ed.), *Communication yearbook 5* (pp. 249-257). New Brunswick, NJ: Transaction.

Rogers-Millar, L. Edna, & Millar, Frank E. (1978). Domineeringness and dominance: A transactional view. *Human Communication Research, 5,* 238-246.

Rogow, Arnold A. (Ed.). (1969). *Politics, personality, and social science in the twentieth century: Essays in honor of Harold D. Lasswell.* Chicago: University of Chicago Press.

Rosenbaum, Howard, & Snyder, Herbert. (1991). An investigation of emerging norms in computer mediated communication: An empirical study of computer conferencing. *ASIS '91: Proceedings of the 54th ASIS annual meeting, 28,* 15-23.

Rosenberg, Stanley D., & Tucker, Gary J. (1979). Verbal behavior and schizophrenia: The semantic dimension. *Archives of General Psychiatry, 36,* 1331-1337.

Rosengren, Karl E. (Ed.). (1981). *Advances in content analysis.* Beverly Hills, CA: Sage.

Rosenthal, Robert. (1987). *Judgment studies: Design, analysis, and meta-analysis.* Cambridge, NJ: Cambridge University Press.

Roter, Debra, Lipkin, Mack, Jr., & Dorsgaard, Audrey. (1991). Sex differences in patients' and physicians' communication during primary care medical visits. *Medical Care, 29,* 1083-1093.

Rothbaum, Fred, & Tsang, Bill Yuk-Piu. (1998). Lovesongs in the United States and China: On the nature of romantic love. *Journal of Cross-Cultural Psychology, 29,* 306-319.

Rothbaum, Fred, & Xu, Xiaofang. (1995). The theme of giving back to parents in Chinese and American songs. *Journal of Cross-Cultural Psychology, 26,* 698-713.

Rowney, Don Karl, & Graham, James Q., Jr. (1969). *Quantitative history: Selected readings in the quantitative analysis of historical data.* Homewood, IL: Dorsey.

Rubin, Rebecca B., Palmgreen, Philip, & Sypher, Howard E. (Eds.). (1994). *Communication research measures: A sourcebook.* New York: Guilford.

Saegert, Susan C., & Jellison, Jerald M. (1970). Effects of initial level of response competition and frequency of exposure on liking and exploratory behavior. *Journal of Personality and Social Psychology, 16,* 553-558.

Salisbury, Joseph G. T. (in press). Using neural networks to assess corporate image. In Mark D. West (Ed.), *Practice in computer content analysis.* Norwood, NJ: Ablex.

Salomon, Gavriel. (1987). *Interaction of media, cognition, and learning.* San Francisco: Jossey-Bass.

Salwen, Michael B. (1986). Effect of accumulation of coverage on issue salience in agenda setting. *Journalism Quarterly, 65,* 100-106.

Sapir, Edward. (1927). Speech as a personality trait. *American Journal of Sociology, 32,* 892-905.

Satterfield, Jason M. (1998). Cognitive-affective states predict military and political aggression and risk taking: A content analysis of Churchill, Hitler, Roosevelt, and Stalin. *Journal of Conflict Resolution, 42,* 667-690.

Schenck-Hamlin, William J., Procter, David E., & Rumsey, Deborah J. (2000). The influence of negative advertising frames on political cynicism and politician accountability. *Human Communication Research, 26,* 53-74.

Schneider, Benjamin, Wheeler, Jill K., & Cox, Jonathan F. (1992). A passion for service: Using content analysis to explicate service climate themes. *Journal of Applied Psychology, 77,* 705-716.

Schramm, Wilbur. (1997). *The beginnings of communication study in America: A personal memoir* (Steven H. Chaffee & Everett M. Rogers, Eds.) Thousand Oaks, CA: Sage.

Schramm, Wilbur, & Roberts, Donald F. (1971). *The process and effects of mass communication* (Rev. ed.). Urbana: University of Illinois Press.

Schreer, George E., & Strichartz, Jeremy M. (1997). Private restroom graffiti: An analysis of controversial social issues on two college campuses. *Psychological Reports, 81,* 1067-1074.

Schulman, Peter, Castellon, Camilo, & Seligman, Martin E. P. (1989). Assessing explanatory style: The content analysis of verbatim explanations and the attributional style questionnaire. *Behavioral Research and Therapy, 27,* 505-512.

Scott, William A. (1955). Reliability of content analysis: The case of nominal scale coding. *Public Opinion Quarterly, 19,* 321-325.

Selltiz, Claire, Jahoda, Marie, Deutsch, Morton, & Cook, Stuart W. (1967). *Research methods in social relations*. New York: Holt, Rinehart & Winston.

Sengupta, Subir. (1996). Understanding consumption related values from advertising: A content analysis of television commercials from India and the United States. *Gazette, 57*, 81-96.

Severin, Werner J., & Tankard, James W., Jr. (1997). *Communication theories: Origins, methods, and uses in the mass media* (4th ed.). New York: Longman.

Shaffer, David R., Pegalis, Linda, & Cornell, David P. (1991). Interactive effects of social context and sex role identity on female self-disclosure during the acquaintance process. *Sex Roles, 24*, 1-19.

Shannon, Claude E., & Weaver, Warren. (1998). *The mathematical theory of communication*. Urbana: University of Illinois Press.

Shapiro, Gilbert, & Markoff, John. (1997). A matter of definition. In Carl W. Roberts (Ed.), *Text analysis for the social sciences: Methods for drawing statistical inferences from texts and transcripts* (pp. 9-34). Mahwah, NJ: Lawrence Erlbaum.

Shapiro, Gilbert, Markoff, John, & Weitman, Sasha R. (1973). Quantitative studies of the French revolution. *History and Theory, 12*(2), 163-191.

Shearer, Robert A. (1999). Statement analysis: SCAN or SCAM? *Skeptical Inquirer, 23*(3), 40-43.

Sherman, Barry L., & Dominick, Joseph R. (1986). Violence and sex in music videos: TV and rock 'n' roll. *Journal of Communication, 36*(4), 76-90.

Shoemaker, Pamela J. (1984). Media treatment of deviant political groups. *Journalism Quarterly, 61*, 66-75, 82.

Shoemaker, Pamela J., & Reese, Stephen D. (1990). Exposure to what? Integrating media content and effects studies. *Journalism Quarterly, 67*, 649-652.

Shoemaker, Pamela J., & Reese, Stephen D. (1996). *Mediating the message: Theories of influences on mass media content* (2nd ed.). White Plains, NY: Longman.

Sigelman, Lee, & Jacoby, William. (1996). The not-so-simple art of imitation: Pastiche, literary style and Raymond Chandler. *Computers and the Humanities, 30*, 11-28.

Signorielli, Nancy, & Bacue, Aaron. (1999). Recognition and respect: A content analysis of prime-time television characters across three decades. *Sex Roles, 40*, 527-544.

Signorielli, Nancy, Gerbner, George, & Morgan, Michael. (1995). Violence on television: The Cultural Indicators Project. *Journal of Broadcasting & Electronic Media, 39*, 278-283.

Signorielli, Nancy, McLeod, Douglas, & Healy, Elaine. (1994). Gender stereotypes in MTV commercials: The beat goes on. *Journal of Broadcasting & Electronic Media, 38*, 91-101.

Simoni, Jane M. (1996). Confronting heterosexism in the teaching of psychology. *Teaching of Psychology, 23*(4), 220-226.

Simonton, Dean K. (1980a). Thematic fame, melodic originality, and musical zeitgeist: A biographical and transhistorical content analysis. *Journal of Personality and Social Psychology, 38*, 972-983.

Simonton, Dean K. (1980b). Thematic fame and melodic originality in classical music: A multivariate computer-content analysis. *Journal of Personality, 48*(2), 206-219.

Simonton, Dean Keith. (1981). The library laboratory: Archival data in personality and social psychology. In Ladd Wheeler (Ed.), *Review of personality and social psychology 2* (pp. 217-243). Beverly Hills, CA: Sage.

Simonton, Dean Keith. (1984). Melodic structure and note transition probabilities: A content analysis of 16,618 classical themes. *Psychology of Music, 12,* 3-16.

Simonton, Dean K. (1987). Musical aesthetics and creativity in Beethoven: A computer analysis of 105 compositions. *Empirical Studies of the Arts, 5*(2), 87-104.

Simonton, Dean Keith. (1994). *Greatness: Who makes history and why?* New York: Guilford.

Singer, Benjamin D. (1982). Minorities and the media—A content-analysis of native Canadians in the daily press. *Canadian Review of Sociology and Anthropology, 19,* 348-359.

Singer, Linda A. (1997). Native Americans on CD-ROM: Two approaches. *Multimedia Schools, 4*(1), 42-46.

Skalski, Paul. (2000). *Distinctive formal features of the World Wide Web.* Unpublished manuscript. Cleveland, OH: Cleveland State University.

Slattery, Karen L., Hakanen, Ernest A., & Doremus, Mark E. (1996). The expression of localism: Local TV news coverage in the new video marketplace. *Journal of Broadcasting & Electronic Media, 40,* 403-413.

Smith, Ann Marie. (1999). *Girls on film: Analysis of women's images in contemporary American and "Golden Age" Hollywood films.* Unpublished master's thesis, Cleveland State University, Cleveland, OH.

Smith, Bruce Lannes. (1969). The mystifying intellectual history of Harold D. Lasswell. In Arnold A. Rogow (Ed.), *Politics, personality, and social science in the twentieth century: Essays in honor of Harold D. Lasswell* (pp. 41-105). Chicago: University of Chicago Press.

Smith, Charles P., (Ed.), in association with Atkinson, John W., McClelland, David C., & Veroff, Joseph. (1992). *Motivation and personality: Handbook of thematic content analysis.* Cambridge, MA: Cambridge University Press.

Smith, Lois J. (1994). A content analysis of gender difference in children's advertising. *Journal of Broadcasting & Electronic Media, 38,* 323-337.

Smith, Raymond G. (1978). *The message measurement inventory: A profile for communication analysis.* Bloomington: Indiana University Press.

Snyder-Duch, Jennifer, Bracken, Cheryl Campanella, & Lombard, Matthew. (2001, May). *Content analysis in communication: Assessment and reporting of intercoder reliability.* Presentation to the International Communication Association, Washington, DC.

Solomon, Michael R., & Greenberg, Lawrence. (1993). Setting the stage: Collective selection in the stylistic context of commercials. *Journal of Advertising, 22*(1), 11-24.

Soskin, William F., & John, Vera P. (1963). The study of spontaneous talk. In Roger G. Barker (Ed.), *The stream of behavior* (pp. 228-281). New York: Appleton-Century-Crofts.

Spak, Michael I. (1990). America for sale: When well-connected former federal officials peddle their influence to the highest foreign bidder—A statutory analysis and proposals for reform of the Foreign Agents Registration Act and the Ethics in Government Act. *Kentucky Law Journal, 78,* 237.

Sparkman, Richard. (1996). Regional geography, the overlooked sampling variable in advertising content analysis. *Journal of Current Issues and Research in Advertising, 18*(2), 53-57.

Sparks, Glenn G., & Fehlner, Christine L. (1986). Faces in the news: Gender comparisons of magazine photographs. *Journal of Communication, 36*(4), 70-79.

Spencer, Gary. (1989). An analysis of JAP-baiting humor on the college campus. *Humor: International Journal of Humor Research, 2,* 329-348.

SRI MAESTRO Team. (2000). MAESTRO: Conductor of multimedia analysis technologies. *Communications of the ACM, 43*(2), 57-63.

Standen, Craig C. (1989, July). What makes a newspaper advertisement effective? Large illustrations, color, headlines and style. *Presstime,* p. 72.

Stempel, Guido H. (1952). Sample size for classifying subject matter in dailies. *Journalism Quarterly, 29,* 333-334.

Stevens, S. S. (1951). Mathematics, measurement, and psychophysics. In S. S. Stevens (Ed.), *Handbook of experimental psychology* (pp. 1-49). New York: John Wiley.

Stevenson, Robert L. (1994). *Global communication in the twenty-first century.* New York: Longman.

Stevenson, Thomas H., & Swayne, Linda E. (1999). The portrayal of African-Americans in business-to-business direct mail: A benchmark study. *Journal of Advertising, 28*(3), 25-35.

Stewart, David W., & Furse, David H. (1986). *Effective television advertising: A study of 1000 commercials.* Lexington, MA: Lexington Books.

Stiles, Deborah A., Gibbons, Judith L., & Schnellmann, Jo. (1987). The smiling sunbather and the chivalrous football player: Young adolescents' images of the ideal woman and man. *Journal of Early Adolescence, 7,* 411-427.

Stiles, William B. (1980). Comparison of dimensions derived from rating versus coding of dialogue. *Journal of Personality and Social Psychology, 38,* 359-374.

Stohl, Cynthia, & Redding, W. Charles. (1987). Messages and message exchange processes. In Fredric M. Jablin, Linda L. Putnam, Karlene H. Roberts, & Lyman W. Porter (Eds.), *Handbook of organizational communication* (pp. 451-502). Newbury Park, CA: Sage.

Stone, Philip J. (1997). Thematic text analysis: New agendas for analyzing text content. In Carl W. Roberts (Ed.), *Text analysis for the social sciences: Methods for drawing statistical inferences from texts and transcripts* (pp. 35-54). Mahwah, NJ: Lawrence Erlbaum.

Stone, Philip J., Dunphy, Dexter C., Smith, Marshall S., & Ogilvie, Daniel M. (1966). *The general inquirer: A computer approach to content analysis.* Cambridge: MIT Press.

Straubhaar, Joseph, & LaRose, Robert. (1996). *Communications media in the information society.* Belmont, CA: Wadsworth.

Stroman, Carolyn A., Merritt, Bishetta D., & Matabane, Paula W. (1989-1990). Twenty years after Kerner: The portrayal of African Americans on prime-time television. *Howard Journal of Communications, 2,* 44-55.

Strong, Pauline Turner. (1996). Animated Indians: Critique and contradiction in commodified children's culture. *Cultural Anthropology, 11,* 405-424.

Sudnow, David. (Ed.). (1972). *Studies in social interaction.* New York: Free Press.

Sutch, Richard. (1975). The treatment received by American slaves: A critical review of the evidence presented in *Time on the Cross. Explorations in Economic History, 12,* 335-438.

Sweeney, Kevin, & Whissell, Cynthia. (1984). A dictionary of affect in language: 1. Establishment and preliminary validation. *Perceptual and Motor Skills, 59,* 695-698.

Switzer, Les. (1990). The ambiguities of protest in South Africa: Rural politics and the press during the 1920s. *International Journal of African Historical Studies, 23*(1), 87-109.

Tak, Jinyoung, Kaid, Lynda Lee, & Lee, Soobum. (1997). A cross-cultural study of political advertising in the United States and Korea. *Communication Research, 24,* 413-430.

Tardy, Charles H. (1988). Interpersonal interaction coding systems. In Charles H. Tardy (Ed.), *A handbook for the study of human communication: Methods and instruments for observing, measuring, and assessing communication processes* (pp. 285-300). Norwood, NJ: Ablex.

Taylor, Charles R., & Bang, Hae-Kyong. (1997). Portrayals of Latinos in magazine advertising. *Journalism and Mass Communication Quarterly, 74,* 285-303.

Taylor, Charles R., Lee, Ju Yung, & Stern, Barbara B. (1996). Portrayals of African, Hispanic, and Asian Americans in magazine advertising. In Ronald Paul Hill (Ed.), *Marketing and consumer research in the public interest* (pp. 133-150). Thousand Oaks, CA: Sage.

Taylor, Charles R., & Stern, Barbara B. (1997). Asian-Americans: Television advertising and the "model minority" stereotype. *Journal of Advertising, 26*(2), 47-61.

Taylor, Charles R., & Taylor, John C. (1994). Regulatory issues in outdoor advertising: A content analysis of billboards. *Journal of Public Policy & Marketing, 13*(1), 97-107.

Te'eni, Daniel R. (1998). Nomothetics and idiographics as antonyms: Two mutually exclusive purposes for using the Rorschach. *Journal of Personality Assessment, 70,* 232-247.

Thompson, Bruce. (1984). *Canonical correlation analysis.* Beverly Hills, CA: Sage.

Thompson, Isabelle. (1996). Competence and critique in technical communication: A qualitative content analysis of journal articles. *Journal of Business and Technical Communication, 10*(1), 48-80.

Thorson, Esther. (1989). Television commercials as mass media messages. In James J. Bradac (Ed.), *Message effects in communication science* (pp. 195-230). Newbury Park, CA: Sage.

Tinsley, Howard E., & Weiss, David J. (1975). Interrater reliability and agreement of subjective judgments. *Journal of Counseling Psychology, 22,* 358-376.

Tracey, Terence J., & Ray, Philip B. (1984). Stages of successful time-limited counseling: An interactional examination. *Journal of Counseling Psychology, 31,* 13-27.

Traub, Ross E. (1994). *Reliability for the social sciences: Theory and applications.* Thousand Oaks, CA: Sage.

Tully, Bryan. (1998). Reliability of criteria-based content analysis of child witness statements: Cohen's kappa doesn't matter. *Legal and Criminological Psychology, 3,* 183-188.

Tunnicliffe, Sue Dale, & Reiss, Michael J. (1999). Talking about brine shrimp: Three ways of analyzing pupil conversations. *Research in Science & Technology Education, 17,* 203-217.

Tweedie, Fiona J., Singh, Semeer, & Holmes, David I. (1996). Neural network approaches in stylometry: The Federalist Papers. *Computers and the Humanities, 30,* 1-20.

U.S. Commission on Civil Rights. (1977). *Window dressing on the set: Women and minorities on television.* Washington, DC: Government Printing Office.

U.S. Commission on Civil Rights. (1979). *Window dressing on the set: An update.* Washington, DC: Government Printing Office.

Urist, Jeffrey. (1977). The Rorschach Test and the assessment of object relations. *Journal of Personality Assessment, 41,* 3-9.

Urist, Jeffrey, & Shill, Merton. (1982). Validity of the Rorschach Mutuality of Autonomy Scale: A replication using excerpted responses. *Journal of Personality Assessment, 46,* 450-454.

Vanden Heuvel, Jon. (1991). *Untapped sources: America's newspaper archives and histories.* New York: Gannett Foundation Media Center.

Vincent, Richard C., Davis, Dennis K., & Boruszkowski, Lilly Ann. (1987). Sexism on MTV: A content analysis of rock videos. *Journalism Quarterly, 64,* 750-755, 941.

Voelker, David H., & Orton, Peter Z. (1993). *Statistics.* Lincoln, NE: Cliffs Notes.

Vogt, W. Paul. (1993). *Dictionary of statistics and methodology: A nontechnical guide for the social sciences.* Newbury Park, CA: Sage.

Vossen, Piek. (1998). Introduction to EuroWordNet. *Computers and the Humanities, 32,* 73-89.

Wactlar, Howard D., Hauptmann, Alexander G., Christel, Michael G., Houghton, Ricky A., & Olligschlaeger, Andreas M. (2000). Complementary video and audio analysis for broadcast news archives. *Communications of the ACM, 43*(2), 42-47.

Ward, L. Monique. (1995). Talking about sex: Common themes about sexuality in the prime-time television programs children and adolescents view most. *Journal of Youth and Adolescence, 24,* 595-615.

Watkins, Patsy G. (1996). Women in the work force in non-traditional jobs. In Paul Martin Lester (Ed.), *Images that injure: Pictorial stereotypes in the media* (pp. 69-74). Westport, CN: Praeger.

Watkinson, John. (1999). *MPEG-2.* Oxford, UK: Focal.

Watt, James H., Mazza, Mary, & Snyder, Leslie. (1993). Agenda-setting effects of television news coverage and the effects decay curve. *Communication Research, 20,* 408-435.

Watt, James H., Jr., & Welch, Alicia J. (1983). Effects of static and dynamic complexity on children's attention and recall of televised instruction. In Jennings Bryant & Daniel R. Anderson (Eds.), *Children's understanding of television: Research on attention and comprehension* (pp. 69-102). New York: Academic Press.

Watts, Mark D., Domke, David, Shah, Dhavan V., & Fan, David P. (1999). Elite cues and media bias in presidential campaigns. *Communication Research, 26,* 144-175.

Watzlawick, Paul, Beavin, Janet Helmick, & Jackson, Don D. (1967). *Pragmatics of human communication: A study of interactional patterns, pathologies, and paradoxes.* New York: Norton.

Weaver, James B., III. (1991). Are "slasher" horror films sexually violent? A content analysis. *Journal of Broadcasting & Electronic Media, 35,* 385-392.

Weber, Robert Philip. (1990). *Basic content analysis* (2nd ed.). Newbury Park, CA: Sage.

Weed, William Speed. (2001, May). Iron bars, silicon chips. *Discover,* pp. 23-24.

Weinberger, Marc G., Spotts, Harlan, Campbell, Leland, & Parsons, Amy L. (1995). The use and effect of humor in different advertising media. *Journal of Advertising Research, 35*(3), 44-56.

West, Mark D. (in press a). The future of computer content analysis: Trends, unexplored lands, and speculations. In Mark D. West (Ed.). *Theory, method, and practice in computer content analysis* (pp. 141-158). Westport, CT: Ablex.

West, Mark D. (Ed.). (in press b). *Theory, method, and practice in computer content analysis.* Westport, CT: Ablex.

Westley, Bruce H., & MacLean, Malcolm. (1957). A conceptual model for communication research. *Journalism Quarterly, 34,* 31-35.

Weyls, Ryan. (2001). *Changing media presentations of adult entertainment.* Unpublished master's thesis, Cleveland State University, Cleveland, OH.

Whissell, Cynthia M. (1994a). A computer program for the objective analysis of style and emotional connotations of prose: Hemingway, Galsworthy, and Faulkner compared. *Perceptual and Motor Skills, 79,* 815-824.

Whissell, Cynthia. (1994b). Objective analysis of text: I. A comparison of adventure and romance novels. *Perceptual and Motor Skills, 79,* 1567-1570.

Whissell, Cynthia. (1996). Traditional and emotional stylometric analysis of the songs of Beatles Paul McCartney and John Lennon. *Computers and the Humanities, 30,* 257-265.

Whissell, Cynthia. (2000). Phonoemotional profiling: A description of the emotional flavour of English texts on the basis of the phonemes employed in them. *Perceptual and Motor Skills, 91,* 617-648.

Whissell, Cynthia, Fournier, Michael, Pelland, Rene, Weir, Deborah, & Makarec, K. (1986). A dictionary of affect in language: IV. Reliability, validity, and applications. *Perceptual and Motor Skills, 62,* 875-888.

Wilkes, Robert E., & Valencia, Humberto. (1989). Hispanics and Blacks in television commercials. *Journal of Advertising, 18*(1), 19-25.

Wilkinson, Gene L., Bennett, Lisa T., & Oliver, Kevin M. (1997). Evaluation criteria and indicators of quality for internet resources. *Educational Technology, 37*(3), 52-58.

Williams, Frederick. (1982). *The communications revolution.* Beverly Hills, CA: Sage.

Williams, Frederick. (1992). *Reasoning with statistics* (4th ed.). Fort Worth, TX: Harcourt Brace Jovanovich.

Willnat, Lars, & Zhu, Jian-Hua. (1996). Newspaper coverage and public opinion in Hong Kong: A time-series analysis of media priming. *Political Communication, 13,* 231-246.

Wimmer, Roger D., & Dominick, Joseph R. (1994). *Mass media research: An introduction* (5th ed.). Belmont, CA: Wadsworth.

Winer, B. J. (1971). *Statistical principles in experimental design* (2nd ed.). New York: McGraw-Hill.

Winter, David G. (1998). The contributions of David McClelland to personality assessment. *Journal of Personality Assessment, 71*(2), 129-145.

Witt, Joseph C. (1990). Face-to-face verbal interaction in school-based consultation: A review of the literature. *Social Psychology Quarterly, 5*(3), 199-210.

Woelfel, Joseph, & Fink, Edward L. (1980). *The measurement of communication processes: Galileo theory and method.* New York: Academic Press.

Wongthongsri, Patinuch. (1993). *A comparative analysis of Thai and U.S. TV commercials.* Unpublished master's thesis, Cleveland State University, Cleveland, Ohio.

Wood, Wally. (1989, January). Tools of the trade: B-to-B's 60% standard. *Marketing and Media Decisions,* pp. 98-99.

Wright, Robert. (1988). *Three scientists and their gods: Looking for meaning in an age of information.* New York: Times.

Wurtzel, Alan, & Lometti, Guy. (1984). Determining the acceptability of violent program content at ABC. *Journal of Broadcasting, 28,* 89-97.

Yale, Laura, & Gilly, Mary C. (1988). Trends in advertising research: A look at the content of marketing-oriented journals from 1976 to 1985. *Journal of Advertising, 17*(1), 12-22.

Yanovitzky, Itzhak, & Blitz, Cynthia L. (2000). Effect of media coverage and physician advice on utilization of breast cancer screening by women 40 years and older. *Journal of Health Communication, 5,* 117-134.

Young, Michael D. (1996). Cognitive mapping meets semantic networks. *Journal of Conflict Resolution, 40,* 395-414.

Ziblatt, Daniel F. (1998). The adaptation of ex-communist parties to post-communist east central Europe: A comparative study of the East German and Hungarian ex-communist parties. *Communist and Post-Communist Studies, 31*(2), 119-137.

Zillmann, Dolf. (1971). Excitation transfer in communication-mediated aggressive behavior. *Journal of Experimental Social Psychology, 7,* 419-434.

Zillmann, Dolf. (1977). Humour and communication: Introduction to symposium. In Antony J. Chapman & Hugh C. Foot (Eds.), *It's a funny thing, humour* (pp. 291-301). Oxford, UK: Pergamon.

Zillmann, Dolf, Bryant, Jennings, & Cantor, Joanne R. (1974). Brutality of assault in political cartoons affecting humor appreciation. *Journal of Research in Personality, 7,* 334-345.

Zillmann, Dolf, Johnson, Rolland C., & Day, Kenneth D. (2000). Attribution of apparent arousal and proficiency of recovery from sympathetic activation affecting excitation transfer to aggressive behavior. In E. Tory Higgins & Arie W. Kruglanski (Eds.), *Motivational science: Social and personality perspectives* (pp. 416-424). Philadelphia: Psychology Press/Taylor & Francis.

Ziv, Avner. (1984). *Personality and the senses of humor.* New York: Springer.

Zuckerman, Milton. (1986). On the meaning and implications of facial prominence. *Journal of Nonverbal Behavior, 10*(4), 215-229.

Zue, Victor. (1999, August). Talking with your computer. *Scientific American,* pp. 56-57.

Zullow, Harold M. (1991). Pessimistic rumination in popular songs and newsmagazines predict economic recession via decreased consumer optimism and spending. *Journal of Economic Psychology, 12,* 501-526.

Zullow, Harold M., & Seligman, Martin E. P. (1990). Pessimistic rumination predicts defeat of presidential candidates, 1900 to 1984. *Psychological Inquiry, 1*(1), 52-61.

Zwick, Rebecca. (1988). Another look at interrater agreement. *Psychological Bulletin, 103,* 374-378.

Author Index

Subject Index

About the Authors

Kimberly A. Neuendorf holds a PhD from Michigan State University. She is Professor and Director of the Communication Research Center at Cleveland State University, where she teaches a variety of courses on media, new technologies, film, and research methods. She has published more than 50 articles, chapters, and research reports. Her recent research focuses on media images of marginalized groups, the diffusion of new technologies, and the relationship of media use to emotion and mood management.

Paul D. Skalski (author of Resources 1 and 3) is a doctoral student in communication at Michigan State University, with a master's degree from Cleveland State University. He is involved in several research projects investigating the social effects of mass media, including a content analysis of televised professional wrestling.